Exploring OREGON'S Wild Areas

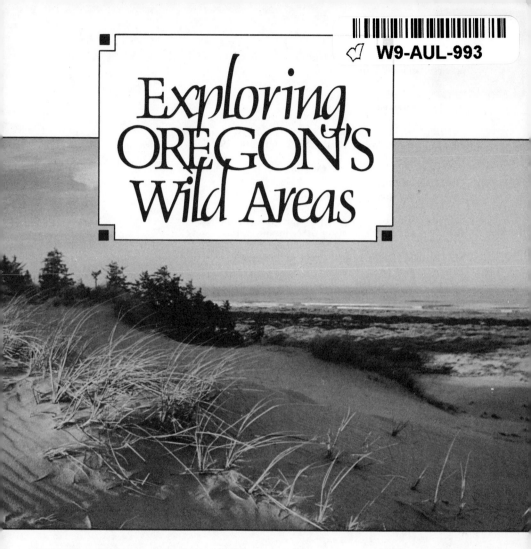

A GUIDE FOR HIKERS, BACKPACKERS, CLIMBERS, XC SKIERS & PADDLERS

WILLIAM L. SULLIVAN

Photographer: Diane Kelsay, In Sync Productions

Research Consultant: The Oregon Natural Resources Council

THE MOUNTAINEERS • SEATTLE

The Mountaineers: Organized 1906 "... to explore, study, preserve, and enjoy the natural beauty of the Northwest."

© 1988 by William L. Sullivan
All rights reserved

Published by The Mountaineers
306 2nd Avenue West, Seattle, Washington 98119

Published simultaneously in Canada by
Douglas & McIntyre Ltd.
1615 Venables Street, Vancouver, British Columbia V5L 2H1

Manufactured in the United States of America
Edited by Jim Jensen
Designed by Constance Bollen
Maps by William L. Sullivan
Cover photo: Lush forests of Oregon's wilderness. Photo by Diane Kelsay. Inset—Author in Smith Rocks State Park (Area 21). Photo by J. Wesley Sullivan.

Library of Congress Cataloging in Publication Data

Sullivan, William L., 1953-
    Exploring Oregon's wild areas : a guide for hikers, backpackers,
XC skiers, climbers, and paddlers / by William L. Sullivan ;
photographer, Diane Kelsay.
        p.   cm.
    Bibliography: p.
    Includes index.
    ISBN 0-89886-144-6 : $11.95
    1. Outdoor recreation--Oregon--Guide-books.   2. Wilderness areas-
Oregon--Guide-books.   3. Oregon--Description and travel--1981- -
-Guide-books.   I. Title.
GV191.42.07S85 1988
917.95--dc 19   88-5188
                                                                        CIP

SAFETY CONSIDERATIONS

Wilderness travel entails unavoidable risks that every traveler assumes and must be aware of and respect. The fact that an area is described in this book is not a representation that it will be safe for you. The routes described herein vary greatly in difficulty and in the amount and kind of preparation needed to enjoy them safely. Some may have changed since this book was written, or conditions along them may have deteriorated. Weather conditions, of course, can change daily or even hourly, especially in mountainous areas. A trip that is safe in good weather or for a highly conditioned, properly equipped traveler may be completely unsafe for a novice or during inclement weather. You can meet these and other risks safely by exercising your own independent judgment and common sense. Be aware of your own limitations and of conditions when and where you are traveling. If conditions are dangerous, or if you are not prepared to deal with them safely, change your plans. Each year, many people enjoy safe trips through the back country. With proper preparation and good judgment, you can too.

The Mountaineers

3 2 1 0 9
6 5 4 3

◆FOREWORD◆

Little more than a century ago, almost all of Oregon was wilderness. The pioneers who sought the promised land of the Willamette Valley or the mother lode of gold in countless places throughout Oregon knew only that the lack of civilization and roads created Herculean obstacles to their hopes and plans. Wilderness defined Oregon.

Today, of course, the Oregon landscape has felt man's hand almost everywhere. We have inverted the map. But with the growing scarcity of wilderness, our awareness of its value and importance has increased. The more we learn about the role these undisturbed watersheds and ecosystems play in producing cold, clean water, providing habitat for fish and wildlife, maintaining ecological diversity and productivity, and providing opportunities for outdoor recreation, the more we appreciate these last vestiges of the original Oregon. This seems especially relevant today as the Northwest economy rapidly shifts away from timber to a more diversified base in which tourism, fishing, and outdoor recreation will play significant roles.

Exploring Oregon's Wild Areas summarizes what we know about Oregon's remaining wilderness. Author Bill Sullivan, working with staff and volunteers of the Oregon Natural Resources Council (ONRC) and others, has created a remarkable and unique book that includes maps, photographs and detailed area-by-area descriptions that tie together in a coherent way the state's entire wilderness resource. Although no single document can cover this topic exhaustively, this one establishes new standards for such endeavors.

The reader needs to be aware that lands that are protected as Wilderness Areas (or the rivers as Wild and Scenic Rivers) receive that special designation from Congress. Consequently, protecting wilderness and wild rivers is a political process. Roadless areas and free-flowing streams that are not classified in some sort of "permanent" system do not survive very long as wild and natural places. If a piece of forested ground is developed, it eventually will be invaded by roads and then probably clearcut. Undisturbed high-desert lands in the Great Basin of southeast Oregon will experience road building, intensive grazing, and perhaps mineral or geothermal development or invasion by off-road vehicles. Free-flowing rivers that lack federal or state protection often end up dammed, diverted, or otherwise degraded; logging and grazing along their banks is almost certain.

In 1980 conservationists estimated that about 4½ million acres of unprotected forested wildlands remained in the state. These are the so-called roadless areas in Oregon's National Forests, Bureau of Land Management forest lands, and Crater Lake National Park. In southeastern Oregon's high desert more than five million acres of such "de facto" (unprotected) wilderness remain. Oregon also contains over 35,000 miles of free-flowing rivers and streams, most of which are not yet protected within the National Wild and Scenic River System or the State Scenic Waterways System.

However, since 1974 significant progress has been made in protecting Oregon's wildlands. From 1964 (the year the Wilderness Act became law) until 1980, Congress designated 14 Wilderness Areas in Oregon. In 1984, with enactment of the Oregon Forest Wilderness bill, 23 more were added to the National Wilderness System. Unfortunately, none of the high-desert rangelands have yet received Wilderness designation. Segments of four Oregon rivers have been classified as federal Wild and Scenic Rivers (the Rogue, Snake, Illinois and Owyhee). Eleven Oregon rivers are currently part of the State Scenic Waterways System, one of the nation's best.

Behind almost every parcel of land and segment of river that have been protected is the story of a local conservation group, comprising citizens who cared enough to work and sacrifice for these very special places. As an association of over 80 local and statewide conservation, sportsmen, outdoor recreation, and business organizations, and more than 3500 individual members, the Oregon Natural Resources Council can keep you posted on issues statewide, and can put you in touch with local grass-roots conservation groups who are responsible for local areas.

The ONRC invites you to become involved in the ongoing endeavor to protect and wisely manage Oregon lands, waters, and natural resources. Your actions could dramatically affect the boundaries of the designated Wilderness Areas and Wild and Scenic Rivers and State Scenic Waterways included in the next edition of this guide! Contact any ONRC office if you'd like to help.

Enjoy this exciting book and use it to see and experience the real Oregon. You'll be glad you did.

James Monteith
Executive Director
Oregon Natural Resources Council
February 1988

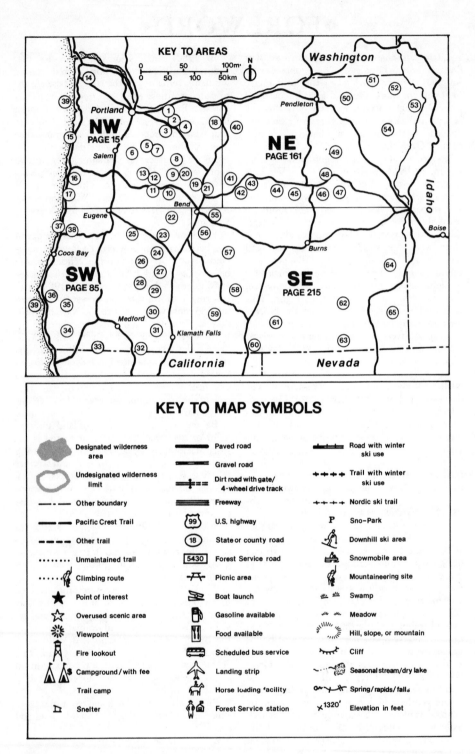

◆CONTENTS◆

◆PREFACE◆

Ever since the Wilderness Act of 1984 boosted the number of designated Wilderness Areas in Oregon from 14 to 37, the need for a comprehensive guidebook to Oregon's wild lands has been felt greatly. Not only have maps and information been unavailable for the many new areas, but also attention has been drawn to the many beautiful wild areas excluded from that legislation.

Word has leaked out that there is good winter hiking on the old-growth forest trails of Hardesty Mountain, a half-hour drive from Eugene; that there are awe-inspiring vistas in the Nez Perce's sacred Joseph Canyon, in northeast Oregon; and that the Bureau of Land Management has hidden all kinds of wilderness surprises in the desert landscape between Bend and Nevada.

This book, for the first time, assembles maps, information, and photographs for 65 wilderness retreats across the state. Scenic lands administered by the Oregon State Parks and Recreation Division, The Nature Conservancy, and a host of federal agencies have not been overlooked. The hiker hunting for new trails within an hour or two of Portland, and the adventurer yearning to prowl the wild lands of Oregon's remote corners will both find enough in this guide to plan many a rewarding trip.

In researching this book, I backpacked 1360 miles across Oregon—from the state's westernmost Pacific shore at Cape Blanco to Oregon's easternmost point in the depths of Hells Canyon. As research consultant, the Oregon Natural Resources Council (ONRC) proofread and checked the maps and information included in this book, drawing on the knowledge of experts from the ONRC's coalition of over 80 local and statewide conservation and outdoor recreational organizations.

Still, new logging roads and developments continue to change Oregon's many unprotected wild areas, and in a project this large, some errors in maps and text are inevitable. Please send corrections for future editions of this book to William L. Sullivan, c/o The Mountaineers, 306 Second Ave. W., Seattle, WA 98119.

In choosing the areas to include in this guide, I have emphasized recreation. In addition, we should remember that many of the benefits of wilderness come to us indirectly—as botanical diversity, pure air and water, and wildlife habitat. The shaded areas on the four quadrant overview maps show the full extent of Oregon's remaining designatable wilderness lands, as judged by the ONRC. The fact that some of these areas are not featured in this guide does not diminish my concern, or the concern of the ONRC, that these areas may also deserve Wilderness Act protection.

There are a number of hard questions left to answer about wilderness. The federal government now allows logging on remote roadless lands, and permits grazing within designated wilderness areas, even though these uses typically cost the public far more money than they provide. Should red-ink commercial use of public wild lands cease, despite the local economic hardships that might result? How much effort should be spent on saving endangered species of wildlife, or on propagating game species? Should the Forest Service continue to manage wilderness for primitive recreation by discouraging new trail construction and allowing shelters to decay? Most importantly, how much wilderness should be preserved at all?

In order to answer these questions wisely, people need to go to the wilderness areas. This guide is dedicated to making that experience as rewarding as possible.

William L. Sullivan
Eugene, 1988

♦INTRODUCTION♦

How can we love Oregon's fragile wilderness without loving it to death? If we intend to walk lightly on the land, we cannot all continue to beat dusty paths to Mt. Jefferson's sorely trammeled Jeff Park, Mt. Hood's Paradise Park, and the Three Sisters' Green Lakes Basin.

Oregon is chock full of alternative trips with both the beauty and the isolation that wilderness is known for. This guide describes more than 600 hikes and 130 cross-country ski tours, as well as prime spots for whitewater rafting, mountaineering, and even hang gliding.

The popular High Cascades wildernesses are all included, of course, but so are less crowded areas in four other major mountain ranges. And there's more: the deepest whitewater river canyons in the world. Fog-bound oceanshore rain forests. Winter hideaways at snowy lakes. Turquoise hot spring pools in stark deserts. Two areas of sand dunes. And thousands of miles of quiet trails.

HOW TO USE THIS BOOK
The Maps

A *locator map* following the Table of Contents identifies the book's 65 areas by number and shows which quarter of the state each area is in. Turn to the appropriate *quadrant overview map* (page 16, 86, 162, or 216) to find the best highway approach to an area.

Individual *area maps* use symbols identified in a key on page 4. Note that solid gray areas denote wilderness designated by act of Congress. Undesignated wilderness—managed

Catching salmon along the Salmon River Trail; area 3. Fishing and hunting are permitted within wilderness areas. State regulations apply.

Old growth forest in the Old Cascades

under quite different rules — is shown only by thin gray borders. Beyond the gray borders lies land unsuitable as wilderness because of clearcuts, roads, private ownership, development, or insufficient size.

Stars denote points of interest, but *hollow* stars indicate scenic spots already badly worn by overuse. Visitors heading for such fragile spots should tread lightly and plan to camp elsewhere.

The maps' north arrows always point to true north; magnetic north lies approximately 20° east of true north in Oregon. In the few instances where north is not at the top of the map, a square of gray shading helps draw attention to the north arrow.

Dirt roads shown with dashed lines are ways — unimproved four-wheel drive tracks that are probably not drivable for passenger cars. The maps do not show all the ways and roads. Particularly in southeast Oregon's desert country, backroads drivers may find the proliferation of unmarked ways confusing. Bureau of Land Management quadrangle maps are good insurance here (see appendix C).

Long-distance recreation trails connecting many of the areas in this book are featured in the *State Trail Plan Map* in appendix A.

The Information Blocks

Each entry begins with a synopsis of the area's facts. The *location* tells the highway mileage and direction from major cities to the closest portion of a roadless area. The *size* reflects the approximate extent (in square miles) of all the roadless lands in each featured area. For state parks, the size is the total extent of parkland. An area's *status* tells how many square miles have been Congressionally designated as wilderness so far, and the dates of those additions to the National Wilderness System. Other, less protective designations are also noted.

Next, each entry notes the roadless area's dominant types of *terrain*, as well as the highest and lowest *elevation* in feet. The *management* listing advises whether a national forest (NF), a district of the Bureau of Land Management (BLM), or some other agency administers the area. These agencies can answer specific questions about road conditions, regulations, and permits. Their addresses and phone numbers appear in appendix B.

An essential back-up for the maps in this book are *topographic maps,* which show landforms by means of contour lines. The best topographic maps are listed first. Appendix C includes detailed information for ordering topographic maps.

The Text Descriptions

An area's *climate* information generally includes average snow levels, temperature ranges, and likeliest seasons to find mosquitoes, wildflowers, or huckleberries. Average annual precipitation reflects the total of rain and melted snow. All of these figures vary substantially from year to year. In addition, some of the data for remote areas are approximate, extrapolated from weather station records. Wilderness visitors should always prepare for inclement weather.

All areas include descriptions of *plants and wildlife* and *geology*. However, only areas with a substantial history of human contact have *history* entries.

A FEW WILDERNESS RULES

The 1964 Wilderness Act defines wilderness as "an area where the earth and its community of life are untrammeled by man, where man himself is a visitor who does not remain." That law established strict rules that govern the 37 Oregon areas Congress has thus far designated as wilderness. These include:

- No mechanical transport. This bans off-road vehicles (ORVs), motorcycles, bicycles, airplane drops, hang gliders, and helicopter landings—except rarely for rescue or fire fighting.
- No new mining claims. Mining on pre-1984 claims, however, continues.
- No commercial enterprises. An exception currently allows some cattle grazing. Guides and outfitters may operate only under permit.
- No motorized equipment (such as generators or chainsaws).
- Fishing and hunting *are* permitted with a state license. Check with the Oregon Department of Fish and Wildlife for regulations.

Many designated wilderness areas have other restrictions as well. The most common "No's" are:

- Cutting, chopping, or clipping of live or dead trees.
- Grazing, picketing, or tying saddle stock within 200 feet of a lake or stream.
- Discharging firearms within 150 yards of a campsite, or across any trail or body of water.
- Smoking while traveling. Stop at a safe spot to smoke.

In addition, some rules extend to all federal lands, wilderness or not:

- Collecting arrowheads or other cultural artifacts is a federal crime.
- Disturbing archeological sites or pictographs is likewise a criminal offense (even making tracings or rubbings of pictographs can damage them).
- National Forests limit campers to 16 days' stay at the same campsite in any 30-day period.
- Permits are required to dig up plants on

Climbers on The Matterhorn in the Eagle Cap Wilderness (photo by William L. Sullivan)

federal land.
- Rare plants and animals are sometimes protected by both federal and state law. Picking wildflowers may in fact be illegal.

HAZARDS IN THE WILDS

The Wilderness Act of 1964 insists a wilderness should offer outstanding opportunities for solitude. One backwoods hiker paraphrased this, suggesting a wilderness should offer outstanding opportunities for death.

Alas, I think the dangers of the wilderness have been overrated. Grizzly bears are extinct in Oregon, so there is no need to decorate backpacks with bear-warning bells. Oregon's black bears huff and scramble out of a hiker's way as fast as their little legs will take them—generally even when the hiker has accidentally passed a mother bear's cubs. In a very few areas (notably the Wild Rogue Wilderness), bears have been trained over the years by careless campers to rip open packs and coolers at night for bacon, tuna, and sweets. Here a standard wilderness precaution will suffice: hang all food from a tree limb, at least 10 feet high and 5 feet away from the trunk. This will also keep food safe from the real scoundrels, chipmunks.

Likewise, rattlesnakes will disappoint the danger seeker. These reptiles are rare enough that I have not seen one in 2000 miles of Oregon hiking. What's more, the aggressive diamond-back species is not found in the state at all. Oregon's subspecies, *Crotalus viridis oreganus,* is a retiring sort, absolutely incapable of such spuriously attributed feats of daring as crawling into a sleeping bag for warmth.

These days, the most threatening beast in the woods is a microscopic paramecium by the name of *Giardia.* This pest, originally from Leningrad, has recently spread to some mountain streams in our country, where it can surprise the drinker of cold, clear water with debilitating diarrhea and nausea. The symptoms appear in 6 to 15 days and only abate after medical treatment. Some commercial filters and chemicals remove *Giardia,* though boiling water for 10 minutes is the surest treatment. It's also possible to second guess the little paramecium. *Giardia* is spread only by mammals (often beavers), enters the water by defecation, and only moves downstream. Thus, water from a spring or a high mountain watershed unfrequented by mammals will have a lower risk of contamination.

Of course, those who enter the wilderness without basic survival gear and skills are bringing hazard with them. Hypothermia is the number one killer in the wilds. It results from being wet and cold too long, and can be prevented by bringing proper clothing and shelter. Useful books and classes abound on preparation for hiking, backpacking, and climbing—with far more detail than this introduction can possibly include. Be prepared for the worst, and one will be able to enjoy the wilderness confidently at its best.

Finally, errors in mileage, trail location, and the like are inevitable in any guidebook—especially when new roads and logging clearcuts are constantly adding confusion. Despite all our effort to the contrary, the author, publisher, and research consultant cannot guarantee the accuracy of the information included here, nor that the trips described are safe for everyone.

Without danger, wilderness would not be wild. Of course, it seems obvious, but visitors in the wild are on their own. Pack some common sense and caution for safety's sake.

A WORD TO HIKERS

The easiest trips in each area are generally described first. Those who rarely hike should look for the nature trails, lakeshore paths, and short riverside hikes listed near the beginning of an area's *hiking* section. Remember that most mileages reflect the one-way length of a trail. Thus, a "1.4-mile trail to Twin Lakes" means a 2.8-mile round-trip hike. Also, the term "easy" is used only in relation to other hikes; someone who puffs climbing a few flights of stairs will not find a 2.8-mile walk easy at all.

And speaking of climbing, pay attention to the *elevation gains*—they warn of steep uphill trails. Many of the hike descriptions mention the elevation gain in feet, but even when they do not, the elevations shown on the maps make gains for most hikes calculable. A 1000-foot gain is an arduous uphill trudge for out-of-shape walkers, particularly if the climb is packed into less than 2 miles. A 2000-foot gain requires frequent rest stops even when hikers are in good condition. Hikers must be in very good shape—strong hearts and strong knees— to handle a 3000-foot elevation gain in a day. And only those in prime condition should tackle the 5000-foot climbs required by trails up Hat Point or South Sister.

A *car shuttle* allows a group with two cars to end their hike at a different trailhead. Drive both cars to the trip's endpoint, leave one there, and then drive in the other to the hike's starting point. A *key-swap hike* requires less driving, but more careful planning. For this arrangement, two carloads of hikers walk the same trail, starting at opposite trailheads. When the two groups meet at a specified time at the trail's midpoint, they swap car keys for the drive home. Better yet, swap duplicate keys before leaving for the hike.

Advanced hikers may be interested in the *cross-country hiking routes* suggested for many areas. Bushwhacking, not to be confused with machete-style trail chopping, can be surprisingly easy and immensely rewarding. It's the only way to hike in Oregon's trailless desert country. And although off-trail travel is more difficult in the dense forests of western Oregon's wildernesses, one needn't bushwhack very far in such terrain before finding true isolation—even in an area billed as crowded. Perhaps the best way to walk lightly on the land is to walk where no one else has.

Cross-country hikers in particular should inform someone of their route before leaving. They should keep a topographic map and compass at hand, and have experience using them. Always carry survival gear.

All hikers—even those on short, well-marked trails—should bring a water-repellent parka and a rucksack packed with the *Ten Essentials:*

1. Extra clothing
2. Extra food
3. Sunglasses
4. Knife
5. Firestarter (candle or butane lighter)
6. First aid kit
7. Matches in a waterproof container
8. Flashlight
9. Map (a topographic map is best)
10. Compass (and knowledge to use it)

Cross-country skiing

Also, always carry some water. Streams and springs shown on the area maps are generally reliable, but expect seasonal streams and lakes (marked with broken lines on the area maps) to be dry in summer and fall. Many hikes pass no water source at all.

Let someone know about the planned hike, so they can call the county sheriff's office to organize a search and rescue, if necessary. Lost hikers should stay put and keep warm.

Trail mileages given in this book are approximate, and may not agree with trail sign mileages (which are often incorrect). Likewise, official signs and maps often offer a confusion of names and numbers for the same trail. This guide generally avoids the debate by identifying trails according to their destination and starting point.

Road directions to trailheads are provided only when the map does not clearly show the route. When several obscure trailheads cluster together, complete car directions may only be given to one of them, with the understanding that drivers can then use the map to find the others.

Finally, remember a few courtesies:

- Step off the trail on the downhill side to let horses pass. Talking quietly to the horses can help prevent them from spooking.
- Leave no litter. Trailside orange peels and eggshells last for decades.
- Do not shortcut switchbacks.
- Divide large groups into independent hiking parties of 12 or fewer.
- Leave pets at home. A dog can dangerously anger bears, porcupines, and other wilderness users.
- Respect private land. This guide makes an effort to steer hikers clear of private property, but even designated wildernesses include some private inholdings.

A WORD TO BACKPACKERS

Wilderness campers face a serious challenge: leaving no trace of their camp. Choosing the right campsite is critical. Savvy campers will not pitch a tent over the wildflower meadow they came to see, but instead will choose a spot in the forest—and never in a hollow where trenching could be a temptation. Likewise, never camp in a fragile alpine area, on a streambank, or within 100 feet of a lake. Choose a less delicate site on sand, snow, or bare pine needle duff. Best of all, bring a gallon's worth of water bottles per camper and pitch a dry camp, away from the water sources that attract camping overuse.

Campfires are a luxury the wilderness can no longer afford to provide. Cook on a lightweight campstove using gas, alcohol, or butane. For warmth, wear more clothing. Even when an emergency requires a campfire, don't build a rock campfire ring; this needlessly blackens stones. Clear a circle of ground to mineral soil. Gather only small pieces of wood that can be broken off by hand. After use, drown the fire, scatter the cold ashes, and restore the site.

Do not bury or burn garbage. Limit the trash that must be packed out by bringing no canned or bottled foods, and by repackaging bulky foods into compact, lightweight plastic bags or containers.

Never wash dishes or bathe with soap directly in a lake or stream. Carry water at least 100 feet away from the shore and wash there.

Bury human waste and toilet paper (or better, leaves) in a small hole dug at least 100 feet from water. Choose a site where no one would ever camp. Fill the hole with dirt and cover the spot with a natural-looking arrangement of rocks or sticks.

When camping at an established site in the wilderness, try to restore it a little. Remove nails and clotheslines from trees. Dismantle racks, benches, or lean-to frames. Pick aluminum foil and trash from campfire rings and scatter the ashes. Remember, campers are visitors in the wilderness; "developed" campsites belong only at automobile campgrounds.

A WORD TO MOUNTAINEERS

This guide identifies mountaineering sites in 17 areas across the state—including Mt. Hood, the world's second most-climbed snowpeak, and Smith Rock, a mecca for technical climbers with 281 named routes. In addition, *hiking* entries describe popular nontechnical

Lightweight backpacking gear includes a nylon tent, a backpacking stove, and dried food (photo by J. Wesley Sullivan)

climbs such as South Sister, Eagle Cap, and Mt. McLoughlin.

Since available guidebooks discuss climbing techniques and safety and describe Oregon's technical climbs in detail, this book restricts itself to noting the chief attractions of each climbing area and the range of difficulty of the most important routes. The rating system used here, known as the Yosemite Decimal System, expresses the climb's overall difficulty first by a Roman numeral, then the climb's athletic difficulty by a number from 1 to 5.13, and finally (when appropriate) the difficulty of available artificial aid by symbols from A1 to A5, as follows:

Overall Difficulty
(length of climb, degree of commitment)
- I— up to 2 hours
- II— up to a half day
- III— a full day
- IV— possibly requires a bivouac
- Oregon has no grade V or VI climbs

Athletic Difficulty
(class of technical skill needed)
- 1— hiking
- 2— scrambling over talus or through brush
- 3— steep slopes or exposed ridges
- 4— rope required
- 5— rope and protection required

Class 5 climbs are broken down from 5.1 to 5.13 to indicate increasingly difficult pitches requiring rope and protection; climbs above 5.7 are demanding even for experts.

Artificial Aid Difficulty
- A1— solid placements
- A2— strenuous placements
- A3— several marginal placements
- A4— many marginal placements
- A5— marginal protection throughout

Thus, the east face of Smith Rock's Monkey Face, rated II-5.7-A3, requires most of a day with advanced free-climbing skills and has several marginally secure aids.

Climbers should not add new bolts to established routes, both to decrease clutter and to preserve a route's challenge.

A WORD TO CROSS-COUNTRY SKIERS

This guide covers most of Oregon's popular cross-country ski touring areas, and many little-known spots as well. In the area maps, hatch marks along trails and unplowed roads indicate feasible winter routes for Nordic skiers. Snowmobile-shaped symbols designate winter ORV staging areas; these have been included on the maps since other winter users may wish to avoid such areas.

"P" symbols along highways represent plowed sno-park lots. From November 15 to April 30, cars parked in or near sno-park lots must display a valid permit or face a $10 fine. Since the permit only costs $9 per season (even less for daily permits), it pays to stop by a sporting goods store, ski shop, or Department of Motor Vehicles office to pick one up.

In some high-use areas the Forest Service marks winter trails. ORV routes are signed with orange plastic diamonds while cross-country ski trails have blue diamonds (though in designated wilderness areas the blue markers are being replaced by less-visible oak signs).

Oregon's extremely variable snow conditions can produce delightful powder, heavy mush, and clattery ice all within a day's time. Waxless skis are usually the boards of choice.

Nordic skiers and snowshoers in Oregon need rain gear, plenty of warm clothing (wool is best), a rucksack with the *Ten Essentials* (see p.10), a full water bottle, a repair kit, and an insulated seating pad for rests. Never set out without a topographic map and compass. Wilderness exploration can be great fun in winter, but the need for caution and survival training is likewise great.

Avalanches, though infrequent in Oregon, may occur during or immediately after a snowstorm or high wind. Avoid slopes of more than 25 percent steepness—especially treeless slopes, since these may have a history as "avalanche chutes." Also beware of frozen lakes. Particularly in the Cascades, heavy snows can insulate the water, preventing it from forming solid ice. Even when skiers succeed in crossing the snow-covered slush, those on foot may fall through.

For Oregon weather reports and road conditions, call (503) 238-8400. For snow recreation information and avalanche forecasts for the Mt. Hood area, call (503) 221-2400; for the Bend area, call (503) 382-6922.

Finally, a few winter manners:
- Yield right of way to downhill skiers.
- Don't stop to rest in a ski track; step aside.
- Don't walk or snowshoe in a ski track; this ruins the smooth grooves.
- Leave pets at home.

A WORD TO BOATERS

This guide describes eight of Oregon's wildest whitewater river runs and numerous quiet spots for canoeing, sailing, or sailboarding. The descriptions use a six-point scale to rate a rapids' difficulty for rafters, kayakers, and drift boaters:

    class 1—easy
    class 2—moderate
    class 3—dangerous. Novices should consider lining or portaging boats.
    class 4—very dangerous. Novices should line or portage.
    class 5—extremely dangerous. Even experts should consider portaging.
    class 6—unrunnable. Portage boats.

Those in decked canoes should add a point to the difficulty of each rapids. For open canoes, add two points.

Note that most of these rivers can only be run when water is high—but not too high. Suitable months for running rivers vary dramatically from year to year. Check with the Water Resources Data Center at (503) 249-0666 for daily updates of river gauge levels.

Since floatboating concentrates visitor impact on the fragile camping beaches of wilderness rivers, it's important to follow the strictest no-trace camping guidelines:

• Cook on camp stoves. Those who require campfires must bring all of their own firewood, build the fire in a firepan they have brought, and then pack up both pan and ashes without a trace.

• Use toilets when provided. When they are not, do not bury toilet paper. Buried human waste decomposes within a few weeks, but paper remains for a year or more in riverbank soils, and can be exposed by wind or water. Burn the paper in a firepan, if available, or pack it out in a plastic bag.

Proper boating skills and safety are essential on wilderness runs where escape or rescue is difficult. Check the references listed at the back of this book for information on these important subjects.

A WORD TO EQUESTRIANS

The role of horses in the wilderness is in transition. A few new routes have been added for horses, but more and more trails bear the sign, "Hiker Only." The National Park Service at Crater Lake bans horses everywhere except on the Pacific Crest Trail, and allows no grazing.

As the no-trace ethic spreads, so have restrictions on saddle stock. Here's a list of guidelines which have grown into iron-clad rules in most wilderness areas:

• Allow no saddle stock within 200 feet of any stream or lake except for loading, unloading, watering, or traveling on a trail.

• Carry all the feed an animal will need. This cuts down on grazing.

• Bring no hay. It spreads weed seeds.

• Feed oats or hay pellets morning and evening from a nose bag, and not from the ground.

• Never tie stock to a tree, even temporarily. Tethers can girdle trees and hooves can dig circular pits.

• Hobble, don't picket stock. This disperses grazing damage.

• Do not build corrals or hitching racks.

• When breaking camp, fill in paw holes and scatter manure.

Gone are the days of campfires, big coffee pots, beans and bacon, and canvas tents. As equestrians limit their loads and their pack strings, their gear increasingly resembles that of the no-trace backpacker: lightweight nylon tents, lightweight campstoves, and freeze-dried food.

Many wilderness visitors who might once have used a pack horse now hire a llama. Llamas must be led on foot, since they can only carry a 60-pound pack. But llamas weigh a fifth as much as a horse, leave only deerlike pellets for droppings, and do a tenth of the damage to trails and meadows.

A FINAL WORD

Once Oregon was all wilderness from the Pacific to the Snake River. Now, only scattered islands of that great wilderness survive, and most of these still lack protection. Use this guide to discover the beautiful but fragile heritage that remains to show Oregon as it once was.

For the areas in this book, there is still time.

Canyon Creek Meadows and Three Fingered Jack, area 9 (photo by William L. Sullivan)

NORTHWEST OREGON

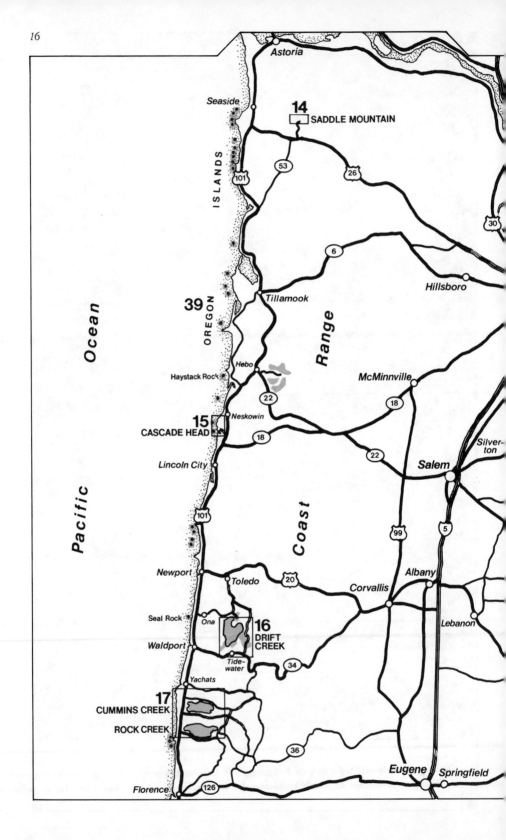

Astoria

Seaside

14 SADDLE MOUNTAIN

53

26

6

30

Hillsboro

Tillamook

39 OREGON

Range

Hebo

McMinnville

Haystack Rock

22

18

15 CASCADE HEAD

Neskowin

18

22

Salem

Silver-ton

Lincoln City

Coast

101

99

5

Newport

Toledo

20

Corvallis

Albany

Seal Rock

Ona

Lebanon

16 DRIFT CREEK

Waldport

Tide-water

34

Yachats

17 CUMMINS CREEK

ROCK CREEK

36

Eugene Springfield

Florence

126

Ocean

Pacific

ISLANDS

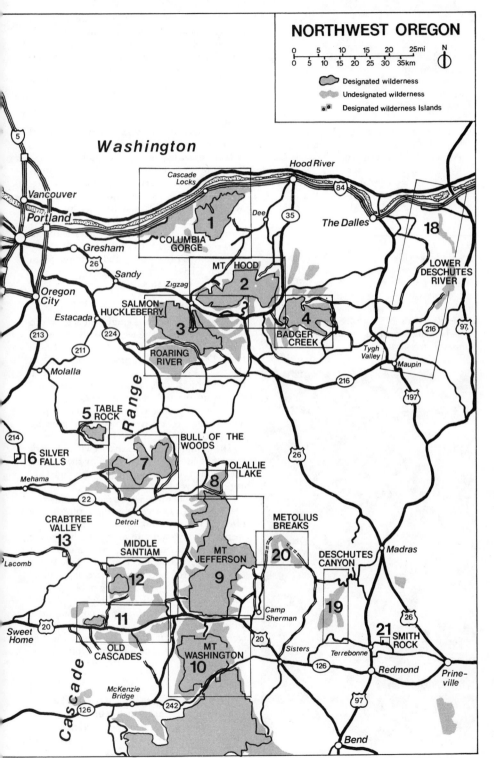

NORTHWEST OREGON

0   5   10   15   20   25mi
0   5   10   15   20   25   30   35km

N

Designated wilderness

Undesignated wilderness

Designated wilderness Islands

Washington

Hood River

Vancouver

Portland

Gresham

Sandy

Oregon City

Estacada

Molalla

Cascade Locks

Dee

The Dalles

84

35

18
LOWER DESCHUTES RIVER

COLUMBIA GORGE

1

MT. HOOD

2

Zigzag

SALMON-HUCKLEBERRY

3

ROARING RIVER

4
BADGER CREEK

Tygh Valley

Maupin

216

97

216

197

213

211

224

26

5
TABLE ROCK

214

6 SILVER FALLS

Mehama

Range

7

BULL OF THE WOODS

OLALLIE LAKE

8

METOLIUS BREAKS

20

22

CRABTREE VALLEY

13

Detroit

MIDDLE SANTIAM

Lacomb

12

MT JEFFERSON

9

Camp Sherman

26

DESCHUTES CANYON

Madras

19

Sweet Home

20

11

OLD CASCADES

20

MT WASHINGTON

10

Sisters

Terrebonne

SMITH ROCK

21

26

126

Redmond

Prineville

Cascade

McKenzie Bridge

126

242

97

Bend

1. Columbia Gorge

LOCATION: 24 mi E of Portland
SIZE: 107 sq mi
STATUS: 62 sq mi designated wilderness (1984)
TERRAIN: cliffs, densely forested canyons
ELEVATION: 100'–4960'
MANAGEMENT: Mt. Hood NF
TOPOGRAPHIC MAPS: Forest Trails of the
   Columbia Gorge, PCT Northern Oregon
   Portion (USFS); Bridal Veil, Bonneville Dam,
   Hood River (Green Trails, 15'); Mt. Hood
   (Geo-Graphics); Bridal Veil, Multnomah
   Falls, Bonneville Dam, Tanner Butte,
   Carson, Wahtum Lake, Mt. Defiance (USGS,
   7.5')

Several worlds collide in the Columbia
Gorge. In the west, moss-covered rain forests
cling to misty green cliffs. A few miles east,
only scrub oaks dot a semiarid scabland. And
in between, a colonnade of more than 20 major
waterfalls separates the alpine meadows of the
Cascade Range from the mudflats of the Columbia River, nearly at sea level.

Rhododendron

In the midst of these colliding ecosystems is
the remarkable Columbia Wilderness. Although it lies a mere half-hour freeway drive
from Portland and overlooks a busy transportation corridor along the Columbia, it remains
delightfully wild, protected by a ribbon of
breathtaking 3000-foot cliffs.

Climate
The annual rainfall varies from a soggy 150
inches in the Bull Run Watershed to 75 inches
at Cascade Locks, and just 29 inches at Hood
River on the eastern end of the gorge. Summers, however, are dry throughout. Snow covers trails over 3600 feet from December to
May, but lower trails may be clear for hiking
even in midwinter. Occasionally, winter ice
storms drape the cliffs with icicles and coat
trees and highways with silvery freezing rain—
a result of warm Pacific clouds dropping rain
through a layer of freezing air blown in from
east of the mountains.

Plants and Wildlife
Between the dense Douglas fir and sword
fern rain forests of the west and the open oak
grasslands of the east, the Columbia Gorge
hosts 12 plant species found nowhere else in
the world—including six strictly confined to
the wilderness lands. Look for rare plants and
flowers on the rock walls of the Gorge's cool
north-facing canyons—there, even alpine
wildflowers are often tricked into growing
nearly at sea level.
   The California condors that Lewis and Clark
reported here in 1805, attracted by the Columbia's salmon runs, are now gone, although bald
eagles may yet be sighted.
   The darling of the gorge's many waterfalls is
the water ouzel, a chubby little bluish-gray
bird that builds its mossy nests in the spray and
spends its days walking along the bottom of
rushing mountain streams, poking about for
mosquito larvae with its deft little bill. When
this robin-sized bird is not marching around
underwater it can be seen doing bobbing knee-
bend exercises on creek rocks or whirring along
just above the water with rapid, constant little
wingbeats. Though common throughout
western North America, this dipper can live
only where water runs wild and white.

Geology
The many layers of columnar basalt exposed
in the cliffs of the gorge are all part of the massive lava outpourings which inundated 50,000
square miles of eastern Washington, eastern
Oregon, and Idaho to a depth of up to a mile 10
to 17 million years ago. These rock floods—a
result of the North American continent over-

Tunnel Falls on the Eagle Creek Trail

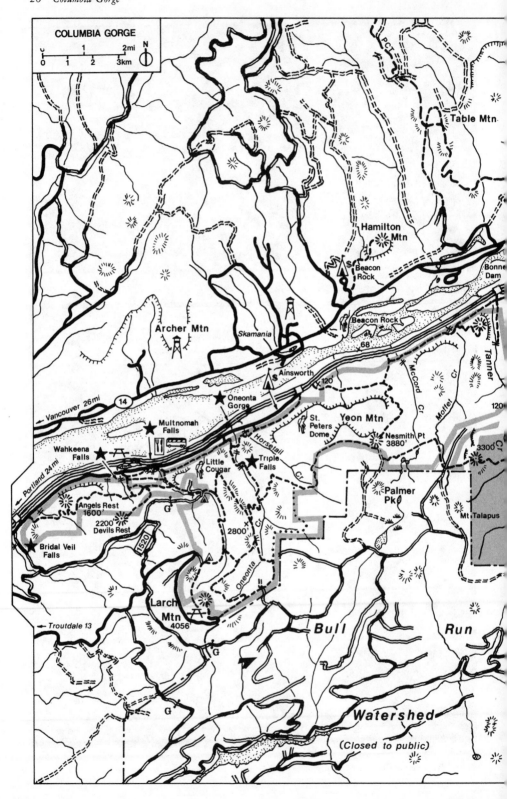

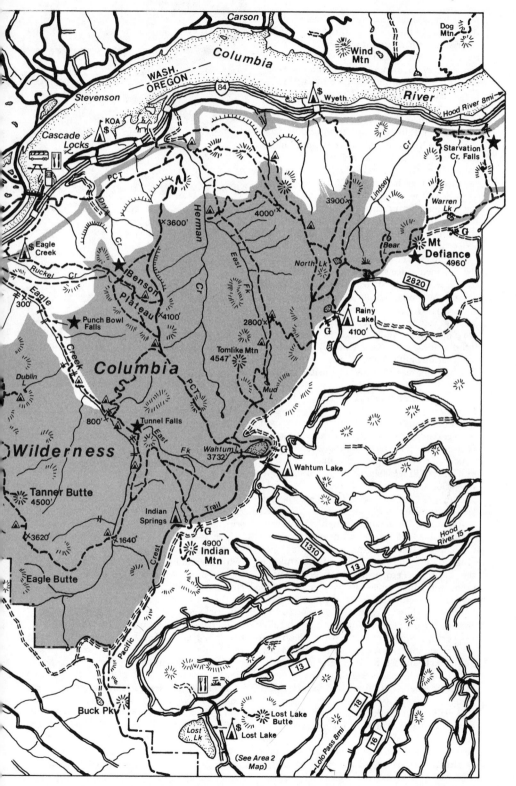

riding the Pacific Ocean floor—surged down the ancient Columbia as far as the sea, pushing the river north to its present location. When the crest of the Cascade Range then gradually warped upward, making those mountains ever higher, the Columbia kept pace by cutting its gorge deeper and deeper. The original surface of the lava flows is now a tilted and well-eroded upland, evident in the 2000-foot plateau above Multnomah Falls and the 4000-foot Benson Plateau. More recent volcanoes—Larch Mountain, Tanner Butte, and Mt. Defiance—protrude above this general silhouette.

During the Ice Age, 20 small glaciers formed on the gorge's southern rim, carving the hanging amphitheaters which lie above many of the waterfalls. Much of the scenery of the gorge, however, can be attributed to a series of monumental Ice Age floods of the Columbia River. These floods occurred when the continental ice sheet then covering Canada temporarily dammed the Clark Fork River in western Montana. The most recent such flood, 13,000 years ago, unleashed a body of water half the volume of Lake Michigan across eastern Washington and through the narrow Columbia Gorge. The flood denuded the gorge to an elevation of 800 feet and undercut the cliffs, leaving the graceful waterfalls visible today.

THINGS TO DO

Hiking

The thorough trail network is heavily used on weekends, particularly in the vicinity of Multnomah Falls and along Eagle Creek. The dramatic elevation gains on many trails (as much as 4000 feet) should be taken into consideration when planning trips.

Oregon's tallest waterfall, Multnomah Falls, has inspired a cluster of trails well suited to day hikes. Paths within roughly a half mile of this noble 620-foot double cascade are paved to accommodate the frequent foot traffic. One of the most popular and spectacular day hikes is the 2.4-mile Perdition Trail between Wahkeena and Multnomah falls; its modest 800-foot climb yields top views of the falls.

Long, slotlike Oneonta Gorge, though lesser-known than neighboring Multnomah Falls, has perhaps equal charm. A 3-mile loop peers down into this mossy chasm from its rim, but it can be more directly experienced by hopping on stepping stones up the narrow creekbed from the old Columbia River Highway bridge.

A half dozen exhilarating day hikes switchback up to viewpoints of the gorge. Angels Rest, atop the 6.4-mile trail between Wahkeena Falls and the Columbia Scenic Highway at Bridal Veil, is one of the most popular of

Oneonta Gorge

these routes, with a moderate 1500-foot elevation gain. Nesmith Point, west of McCord Creek, is an ambitious 3700-foot climb to a stunning view. Short but steep scramble trails leading to viewpoints of the Bonneville Dam area include Munra Point and Wauna Point (west and east of the mouth of Tanner Creek, respectively) and the Ruckel Ridge Trail, which begins at the Eagle Creek Campground.

The spectacular Eagle Creek Trail features seven waterfalls, a high bridge, and one tunnel (which actually goes *behind* Tunnel Falls). Blasted out of the sheer cliffs in the 1910s, this trail is now very popular. A day trip can hardly do the trail justice; it is better seen on a two-day backpack, perhaps returning via the beautiful Benson Plateau, or the quiet Tanner Creek or Herman Creek trails. Camping along the Eagle Creek Trail is restricted to designated sites; on summer weekends space can be tight.

Three long-distance trail routes cross the Columbia Wilderness. The 22-mile low-elevation Gorge Trail, between Multnomah Falls and Herman Creek, avoids the steep climbs found on many other trails and is snowfree year round. It is used primarily to connect other trails, but it makes good hiking from end to

end. And because of the Gorge Trail's many trailheads along the Columbia River Highway, sections of the path make for accessible and undemanding day hikes.

A higher elevation route, the Talapus Trail, winds 38 miles from 4056-foot Larch Mountain to 4960-foot Mt. Defiance. Together with the low-elevation Gorge Trail, this route makes it possible to convert any of the area's 15 north-south trails into scenic loop hikes. Hiking the length of the Talapus Trail is a challenging four-day backpack; the route zigzags across several steep canyons in the most remote part of the wilderness.

The third long-distance trail in the Gorge is the Pacific Crest Trail, which passes Wahtum Lake and crosses the Benson Plateau. Those who just can't wait to see the summer display of alpine wildflowers will find them blooming as early as June on the 4000-foot, two-square-mile Benson Plateau. Huckleberry aficionados can profitably prowl about Wahtum Lake in late August.

For those able to arrange a car shuttle between trailheads, Larch Mountain and Mt. Defiance can be the starting points of dramatic, downhill day hikes. The Larch Mountain Trail drops 4000 feet in 6.8 miles to the Multnomah

Falls Lodge. The Mt. Defiance Trail loses fully 4800 feet elevation to Starvation Creek Falls in just 5.5 miles. Both mountains offer dramatic views of Mt. Hood, Mt. Adams, and Mt. St. Helens.

Throughout the Columbia Gorge, hikers should remember that poison oak is common below 800 feet elevation, that trailside cliffs make some paths inappropriate for unsupervised children, and that underbrush and steep slopes virtually prohibit cross-country travel. Only the wider, well-graded Herman Creek and Pacific Crest trails are open to horses or pack stock. The Bull Run Watershed to the south, the source of Portland's water supply, is closed to the public except specifically for travel on the PCT.

Climbing

The Columbia Gorge is a center for testing technical climbing skills. For starters, good conditioning hikes include the nearly 5000-foot climb from Starvation Creek Falls to Mt. Defiance and the numerous trails up to the 4000-foot Benson Plateau. Then, 3 miles west of Bridal Veil Falls are Rooster Rock (a 200-foot pinnacle with routes varying in difficulty from level I-4 to II-5.6-A3) and Crown Point (a 700-foot bluff with routes of difficulty II-5.4 and III-5.6). The Pillars of Hercules, a group of 100-foot basalt towers immediately west of Bridal Veil, rate difficulty levels from I-5.2 to II-5.8.

Little Cougar, a small thumb of rotten rock at 1300 feet elevation 1 mile east of Multnomah Falls, is a level I-4 or I-5.4 climb, depending on the route taken. St. Peters Dome, 1 mile east of Ainsworth State Park, consists of similarly poor rock but requires level II-5.6 or III-5.6-A3 skills. It is a 200-foot thumb at 1525 feet and was unclimbed until 1940.

The greatest of all climbing challenges in the area is Beacon Rock, just across the Columbia River from St. Peters Dome. This impressive 848-foot andesite monolith requires about five rope lengths of skilled climbing. Difficulty levels of II-5.6 to IV-5.11 are encountered on a total of 45 named routes and variations.

Multnomah Falls

Mount Hood from the trail to Elk Meadows

2. Mount Hood

LOCATION: 34 mi E of Portland
SIZE: 115 sq mi
STATUS: 74 sq mi designated wilderness (1964, 1978)
TERRAIN: glaciated peak, alpine meadows, forested slopes
ELEVATION: 1800'–11,237'
MANAGEMENT: Mt. Hood NF
TOPOGRAPHIC MAPS: Mt. Hood (Geo-Graphics); Mt. Hood Wilderness, PCT Northern Oregon Portion (USFS); Government Camp, Mt. Hood (Green Trails, 15'); Rhododendron, Bull Run Lake, Government Camp, Mt. Hood N, Mt. Hood S, Dog River, Badger Lake (USGS, 7.5')

Oregon's tallest peak dominates this popular wilderness. Hikers meet alpine vistas of Mt. Hood from every path of the area's well-developed trail network. The dormant volcano's summit, ringed with 11 active glaciers, is the goal of 10,000 climbers a year.

But the peak is not the area's only attraction. The 38-mile Timberline Trail circles the mountain through a succession of stunning alpine meadows filled with wildflowers. Ramona, Tamanawas, and a dozen other waterfalls grace heavily forested river valleys. Zigzag Canyon is an impressive 1000-foot-deep gorge

on the mountain's flank. And 5000-foot Zigzag Mountain, an 8-mile-long western spur of Hood, offers lakes and ridges of its own.

Climate

The area's 100 inches of annual precipitation come largely as snow between October and April. Skiers and snowshoers will find the snow drier, and the skies often bluer, on Hood's east and southeast slopes. Snow melts off lower trails (up to 4000 feet) by about June 1, and off higher trails (up to 7000 feet) by mid-July. July and August yield warm days and cold nights. Sudden storms can bring snowfall in any month—a fact which has led to climbing tragedies.

Plants and Wildlife

Dense Douglas fir forests blanket lower areas of the wilderness, with an understory of Oregon grape, salal, and rhododendron (blooms late May). Higher forests are of mountain hemlock, noble fir, and subalpine fir. Near timberline (6500 feet), gnarled whitebark pines frame meadows of blue lupine, red Indian paintbrush, beargrass plumes, penstemon, purple Cascade aster, and western pasque flower ("old-man-of-the-mountain"). Profuse displays of white avalanche lilies decorate Paradise Park in July and Elk Cove in August. Huckleberries (ripe late August) dominate the ridges of Zigzag Mountain.

A bird checklist for Hood's south slope notes 132 species, from hummingbirds to bald ea-

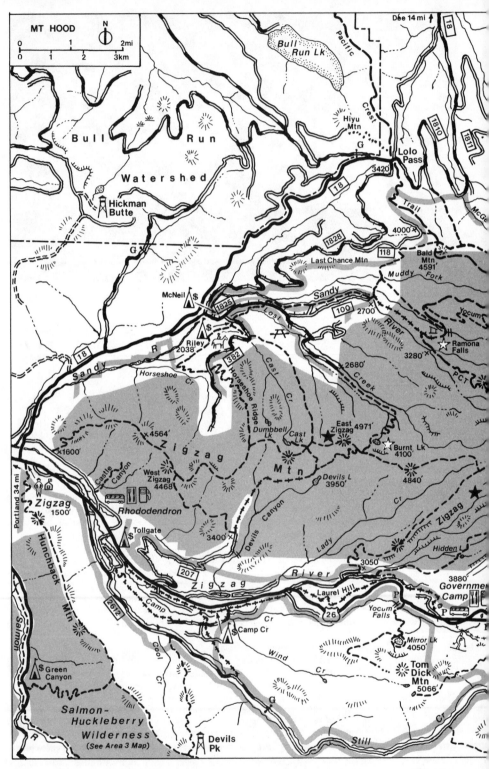

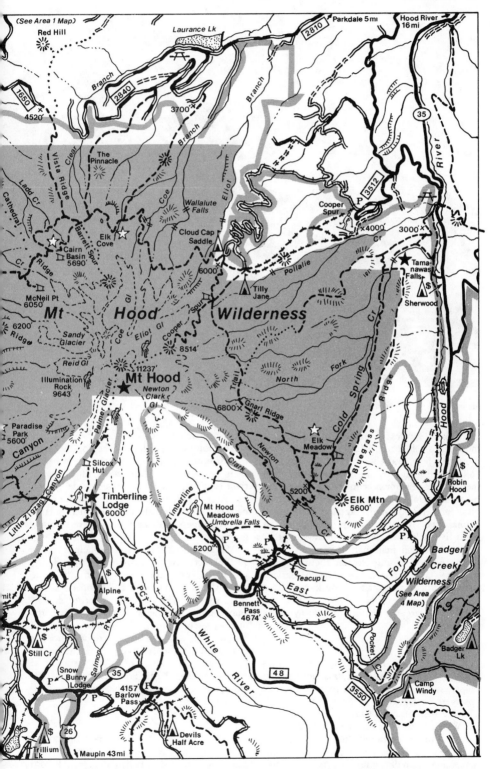

Mount Hood from the Pacific Crest Trail near Timberline Lodge

gles. Forty species of mammals live on the mountain's slopes, including black bear, mountain lion, and elk.

The whistling, squirrellike animals often met on Hood's rocky timberline slopes are pikas. Pikas (also known as conies or rock rabbits) are round-eared, apparently tailless animals the size of guinea pigs. Colonies of pikas live at higher elevations than any other North American mammal, cutting and sun-drying bushels of grass to last them through nine snowbound months without hibernation. Yellow-bellied marmots also live in rockslides and whistle to each other for warning, but they are much larger, resembling bushy-tailed beavers.

Geology

Mt. Hood is the most recently active of all Oregon volcanoes. In the 1800s, four minor eruptions of steam, ash, and magma alarmed observers as far away as Portland. In 1907 glowing rock near the summit melted part of the White River Glacier, causing floods. Even today, climbers encounter hot rock, scalding steam vents, and a powerful sulfur smell in the depression south of the summit, between Steel Cliff and Crater Rock.

The volcano itself had its beginnings after the surrounding hills and rivers were in nearly their present form. Lava flows filled nearby river canyons, forcing the rivers aside. When the rivers eroded the softer rock around the hard lava, the original valleys were left as lava-topped ridges—an example of "reverse topography."

Mt. Hood reached its greatest height, about 12,000 feet, just prior to the Ice Age. Then, glaciers removed the crater and much of the north slope. Barrett Spur and Cooper Spur remain to show the mountain's earlier dimensions, indicating the ancient crater was north of the present summit. Crater Rock, south of the summit, was long thought to be a remnant of the volcano's central plug. In fact it is a recent side vent's lava dome, the creation of which smothered the Timberline Lodge area with cinder-and-mud avalanches just 2000 years ago.

History

Spotted in 1792 by a Lieutenant Broughton under explorer Vancouver's command, Mt. Hood was named for British admiral Lord

Hood. In 1845 Sam Barlow laid out Oregon's first road around the south base of Mt. Hood, leading Oregon Trail wagons from The Dalles to Sandy over Barlow Pass. The route spared settlers the expense of a raft trip on the Columbia, but subjected them to the miseries of Laurel Hill, 3 miles west of Government Camp, a slope so steep that wagons had to be skidded down with wheels removed.

A 4-mile section of the Barlow Road over Laurel Hill was rebuilt as a hiking and equestrian trail by the Civilian Conservation Corps in 1935. Other Depression-era work projects include the artistically designed Timberline Lodge and the Timberline Trail with its scenic stone shelters.

THINGS TO DO

Hiking

The marvels of Mt. Hood are so close to Portland that overuse is a real concern. The many meadows, with their wildflower displays and mountain views, have had to be protected by a complete ban on camping. Backpackers must seek out less fragile sites in forested areas—and even the forested "islands" in Elk Meadows and Elk Cove have been placed off limits to tents or fires. The small lakes of Zigzag Mountain, popular for their reflections of Mt. Hood, are included in a general ban on camping within 200 feet of any lake's or stream's shoreline. Camping is not allowed within 500 feet of popular Ramona Falls, and fires are forbidden within 500 feet of McNeil Point—to save the gnarled dead wood at timberline for its own beauty.

This list of relatively crowded areas, however, also reads as a list of the wilderness area's top attractions, worth visiting for day hikers or careful backpackers.

Start with Ramona Falls, an easy 4.4-mile loop hike through the old growth forests along the Sandy River to a mossy, 100-foot falls on a stairstepped cliff of columnar basalt. Complete the loop by returning via the Ramona Creek Trail to Forest Road 100. A comparable, but lesser-known day hike on the east side of Mt. Hood leads an easy 2 miles (one way) from Sherwood Campground to 100-foot Tamanawas Falls.

The prime hike through Hood's alpine meadows is the 37.6-mile Timberline Trail, a three- to five-day trip usually begun at Timberline Lodge and undertaken clockwise around the mountain, so as to finish up at the showers and swimming pool (suit rentals available) at the classic old lodge. Five unbridged creek crossings on the route can be hazardous in the high water of June and July snowmelt: Zigzag River, Sandy River, Muddy Fork, Eliot Branch, and White River. Water is lower in August and during the mornings.

No fewer than 21 trails lead up the flanks of Mt. Hood to the Timberline Trail, making all manner of loop hikes and day trips possible. Many of these tributary trails ascend ridges that are scenic in their own right—notably Gnarl Ridge on Hood's east slope, the Hidden Lake Trail and Zigzag Canyon Trail on the mountain's southwest slope, and Vista Ridge and The Pinnacle on Hood's north flank. All make excellent day trips for the fit hiker; distances average 3 to 5 miles one way with 2000-foot elevation gains.

Hikers who shy from such climbs can still sample the Timberline Trail's charms from two high-elevation trailheads. Timberline Lodge, set among wildflowers itself, is a good starting point for an easy 2.6-mile traverse to Zigzag Canyon, an impressive 1000-foot-deep erosional gash into Hood's volcanic scree. On the mountain's northeast flank, Cloud Cap Saddle Campground touches the Timberline Trail amidst 6000-foot-elevation meadows; the popular meadow at Elk Cove is a 4.9-mile hike west.

The adventurous hiker can climb well above timberline to view Hood's glaciers close-up at several points. By far the highest trail is 8514 feet up Cooper Spur, overlooking Eliot Glacier, 3 miles from Cloud Cap Saddle. A trail up from Timberline Lodge passes Silcox Hut before petering out at 8000-feet. Yocum Ridge and the McNeil Point shelter are atop other high trails; Barrett Spur's viewpoint is a cross-country scramble above the Timberline Trail. Climbing beyond these points is technical, requiring special gear and climber registration.

West of Mt. Hood, Zigzag Mountain is another popular hiking center, with four lakes, two lookout tower sites (West and East Zigzag), and six trailheads. The Devils Canyon trailhead provides the gentlest grades up to the area's best viewpoints—2.5 miles to West Zigzag and 4 miles to East Zigzag. The two most popular day hikes are probably the 3.5-mile trail to Burnt Lake and the 4.3-mile trip from Road 382 to Cast Lake. Ridgetops south of both lakes offer views worth the extra climb.

East of Hood, Elk Meadows is another popular destination, with its fine mountain view. Reach the meadow's three-sided shelter either up the 2.5-mile trail from Hood River

Meadows or along the heavily forested 6.2-mile Cold Spring Creek Trail from the Polallie Picnic Area on Highway 35. One of the best hikes for a foggy, viewless day is the 4.1-mile East Fork Hood River Trail, a level forest walk between Robin Hood and Sherwood campgrounds.

Most equestrian use in the wilderness begins at the horse-loading facilities at Riley Campground, west of Mt. Hood. Signs mark the fragile or hazardous trails closed to pack and saddle stock: the non-Pacific Crest Trail portion of the Timberline Trail, Cathedral Ridge, Vista Ridge, Pinnacle Ridge, Elk Cove, Paradise Park Loop, Castle Canyon, Yocum Ridge, Burnt Lake, and the Sandy River portion of the Ramona Falls loop.

Climbing

First climbed in 1857, Mt. Hood has become the second most climbed snowpeak in the world—after Japan's sacred Mt. Fuji. Portland's outdoor club, the Mazamas, was organized in 1894 by 193 climbers who convened on the summit in inclement weather. Hood has been scaled by a woman in high heels and by a man with no legs. Climber Gary Leech once raced from Timberline to the summit in 85 minutes.

But Hood is still a technical climb, over crevassed glaciers and loose, rotten rock. Lack of caution and the area's volatile weather have given Hood one of the highest accident rates of any peak in the country. An ice ax, crampons, and rope are essential; helmets are recommended. And all climbers must register either at Timberline Lodge or at Cloud Cap Inn.

The easiest and most popular route to the top, the "South Side" route, proceeds at a true 5° compass bearing from Silcox Hut to the Hot Rocks, a geothermal area between Crater Rock and Steel Cliff. A snow hogback north of Crater Rock leads to the summit wall, where a large crevasse must be circumvented before continuing to the summit. The climb takes 4 to 10 hours, and is begun in the predawn dark to avoid the afternoon's slushy snow. A descent in poor visibility must be undertaken by compass; the tendency to return "straight down" often leads climbers southwest toward Zigzag Canyon.

The second most common summit route, also rated level I-2, ascends the 45° snow slope above the Cooper Spur viewpoint on the mountain's east face. Avalanches can be a hazard here.

There are 12 additional ascent routes varying in difficulty from I-3 to III-5.6.

Illumination Rock, a 9543-foot crag between the Reid and Zigzag glaciers southwest of Hood's summit, offers some interesting climbing topography. Five level I routes, of classes 4 to 5.4, explore the rock's pinnacles and a summit "skylight" hole.

Winter Sports

Mt. Hood offers the largest selection of Nordic ski routes in the state. Highways 26 and 35 are plowed in winter, providing access to five developed downhill ski areas and 12 plowed sno-park lots. Snow Bunny Lodge and all of the downhill areas, except Timberline Lodge, rent cross-country skis.

From Timberline Lodge, Nordic skiers can traverse 2.6 miles to the brink of Zigzag Canyon on the PCT, or choose one of three heavily used routes for the 4-mile glide down to Government Camp. From Government Camp, numerous short trails lace the level area between Multorpor Meadows and the snowed-under Still Creek Campground. More advanced skiers can tackle the 6.3-mile Yellowjacket Trail, traversing from the junction of Highway 26 and the Timberline Lodge Road to the White River sno-park on Highway 35.

Snow Bunny Lodge, a snow play center without downhill skiing facilities, is the starting point for the many Nordic routes on snowed-under roads around scenic Trillium Lake. The easiest trip is to Summit Meadows, north of Trillium Lake, where the graves of Barlow Road pioneers are marked by white crosses.

The winding 2.4-mile section of old highway at Barlow Pass makes a pleasant ski route; the Giant Trees loop trail between the old and new highways explores an old growth grove. Trailless exploration of the scenic White River Canyon is relatively easy from the White River sno-park on Highway 35.

Nordic ski routes from Bennett Pass head southeast along roads toward the Badger Creek Wilderness or upper Pocket Creek (beware of avalanche-prone steep slopes in this area). From the parking lots of nearby Mt. Hood Meadows, Elk Meadows makes a spectacular winter goal, but bring map and compass for safety on the 2.4-mile trail. Robin Hood Campground's sno-park offers good level skiing along the East Fork Hood River Trail, as well as on roads to the west, through Horsethief Meadows toward Bluegrass Ridge.

From the Cooper Spur Ski Area's sno-park, the challenging Cooper Spur Ski Trail climbs 1800 feet in 3 miles to the snowed-under Tilly Jane Campground; a return loop is possible via

Timberline Lodge

Sahalie Falls, two miles west of Bennett Pass

the 8.6-mile Cloud Cap Road.

Although there are no sno-parks on the west side of Mt. Hood, the lower portion of Road 18 is typically snowfree, allowing access to good ski-touring country. Drive to the snow gate at McNeil Campground, then ski 5.7 miles east to beautiful Ramona Falls. Another trip from the snow gate tours 4 miles south up Road 382 into Horseshoe Canyon. In spring, when higher snow levels open Road 18 farther, drive to the snowline and continue on skis along Road 18 to Lolo Pass, where views open up in all directions. For a genuine challenge, ski the 9.2 miles back to McNeil Campground on Road 1828, around Last Chance Mountain.

3. Salmon-Huckleberry and Roaring River

LOCATION: 32 mi SE of Portland
SIZE: 164 sq mi
STATUS: 70 sq mi designated wilderness (1984)
TERRAIN: densely forested river canyons, ridges, lake basins
ELEVATION: 980'–5159'
MANAGEMENT: Mt. Hood NF
TOPOGRAPHIC MAPS: Mt. Hood (Geo-Graphics); PCT Northern Oregon Portion (USFS); Cherryville, Government Camp, Fish Creek Mountain, High Rock, Mt. Wilson (Green Trails, 15'); Wildcat Mountain, Rhododendron, Government. Camp, Three Lynx, High Rock, Wolf Peak, Wapinitia Pass, Mt. Mitchell, Fish Creek Mountain (USGS, 7.5')

Less than an hour's drive from Portland, this spacious wilderness remains virtually undiscovered. Hidden here are the spectacular Salmon River waterfalls and the delightful subalpine lakes of the Rock Lakes Basin. Yet the area's greatest charms are more subtle: fog-draped ridgecrests of ripe huckleberries and lonely whitewater canyons lined with mossy maples.

Climate

Trails below 2000 feet are usually snowfree in winter; ridge trails and the Pacific Crest Trail remain under snow from November to May. Spring and fall rains account for a share of the area's 80-inch annual precipitation. Summers are generally clear and dry.

Plants and Wildlife

Major runs of steelhead, Chinook, and coho salmon return annually to the aptly named Salmon River. The Roaring River's thunderous torrent is home to hardy anadromous fish and cutthroat trout as well, while every lake of size in the area supports brook trout.

Elk and blacktail deer rely on the area's extremely rugged, snowless lower canyons for winter range. The large, trailless upper Roaring River valley shelters several shy wildlife species, including cougar, fisher, and marten. Listen for the flute-like call of the hermit thrush in June and July. Water ouzels whir along streams year round.

The dense western hemlock and Douglas fir forests of the canyon bottoms are interspersed with droopy-branched western red cedar and red alder. Creekside vine maple adds brilliant scarlet foliage in fall. Rare Alaska cedar can be found on the fringes of Salmon River Meadows.

Ridgetops are mostly open, decorated in June with showy Washington lily and the white plumes of beargrass. The area's famed huckleberries, once the goal of annual harvest treks by Indians and pioneers alike, are ripe in late August. Hikers and black bears still seek out the abundant blue fruit around Veda Lake and on Indian Ridge, Huckleberry Mountain, Old Baldy, and Devils Peak.

Geology

The ridges of this area belong to the Old Cascades, a broad volcanic mountain range that erupted 10 million years before the High Cascades, and which now forms the rugged western foothills for those taller, snow-capped peaks. Devils Peak and Salmon Butte are probably remnants of once-tall volcanoes, but the erosive power of water and ice have reduced them to ridges. Broad, U-shaped glacial valleys, now filled with meadows and lakes, are recognizable at Rock Lakes, Squaw Lakes, Plaza Lake, and Serene Lake.

THINGS TO DO

Hiking

Two very easy day hikes with views of Mt. Hood are the 1.2-mile trail into Mirror Lake (1 mile west of Government Camp) and the 1.2-mile Veda Lake Trail (8 miles south of Government Camp on Road 2613). The lower part of the Salmon River Trail, paralleling Road 2618 for 2.6 miles, to Green Canyon Campground, makes another pleasant warm-up trip.

The Salmon River Trail upriver of Green Canyon Campground enters wilder country: a densely forested canyon with a string of hidden waterfalls. The trail stays at water level for 2 miles to Rolling Riffle Camp, then contours several hundred feet above the river on steep slopes. Between 3 and 4 miles in, rough, un-

The lower part of the Salmon River Trail

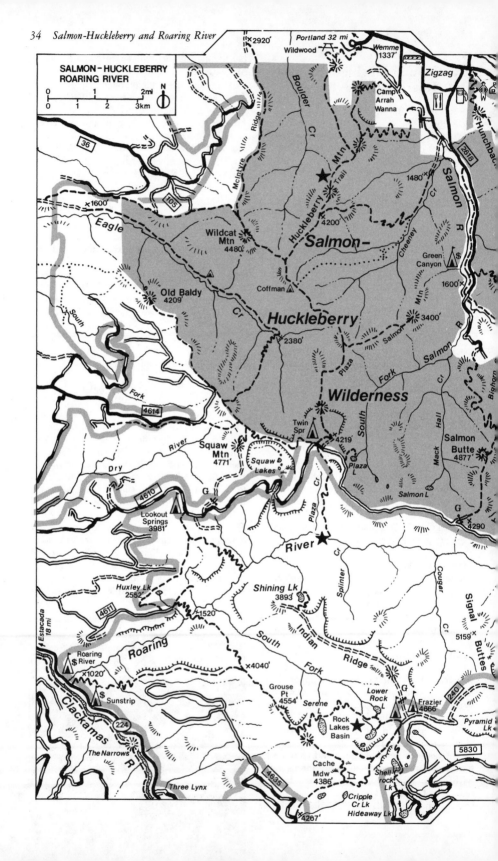

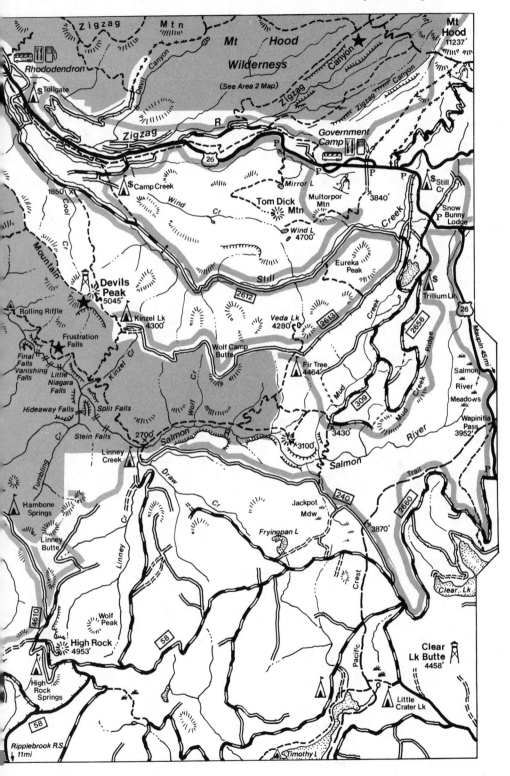

marked side trails lead steeply down to viewpoints of the rugged inner canyon and secluded falls. Plan a car shuttle to hike the Salmon River Trail from Road 2618 to any of four higher trailheads. (Kinzel Lake is 7 miles; Linney Creek, 8; Fir Tree, 13; and Mud Creek Road, 13).

The 7.7-mile Rock Basin loop trail offers the attractions of a High Cascades hike, without the crowds. The loop passes three subalpine lakes, a clifftop viewpoint, and Cache Meadow's somewhat rundown log hut. Side trails from the loop plunge toward the Roaring River. To reach the trailhead at Frazier Turnaround (a primitive campground with no water) take Highway 224 southeast of Estacada 26 miles, turn left just after Ripplebrook Ranger Station onto Road 57, turn left again after 8 miles onto Road 58, head left after another 7 miles onto Road 4610 past High Rock, then after 2 more miles, continue straight on Road 240 to its end. From the same trailhead, try the 1-mile jaunt down to Shellrock Lake, or hike the scenic abandoned road 4.7 miles to Shining Lake.

The Salmon-Huckleberry Wilderness has no fewer than five panoramic ridges with trails; most of these hikes begin with long climbs. The closest to Portland is Wildcat Mountain, a 5-mile trip (one way) gradually gaining 2900 feet up McIntyre Ridge to views of Mt. Hood. The trailhead is 3.5 miles up Wildcat Creek Road, which begins just beyond milepost 36 on Highway 26, east of Portland.

Four good routes ascend Huckleberry Mountain, though two of them begin on private roads (the trails at, and immediately south of, Camp Arrah Wannah).

The best view of all is from the lookout tower on Devils Peak; it can be reached either by the 4-mile Cool Creek Trail from Road 2612, the new 5-mile Green Canyon Trail from Road 2618, or the 8.5-mile Hunchback Ridge Trail from the Zigzag Ranger Station. Since all these routes gain over 3000 feet in elevation, most day hikers feel justly satisfied with the excellent viewpoints of Mt. Hood short of the actual lookout.

The views from the open, rocky summit of Salmon Butte are reached either by a woodsy 4.3-mile trail climbing 2700 feet from a spur near the end of Road 2618, or by a less pleasant, but nearly level, 2-mile route on a barricaded road off Road 4610.

Another trail center is Twin Springs Campground; drive 7 miles southeast of Estacada on Highway 224, then turn left on Road 4610 for 19 miles. Twin Springs is atop "The Plaza," a 1-square-mile plateau surrounded by ridges and glacial valleys. Follow The Plaza Trail 1.5

miles north to the Sheepshead Rock viewpoint at the tip of The Plaza; then hike down another 3.5 miles northeast for the view on Salmon Mountain.

The Roaring River is one of the wildest and most remote streams in northwest Oregon. Quiet trails switchback down to the river from Lookout Springs Campground (3 miles) and Twin Springs Campground (2.3 miles). On either route, hikers must return the way they came, regaining 2000 feet elevation. No trails or easy bushwhacking routes follow the river itself through its rugged canyon.

The Eagle Creek Trail follows a rushing stream through a towering old growth rain forest. A meadow at 3.5 miles makes a logical stopping point for day hikers. A Mt. Hood National Forest Map is necessary to locate the trailhead, 15 miles east of the town of Eagle Creek.

Winter Sports

Three excellent cross-country skiing centers border the area. Most popular is the Snowbunny Lodge sno-park on Highway 26, from which a wide variety of tours are possible into the Trillium Lake Basin. Several short trips are described in the Mt. Hood entry; longer tours follow Road 2613 5.5 miles to a view on the Veda Lake Trail, or prowl the roads and clearcuts along Mud Creek and Mud Creek Ridge. Numerous loop routes are possible by going cross-country between roads—remember a compass and topographic map.

The second major Nordic skiing area focuses on four sno-parks, located 0.5, 1.5, 2.7, and 4.4 miles south of Wapinitia Pass on Highway 26. The area features road tours around scenic Clear Lake and Frog Lake. A short, often overlooked trip is the half-mile jaunt to spacious Salmon River Meadows, 1.6 miles north of Wapinitia Pass on Highway 26, but hidden from the road by trees.

The high country southeast of Roaring River offers solitude for cross-country skiers. This area begins near the Ripplebrook Ranger Station 26 miles southeast of Estacada on Highway 224. Winter plowing extends as far as the Silvertip Work Center, 3 miles up Road 4630 from Ripplebrook, so after heavy midwinter snows, tours start there. It is 11.4 miles up Road 4635 to Cache Meadow—a worthy overnight trek for the prepared. When the snowline reaches 3000 feet in spring (call Ripplebrook Ranger Station for snow information), skiers can drive 8 miles east of Ripplebrook on Road 57, then turn left on Road 58 another 3 miles. From that point, tours on Roads 58 and 5830 extend to Shellrock Lake and High Rock.

4. Badger Creek

LOCATION: 65 mi E of Portland, 44 mi SE of
  The Dalles
SIZE: 45 sq mi
STATUS: 36 sq mi designated wilderness (1984)
TERRAIN: forested canyons
ELEVATION: 2100'–6525'
MANAGEMENT: Mt. Hood NF
TOPOGRAPHIC MAPS: Mt. Hood, Flag Point
  (Green Trails, 15'); Mt. Hood (Geo-
  Graphics); Badger Lake, Flag Point, Friend,
  Post Point (USGS, 7.5')

Draped across the eastern foothills of Mt.
Hood, the Badger Creek canyonlands form the
remarkable transition zone between High Cascade forest and Columbia Plateau steppe. The
area's 80 miles of trails connect with the Mt.
Hood Wilderness nearby.

Climate

Lying east of the Cascade Crest, Badger
Creek is often sunny when western Oregon is
suffering drizzle. Though the area measures
just 12 miles end to end, annual precipitation
ranges from 70 inches on the windy western
ridges to 20 inches in the dry eastern lowlands.
Snows close the lower trails from December

through February. The ridges' relatively light
winter snowpack melts from the highest trails
by mid-June. Afternoon thunderstorms occasionally interrupt hot summer days.

Plants and Wildlife

The higher elevations of Badger Creek share
the alpine rock gardens and Hudsonian forests
of Mt. Hood, but the eastern lowlands exhibit
a pine-oak biologic zone unique in Oregon wilderness. This open, parklike ecosystem of ponderosa pine and Oregon white oak extends only
a short distance north and south of the Columbia River between Hood River and The Dalles.

Nowhere is the pine-oak zone's spring wildflower display as spectacular as on the School
Canyon Trail, west from Road 27 over Ball
Point. Tall purple larkspur bloom in mid-
April, with pink shooting star in damp areas.
By late May, great fields of lupine turn the hillsides blue, splashed yellow at places by balsamroot. By July, white death camas and purple
onion remain among the yellow, withered
grass.

By late July the wildflowers of the pine-oak
zone are gone, but the rock gardens of the alpine zone are at their peak. Amble along the
Divide and Gunsight Butte trails for showy
penstemon, Indian paintbrush, avalanche
lilies, and stonecrop.

The Portland Audubon Society has com-

Gunsight Butte and Gumjuwac Saddle, seen from Mount Hood

piled lists for Badger Creek showing 46 butterfly species, 101 lichens, and 157 birds —surprising diversity for such a compact area.

Geology

Volcanism from Mt. Hood provided the raw material for the Badger Creek area. An Ice Age glacier scoured a curving, 2500-foot-deep, U-shaped valley from its cirque at Badger Lake down Badger Creek, leaving the dramatic cliffs below the Divide Trail. A second glacier cut the valley of Boulder Creek; its cirque lake, below Camp Windy, has filled with sediment to become Crane Prairie. Stream erosion since the Ice Age cut the precipitous, narrow gorges of lower Badger Creek and Little Badger Creek, leaving interesting badlands and pinnacles of more resistant rock.

THINGS TO DO

Hiking

The steep 2.5-mile route up from Robin Hood Campground on Highway 35 to Gumjuwac Saddle climbs 1700 feet through forest to the intersection of four Badger Creek trails, all suitable for day hikes or longer treks.

Southeast of Gumjuwac Saddle, the Gunsight Trail parallels Road 3550 for 5 miles to the junction of Road 4891, following a ridgetop packed with rock gardens, interesting rock formations, and viewpoints of Mt. Hood. Due south of Gumjuwac Saddle is the 2-mile trail down to Badger Lake.

A trail heading east from Gumjuwac Saddle drops 1300 feet in 2 miles to the Badger Creek Trail; from there, Bonney Crossing Campground is an enchanting 9.5-mile backpack downstream, past old growth Douglas fir, green-pooled cascades, and finally, oak-fringed cliffs. Yet another trail from Gumjuwac Saddle climbs 2.5 miles northeast to 6525-foot Lookout Mountain, the finest viewpoint in the area.

It is possible to drive to the trail crossing at Gumjuwac Saddle by following Road 3550 from Highway 35 at Bennett Pass, but it's a slow, rough dusty drive.

To reach the trailhead to Crane Prairie, in the lovely valley of Boulder Creek, leave Road 3550 4 miles from Bennett Pass, continuing straight 0.25 mile on Road 4891. Another mile down Road 4891 is Bonney Meadows Campground, which offers several trails, including the pleasant 2-mile day hike to Boulder Lake.

The northern portion of the Badger Creek Wilderness features the Divide Trail, a 3-mile route between the Flag Point fire lookout and

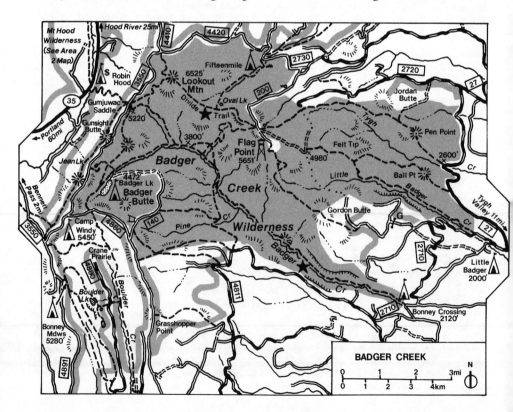

Badger Lake from the trail to Gumjuwac Saddle (photo by Wendell Wood)

Lookout Mountain. The path is a stunning series of cliff-edged viewpoints, rock formations, and wildflower gardens. Reach it by driving east from Highway 35 on paved Road 44, 2 miles north of Robin Hood Campground. After 3 miles, turn right onto dirt Road 4410; follow this 5 miles to its junction with Road 3550. This junction is the trailhead for an easy 1-mile hike up an abandoned road to the spectacular viewpoint atop Lookout Mountain, and to the Divide Trail.

On the eastern edge of the wilderness, four trails set out through the unique pine-oak forest. The 11.5-mile Badger Creek Trail to Badger Lake is more than a day hike, but worth it. The Little Badger Creek Trail fords its creek seven times in the first 3 miles of its rugged canyon; crossings during spring runoff can be cold and awkward. Access to the eastern Badger Creek trailheads is via Tygh Valley, a town on Highway 197. Bear west from town past the fairgrounds onto what will become Road 27; Little Badger Campground is 11 miles.

Winter Sports

Cross-country skiers can follow Road 3550 from the sno-park at Bennett Pass toward a number of destinations: Bonney Meadows (5.8 miles), Gunsight Butte (7.2 miles), and Badger Lake (7.4 miles via the trail at Camp Windy).

5. Table Rock

LOCATION: 19 mi SE of Molalla, 50 mi S of
   Portland
SIZE: 9 sq mi
STATUS: 9 sq mi designated wilderness (1984)
TERRAIN: forested ridges
ELEVATION: 1300'–4881'
MANAGEMENT: Salem District BLM
TOPOGRAPHIC MAPS: Rooster Rock, Gawley
   Creek (USGS, 7.5')

This pocket wilderness, close to the populous Willamette Valley, offers year-round hiking on quiet forest trails. Table Rock's basalt
mesa is the area's high point, with a view worth
the climb.

Climate
Table Rock is mild and wet (80 inches of annual precipitation), with sunny summers.
Winter snows cover trails above 3000 feet from
about December to March.

Plants and Wildlife
The virtually unbroken forest cover is
Douglas fir and western hemlock, with noble
fir at higher elevations. Pink-blossomed
rhododendron crowd lower slopes. The small,
sparsely petaled Gorman's aster found on rockslides is a candidate for endangered species
status, as is Oregon sullivantia, a saxifrage of
cliff seeps. White Clackamas iris, showy
Washington lilies, and delicate calypso orchids
are endangered primarily by indiscriminate
flower pickers.

Hawks, eagles, and owls top the list of
birds. Deer and coyotes frequent the higher
ridgetop trails.

Geology
The dramatic rock pillars on Table Rock's
sheer northern cliff are remnants of a hard
basalt lava flow which once capped the entire
area. All local rocks date from the Old Cascade's eruptions 16 to 25 million years ago.

History
Table Rock was in the hunting grounds of
the Northern Molalla, a small tribe confined to
the rugged foothills between the Willamette
Valley and the High Cascades. Because the
Molalla spoke a Sahaptin language similar to
that of the Nez Perce, they are thought to have
been driven from an eastern Oregon homeland
centuries ago to this unlikely range.

Table Rock Trail (photo by Salem District BLM)

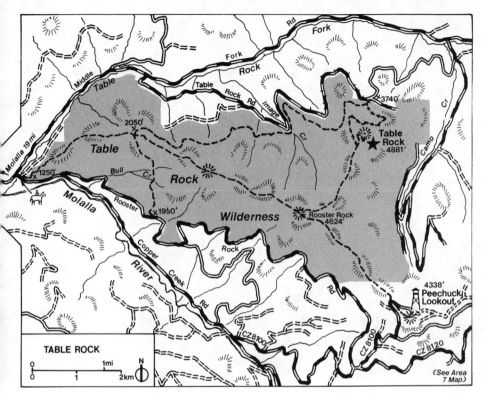

The east-west trail from the Molalla River to Peechuck Lookout is a remnant of a Molalla trail leading from the lowlands to Bull of the Woods and the High Cascades. Three archeological sites—evidently Molalla camps—have been identified in the area.

THINGS TO DO

Hiking

Seldom are wilderness viewpoints as sweeping and accessible as the one atop Table Rock, a pleasant 2.3-mile hike away from the Table Rock Road. On its 1100-foot climb, the trail winds about the impressive basalt cliffs of Table Rock's north face, then switchbacks up the gentler west slope. The panorama extends from Mt. Rainier to the Three Sisters, including views into the Bull of the Woods Wilderness and the Willamette Valley.

The 1.5-mile trail between Table Rock and Rooster Rock is a little rough where it dips briefly into a steep valley. Rooster Rock affords lesser views, but protrudes from a scenic heather-topped ridge. The hiker who has planned a car shuttle can continue past Rooster Rock on this ridge to the Molalla River trailhead —an 8.8-mile trip in all. Peechuck fire lookout, though no longer in use, is another interesting goal.

There are no reliable water sources on the area's trails. Equestrians will want to avoid the rough rock talus slope directly north of Table Rock; a snow patch can linger here until July.

All trailheads are reached by Highway 211 via the town of Molalla, 30 miles south of Portland. From the east edge of Molalla, turn south off Highway 211 onto South Mathias Road. After 0.3 mile curve left onto South Feyrer Park Road; after another 1.8 miles turn right onto South Dickey Prairie Road. For 5 miles follow this road, which turns right at Dickey Prairie and finally crosses the Molalla River bridge. Continue on the South Molalla Road 12.5 miles to a junction with the Middle Fork Road. The low elevation Table Rock trailhead is a stone's throw to the east.

Winter Sports

From December to March it is pleasant to drive to snowline on the Table Rock Road, park to one side, and ski up the road and Table Rock Trail to the base of Table Rock's ice-encrusted cliffs for the fine view. The distance varies from 2 to 4 miles, depending on the snow level on the road.

South Falls

6. Silver Falls

LOCATION: 26 mi E of Salem
SIZE: 13 sq mi
STATUS: state park
TERRAIN: forested gorge, waterfalls
ELEVATION: 760′–2400′
MANAGEMENT: Oregon Parks and Recreation Division.
TOPOGRAPHIC MAPS: Silverton, Scotts Mills, Stayton NE, Drake Crossing (USGS, 7.5′)

Waterfalls are the specialty of this very popular state park. Trails lead through a steep-sided, scenic canyon past 10 falls, 5 of which are over 100 feet tall. In 3 cases, trails actually lead through mossy caverns *behind* waterfalls.

Climate

The mild, wet weather of this relatively low elevation park allows hiking in any season. In fact, the falls are most spectacular in winter, when silvery icicles and snow add a delicate beauty missed by the summer crowds.

Plants and Wildlife

Dense Douglas fir forests and streambank maples shelter a lush undergrowth of ferns, Oregon grape, salal and many forest wildflowers. Though most wildlife species shy away from the park's populous trails, look for gray, robin-sized water ouzels dipping or flying along the creek. Hikers often marvel at the area's spectacular anthills, some 4 feet tall.

Geology

Silver Creek Canyon's cliffs are part of the Columbia River basalt flows which inundated this area about 15 million years ago, leveling the landscape. When the area was then tilted upward with the rising Cascade Range, Silver Creek cut through the resistant basalt. The basalt now forms the lips of the waterfalls. Many of the splash pools have eroded caverns into the soft rock beneath the basalt. Cylindrical indentations in the roofs of these canyons are "tree wells" left when the Columbia River lava flows surrounded tree trunks, which then burned.

Another feature of the basalt is its interesting six-sided columnar jointing. When basalt cools slowly, it cracks into a honeycomb of pillars perpendicular to the cooling surface. Look for these pillars in the cliffs.

History

The Silverton Fire, largest in Oregon history, burned this area in 1865. Silver Falls City, on the site of the present park headquarters, was founded as a logging camp in 1888. Stumps attest to early logging activity. State park status came in 1931. The canyon trails, lodge, shelters, highway overlooks, and two nearby youth camps were built by 200 Civilian Conservation Corps employees stationed near North Falls from 1935 to 1942.

THINGS TO DO

Hiking

Long, graceful waterfalls appear at nearly every bend along the beautiful 4.2-mile canyon trail from South to North Falls. Side trails create loop hike possibilities ranging in length from 0.5 to 6.7 miles. Trails are wheelchair accessible.

Most loop hikes begin at 177-foot South Falls, the tallest and most popular of the cascades. A paved, heavily used half-mile loop winds through the cavern behind the waterfall, crosses a footbridge, and returns to the South Falls picnic area. A quieter 2-mile loop extends the shorter hike as far down the canyon as 93-foot Lower South Falls.

A 5-mile circuit of the canyon continues past Lower South Falls to Lower North, Double, Drake, and 106-foot Middle North falls before crossing a footbridge and climbing to the parking area on Highway 214 above Winter Falls; from there a 1.5-mile hiking trail through a large Douglas fir forest parallels the highway back to the South Falls picnic area. The longest loop hike, 6.7 miles, follows the canyon from South Falls to 136-foot North Falls and returns on the trail near the highway.

A paved 4-mile bicycle path beginning at Silver Falls Campground is also hikable; it passes South Falls and prowls the forest above Winter Falls. Another 14 miles of hiking and equestrian trails begin at the hitching rails and horse-loading ramp at the southwest park entrance on Highway 214. This trail network consists primarily of logging roads maintained for recreation.

The most remote portion of the park is the lower 2.5 miles of Silver Creek Canyon, a trailless gorge with four rarely visited waterfalls.

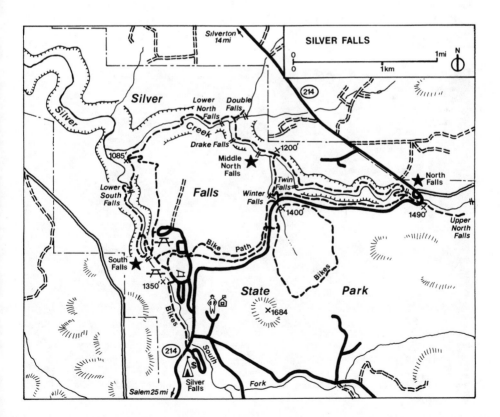

7. Bull of the Woods

LOCATION: 68 mi SE of Portland, 64 mi E of
Salem
SIZE: 80 sq mi
STATUS: 54 sq mi designated wilderness (1984)
TERRAIN: densely forested mountain ridges,
valleys
ELEVATION: 2000'–5710'
MANAGEMENT: Mt. Hood NF, Willamette
NF
TOPOGRAPHIC MAPS: Battle Ax (Green
Trails, 15'); Bagby Hot Springs, Bull of the
Woods, Mother Lode Mountain, Battle Ax,
Elkhorn, Rooster Rock (USGS, 7.5')

Hidden high in the Cascade foothills, this
uncrowded area features subalpine mountains
and a dozen lakes amidst dense, steep forests.
At the center of the well-developed trail network is the Bull of the Woods lookout tower,
elevation 5523 feet, with a sweeping view of
the high country from Mt. Hood to Mt. Jefferson and beyond. Bagby Hot Springs, with
their steaming pools, provide a relaxing stop.

Climate
Trails below 3000 feet are usually snowfree
from April into December; the highest trails
are clear from June through October. Lack of

plowed winter access limits cross-country skiing. Despite 100 inches of annual precipitation, summers are sunny.

Plants and Wildlife
Bull of the Woods is one of the last great old
growth forest reserves of western Oregon.
Towering western hemlock and Douglas fir remain in the valleys, with a complex ecosystem
of lichens, birds, insects, and mosses. Elegant
white trillium and yellow-clustered Oregon
grape bloom in the deep forest in April; tangles
of rhododendron erupt in pink blossoms early
in July.

Here the patient observer may sight a northern spotted owl, the huge, shy bird threatened
by reductions in its old growth habitat. By day
the owl remains in its nest, high in the re-
sprouted top of a broken conifer—or it may
perch like an 18-inch-tall, earless statue on a
branch near the trunk, where the owl's mottled, white-spotted feathers camouflage it perfectly against the tree's bark. At night, however, this owl glides through the forest on its
3.5-foot wingspan, catching wood rats, mice,
and flying squirrels. In the dark it answers
readily to its own recorded call, a high-pitched
"hoo, hoo-hoo" (occasionally a human imitation will do). Then a flashlight held at the observer's eye level will reflect off the owl's dark
eyes, revealing its location.

Five other species of owls share the area: the

Spotted owl

Elk Lake

larger, ear-tufted great horned owl, the robin-sized screech owl, the day-hunting pygmy owl, the small saw-whet owl, and the dark-eyed flammulated owl. A good range for owling indeed!

Geology

Erosion has uncovered quartz veins containing small amounts of copper and silver in this section of the 16- to 25-million-year-old "Old Cascades." A relic of the Elkhorn Mining District, which once brought a rush of prospectors to the area, survives in the small mines scattered along Battle Ax Creek at Jawbone Flats. Abandoned prospects can be found throughout the area, notably above Pansy Lake.

Ice Age glaciation carved the area's many bowl-shaped lake valleys. A vanished Ice Age glacier carved Elk Lake's basin and polished the smooth bedrock visible along the trail on the eastern slope of Battle Ax.

THINGS TO DO

Hiking

This untrammeled area, often called the "Hidden Wilderness," has ample room for satisfying two- and three-day backpacking trips, yet it is small enough to be explored by day hikers as well.

The easy 1.5-mile hike to Bagby Hot Springs, leading through a huge, old growth forest, is the area's most popular day trip. Although the hot springs' legendary shake-roofed bathhouse, complete with cedar-log tubs, burned in 1979, rock-rimmed pools in the Hot Springs Fork provide any blend of freezing or scalding water desired. A resident ranger enforces a ban on camping extending from the trailhead to a quarter mile beyond the springs. Visit in midweek to avoid crowds.

Reach the hot springs trail by driving 26 miles southeast of Estacada on Highway 224 to a junction just past Ripplebrook Campground. Turn right onto Road 46 for 3.6 miles, continue to the right on Road 63 another 3 miles, then turn left on Road 70 for 5.5 miles to the trailhead, 0.5 mile beyond Pegleg Falls Campground.

Pansy Lake is another rewarding, easy hike, passing a small wildflower meadow on its 1.2-mile route to a swimmable lake in a forested cirque. The drive to this trailhead starts out the same as to the hot springs, but follows Road 63 for 5.5 miles before turning left onto Road 6340 for 7.7 miles, and then right onto Road 6341 for 3.5 miles, to the Pansy Basin Trail.

Several outstanding, but more strenuous, day hikes seek out viewpoints. Chief among these is Bull of the Woods, the only area peak still topped by a lookout tower. Here the view across beargrass-dotted meadows stretches from Mt. Rainier to the Three Sisters. Staffed only in times of extreme fire danger, the tower also serves as an emergency shelter. The Pansy Basin Trail extends to the Bull of the Woods lookout—a 3.6-mile route in all—but the Bull of the Woods Trail from Road 6340 (past the Dickey Peaks) climbs 1200 feet less and is a half mile shorter.

Two craggy peaks contend for the title of best viewpoint in the southern end of this wilderness: Battle Ax and Mt. Beachie. Both are reached by driving 52 miles east of Salem on Highway 22 to Detroit, turning left for 4.5 miles on Road 46, then turning left onto Road 2209 for 6 miles to the Elk Lake Campground. The 1-mile dirt track from the campground to the trailheads at Beachie Saddle is too rough for most vehicles; park and walk.

To the north from Beachie Saddle, a 2-mile trail switchbacks up to the clifftop views at Battle Ax's old lookout site, gaining 1200 feet elevation. The lookout's old water trail continues north, making a loop trail possible back to the Elk Lake Campground—a pleasant 6.5-mile hike in all.

To the southwest from Beachie Saddle, a 1.5-mile trail traverses to a lovely ridge topped by Mt. Beachie, gaining just 900 feet to reach views of Elk Lake, Mt. Jefferson, and beyond.

Whetstone Mountain, a former lookout site in the seldom visited western end of this wilderness, is the quietest viewpoint of all. The easiest route up, a 2.5-mile trail on the mountain's north flank, begins on Road 7020, 9 miles south of the Bagby Hot Springs trailhead.

A much more arduous trail up Whetstone Mountain—gaining 3000 feet in 4.5 miles—is the route of choice for some hikers because of its easier trailhead access from Salem. To reach it, drive 22.8 miles east of Salem on Highway 22 to Mehama, turn left on the Little North Fork Road for 16 miles to Elkhorn, continue 1.5 miles on Road 2207, then keep left on Road 2209 another 4.5 miles to a locked gate. Walk the mining road a half mile past the gate and turn left on a side road another half mile up Gold Creek to the trail.

For a hike through the old-growth forest along Opal Creek, park at the locked gate on Road 2209. Walk or bicycle 3 miles up the road along the Little North Fork Santiam River to Jawbone Flats, past 700-year-old Douglas firs and interesting private mining shacks. When the road crosses Battle Ax Creek, take a spur road right a quarter mile to jewel-like Opal Pool. Continue another quarter mile up the road to a switchback with a metal culvert. From here follow a rough water line trail across a creek, and then continue on a steep path over a ridge to Opal Creek. The trail continues 2 miles upstream to a stand of 7-foot-thick red cedars. Round-trip distance from the gate to the cedar grove is 13 miles; bicycling to Jawbone Flats saves 6 miles.

Another good old-growth forest walk follows an easy 4-mile trail from Elk Lake to the Battle Creek shelter, where two woodsy streams join.

Most of the small, scenic lakes in this wilderness are just far enough from trailheads to be the destinations either of very challenging day hikes or very pleasant overnight trips. For instance, the Welcome Lakes are 5 miles in and 2000 feet up from the Road 6380 trailhead—a rugged 10-mile round-trip day hike through old growth forest. But the backpacker can pitch his tent near Upper Welcome Lake and still have energy left to hike another mile up to the Bull of the Woods lookout, or to prowl the interesting ridges and meadows along nearby trails.

Likewise, Big Slide Lake is 5 miles in and

1600 feet up the rhododendron-lined Dickey Creek Trail from Road 6340-140. A base camp at the lake will allow the backpacker to continue out Big Slide Mountain's ridge to Lake Lenore's clifftop cirque.

Another pretty lake destination is Silver King Lake. It's a 4.7-mile hike from Road 7020 along the Whetstone Mountain Trail's scenic ridgetop—a little more if one takes the worthwhile side trip to Silver King Mountain. Those who can arrange a short car shuttle can camp at the lake, then hike 7.7 miles down the Bagby Trail the second day through old growth forest to Road 70, stopping at the hot

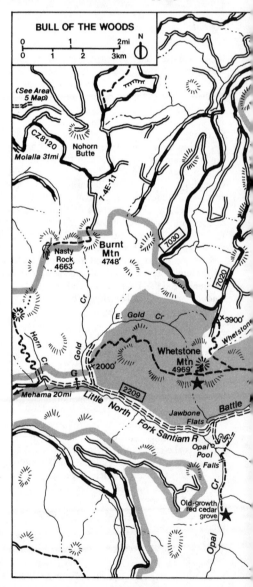

springs for a dip on the way.

Finally, the Twin Lakes make a good hiking goal. Start out from Road 2209 near the Elk Lake Campground, climbing to a scenic ridgetop trail north of Battle Ax. Camp after 5.5 miles at Upper Twin Lake. The second day, either stroll 4.5 miles to an easy camp at the Battle Creek Shelter or hike 4 miles past the shelter, back to Elk Lake.

Climbing

Nasty Rock and a small unnamed pinnacle to the southwest offer some technical rock pitches. Many of the routes on these remote volcanic crags are untested. To reach the 2-mile BLM trail to Nasty Rock, follow the road directions from Molalla given in the Table Rock Wilderness description. Drive below Peechuck Lookout, continuing on CZ 8200 to BLM Road 7-4E-1.1; the trail is at the end of this road.

Winter Sports

Though adjacent roads are unplowed in winter, skiers park at snowline on Road 2209 and ski to Elk Lake. In spring the trip is usually 3 to 4 miles one way, with Beachie Saddle a tempting additional 1.5-mile climb.

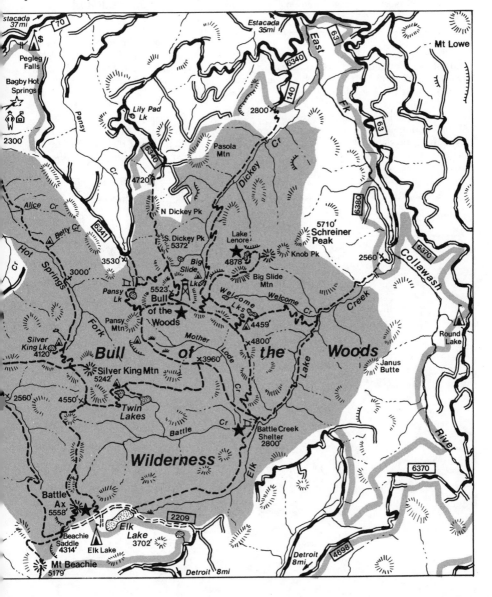

8. Olallie Lake

LOCATION: 80 mi SE of Portland, 69 mi E of Salem

SIZE: 36 sq mi

STATUS: 17 sq mi Forest Service scenic area, 14 sq mi Indian reservation

TERRAIN: forested, lake-dotted plateau

ELEVATION: 2100'–7215'

MANAGEMENT: Mt. Hood NF, Confederated Tribes of the Warm Springs Indian Reservation

TOPOGRAPHIC MAPS: Breitenbush (Green Trails, 15'); Northern Oregon Portion (USFS); Olallie Butte (USGS, 7.5')

In the shadow of Mt. Jefferson, this forested region of 200 lakes and ponds is one of the most accessible portions of the Cascade's high country. Short, nearly level trails from seven developed campgrounds along Skyline Road 4220 lead to the larger lakes, while the open, lodgepole pine and mountain hemlock forests invite easy cross-country hikes to more remote lakeside campsites.

Climate

A very heavy winter snowpack keeps most trails, and Road 4220, closed from about mid-October to the first of July. As lingering snow melts during the peak wildflower month of July, mosquitoes are so profuse that headnets are advisable. By late summer, cross-country hikers may stumble on ground-nesting yellowjackets.

Plants and Wildlife

Low huckleberry bushes provide a carpet beneath the forests of lodgepole pine and mountain hemlock. Watch for mink, otter, and eagles at the many fishfilled lakes.

Geology

This Cascade Range upland has been dotted by geologically recent cinder cones such as Olallie Butte and Potato Butte. A broad Ice Age glacial ice sheet left the many shallow lake basins.

History

The Indians who once trekked here each fall to hunt deer and gather the abundant huckleberries named the largest lake *Olallie*—the

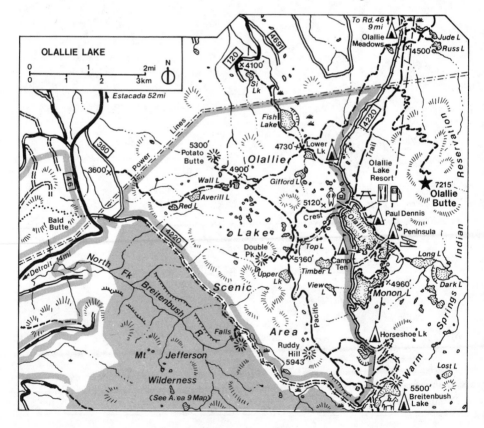

The Pacific Crest Trail along Olallie Lake

Chinook jargon word for "berry." Seven bands of central Oregon Indians were granted the eastern portion of this area when the Warm Springs Indian Reservation was created by a treaty in 1855.

THINGS TO DO

Hiking

Short trails and frequent lakes make the area well suited for beginning backpackers and families with young hikers. A good day hike for children is the 0.9-mile Russ Lake Trail from wildflower-filled Olallie Meadows. Hiking the shore trails around Olallie or Monon Lakes is also fun with children, and yields first-rate views of Olallie Butte and Mt. Jefferson. It's 2.7 miles around Monon Lake, and 2.9 around Olallie Lake.

The pleasant 2.8-mile trail from Si Lake past cliff-rimmed Fish Lake and 73-foot-deep Lower Lake climbs 700 feet on its way to the Lower Lake Campground.

Good camping lakes appear at nearly every bend in the 5.8-mile Red Lake Trail between Road 380 and Olallie Lake. A worthwhile side trip to this east-west route is the 1-mile climb to the viewpoint atop Potato Butte.

The most interesting section of the Pacific Crest Trail here is the 6.1 miles between Olallie Lake Guard Station and Road 4220 just west of Breitenbush Lake. At either end, this section follows cliffs and ridges with good views.

Olallie Butte has the best view of all, atop a trail climbing 2600 feet in 3.8 miles. The former lookout site not only overlooks the entire Olallie Lake area, it offers an eye-level view of Mt. Jefferson and a long look into central Oregon.

Cross-country hiking to trailless lakes avoids the crowds of the best hiking months, August and September. Beginners in the art of finding routes with map and compass can practice by bearing south from crowded Lower Lake to quiet Gifford Lake, or from Timber Lake to View Lake (the view is of Olallie Butte). Then try bushwhacking on compass bearings along

the string of small lakes that form a 1-mile-diameter circle about the northern base of Double Peaks. It is difficult to become hopelessly lost anywhere in the area, since a trail or road is never over a mile away.

Camping is prohibited within the Warm Springs Indian Reservation, except specifically at Breitenbush Lake. Anglers on reservation lands must have a state fishing license, tribal fishing permit, and a copy of the Warm Springs fishing regulations. Violators are subject to a $200 fine or 90-day imprisonment.

To reach the Olallie Lake area from the north, follow Highway 224 and then paved Road 46 a total of 51 miles past Estacada. Turn left on gravel Road 4690 for 8 miles, then turn right on dirt Road 4220 for 6 miles to Olallie Lake. Beyond Horseshoe Lake, Road 4220 becomes a very slow, badly rutted track, unsuited for trailer travel. The Fish Lake trailhead is only 6 miles from Highway 46; drive 3.5 miles up Road 4690, turn right on Road 4691 for 1.5 miles, then turn right on Road 120 for another mile.

Drivers approaching from Salem can take Highway 22 to Detroit, follow paved Road 46 for 17 miles, then turn right on treacherously rutted Road 4220 for 7.5 miles to Breitenbush Lake. Those without four-wheel drive should consider continuing on paved Road 46 another 7 miles before turning right on Road 4690 toward Olallie Lake.

Winter Sports

Road 46, plowed in winter, allows cross-country ski access to the area's lakes via snowed-under Roads 4220 and 4690. Snowmobiles are allowed on these routes. The 7.5-mile distance to Breitenbush Lake makes an overnight trip in order, perhaps to one of the two shake-roofed stone shelters beside the lake.

Boating

A resort at Olallie Lake rents rowboats, and Peninsula Campground offers a boat ramp. Motors are prohibited on all of the area's lakes.

9. Mount Jefferson

LOCATION: 64 mi E of Salem, 37 mi NE of
Bend
SIZE: 273 sq mi
STATUS: 174 sq mi designated wilderness
(1968, 1984)
TERRAIN: glaciated peak, forested ridges, lake
basins
ELEVATION: 2400'–10,497'
MANAGEMENT: Willamette NF, Deschutes
NF, Mt. Hood NF, Confederated Tribes of
Warm Springs Indian Reservation
TOPOGRAPHIC MAPS: Mt. Jefferson
Wilderness, PCT Northern Oregon Portion
(USFS); Mt. Jefferson, Whitewater River
(Green Trails, 15'); Mt. Jefferson (Geo-
Graphics)

Mt. Jefferson ranks as Oregon's second
highest peak (after Mt. Hood), and forms the
centerpiece of Oregon's second most visited
wilderness (after the Three Sisters).

The top attractions are 150 mountain lakes,
ranging from heavily visited, half-square-mile
Marion Lake to the delicate tarns of Jefferson
Park's popular alpine wildflower meadows.
Three Fingered Jack, an impressive 7841-foot
crag, dominates the southern end of the wilderness with its own collection of alpine lakes
and meadows.

Climate

Winter snows, commencing early in November, total from 230 to 690 inches at Santiam Pass. The spring melt typically opens
trails up to 3500 feet elevation by mid-May,
up to 4500 feet by mid-June, up to 5500 feet
by mid-July, and up to 6500 feet by August 1.
Mosquitoes are troublesome for two to three
weeks following the final snowmelt in each
region.

Storms occasionally interrupt clear, dry
summer weather. The eastern slopes, with 40
inches of annual precipitation, are often sunny
even when the western slopes, with 80 inches
of precipitation, are lost in clouds.

Plants and Wildlife

Deer, elk, black bear, and coyotes are numerous enough to be seen frequently. Bald eagles can be spotted fishing in the lakes.

The area's lower western valleys shelter old
growth Douglas fir forests. Spire-shaped subalpine fir and mountain hemlock cluster at
higher elevations. Descending the area's drier
eastern slopes is a remarkably compact se-
quence of forest zones, from mountain hem-

lock to lodgepole pine, and finally to the long-
needled ponderosa pine of the Metolius Valley.

Fields of blue lupine and red Indian paintbrush attract day hikers to Canyon Creek
Meadows, Jefferson Park, the Eight Lakes Basin, and the Santiam Lake area in July.

Also in July, the white, 4-foot-tall plumes
of beargrass may be profuse along ridges, on
slopes, and in lodgepole pine forests. This
bunchgrasslike plant fills the wilderness with
its fragrant blooms most years, but mysteri-
ously chooses not to flower at all in other years.
An unlikely-looking member of the lily family, beargrass blooms consist of hundreds of
tiny, six-petaled flowers. Bears unearth and eat
the plant's succulent root, which, when

boiled, is said to make a substitute for soap. Indians gathered the plant's 2-foot-long leaves and wove them into useful baskets.

Geology

Mt. Jefferson and Three Fingered Jack are both heavily eroded remnants of apparently extinct volcanoes. On Three Fingered Jack, only the hard lava plug, or central core, survives, flanked by ridges of the old volcano's subsidiary lava dikes. Mt. Jefferson is also topped by a lava spire, but it is not the mountain's ancient plug. Glaciation has removed the western third of the mountain, including the ancient summit. The current summit rock was once a flank lava flow.

Geologically recent cinder cones (including Pyramid Butte, South Cinder Peak, and Maxwell Butte) and two large 6500-year-old lava flows 6 miles southeast of Mt. Jefferson prove that the area is not volcanically dead.

History

Lewis and Clark sighted Mt. Jefferson from the mouth of the Willamette River in 1806 and named it after the president who had sent them on their expedition. Three Fingered Jack apparently won its name because its summit spires reminded pioneers of a renowned, mutilated cohort of California Gold Rush bandit Joaquin Murietta.

Two failed transportation routes across the

Three Fingered Jack from the Pacific Crest Trail near Santiam Pass

MT JEFFERSON

0   1   2mi
0   1   2   3km

Warm   Springs

Whitewater

Camp Creek
Butte

Bald Peter
6574'

Lionshead
6110'

Shitike

Indian   Reservation

Milk   Cr

Parker

L Sarah

Cr

Jefferson

L a v a

Jefferson L
5905'

Harvey L

Kuckup
Park

River

Hole-in-the-
Wall Park

Breitenbush LK
×5650'

Pacific

Whitewater   Glacier

Waldo Gl

Goat
Pk

5470'
Table L

Patsy
L

Jefferson
Park

Mt Jefferson
10,497'

The Table

Pyramid Butte

6900'
Park Butte

Russell L

Jeff Park
Gl

Cathedral Rocks
6100'

Hunts
Cove

(See Area
8 Map)

Mt

Scout L
×5800'

Russell Glacier

Jefferson

Hunts
L

Hanks
L

5600'

Bays L

Russell

Crest

Bear Point
6043'

R

Whitewater

Milk

Trail

4350'×

3884'
Pamelia Lake

Grizzly Pk
5799'

Claggett L

Breitenbush

Cr

Lizard

Ridge

4852'×   Crown L

3100'×

4700'×   4080'

×4400

3120'×

Grizzly

Minto Mtn

Ridge

Bingham   Cr

Fork

4685

4400'×

Cheat

Cr

Woodpecker

Cr

Marion
Forks

2253

Minto

870

Boca Cave

2940

040

2246

Devils
Pk
×4528

Spire
Rk

5434'
Triangulation
Peak

2243

Pamelia

S

×2450

×4960'

Whitewater

Riverside

Estacada 60 mi

Breitenbush Hot
Springs

650

Creek

North   Santiam

River

2233

2231

22

Detroit 9 mi   Detroit 9 mi

Pamelia Lake and Mount Jefferson

Cascade Range left their mark on the wilderness here. Minto Mountain and Minto Lake recall Salem pioneer John Minto, who urged in vain that a wagon road be built over Minto Pass in the 1870s.

The designated wilderness boundary between Santiam Pass and Lost Lake follows a bit of railroad grade built in the 1880s by entrepreneur Colonel T. Egenton Hogg. Hogg dreamed of a transcontinental line from Corvallis east, but his London financiers doubted a crossing of Santiam Pass was feasible. Undaunted, he ordered Chinese laborers to build 11 miles of grade, lay 300 feet of track, and pack a disassembled boxcar to the site. Mules pulled the car across the pass, allowing Hogg to tell his investors, straight-faced, that his train already had crossed the Cascades. The grade is still hikable from Santiam Lodge partway around the sheer cliffs of Hogg Rock.

THINGS TO DO

Hiking

With 200 miles of trails, the Mt. Jefferson area offers a dazzling variety of day hikes and backpacks. The open high country and many off-trail lakes invite cross-country exploration as well—the surest way to find solitude.

On July and August weekends, it is not unusual to find 500 people in the beautiful Jefferson Park area and 300 people at Marion Lake. Visit these and other popular areas (marked with hollow stars on the map) in midweek or in other months.

Overuse has led the Forest Service to ban camping on Marion Lake's small northwest peninsula and on the peninsula of Scout and Bays lakes. Camping, campfires, and stoves are prohibited within 100 feet horizontal distance of the high water mark of Marion, Pamelia, Hanks, and Hunts lakes. Livestock may not be grazed or picketed within 200 feet of any lake. Wilderness rangers patrol the area in summer.

Overnight camping is banned within the Warm Springs Indian Reservation, except specifically at Breitenbush Lake.

Among the easiest day hikes is the 2.3-mile trail from Road 2246 along a splashing creek under towering Douglas firs to Pamelia Lake. In early June the lake is ringed with pink rhododendron blooms. The area's best mountain view is 2.8 miles farther, at the old lookout site atop Grizzly Peak, 1900 feet above the lake and breathtakingly close to Mt. Jefferson.

Marion Lake is an easy 2.6-mile walk (one way) from Road 2255 along a wide and occasionally dusty path. Hikers can pack in inflatable boats to cruise the 360-acre, 180-foot-deep lake. A scenic trail around the lake is interrupted by a cold ford at the inlet creek to the southeast. Fishing is prohibited between the lake's outlet and picturesque little Marion Falls.

Square Lake, nestled in the forest at the foot of Three Fingered Jack, is a pleasant 2-mile day hike either from the Pacific Crest Trail's Santiam Pass trailhead on Highway 20 or from the Round Lake Campground.

Wildflowers and a close-up view of Three Fingered Jack highlight the 2-mile walk into Canyon Creek Meadows. The trail begins at the Jack Lake Campground at the end of Road 1234; a 2.3-mile trail along Canyon Creek makes a loop trip possible past that creek's pair of 20-foot falls. From the meadows, an additional 1.5-mile track leads steeply up a glacial moraine, past an ice-filled cirque lake, to a viewpoint saddle overtowered by Three Fingered Jack's summit pinnacles.

The fire lookout structures which once topped five peaks in this wilderness have been removed, but their panoramic views remain, an enticing goal for invigorating day hikes. Bear Point's view of Mt. Jefferson is 4 miles away, and 2900 feet up, from Road 4685, which joins Road 46 a mile east of Breitenbush Hot Springs.

Triangulation Peak is surrounded by several interesting rock spires and a cave. The huge mouth of Boca Cave, a protected archeological site, can be reached by scrambling several hundred yards down the rugged east side of the summit. Triangulation Peak is an easy 2.2-mile walk from Road 2233-650, but the Cheat Creek trailhead on Whitewater Creek Road 2243 is easier to find, and its 6.3-mile route passes a lovely meadow and scenic ridge during its 2500-foot climb to the peak.

Marion Mountain, the area's lowest lookout site, is a 2.8-mile side trip up from Marion Lake, or a 4.2-mile hike from the Camp Pioneer trailhead on Road 2261. Maxwell Butte, a cinder cone overlooking the Santiam Pass area, is 4.8 miles up from Road 080, off Highway 22; at the dry trail's midpoint, Twin Lakes offer an irresistible swimming opportunity.

Another viewpoint worth the hike involves following the PCT 5 miles from Santiam Pass to Three Fingered Jack. After a 1600-foot climb the PCT crests a ridge with views south along the Cascades, then traverses almost directly below Three Fingered Jack's sheer west face.

Many of the most spectacular areas are reached either by very long day hikes or by leisurely backpacking trips. The best example is Jefferson Park, a square-mile plain of lush wildflowers and swimable alpine lakes set so close to Mt. Jefferson the snowy mountain seems to fill the sky.

Three routes reach Jefferson Park. The easiest trail climbs 5 miles from Whitewater Creek Road 2243 along a pretty ridge. The PCT also reaches Jefferson Park, climbing to breathtaking viewpoints on Park Butte's 6900-foot ridge; the 5.6-mile route begins at Skyline Road 4220 near Breitenbush Lake. A third, much less used route to Jefferson Park climbs 6.2 miles along the South Breitenbush Trail from Road 4685. Because Jefferson Park's alpine flora is so fragile, backpackers are urged to make low-impact camps in the area's sparsely visited northwest and southeast corners, away from lakes.

Hunts Cove is a similar, but much smaller alpine basin on the south side of Mt. Jefferson. The two main lakes, Hunts and Hanks, are 6 miles up from Road 2248 via Pamelia Lake. Backpackers based at Hunts Cove can climb to the PCT and prowl the interesting crags of Cathedral Rocks.

Duffy, Mowich, and Santiam lakes lie in a plateau of open lodgepole pine forests and wildflower meadows at the foot of Three Fingered Jack. From Road 2267, a 3.5-mile day hike (one way) through the dry forest along the North Fork Santiam River will reach Duffy Lake; Mowich Lake, with its large island, is another mile. Santiam Lake is a 5.5-mile walk from Highway 20 at Santiam Pass (or start at Santiam Lodge, and avoid the dusty PCT).

Just 1.8 miles past Mowich Lake is the Eight Lakes Basin, a patchwork of meadows and forest renowned for its wildflowers, pretty lakes, and July mosquitoes. The five nearest trailheads are 6.8 to 8.6 miles distant; a car shuttle arrangement would allow backpackers at the Eight Lakes Basin to choose a different trail on the trip out.

Trails on the east side of the wilderness are often sunnier but are much less used because of the longer gravel road access. The Bear Valley Trail from the end of Road 1235 gains 2000

Three Fingered Jack (photo by William L. Sullivan)

feet on its 4-mile route to Rockpile Lake, where there are views and alpine rock gardens. Equestrians often begin the Bear Valley Trail at the Sheep Springs Horse Campground or the campgrounds along the Metolius River.

Carl Lake, a forest-rimmed rock basin, is 5 miles up the Cabot Creek Trail from Road 1230. Hike 2 miles past Carl Lake to reach the sweeping viewpoint atop South Cinder Peak.

Table Lake lies at the center of a fascinating, rarely visited landscape of wildflower-filled mesas, sudden canyons, cinder cones, and lava flows. Backpack to Table Lake via Carl Lake (10 miles from Road 1230), via the long uphill climb of Sugarpine Ridge (10.5 miles from Road 1292), or on the Jefferson Lake Trail, skirting a lava flow (10.1 miles from Road 1292).

Another rewarding, longer backpack is the 20-mile circuit around Three Fingered Jack, following the PCT from Santiam Pass and returning via Jack and Square lakes; plan to take three days.

For an even greater challenge, try the 36-mile stretch of PCT south of Breitenbush Lake. After crossing Jefferson Park and skirting halfway around Mt. Jefferson, the wide, well-graded PCT follows a high, scenic ridgecrest south 10 miles to Minto Pass, passing lots of viewpoints, but no water. Then the PCT climbs high along the side of Three Fingered Jack before dropping to Santiam Pass—a spectacular three- to six-day hike.

Climbing

Mt. Jefferson is the most difficult of Oregon's Cascade peaks, both because of the relentless 4000- to 6000-foot elevation gains from base camps and because of the 400-foot summit pinnacle of crumbly lava, a class 4 climb in itself.

A dozen routes ascend as far as the summit pinnacle, with difficulties ranging from I-2 to

Pamelia Creek

III-5.2. The three easiest are from Jefferson Park across Whitewater Glacier to the ridge west of Waldo Glacier, from Pamelia Lake straight up the mountain's southwest ridge, and from the PCT above Hunts Lake directly toward the summit.

In the 19th century, Mt. Jefferson was believed unclimbable. A reputed "first ascent" in 1888 probably did not reach the summit. When a group led by Salem lawyer Charles E. Robin really did scale the peak in 1899, their photographer had put in his film backwards, and skeptics drove Robin to climb it again a week later.

Three Fingered Jack, though much lower and easier, was first climbed on Labor Day, 1923, by six Bend boys, four of whom had been first to the top of Mt. Washington the previous weekend.

A popular, level I-4 route follows a well-defined climber's trail up the south ridge, passes to the east of a gendarme spire at 7600 feet, and continues 300 feet to a rough 40-foot recessed wall in the summit block.

The West Face Direct route is a level II-5.6-A1 climb, while a northeast route, above Canyon Creek Meadows, is rated III-5.4. Both cross dangerously rotten rock.

Winter Sports

Santiam Pass typically has enough snow to ski by late November. Starting from the sno-park near Santiam Lodge, a marked trail leads 0.5 mile through the woods to the PCT trailhead. From there, Square Lake is a nice 2.2-mile goal, with views of Three Fingered Jack across the frozen lake. The PCT toward Three Fingered Jack climbs steadily, requiring downhill skiing skills on the return. The 3.6-mile trail from the Santiam Lodge sno-park to Lower Berley Lake crosses pleasant, rolling terrain, and can be combined with the PCT to form a loop.

Map and compass are essential on all wilderness trail routes. Consult the Mt. Washington entry for ski tours south from Santiam Pass.

When the snow level drops to 4000 feet, the 1-mile road along the shore of Lost Lake is popular with beginners. After December, routes lower in the North Santiam River canyon become skiable.

Twin Lakes is an uphill 2.6-mile tour from plowed Highway 22; a few brave souls venture on by compass to the summit of Maxwell Butte. Road 2257 is an even more popular skiing route, leading 3 easy miles to Fay Lake. On the way, the road passes just west of Big Meadows, with large openings good for exploring.

Marion Lake and Pamelia Lake are both dramatic goals. In midwinter, when the access roads are snowed in all the way down to Highway 22, Pamelia Lake is 6.5 miles (one way) and Marion Lake is 7. By March the snow melts off the access roads and shortens the ski trip to these lakes. Spring often brings sunny, shirtsleeved skiing weather, but the wet, heavy snow can be difficult for beginners.

10. Mount Washington

LOCATION: 70 mi E of Eugene, 31 mi W of Bend

SIZE: 111 sq mi

STATUS: 82 sq mi designated wilderness (1964, 1984)

TERRAIN: lava plains, high forest, peak

ELEVATION: 2800'–7794'

MANAGEMENT: Deschutes NF, Willamette NF

TOPOGRAPHIC MAPS: Mt. Washington Wilderness, PCT Northern Oregon Portion (USFS); Three Sisters (Geo-Graphics); Three Sisters 2 SW, Three Sisters 2 SE, Three Sisters 3 NW, Three Sisters 3 NE (USGS, 7.5')

Sometimes called the "Black Wilderness" because of its 38 square miles of rugged lava flows, the Mt. Washington area also features sweeping forests and scores of small lakes. All around are mountain vistas, not only of Mt. Washington's craggy spire, but of a half dozen snowpeaks in the adjacent Three Sisters and Mt. Jefferson areas.

Climate

Santiam Pass, with an average snowfall of 230 to 690 inches, is plowed throughout winter. Highway 242 over McKenzie Pass is closed from November or December to May or June. Trails are clear of snow from mid-June to mid-October. Summers are warm and dry.

Plants and Wildlife

The barren lava fields support little more than an occasional, bonsaied whitebark pine.

But the high plains surrounding the lava are evenly covered by mountain hemlock and true fir on the west and by lodgepole and ponderosa pine on the east. Blacktailed deer wintering in the Old Cascades and mule deer wintering in the Metolius Valley often make Mt. Washington their summer range.

Geology

At least 125 eruptive centers produced cinder cones and basalt lava flows in this area since the Ice Age—an average of one major eruption every century. The most recent flow, 1300 years old, streamed 12 miles from Belknap Crater's flank to divert the McKenzie River south of Koosah Falls.

Clear Lake was formed when a lava flow from a cone south of Sand Mountain succeeded in damming the McKenzie River and drowning a forest. The lake's water is so cold and clear that the branchless forest can still be seen as much as 100 feet below the lake surface—a source of fascination for boaters (no motors permitted) and wet-suited scuba divers. Radiocarbon dating of the wood indicates the lake and lava flow are 3000 years old.

The intensely jumbled, almost uncrossable surface of the area's lava resulted as the cooled crust of molten flows was broken up by lava continuing to flow underneath. Where molten lava flowed out from under an intact crust, lava tubes formed, such as Sawyers Cave and Skylight Cave. Permanent ice and smooth lava stalactites can be seen in these long caves and in the collapsed lava tubes filling the summit crater of Little Belknap.

Though at least 100,000 years older than Belknap Crater, Mt. Washington began as a similarly broad shield volcano. It went on to

Mount Washington and McKenzie Pass lava fields

add a cone as large and symmetrical as any of the Three Sisters, but then was stripped to its central lava plug by glaciation.

History

The Santiam Wagon Road, built in 1866 to allow the grazing of Willamette Valley livestock in central Oregon, can still be traced between Fish Lake and the 1896 Cache Creek Toll Station site.

Around 1871, John Craig built a wagon route over McKenzie Pass, arduously chipping and leveling the lava roadbed still visible in the rugged basalt flows around Hand Lake and near Dee Wright Observatory at McKenzie Pass. Craig contracted to carry mail across his wagon road through the winter on skis. In an 1877 storm he froze to death in a cabin at Craig Lake. Since the 1920s, an annual John Templeton Craig ski tour and ski race has carried specially marked mail on the 18-mile route across McKenzie Pass each April.

THINGS TO DO

Hiking

The area has many excellent trails, but lacks running water; hikers must carry what they need or purify lakewater.

The most popular day hike is the half-mile walk through subalpine wildflower meadows from Highway 242 to the Hand Lake shelter, a trip often combined with the pleasant 1.5-mile trail between Hand and Scott lakes. Scott Lake's reflection of the Three Sisters is especially photogenic.

Another heavily used trail climbs 400 feet in 1.4 miles from the Scott Lake Campground to Benson Lake, a deep, blue jewel partly rimmed by cliffs. One mile past Benson Lake are the similarly scenic and popular Tenas Lakes. Hikers seeking solitude should head for one of the many off-trail lakes in this area. Bring a map and compass.

The Patjens Lakes, with wildflower meadows and reflections of Mt. Washington, are on a 5.3-mile loop through rolling forest from the gate on paved Road 2690 at Big Lake. An equally swimmable, but far less visited lake is Robinson Lake, on an easy 0.3-mile trail from Road 2664.

Day hikers often follow the Pacific Crest Trail south from Lava Camp Lake Campground to South Matthieu Lake, then take the abandoned Skyline Trail back via North Matthieu Lake—a 6-mile loop through both lava and forest.

The lava fields at McKenzie Pass are so impressively rugged that many visitors only hike the paved half-mile Lava River nature trail around the Dee Wright Observatory's basalt-

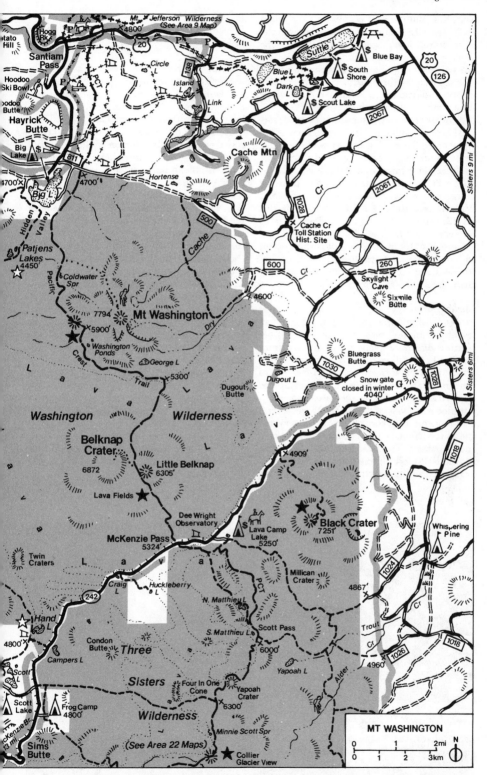

block hut. But the PCT climbs on a very good grade from the same trailhead through the heart of the lava's spectacular barrens. The panoramic view atop Little Belknap is 2.6 miles via a short spur trail. From the spur trail, Belknap Crater's three distinct summit craters are an additional 0.7-mile cross-country climb, mostly through forest.

Another good view, atop shield-shaped, forested Scott Mountain, is reachable from seven different trailheads. The best view of the Three Sisters is at Black Crater, on a trail climbing 2400 feet in 4 miles from Highway 242.

The PCT leads to views up and down the Cascades from wildflower meadows on Mt. Washington's shoulder. Carry water on this dry 12.4-mile section of the PCT north from McKenzie Pass to Road 811.

Cross-country hiking, though impractical on lava, is pleasant both through the open forest and along the beachlike cinder strips separating lava flows from forest.

Climbing

Mt. Washington's eroded lava plug offers several technical climbs. To take the level I-4 North Ridge route, pioneered by six boys from Bend in 1923, follow the PCT 2 miles south of Road 811. Follow tree blazes cross-country to the mountain's north ridge, then hike up the ridge to a small saddle at the base of the summit pinnacle. West of the saddle 25 feet ascend a 30-foot chimney, then climb 30 feet upwards and to the left on the rough, rotten rock of the "nose." Atop the nose, a steep hike leads to an additional 20-foot chimney and the summit.

A dozen additional climbing routes increase in difficulty to the level III-5.7 East Face Direct and the west face's level II-5.8 Chimney of Space.

Winter Sports

Santiam Pass is a major Nordic skiing center, while McKenzie Pass offers a few longer, more remote trips. See area 9, Mt. Jefferson, for routes north of Santiam Pass.

A network of marked cross-country ski trails converges at the Ray Benson sno-park on Big Lake Road 2690. Three shelters make easy goals in the rolling, often clearcut terrain. Nordic routes occasionally cross or parallel marked snowmobile routes. Cross-country skis, lessons, and groomed trails are available for a fee at Hoodoo Ski Bowl nearby.

Another marked Nordic route climbs 1000 feet in 3 miles from the Road 830 sno-park to the view atop Potato Hill. A 4-mile loop trail south of Potato Hill requires less of a climb.

McKenzie Pass is typically plowed only a week or so past the first snowfall, usually in November. Once the snow gates are closed, it's 9 miles to the pass—hiking and/or skiing—from either side.

A rewarding, and demanding, trip from the west side's snow gate at the Alder Springs Picnic Area leads 6 miles up hairpin curves on Highway 242 to the Hand Lake shelter. The generally unplowed side roads from Highway 126 are skiable, especially Road 2664 to Robinson Lake (4 miles one way), and Road 2649 to Melakwa Lake (10 miles one way). Those prepared for a snow camp will find the 18-mile crossing of McKenzie Pass unparalleled in scenic splendor.

Sunrise at Scott Lake

Photographing along the Cone Peak Trail

11. Old Cascades

LOCATION: 45 mi E of Albany
SIZE: 74 sq mi
STATUS: 8 sq mi designated wilderness (1984)
TERRAIN: densely forested ridges, ridgetop
  meadows, rock pinnacles
ELEVATION: 1230'–5830'
MANAGEMENT: Willamette NF
TOPOGRAPHIC MAPS: Upper Soda, Harter
  Mountain, Echo Mountain, Cascadia (USGS,
  7.5'); Cascadia, Echo Mountain (USGS, 15')

Six separate roadless areas along Highway 20 remain to show the scale of the wild forests which once blanketed the western foothills of the Cascade Range. Here are broad ridges, subalpine meadows, and views of the High Cascades' snowpeaks, all within an hour's drive of the Willamette Valley.

Climate

The area's 80 inches of annual precipitation come as snow from December through March, and rain in spring and fall. Trails over 4000 feet are usually clear of snow by May.

Plants and Wildlife

The Old Cascades' remarkable botanic diversity is best seen in early summer on the Echo Mountain - Iron Mountain ridge. A study of this site found 60 plant species that are rare or unusual in the Western Cascades, including spectacular penstemon and other wildflowers. Nowhere in Oregon are there more varieties of conifers in such a compact area—17 species, from water-loving western red cedar to drought-tolerant juniper and rare alpine Alaska cedar.

Lower elevations of the Old Cascades include pockets of old-growth western hemlock and Douglas fir; higher elevations are dominated by flexible-limbed, snow-resistant Pacific silver fir and noble fir. Stumps in a 1986 clearcut 3 miles south of House Rock Campground indicate the area held Oregon's oldest trees.

Fishing is banned in Hackleman Creek to protect that stream's unique strain of cutthroat trout.

Geology

The Old Cascades are a chain of volcanoes predating the peaks of the High Cascades by 10 million years. It was the Old Cascades which originally made eastern Oregon the semiarid area it is today, and which filled ancient inland seas with rhyolite ash, preserving the John Day area's famous fossils.

Time and erosion have reduced the Old Cascades' once-tall volcanic cones to a dissected canyonland, studded with the cliffs and pinnacles of resistant lava intrusions. The Menagerie is a collection of two dozen such rock spires, including three natural arches and a 300-foot tower called Turkey Monster.

History

The Santiam band of Kalapuya Indians once had a summer hunting and gathering camp at House Rock. White settlers built the Santiam Wagon Road through the area between Albany and central Oregon in 1861-68. The state purchased the heavily used toll route in 1927. Construction of Highway 20 largely bypassed the old wagon route, which is now being developed between Fernview Campground and Santiam Pass as a trail for hikers and equestrians.

THINGS TO DO

Hiking

All six of the Old Cascades areas have good hiking trails. In the east, the 4-mile Crescent Mountain Trail crosses broad, grassy slopes of alpine wildflowers on its 2000-foot climb to an excellent viewpoint. The first 1.5 miles to Maude Creek make a less strenuous, but also rewarding walk among old-growth Engelmann spruce.

Two trails climb through the forests and wildflower meadows near Iron Mountain's dramatic cliffs: the popular, somewhat steep, 1.6-mile Iron Mountain Trail from Tombstone Pass, and the 3.4-mile Cone Peak Trail from Tombstone Prairie. Iron Mountain's lookout building was blown off the peak by a 1976 winter storm. The Forest Service repaired the structure and returned it by helicopter. It is one of only three remaining lookouts in the Willamette National Forest staffed each summer. An outstanding cross-country hiking route follows the ridge from Cone Peak past Echo Mountain and North Peak, and descends to Road 508 along Maude Creek.

Two trails lead to the fern meadows of Browder Ridge—the 1.5-mile Browder Ridge Trail from Road 080 and the 2.5-mile Gate Creek Trail from Road 1598. Hikers can traverse the ridgetop between trails, following an unmaintained, 3-mile trail. The route's highest point, above scenic Heart Lake, offers spectacular views of the major Cascade peaks and Echo Mountain Ridge.

The Old Santiam Wagon Road, occasionally overgrown by young hemlock and cedar, is eas-

ily hiked and makes an interesting historical route. Old mileposts and signs should be left undisturbed. Find the unmarked Sevenmile Creek segment of the wagon trail by walking along either Road 2024, 6 miles east of House Rock Campground via Highway 20, or along Road 245, 3 miles west of Tombstone Pass.

An easier-to-find section of the old wagon route is part of House Rock Campground's marked trail network. Follow the wagon trail 0.6 mile east from the campground to a waterfall on the South Santiam River, or explore the old route west from the campground 1.5 miles to a private property boundary.

The fascinating rock pinnacles of The Menagerie can be reached by two developed trails, both of which climb 2200 feet through old-growth Douglas fir forests to a dry upland forested with madrone and chinkapin. The 2.4-mile Trout Creek Trail begins at the Trout Creek Campground, while the steep 2.1-mile Rooster Rock Trail starts at Fernview Campground. An abandoned fire lookout shack, wedged in a rock crack near the top of Rooster Rock's impressive spire, was once reached by a long ladder.

The prolific wildflowers of Gordon Meadows are a good hiking goal. Gordon Lakes and

the nearby meadows exhibit stages in the natural plant succession from lake to forest. The meadows are 4 miles through the old growth forests of the Falls Creek Trail from Road 2032, or 3 miles from Road 230, past scenic Gordon Lakes and the impressive cliffs of Soapgrass Mountain.

Moose Lake, snowfree most winters, makes a nice destination in spring, when the moss of Moose Creek's boulder-strewn rapids glows a brilliant green. Reach the steep 1-mile Moose Lake Trail by turning off Highway 20 onto the Moose Creek Road, 2.5 miles east of Cascadia. Promptly turn right on Road 2027 for 5.5 miles, fork left onto Road 720 for 0.25 mile, and park at a wide spot in the road to find the trailhead.

Climbing

The two dozen spires of The Menagerie provide popular technical climbing challenges. Rooster Rock's abandoned lookout can be reached with class 5.4 skills; three other routes up that crag range in difficulty to level II-5.8. Nearby are Roosters Tail, Chicken Rock, and Hen Rock, with routes of similar difficulty.

Clustered a mile north of Rooster Rock, but composed of slightly lower quality rock, are two natural arches (Big Arch is a level II-5.7-A1 climb) and six additional spires, including 265-foot South Rabbit Ear (a III-5.7 climb) and North Rabbit Ear (III-5.7-A2).

A dozen other crags and spires dot the slope above Keith Creek, a half mile east of Rabbit Ears. The first of these is Turkey Monster, unclimbed until 1966. This 300-foot column has level III-5.6-A3 and IV-5.7-A3 routes. Other difficult spires include The Porpoise (I-5.8) and The Bridge (II-5.9).

Elsewhere in the area, the Santiam Pinnacle, above Highway 20, offers four routes of level I-4 to II-5.6 difficulty. And although a trail ascends Iron Mountain's west slope, the 400-foot cliff on the south face is a level I-5.6 climb.

Winter Sports

Plowed Highway 20 provides access to some cross-country ski opportunities on trails and side roads in the Tombstone Pass area. Skiable snow can be expected in January and February. Beginners often practice on Tombstone Prairie. The steep 1.6-mile Iron Mountain Trail, though scenic, requires good balance and downhill skiing skills. The 3.4-mile Cone Peak Trail, steep at first, leads to an open plateau with good skiing.

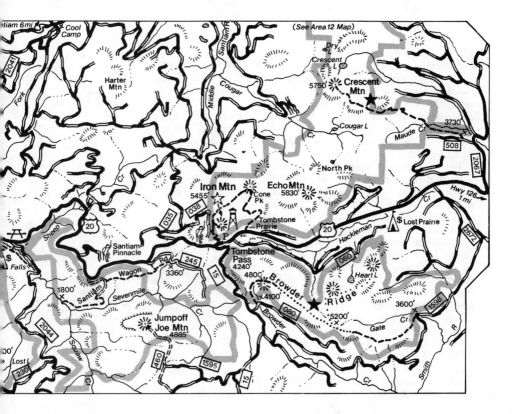

12. Middle Santiam River

LOCATION: 56 mi E of Albany
SIZE: 40 sq mi (including the Pyramids)
STATUS: 13 sq mi designated wilderness (1984)
TERRAIN: densely forested river valley, peaks
   with meadows
ELEVATION: 1300'–5618'
MANAGEMENT: Willamette NF
TOPOGRAPHIC MAPS: Chimney Peak, Coffin
   Mountain, Echo Mountain, Harter
   Mountain, Quartzville (USGS, 7.5'); Detroit
   (Green Trails)

Hidden along the remote headwaters of the Middle Santiam River is one of Oregon's largest low-elevation old growth forests. Great Douglas firs, western hemlocks, and western red cedars tower above the steep, mist-shrouded valley, where the green-pooled river cascades between mossy banks.

Climate

Though the river's canyon seldom sees snow, access roads and trails cross higher elevations, and are blocked from about December through March. Annual rainfall averages 80 inches; only summers are reliably dry.

Plants and Wildlife

Pockets of extremely old forest (over 450 years old) throughout the area form a spectacular 200-foot-high canopy above a shady world of rhododendrons, lichen-covered snags, and huge rotting logs. Old-growth forests, now rare in Oregon, are the optimum habitat for 137 vertebrate species, including the spotted owl and 85 other types of birds.

Fallen old-growth trees across the Middle Santiam River create the river's siltfree, gravel-bottomed pools—the spawning sites of a third of the Santiam drainage's Chinook salmon.

While marveling at the Middle Santiam's old-growth trees, it is worth remembering that a $100 reward has been posted for discovering the world's largest Douglas fir in Oregon. Although the Douglas fir is Oregon's state tree, the current champion is a Washington giant measuring 211 feet tall, 45.5 feet in circumference at breast height, and 61 feet in average crown spread. For information about measurement requirements and the reward contact Big Tree Hunt, Oregon Department of Forestry, 2600 State St., Salem, OR 97310.

The Pyramids host higher-elevation plant species: wildflowers in subalpine meadows and old growth noble fir.

Geology

In the east, the Three Pyramids are relatively recent volcanoes associated with the High Cascades. The remainder of the area consists of ancient, heavily eroded Old Cascades volcanics. Chimney Peak is an Old Cascades lava plug. Traces of gold and silver brought prospectors to Quartzville Creek in the 19th century.

Cliffs left by immense landslides extend from Scar Mountain to Knob Rock. One of these ancient slides dammed Donaca Lake. A more recent 100-acre slump triggered by clear-cut logging, closed Road 2041 a half mile from the Middle Santiam River bridge. The area's steep, unstable clay soils make road construction so expensive that many of the valuable old-growth forests could only be cut at a net loss.

THINGS TO DO

Hiking

In the east, forest-rimmed Daly, Parish, and Riggs lakes are each at the end of easy half-mile trails suitable for day hikes with children. Drive to the trails via Road 2266, which joins Highway 22 about 8 miles north of the Highway 20 junction.

Viewpoints and alpine rock gardens at the summit of Middle Pyramid climax a more challenging 3.1-mile trail uphill from Road 560. Get there via Lava Lake Road 2067, which meets Highway 22 about 5 miles from the "Y" junction with Highway 20.

Chimney Peak, site of a former fire lookout, commands views across valley after valley of old-growth forests, as well as many devastating clearcuts. The quickest way to the top is to bushwhack a mile southeast along the ridgetop from the clearcut at the end of Road 1142. The 7-mile McQuade Creek Trail also leads to the peak, through deep forest and past a well-preserved shelter. For both routes, turn north from Highway 20 onto the Quartzville Road 5

Daly Lake

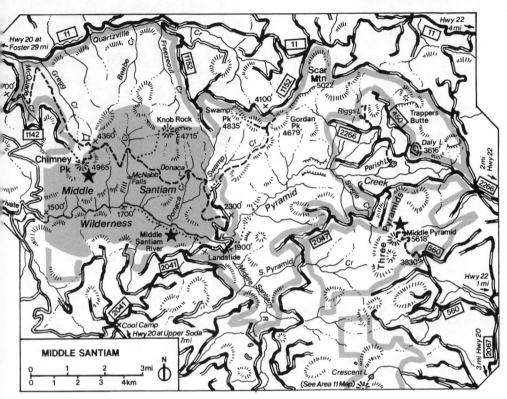

miles east of Sweet Home. After 25.5 miles, at the National Forest boundary, the Quartzville Road becomes paved Road 11. Continue 2 more miles, then turn right onto steep, winding Road 1142 for 4 miles to the McQuade Creek trailhead; the end of Road 1142 is 5 miles farther.

To hike into the heart of the Middle Santiam's old growth forests, try one of the trails or cross-country routes starting from remote Road 2041. This road, long blocked by a huge landslide 0.5 mile before the Middle Santiam bridge, has been rerouted below the slide. The best route to the river is an angler's trail down a sharp forested ridge just west of the slide. The flats along the Middle Santiam feature towering Douglas firs, mossy bigleaf maples, and frequent glimpses of Chimney Peak and the Pyramids. A cross-country route follows the south bank downstream 3 miles; west of Fitt Creek the canyon becomes too narrow for easy passage.

An unofficial but easily followed trail explores Pyramid Creek's remote roadless valley. Drive 100 yards past the Middle Santiam bridge on Road 2041 and park at the gravel quarry on the right. Hike to the top of the gravel pit and follow the rough trail straight uphill. After 100 yards, a right fork heads to the Middle Santiam River. The left fork leads up Pyramid Creek and crosses at a huge log a mile upstream.

The well-marked Chimney Peak Trail begins 1.7 miles past the Middle Santiam bridge on Road 2041. Blue-green Donaca Lake, 2.5 miles, makes a good day-hike goal. Backpackers will be able to camp at the lake and continue on 5.5 miles to Chimney Peak, perhaps making cross-country side trips to 75-foot McNabb Falls or the viewpoint at Knob Rock.

The Gordan Peak Trail follows a quiet ridge 6.5 miles between Roads 2041 and 1152, but is difficult to locate at either end due to clearcuts.

To reach these hikes from Road 2041, turn north off Highway 20 at Mountain House, 25 miles east of Sweet Home. Follow Road 2041 carefully from here north, avoiding side roads. It is 8 miles up to a pass at Cool Camp, where five roads meet (see area 11 map). From Cool Camp continue on Road 2041 downhill another 6 miles to the landslide (see area 12 map).

13. Crabtree Valley

LOCATION: 42 mi E of Albany
SIZE: 2 sq mi
STATUS: undesignated
TERRAIN: old-growth forest valley
ELEVATION: 2850'–4443'
MANAGEMENT: Salem District BLM
TOPOGRAPHIC MAP: Yellowstone Mountain
   (USGS, 7.5')

Crabtree Lake (photo by Wendell Wood)

Oregon's oldest trees—perhaps 1000 years old—grow undisturbed in this secluded Western Cascades valley.

Climate

Snow typically blocks the roads from December to April. Annual precipitation is 70 inches.

Plants and Wildlife

Crabtree Valley's claim to Oregon's oldest trees remains unproven, since the very largest trunks are too wide for growth rings to be counted by the usual method—drilling out a core sample with an incremental borer. King Tut, a monumental Douglas fir, is a prime candidate for 1000-year honors. The majority of

the Douglas fir, western hemlock, and western red cedar forming a canopy across the valley are over 800 years old. Such age is unusual in the Western Cascades, where forests rarely live 200 years before being overswept by fire.

The valley was preserved from logging when a 1985 land swap transfered a square mile of private land to the Bureau of Land Management.

Geology

A glacier filled this valley during the last major Ice Age, which ended about 10,000 years ago. The ring of glacier-carved cliffs along the valley's rim has served as a natural firebreak, protecting the aged forest within.

THINGS TO DO

Hiking

The valley lends itself to short, cross-country trips. Crabtree Lake, Waterdog Meadow, or cascading Schafer Creek may be the destinations, but the huge old growth forests are always the real goal. Fall mushrooms provide another good excuse to roam these grand woods.

To drive to Crabtree Valley, turn north off Highway 20, 4 miles east of the Sweet Home Ranger Station onto the Middle Santiam River Road (County Road 912) at a sign for Quartzville. Continue 20.5 miles east on what becomes the Quartzville Access Road along Green Peter Reservoir. About 3 miles past the reservoir turn left on Yellowstone Access Road (Road 11-3E-35.1) for 6.7 miles to the end of pavement. Turn left (following the sign for Snow Peak Camp) and 0.8 mile farther turn left again (avoiding Road 11-3E-18.1, which goes up steeply to the right). Continue 1.3 miles around a switchback, dropping steeply into Crabtree Valley with Crabtree Lake and a beaver pond in Waterdog Meadow visible below on the left. At the bottom of the hill make the first possible left turn, park, and walk the dirt road 0.7 mile to Crabtree Lake.

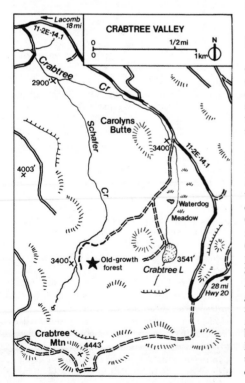

CRABTREE VALLEY

← Lacomb 18 mi
11-2E-14.1

0   1/2 mi
0   1km   N

Crabtree Cr
2900'×
Schafer
Carolyns Butte
3400'
11-2E-14.1
4003'×
Cr
Waterdog Meadow
3400'× ★ Old-growth forest
3541'
Crabtree L
28 mi Hwy 20
Crabtree Mtn 4443'

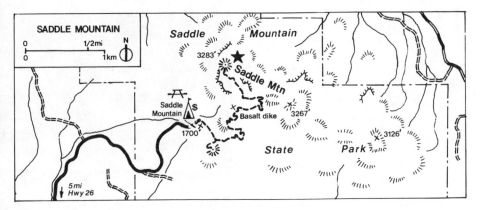

14. Saddle Mountain

LOCATION: 73 mi NW of Portland, 21 mi E of Seaside
SIZE: 4 sq mi
STATUS: state park
TERRAIN: meadow-topped mountain
ELEVATION: 900'–3283'
MANAGEMENT: Oregon Parks and Recreation Division
TOPOGRAPHIC MAP: Saddle Mountain (USGS, 7.5')

From the summit of this saddle-shaped mountain, highest point in the northern Oregon Coast Range, views sweep from Mt. Rainier to the Columbia River and to ships far out at sea.

Climate

The area's mossy rain forest results from over 100 inches of annual precipitation. Storms briefly cover the peak with snow and ice in midwinter.

Plants and Wildlife

Saddle Mountain features 301 identified species of flora, some of which have chosen this singular, tall peak as their sole Coast Range habitat. Trilliums and pink coast fawn lilies spangle the lower slopes in April and May. Summit wildflower displays peak in mid June. Patterson's bittercress, a delicate, pink-petaled mustard, is known only from Saddle Mountain and nearby Onion Peak.

Herds of up to 70 elk have been sighted on the peak. The Sitka spruce and western hemlock rain forest about the mountain's base is regrowing from 1920s logging and from fires in 1936 and 1939.

Geology

Saddle Mountain erupted as a seafloor volcano about 20 million years ago. Lumpy, "pillow basalt" lavas exposed about the mountain are typical of underwater flows, much like the flows forming many Oregon coastal headlands. Later, basalt oozed into cracks in the Saddle Mountain volcano, forming resistant, wall-like dikes. One dike along the summit trail fractured hexagonally due to slow cooling; it now resembles an immense stack of cordwood. The Coast Range has been rising from the seafloor for 35 million years.

THINGS TO DO

Hiking

The exhilarating 3-mile summit trail traverses 0.6 mile through dense forest, then switchbacks up to a cliff-edged saddle before crossing meadows to the taller of the mountain's two peaks, the former site of a fire lookout cabin. The 1600-foot elevation gain leaves hikers glad for a rest or lunch break on top. Bring binoculars to spot the Olympic Mountains and Astoria's Columbia River Bridge.

The park's paved 7-mile access road turns off Highway 26 near milepost 10, 66 miles from Portland.

Saddle Mountain

15. Cascade Head

LOCATION: 7 mi N of Lincoln City, 56 mi W of Salem
SIZE: 10 sq mi
STATUS: scenic-research area; islands are designated wilderness
TERRAIN: clifftop meadows, rain forest
ELEVATION: 0'–1783'
MANAGEMENT: The Nature Conservancy, Siuslaw NF
TOPOGRAPHIC MAP: Neskowin (USGS, 7.5')

Surf-pounded cliffs surround the wildflower meadows on Cascade Head's steep headland. Craggy islands crowded with birds dot the sea. On either hand, 20 miles of beaches and headlands diminish into blue silhouettes. Yet just behind the meadows lie dark green rain forests of dense salal and Sitka spruce, where it is easy to imagine oneself far from the ocean.

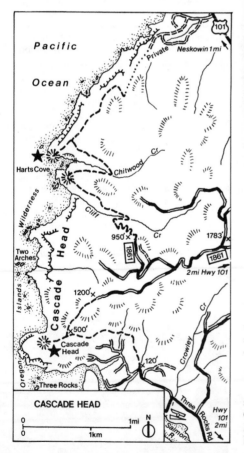

CASCADE HEAD

Climate

Rain falls at Cascade Head on more than 180 days per year. Cool fog shrouds the headland most of the summer, particularly when temperatures in the Willamette Valley are high. Fog drip brings the annual precipitation to over 100 inches in the forests, although rainfall only totals 69 inches on the beach. Winters are snowless; fall and spring have the most clear days.

Plants and Wildlife

The area's many offshore crags, roosting sites for a multitude of seabirds, are part of the Oregon Islands Wilderness (see area 39). Sea lions are usually lounging on the inaccessible beaches below the cliffs of Harts Cove. Cascade

Old growth spruce on the trail from Three Rocks Road to Cascade Head

Head is also an ideal lookout from which to spot the spouts of migrating gray whales from December to May. Cascade Head's meadow is one of only three locations worldwide that supports a stable population of the threatened, orange-and-brown mottled, Oregon silverspot butterfly.

The headland meadows are filled with summer asters and Indian paintbrush reminiscent of an alpine environment. Several species of these wildflowers grow only in the windswept meadows of coastal headlands. Wind has sculpted the oceanfront Sitka spruce into a waist-high mat, but only a short distance inland, Sitka spruce grow as much as 7 feet thick and 240 feet tall. The mossy western hemlock and Sitka spruce rain forest has one of the fastest growth rates for trees and one of the highest biomass-per-acre ratios of any area in the world. At its densest, the forest has 24 square meters of leaf surface for every square meter of sunlight.

The Cascade Head Experimental Forest, a research facility overseeing National Forest land on the headland, pioneered Northwest forestry's clearcutting and herbicide-spraying techniques.

Geology

The rocks here formed on the seafloor about 50 million years ago when sand and mud became interlayered with submarine basalt lava flows. As the Coast Range rose from the sea, areas with exposed mudstone and soft sand-

Mouth of the Salmon River from Cascade Head

stone quickly eroded to create low beaches; Cascade Head's much more resistant basalt, however, remained as a headland.

THINGS TO DO

Hiking

Most popular of area trails is the 2-mile Nature Conservancy path from the Lower Salmon River Road to Cascade Head. After a half mile through a lush forest of sword fern, salmonberry (edible orange berries ripe in June), and red alder, the route breaks out into steep meadows with breathtaking views across the Salmon River estuary and offshore islands. The fragile flora of the headland's low, final bluff is protected by a fence. The Nature Conservancy purchased 300 acres of the headland's tip in 1967.

To reach this trail, drive one mile north on Highway 101 from the junction with Highway 18. Turn left on the paved Three Rocks Road for 2.5 miles, then continue straight on the Lower Salmon River Road 0.4 mile to the Nature Conservancy sign and trailhead.

A less-used, upper trailhead for the same trail begins in a deep hemlock forest. Get there by driving 3.5 miles north of the Highway 18 junction on Highway 101. Turn left on Road 1861 for 2.5 miles, then keep left on an unnumbered road another mile.

Harts Cove is a cliff-rimmed bay where the crashing of the surf competes with the barks of sea lions, the cries of sea gulls, and the rush of Chitwood Creek's waterfall. The 2.6-mile downhill trail to the meadow overlooking the cove is far less used than the better-known Cascade Head trails. After wet weather, the path can be too muddy for tennis shoes.

Except on Cascade Head's meadow, cross-country hiking is generally impractical because of dense salal bushes—a plant whose tough-skinned, dark blue berries were used by pioneers for preserves. Seaside cliffs prevent all access to the headland's few, rocky beaches.

16. Drift Creek

LOCATION: 12 mi E of Waldport, 57 mi W of
Corvallis
SIZE: 18 sq mi
STATUS: 9 sq mi designated wilderness (1984)
TERRAIN: steep valleys, rain forest
ELEVATION: 80'–2100'
MANAGEMENT: Siuslaw NF
TOPOGRAPHIC MAPS: Tidewater, Hellion
Rapids (USGS, 7.5')

Drift Creek features the Coast Range's largest remaining stands of old-growth rain forest. The rushing creek's steep-sided canyon gives the area a mountainous feel, although it is actually close to tidewater.

Climate
Temperatures are mild year round. Heavy rainfall can be expected from fall through spring (74 inches annually in the west, 120 inches at Table Mountain). Winter snow is rare even at high elevations.

Plants and Wildlife
Sitka spruce, Douglas fir and western hemlock grow 7 feet thick at many places in the area, particularly along the northern portion of the Horse Creek Trail. Creekbanks are overhung with bigleaf maple trees, their spreading branches cushioned by a 6-inch-deep layer of moss and licorice ferns.

In summer look for edible berries in the rain forest undergrowth: orange salmonberry, red thimbleberry, blue and red huckleberries, and dark blue salal. Sourgrass, or oxalis, is edible in small quantities and tart as a lemon. Its shamrock-shaped leaves often carpet the forest floor. Swampy areas brighten in April with the huge yellow spathes of skunk cabbage. Disturbed hillsides sprout 6-foot-tall spires of red and white foxglove throughout summer.

Several pairs of northern spotted owls and bald eagles, both threatened in Oregon, nest in the old-growth forest. Expect to find tracks or scat of Roosevelt elk or black bear.

Though Drift Creek is not ranked as a river, it supports river-sized runs of native fish. Chinook salmon, coho salmon, steelhead, and cutthroat trout return each fall, while a much smaller Chinook run comes in spring. Hatchery fish have never been stocked.

Geology
This area's crumbly sandstone and siltstone weather to slippery clay, making roads and trails susceptible to landslides. The rock began as oceanic deposits of mud and sand; the rise of the Coast Range lifted this section of seafloor from the waves.

History
Drift Creek was once the hunting and gathering grounds of the Waldport Bay-based Alsea Indians. Some meadows show the attempts of failed, pre-World War II homesteads.

Drift Creek (photo by K. Norman Johnson)

THINGS TO DO

Hiking

Three paths descend through forest to the shady, green banks of Drift Creek. The trails can be connected by wading 20-foot-wide Drift Creek in summer or fall, when it is only knee deep.

The southern part of the Horse Creek Trail loses over 1200 feet on its 2-mile route to the creek. The recently built Harris Ranch Trail drops 1000 feet in 2 miles to a large, campable creekside meadow. A path along the creek, requiring two fords, makes a pleasant 5.5-mile trip for those who can shuttle cars between the southern Horse Creek and Harris Ranch trailheads.

The third route to Drift Creek, the 3-mile-long northern portion of the Horse Creek Trail, traverses spectacular old-growth forest. Hikers starting on this trail usually return the

way they came, since a car shuttle to the southern end of the Horse Creek Trail requires a 23-mile drive on gravel roads over Table Mountain. Good campsites are on either side of Drift Creek at the Horse Creek Trail crossing.

An angler's trail scrambles along the north bank of Drift Creek from the Horse Creek Trail, crossing as far as a campable site across from the mouth of Boulder Creek. Bushwhacking along other creeks and ridges is just difficult enough to ensure solitude.

Reach the northern Horse Creek trailhead from Highway 101 by turning inland on Beaver Creek Road at Ona Beach State Park, just north of Seal Rock. After 3.8 miles, turn right on paved Road 51. After 5.8 more miles, turn left on Road 50 for 1.3 miles, then turn right onto Road 5087 for 3.4 miles to the marked trailhead.

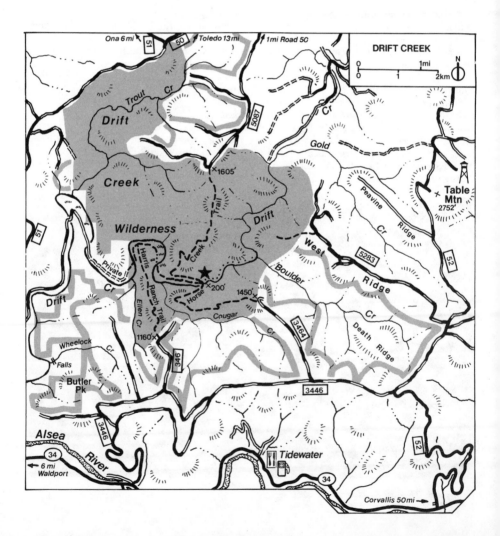

View south from Cape Perpetua

17. Cummins Creek and Rock Creek

LOCATION: 15 mi N of Florence
SIZE: 26 sq mi
STATUS: designated wilderness (1984)
TERRAIN: steep valleys, rain forest
ELEVATION: 0'–2300'
MANAGEMENT: Siuslaw NF
TOPOGRAPHIC MAPS: Yachats, Heceta
  Head, Cummins Peak, Cannibal Mountain
  (USGS, 7.5')

On this wild stretch of coast, pristine rain forest canyons pour a half dozen clear creeks between the cliff-tipped headlands of 2000-foot-tall ridges. Here, hikers can alternate prowling the old-growth forests with studying tide pools or picnicking on a secluded beach.

Climate

Annual rainfall varies from 60 inches on the beach to over 80 inches in the interior. Cool fogs line the coast and fill the valleys most of summer. Winters are snowless; fall and spring have the most clear days.

Plants and Wildlife

The ridge between Rock Creek and Big Creek is one of only three locations worldwide to support a stable population of the threatened, orange-and-brown mottled, Oregon silverspot butterfly. Cape Perpetua is a popular lookout from which to spot the spouts of migrating gray whales from December to May. Low tides expose sea urchins, sea anemones, and other marine life in the tide pools of the rocky coastline between the Devils Churn and Captain Cook Point.

Sitka spruce as large as 9 feet in diameter dominate the valley slopes within 2 miles of the ocean. Farther inland the forest gradually shifts to old-growth Douglas fir. Undergrowth of rhododendron (blooms in May), salal, sword fern, and salmonberry is so dense that even shade-tolerant western hemlock seedlings often must sprout atop rotting old-growth "nursery logs" to survive. Red alder, mossy bigleaf maple, and autumn-reddening vine maple overhang creeks. Wildflowers include yellow monkeyflower, purple aster, white candyflower, and the tall red spires of foxglove. Wild lily-of-the-valley carpets the forest with heart-shaped leaves.

The area supports larger native runs of

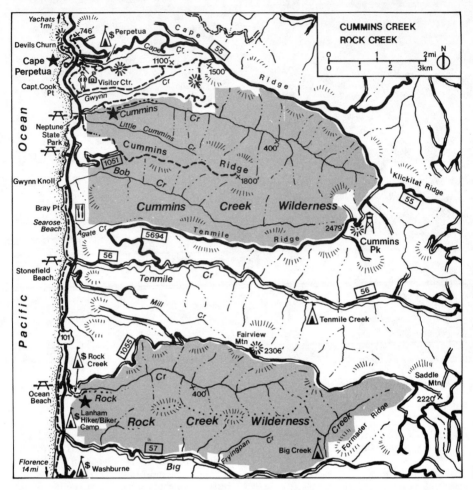

salmon, steelhead, and cutthroat trout than any other similar-sized watershed in Oregon. A fish count in late June, 1979, found an average of 50 coho salmon per 100 feet on the lower two miles of Cummins Creek.

Geology

The area's basalt bedrock began as undersea lava flows. As upfaulting lifted the Coast Range from the ocean, creeks eroded the face of the fault block into steep, shallow-soiled canyons. Small oceanfront fractures have been widened by wave action into slot-shaped spouting horns and the Devils Churn.

THINGS TO DO

Hiking

Seven trails suitable for day hikes originate at the Cape Perpetua Visitor Center. The most heavily used of these are paved, and several are equipped with interpretive signs. Loop hikes of less than a mile extend to the Devils Churn

and Captain Cook Point's spouting horns and tide pools. A 1.5-mile trail (one way) climbs 700 feet to a viewpoint atop Cape Perpetua. A 1-mile trail follows the south bank of Cape Creek, past the Perpetua Campground, to a giant spruce tree. Cassette-guided tours are available for a 1-mile nature trail loop up the ridge southeast of the visitor center. Cape Perpetua's most ambitious hike is a 6.5-mile loop from the visitor center up quiet Gwynn Creek and back along a ridge with ocean views.

A lovely trail along Cummins Creek emerges at intervals from lush, valley-bottom rain forest to pass creekside gravel bars ideal for picnics. To start, turn off Highway 101 immediately north of Neptune State Park at a sign reading, "Cummins Creek Trailhead ¼ mile." The trailhead is a barricade blocking Road 1030. Hike up the abandoned road 250 yards and take an unmarked spur to the right; this is the 1-mile-long creek trail. An elk trail continues upstream another half mile.

For another hike from the Cummins Creek trailhead, walk up the abandoned road through deep forest 2.3 miles, and then take a marked 1-mile trail to the left, climbing past several viewpoints. At a ridgetop trail junction, hikers can either head right 0.2 mile to Road 55 or left 3.6 miles down the scenic Gwynn Creek canyon to Highway 101. A 0.3-mile connector trail between Gwynn Creek and Road 1030 makes a 7.4-mile loop hike possible from the Cummins Creek trailhead.

Three trails explore the old-growth Sitka spruce forest on Cummins Ridge. One begins at the white concrete posts beside Highway 101 immediately south of the Neptune State Park entrance and climbs a half mile before petering out. Two others begin at the well-marked Cummins Ridge Trailhead at the barricaded end of Road 1051. The official trail from this barricade continues east along the ridgetop 3.5 miles, following the abandoned road. An unofficial trail heads north from the Road 1051 barricade on a spur road. Keep left on this spur a half mile to a park-like bench of old-growh Sitka spruce. Adventurous hikers can bushwhack onward down the ridge to Highway 101.

Hikers heading up Rock Creek start at the Rock Creek Campground and walk east along a short Forest Service road and through a meadow that was once the site of a homestead. The impromptu trail quickly becomes a bushwhacking route. Wear tennis shoes and walk up the middle of the chilly (average 56° F) creek, to continue.

The Oregon Coast Trail, which is being developed along the length of this shore, will eventually provide paths around headlands, connecting the many already hikable beaches.

Spouting horn at Cape Perpetua

18. Lower Deschutes River

LOCATION: 14 mi E of The Dalles
SIZE: 38 sq mi
STATUS: state scenic waterway
TERRAIN: rimrock-lined river canyon
ELEVATION: 150'–2500'
MANAGEMENT: Oregon Parks and Recreation
   Division, Prineville District BLM
TOPOGRAPHIC MAPS: Lower Deschutes
   River (BLM); Wishram, Emerson, Locust
   Grove, Erskine, Summit Ridge, Sinamox,
   Sherars Bridge, Maupin (USGS, 7.5')

Roaring whitewater and cliff-rimmed canyons highlight the final 51 miles of the Deschutes River, popular for two-day float trips.

Climate
With just 10 inches of annual precipitation, the area boasts reliable sunshine. Summers are hot, but frost is common at night and throughout winter.

Plants and Wildlife
Sagebrush dominates this canyonland. Mule deer, coyotes, and rattlesnakes are common. The river's famous steelhead include a native Descutes strain (6-8 pounds), which swim up the river from June to September, and a Clearwater River strain (up to 22 pounds), which often visit the cool Deschutes, seeking respite from the warmer Columbia on their way to spawning grounds in Idaho.

Geology
The canyon walls have many layers of 25- to 100-foot cliffs—lava flows of the 13- to 16-million-year-old Columbia River Basalts.

History
Warm Springs Indians maintain a centuries-old tradition by dipnetting migrating salmon each spring and fall from rickety wooden platforms overhanging 15-foot Sherars Falls. Explorer Peter Skene Ogden lost five horses through an Indian bridge at the falls in 1826. A toll bridge built there in 1860 connected The Dalles with the rich Canyon City gold fields in central Oregon. The old county bridge at Freebridge was apparently dynamited in 1912 by competing toll bridge owners.

Although an 1855 Army engineering survey reported that a railroad grade was impossible along the Lower Deschutes, rivalry between railroad magnates James Hill and Edward Harriman resulted in *two* rail lines being built up the "impossible" canyon to Bend in 1909-11. Hill's Oregon Trunk Railway remains on the west bank; track has been removed from the east bank grade.

THINGS TO DO

Hiking
The open sagebrush lands along the river are so easily hiked that trails are unnecessary. Primitive campsites are plentiful, but stays are limited to four days and campfires are prohibited. Anglers must use barbless hooks and release all native steelhead; hatchery fish can be identified by a clipped fin.

The most popular riverbank hike starts at the Deschutes River State Park campground and passes scenic Gordon Ridge Rapids; private land stops hikers after 12 miles on either shore, beyond Harris Canyon.

Boating
The popular 51-mile drift trip from Maupin to the Columbia River encounters three thrill-

ing class 4 rapids, dozens of lesser riffles, and one impassable falls.

Four miles below the Maupin City Park boat ramp, class 4 Oak Springs Rapids splits the river into three channels; stop to look it over, then avoid the right-hand channel. After another 3.5 miles, all craft *must* portage around unnavigable Sherars Falls. Just 150 yards beyond the portage, boaters are faced with class 3 Upper Bridge Rapids, and, in another 0.2 mile, the dangerous Lower Bridge Rapids. Scout this class 4+ whitewater from the right bank, then paddle hard to stay in the smaller right-hand channel.

Downriver 3.6 miles, the class 3 Wreck Rapids introduces a 34-mile stretch of calmer water with a steady 5 mile-per-hour current, past some of the canyon's most spectacular basalt rimrock.

The pace picks up for the river's final 6 miles. First comes Gordon Ridge Rapids, a long class 2+ ride with outcroppings of columnar basalt in midriver. Scouting is required. A mile and a half downstream comes class 3 Colorado Rapids, with a treacherous standing wave and suckhole on the left-hand side. Class 4 Rattlesnake Rapids is only 1.2 miles farther. Three drownings testify to the danger of this narrows, where boaters must thread their way between rocks on the river's left side and a gigantic suckhole in the river's middle. Two miles farther on, the class 2 Moody Rapids delivers boaters to the backwater of The Dalles Dam.

All boaters must carry a Deschutes River Boater Pass, available at local sporting goods stores. Fishing is prohibited from any floating device in the river. Campfires are permitted only in firepans, and only from October 1 to June 1. Campsites between Macks Canyon and Deschutes River State Park campground have a four-day stay limit. No camping is allowed on islands. Boaters can recognize the beginning of private, off limits shorefront by watching for posts marked with circles; posts with triangles signal the return to public lands.

Lower Deschutes float trips are often coupled with the two-day, 45-mile drift of the central Deschutes River, from the Highway 26 bridge near Warm Springs to the boat landing at Maupin.

Jet boats are allowed, and common everywhere except bordering the Warm Springs Indian Reservation on the central Deschutes River.

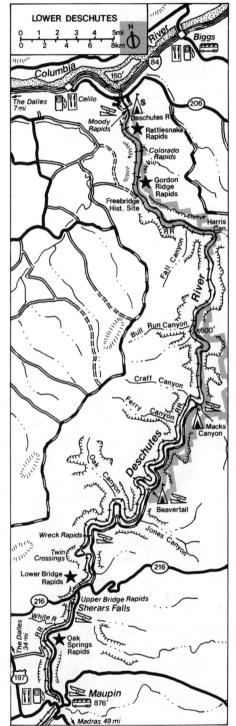

Whitewater below Sherars Falls (photo by Don Tryon)

19. Deschutes Canyon

LOCATION: 32 mi N of Bend
SIZE: 29 sq mi
STATUS: undesignated wilderness
TERRAIN: cliff-lined canyons, desert plateaus
ELEVATION: 1945'–2950'
MANAGEMENT: Crooked River National
   Grassland
TOPOGRAPHIC MAPS: Central Oregon
   (BLM), Steelhead Falls, Squaw Back Ridge,
   Round Butte Dam (USGS, 7.5')

The Deschutes River roars through this seldom-visited 700-foot-deep canyon, beneath sagebrush mesas with views of the High Cascade snowpeaks.

Climate

Sunshine is the rule in this steppe, which gets only 10 inches of annual rainfall. Summers are hot, but frost is common at night and in winter.

Plants and Wildlife

Heavy grazing on the tablelands has converted an historic grassland to sagebrush, cheat grass, and tumbleweed. The steep canyons, however, preserve native bunchgrasses. The river itself creates a narrow oasis dotted with ponderosa pine and vine maple. Coyote and mule deer abound.

Geology

The canyon's layer-cake-style cliffs consist of 13- to 16-million-year-old Columbia River Basalt lava flows. These lavas erupted from fissures near Hells Canyon, burying most of northern Oregon and eastern Washington, in places 5000 feet deep. Slow cooling allowed the basalt to fracture into a distinctive pattern of hexagonal pillars. The slopes between cliff layers, sometimes eroded into multicolored pinnacles, are composed of volcanic ash,

gravel, and soil that accumulated between the devastating basalt floods, which were often 100,000 years apart.

THINGS TO DO

Hiking

Cross-country hiking is easy and views are best along the rims of the open tablelands. Hardy hikers will find the rimrock broken in many places, allowing steep hiking on deer trails into the canyon itself. The canyon bottom is more easily reached by boat at the head of the Lake Billy Chinook reservoir.

To the south, massive Steelhead Falls is a half-mile hike from poorly marked dirt roads. Roads in the extensive Crooked River Ranch subdivision north and east of Steelhead Falls are open to public use.

To the southwest, dirt Roads 6360 and 6370 descend to Squaw Creek, a grassy canyon bottom with spring wildflowers. A rewarding 1-mile cross-country route from Road 6370 follows Squaw Creek to the hidden oasis of Alder Springs, a grassy basin ringed by rimrock. The remote canyon abyss where Squaw Creek and the Deschutes River join lies a difficult 1.5-mile scramble downstream. While Squaw Creek can be forded nearly everywhere, the raging Deschutes River is nowhere crossable.

To find Road 6360 from Sisters, drive 4.5 miles east on Highway 126, turn left toward Lower Bridge, and continue 8 miles on pavement to a dirt turnoff on the left. To reach Road 6360 from Highway 97, turn west at Terrebonne, pass Lower Bridge, and continue 6.5 miles on pavement to the dirt turnoff.

Boating

Big Falls and Steelhead Falls stop all whitewater boating on the Deschutes. Kayaks carried to the base of Steelhead Falls face 7.5 miles of apparently runnable rapids.

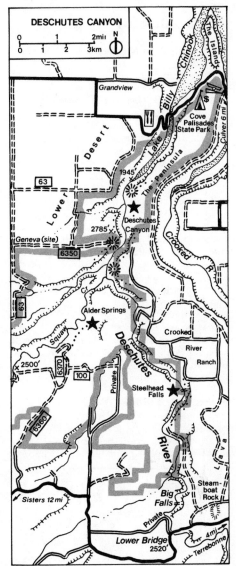

Deschutes Canyon and the Three Sisters (photo by William L. Sullivan)

20. Metolius Breaks

LOCATION: 45 mi N of Bend, 32 mi W of Madras
SIZE: 17 sq mi
STATUS: undesignated wilderness
TERRAIN: steep, forested river canyon
ELEVATION: 2000'–5050'
MANAGEMENT: Deschutes NF
TOPOGRAPHIC MAPS: Whitewater River (Green Trails, 15'); Shitike Butte, Prairie Farm, Fly Creek (USGS, 7.5')

The Metolius River is the most magical of all Oregon rivers. From the arid base of Black Butte it springs fully grown, at an identical temperature and volume year round, then slides swiftly through 29 miles of rugged canyons and vanishes into the backwaters of the Lake Billy Chinook reservoir. The Metolius Breaks are the wilderness canyon slopes of the remote lower river.

Climate

Though mostly sunny and dry (20 inches of annual precipitation), the area receives snow from about December to February. Snow lingers on Green Ridge till April.

Plants and Wildlife

Orange-trunked ponderosa pine and autumn-red vine maple flank the river. Bitterbrush and rabbit brush (bright yellow blooms in fall) form a sparse ground cover. On the east-

ern ridges, gnarled juniper reign.

The river's name comes from the Warm Springs Indian *Mpto-ly-as,* "white fish." The light-fleshed salmon which prompted this name are gone; however, introduced Kokanee salmon and abundant hatchery trout attract eagles, bears, and other anglers.

Geology

Green Ridge, a 16-mile-long, 2500-foot-tall fault scarp, gave rise to Black Butte's volcanic cone on the south and displaced the Metolius River to the north. Later Columbia River basalt flows created the adjacent Metolius Bench tablelands, with their dramatic rimrock.

THINGS TO DO

Hiking

A 1.5-mile trail in the heart of the area traverses a dense forest along the rushing Metolius River. The trail's eastern terminus is the end of Road 64, reached by driving west from Madras through Cove Palisades State Park and Grandview. To reach this trailhead from Sisters, drive 5 miles west on Highway 20, turn north onto Road 11 for 18 miles, turn right onto Road 1170 for 5 miles, and then take Road 64 to the left for 12 miles to its end. To reach the western trailhead, turn north from Highway 20, 10 miles east of Santiam Pass. Follow paved Road 14 for 13 miles to Lower Bridge Campground, then continue north on badly rutted dirt Road 1499 (4-wheel drive vehicles recommended) for 10 miles to its end.

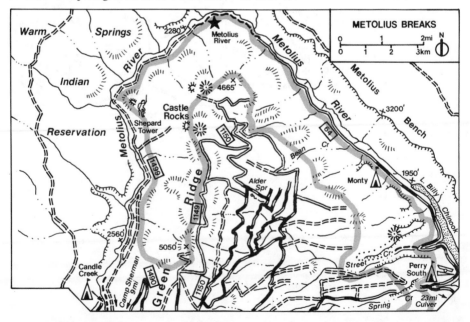

The Metolius River from the river trail (photo by William L. Sullivan)

Excellent views of Mt. Jefferson and the craggy Castle Rocks await cross-country hikers willing to scale the persistent slopes of Green Ridge. The open forest presents no obstacle.

A nice hike in the east of the area follows an unmarked half-mile-long trail up Street Creek. To find Street Creek, drive 2 miles past Perry South Campground on road 64 to a sign reading, "Monty Campground 3 miles." The trail itself, easy to spot, follows the creek's north bank. At trail's end, adventurous hikers can continue 1.5 miles upstream cross-country past ash formations and a cave, hike north up a side canyon, and walk east along the rimrock's edge to a viewpoint.

The Metolius River forms the southern boundary of the Warm Springs Indian Reservation. Entry to tribal lands is completely prohibited here.

Climbing

Shepard Tower of the Metolius, a half mile uphill from Road 1499 (14.5 miles north of Camp Sherman) offers four routes via chimneys and ledges. Difficulty levels are I-3 to I-5.4.

Boating

Clear, deep, and cold (46° F year round), the Metolius races along at between 5 and 10 miles per hour, with three class 3 rapids. In 26 miles of free-flowing water between Riverside Campground (1.5 miles south of Camp Sherman) and Lake Billy Chinook, the chief hazards are fallen pine trees, which may span the river, and Wizard Falls (6.5 miles from the start). A bridge immediately before the falls signals the portage. The last bridge across the river, Lower Bridge, is at river mile 9. Float trips end at Monty Campground, since the inlet of Lake Billy Chinook is on private land, and reaching Perry South Campground's boat ramp means paddling another 3.5 miles across the reservoir.

21. Smith Rock

LOCATION: 8 mi N of Redmond
SIZE: 1 sq mi
STATUS: state park
TERRAIN: river peninsula with rock formations
ELEVATION: 2620'–3500'
MANAGEMENT: Oregon Parks and Recreation
    Division
TOPOGRAPHIC MAPS: Redmond, Opal City,
    O'Neil, Gray Butte (USGS, 7.5')

The orange rock walls and pinnacles of
Smith Rock tower above an oasislike riverbend
at the edge of central Oregon's sagebrush
plains. The spectacular formation is both a reliably rainless hiking destination and the best
technical rock climbing site in Oregon.

Climate

With just 10 inches of annual precipitation,
Smith Rock is usually sunny even when the
trails of the High Cascades are beset with rain
or snow. Midwinter brings a few dustings of
snow, and midsummer brings blazing heat.

Plants and Wildlife

Visit in spring for high desert wildflowers.
Admire, but do not pick, the riverbank's wild
asparagus and wild onions. Climbers should
take pains not to disturb birds of prey nesting
on the crags.

Geology

The western vanguard of the Ochoco Mountains, Smith Rock consists of welded rhyolite
ash. This ash erupted from the Old Cascades,
settled in a large inland sea, and fused to form
rock by heat and pressure. More recent lava
flows pushed the Crooked River up against
Smith Rock, leaving an arid plain and basalt
rimrock on the river's south shore.

THINGS TO DO

Hiking

The popular riverbank trail meanders below
the orange cliffs for 2.8 easy miles to Monkey
Face, a 300-foot rock monolith topped by a remarkable natural sculpture of a monkey's head.
A short scramble to the base of the tower not
only gives a better look at the rock climbers
usually found there, but also yields a view
across central Oregon to the Cascade snowpeaks.

A second hike, also starting at the picnic
area parking lot, follows the river in the opposite direction, climbs the Burma Road, and descends a ridge above the cliffs. This 3.6-mile
route (one way) passes numerous viewpoints of
the Cascades and ends at an overlook of Monkey Face.

To reach the park, turn east off Highway 97
at Terrebonne, 6 miles north of Redmond, and
follow state park signs for 3 miles. The route
passes Juniper Junction, a shop known for its
refreshing huckleberry ice cream.

Climbing

With more than 3 miles of rock faces and
281 named routes, Smith Rock ranks first

The Crooked River and Smith Rock

among Oregon's technical climbing sites. It was here, on routes up to level IV-5.12, that many well-known Yosemite climbers first honed their skills. Good weather and easy access add to the area's popularity. But Smith Rock's enduring charm is its scenery: orange, yellow, and purple walls tower above the green-banked river, while white-capped Cascade peaks line the horizon.

By dawn on weekend mornings the parking lot teems with climbers checking their gear; an early start helps avoid the afternoon's scorching sun. Heavy use, however, has necessitated sev-

eral rules: use removable nuts and "friends" on climbs instead of pitons or bolts. Leave existing pitons and bolts in place. Stay on established trails as much possible. Camping is allowed only in the designated bivouac area. Campfires are prohibited.

Large climbing classes and search-and-rescue practice groups should strive to minimize their impact by climbing in beginner areas. The 30-foot basalt rimrock cliffs on the opposite shore of the river from The Monument are easily accessible and offer technical pitches. Beginners intent on trying rhyolite

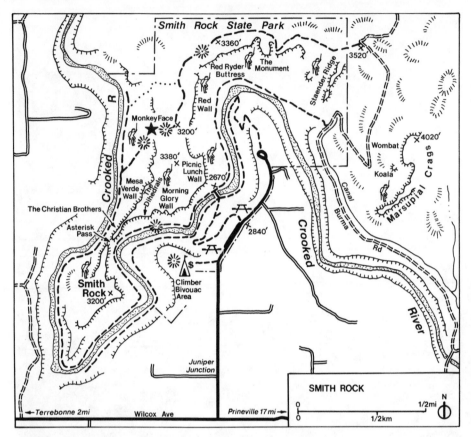

will find a good practice boulder on the river-bank opposite Morning Glory Wall.

The area's most spectacular challenge is Monkey Face, a 300-foot tower overhanging on all sides, first climbed on January 1, 1960. There are 27 routes and variations, including the level II-5.11 Monkey Space route behind the monkey's head, and the level II-5.7-A1 Pioneer Route past Panic Point, on the monkey's Mouth Cave. Climbers sometimes hike to the tower by crossing the Smith Rock Isthmus at Asterisk Pass, or via a steep trail up Misery Ridge, between Red Wall and Red Ryder Buttress.

Other major climbing areas include Picnic Lunch Wall (10 routes), Morning Glory Wall (8 routes), The Dihedrals (15 routes), The Christian Brothers (25 routes), Smith Rock promontory (25 routes), Mesa Verde Wall (13 routes), Red Wall (19 routes), Red Ryder Buttress (5 routes), The Monument (4 routes), Staender Ridge (29 routes), and, on private land outside the park, Marsupial Crags (26 routes).

Descriptions of individual routes, with levels of difficulty, are available in *Oregon Rock:* *A Climber's Guide,* by Jeff Thomas (The Mountaineers, 1983).

Above, Stoney mountaineering at Smith Rock
Right, the Pacific Crest Trail at the foot of Red Buttes (photo by William L. Sullivan)

SOUTHWEST OREGON

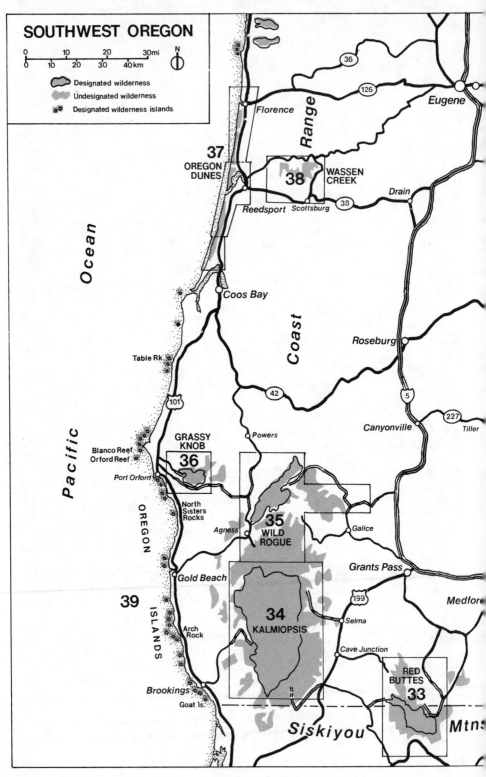

SOUTHWEST OREGON

0   10   20   30mi   N

0   10   20   30   40km

Designated wilderness

Undesignated wilderness

Designated wilderness islands

Eugene

36

126

Florence

37
OREGON
DUNES

38
WASSEN
CREEK

Drain

Reedsport   Scottsburg

38

Ocean

Coos Bay

Coast

Range

Roseburg

5

Table Rk.

42

Canyonville

Tiller

227

101

Powers

GRASSY
KNOB

36

Blanco Reef
Orford Reef

Port Orford

North
Sisters
Rocks

35
WILD
ROGUE

Galice

Agness

Grants Pass

Pacific

Gold Beach

39

OREGON

199

Medfor

34
KALMIOPSIS

Selma

Arch
Rock

Cave Junction

ISLANDS

RED
BUTTES

33

Brookings

Goat Is.

Siskiyou

Mtns

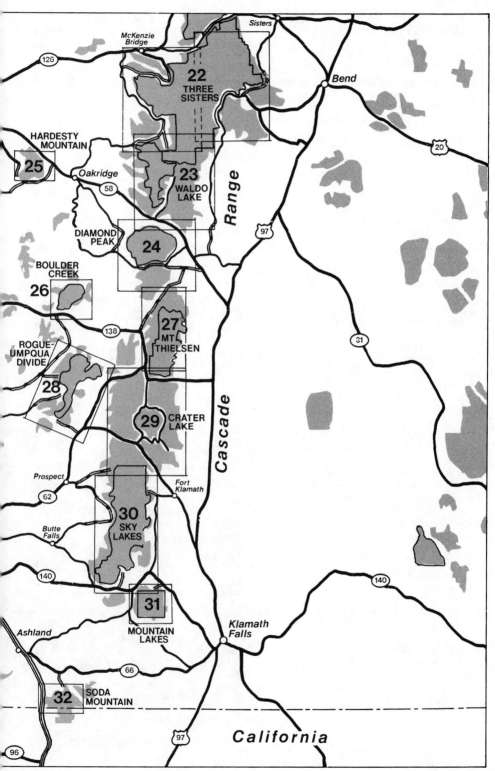

22. Three Sisters

LOCATION: 52 mi E of Eugene, 26 mi W of Bend

SIZE: 580 sq mi, including Century Lakes, Chucksney Mountain, and McLennen Mountain

STATUS: 443 sq mi designated wilderness (1964, 1978, 1984)

TERRAIN: snowpeaks, lava, forests, lakes, valleys

ELEVATION: 1850'–10,358'

MANAGEMENT: Deschutes NF, Willamette NF

TOPOGRAPHIC MAPS: Three Sisters (Geo-Graphics); Three Sisters Wilderness, PCT Northern Oregon Portion (USFS)

A cluster of glacier-clad volcanoes highlights Oregon's most visited wilderness. This large area contains four very different geographic zones.

In the alpine region ringing the Three Sisters and craggy Broken Top, wildflower meadows alternate with lava formations. But to the south, the Cascade Crest is a rolling forest of pine and mountain hemlock interwoven with hundreds of lakes. To the west, foggy, low-elevation canyons brim with old-growth Douglas fir. To the southeast, sparse forests of lodgepole pine and beargrass carpet arid lands beyond the Century Lakes.

Climate

The uplands receive as much as 20 feet of snow per year. In the east the snow falls dry, providing the state's best powder skiing. Even the lowest trails remain blocked by snow until May; trails to 5000 feet are clear by about mid-June and trails at 6500 feet are usually clear by August, though snowstorms can occur in any month.

The area's western slopes receive 90 inches of annual precipitation, but the eastern slopes receive less than 20 inches. The Mink Lake and Horse Lake basins especially are plagued by mosquitoes in July and early August.

Plants and Wildlife

The area's size makes it a refuge for large, shy animals such as wolverine, mink, cougar, and bald eagle. Geographic diversity makes the area home to more plant species than any other Oregon wilderness.

Subalpine wildflower displays in July and early August include blue lupine and red Indian paintbrush. Snowmelt zones teem with white avalanche lily, marsh marigolds, and fuzzy pasque flower. Wet areas have red elephanthead, shooting star, yellow monkeyflower, columbine, and larkspur. Drier fields host fuzzy cats-ears and wild sunflower.

Pink rhododendron displays brighten the lower western slopes in early June. Ripe wild huckleberries line forest trails through 5000 to 6500 feet elevation in late August.

Geology

Although a 1925 theory claimed the taller peaks were remnants of an exploded supervolcano, "Mt. Multnomah," more recent study shows the mountains formed separately, all within the past 100,000 years, along the High Cascades fault zone.

Oldest peaks in the group are North Sister, which has lost a third of its bulk to glacial erosion, leaving its central plug as a summit spire, and Broken Top, eroded so severely it offers a good cut-away view of a composite volcano's interior structure—alternating red and black

bands of cinder and lava. Broken Top's violent past has left the area strewn with interesting, drop-shaped "lava bombs," football-sized bits of exploded magma which cooled in flight.

Middle Sister's Collier Glacier was once the state's largest, but a one-mile retreat since 1900 has transferred the honor to South Sister's Prouty Glacier. South Sister is geologically "young" enough to have kept its uneroded conical shape. Its summit crater cups the state's highest lake, Teardrop Pool. Mt. Bachelor, another "youthful" volcano, harbors inner fires which create small snow wells on the mountain's north slope, a hazard for skiers.

Collier Cone erupted some 15,000 years ago directly in the path of the mighty Collier Glacier, commencing a battle of fire and ice. One of the cone's fresh-looking lava flows traced the White Branch valley for 8.5 miles, damming Linton Lake.

Flows of glassy, black obsidian are exposed both below Sunshine, near North Sister, and at Green Lakes, near South Sister. Another kind of high-silica-content eruption formed the frothy, lighter-than-water pumice of Rock Mesa. A California company's mining claim on Rock Mesa's pumice, which would have converted this prominent wilderness feature to cat litter, ended with a $2 million buyout by Congress in 1983.

Ice Age glaciers formed the steep U-shaped valleys of the South Fork McKenzie River and Separation Creek. Sand-pile moraines left by retreating glaciers dammed several alpine lakes.

History

Once a popular autumn camp for Indians, the area provided huckleberries, venison, obsidian for arrowheads, and beargrass for basketry. Antler-shaped petroglyphs across Highway 46 from the east end of Devils Lake are federally protected.

Many place names in the area recall Chinook

North Sister and Middle Sister from McKenzie Pass lava field

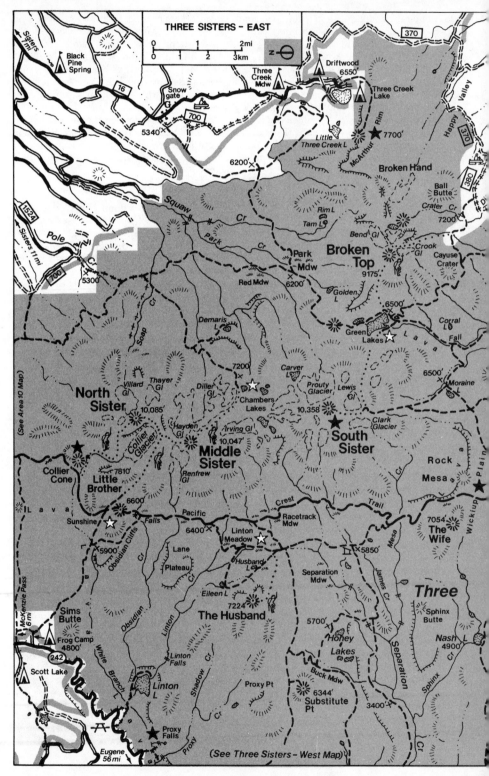

THREE SISTERS - EAST

(See Three Sisters - West Map)

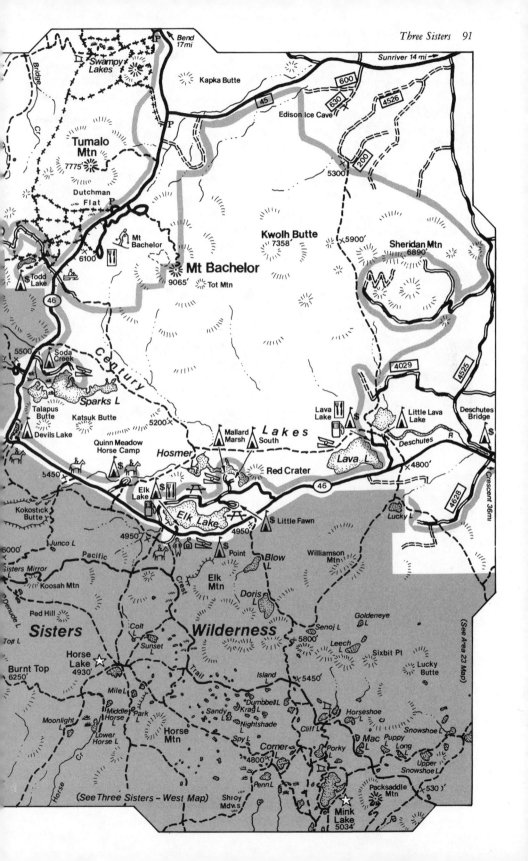

Upper Proxy Falls

jargon, an Indian trade language once widely used by Indians and settlers of the Oregon frontier. Hikers can cross Skookum ("powerful") Creek, camp in Olallie ("berry") Meadows, climb Koosah ("sky") Mountain, and spot Cultus ("worthless") Lake.

Visitors to the area sometimes smile at the Three Sisters' "family" of lesser peaks—Little Brother, The Husband, and The Wife. Few realize there are also a Chinook aunt and uncle (Kwolh Butte and Tot Mountain) hiding behind Mt. Bachelor. Other Chinook names in the area are Tipsoo ("grassy") Butte, Hiyu ("big") Ridge, Moolack ("elk") Mountain, Kokostick ("woodpecker") Butte, Talapus ("coyote") Butte, and Sahalie ("upper") Falls.

THINGS TO DO

Hiking (East Map)

The area is so large most hikes take a full day, and many demand overnight gear. Nonetheless, on August weekends, as many as 200 backpackers make the 4.4-mile climb to the small, fragile meadows by Green Lakes. Even more day hikers make the 9.6-mile round-trip to the alpine views of North Sister at Sunshine Meadow, where overuse has forced a ban on

camping. Horse Lake is 3.8 miles from the nearest road—and Mink Lake is 7.9 miles from a road—yet both of these beautiful lakes are so heavily visited that trails there are deep with dust by late summer.

To find solitude, visit "star attractions" in fall, or in midweek, and camp at the hundreds of overlooked forest lakes, meadows, and viewpoints along less-used trails. Better yet, strike off cross-country by compass; it's not hard through the high country.

Two of the area's easiest hikes are the half-mile walk to feathery Proxy Falls and the level 1-mile trail to Linton Lake. Both paths start from Highway 242 west of McKenzie Pass.

The very popular 4.8-mile Obsidian Trail uphill to Sunshine Meadow begins at Frog Camp on Highway 242. Day hikers should not miss the loop past Obsidian Cliffs and Obsidian Falls. Following the Pacific Crest Trail either direction from Sunshine makes for memorable backpacking trips. Two miles north of Sunshine, the PCT crosses lava to Collier Cone and a viewpoint of the huge Collier Glacier. Five miles south of Sunshine, side trails of the PCT reach Linton Meadow, nestled between Middle Sister and the crags of The Husband.

The 7000-foot-high Chambers Lakes, surrounded by the glaciers of Middle Sister and South Sister, often have drifting ice throughout summer. Gnarled whitebark pines are the only trees. The dramatic lakes are 6.9 miles from the Pole Creek Spring trailhead at the end of Road 1524. From the town of Sisters, drive west 1.5 miles on Highway 242, then turn left onto Road 15 for 5 miles to Road 1524.

Park Meadow features panoramic views of four mountains. Nearby, easy cross-country hikes lead to other wildflower havens higher on the slopes of Broken Top and South Sister. Park Meadow is an almost level 4.6 miles from the end of pavement on Road 16, a road which begins at Highway 20 in downtown Sisters.

Cliff-edged Tam McArthur Rim rises from the ponderosa pine forests of central Oregon. A 3-mile trail climbs from the Three Creek Lake Campground at the end of Road 16 to the rim viewpoint, where snow lingers through August. From there, the rim's above-timberline crest lures hikers on toward Broken Hand and increasingly grand views.

A dozen popular campgrounds and trailheads line Century Drive (Highway 46). West of Bend 21.5 miles on this route is the trail to Tumalo Mountain, a 1.4-mile track climbing 1400 feet up the conical, sparsely forested butte to a former fire lookout site.

The most heavily used trail in the area, and one of the most scenic, climbs 4.4 miles from Sparks Lake to the Green Lakes Basin at the foot of South Sister. The route follows rushing Fall Creek around a blocky lava flow to the high lakes, which really are green, colored by finely ground silt from nearby Lewis Glacier. Open campfires are banned within a mile of Green Lakes.

A more nearly level route into the Green Lakes is available once August snowmelt opens Road 370 from Todd Lake to Crater Creek Ditch. The 4.3-mile Ditch Trail from spur Road 380 contours around Broken Top, offering viewpoints at every turn. A worthwhile cross-country trip from the same trailhead follows Crater Creek up to its head at an ice-filled lake inside Broken Top's ruined crater.

Scaling South Sister may sound too ambitious for a hike, but in fact Oregon's third tallest mountain requires no technical climbing skills or equipment. The hike gains 4,800 feet in 5.6 miles to the view of a lifetime. Begin at Highway 46 beside Devils Lake and head directly for the summit. The unofficial trail peters out at the edge of Lewis Glacier, but hiking is easy from there to the summit. Be sure to keep west of Lewis Glacier on the way up (snowfields can be mistaken for this crevassed, dangerous ice field). Do not attempt

the trip in anything less than perfect weather. A good consolation goal is Moraine Lake, surrounded by an ancient, sandy glacial terminus.

South Sister rises like a wall from the edge of Wickiup Plain, a square mile of cinders and bunchgrass located 1.5 trail miles from Devils Lake. LeConte Crater, a perfect little cinder cone at the plain's edge, makes a fun climb. The scenic plain has no water, so the meadows a mile farther west, at Sisters Mirror Lake, see heavy camping use. This area is quite fragile; explore the interesting surrounding terrain for campsites well away from trailside lakes.

Horse Lake, an easy 3.8-mile hike west of Highway 46 at Elk Lake, is the most heavily visited of a broad basin of lakes. Trails radiate from Horse Lake toward dozens of more peaceful lake destinations, all with views of South Sister above their forested shores.

Mink Lake is the largest of another cluster of forest-rimmed lakes. A popular 8.4-mile route to Mink Lake begins on Highway 46 a mile south of Elk Lake. Expect crowds at cliff-lined Blow Lake, 1.2 miles along this trail, and 90-acre Doris Lake, 1.5 miles farther. At a junction 5.5 miles from the trailhead, the PCT leads to other heavily used lakes: Mac, Horseshoe, Cliff, Island, and Dumbbell. Lake lovers can easily find solitude at the hundreds of

South Sister from the trail to Moraine Lake

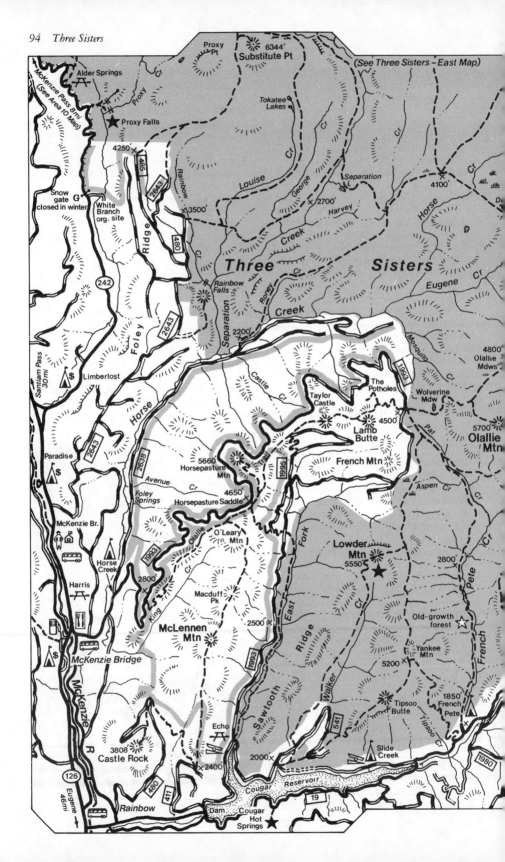

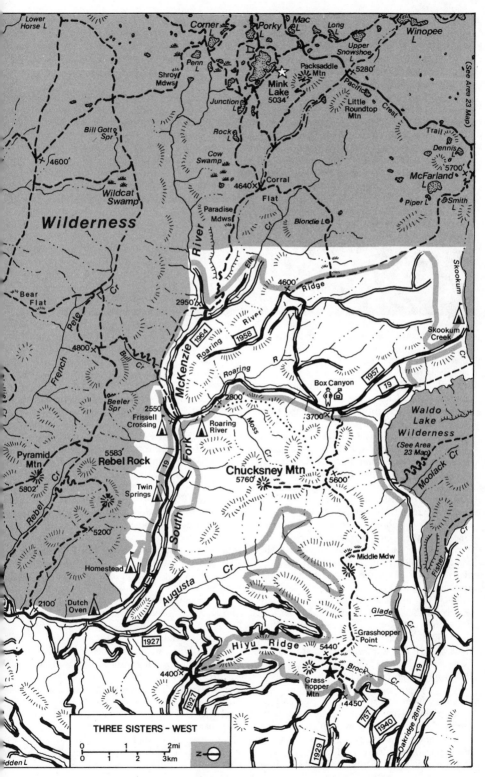

THREE SISTERS - WEST

0   1   2mi

0   1   2   3km

Broken Top from Moraine Lake (photo by Diane Kelsay and Bob Harvey)

quieter lakes nearby.

Equestrians should keep in mind that pack and saddle animals are not permitted within 200 feet of any lake in the designated wilderness except for watering, loading, or traveling on established trails.

Trails in the Century Lakes area, often used by equestrians, are also suitable for hikers. The 8-mile route from Quinn Meadow Horse Camp to Soda Creek Campground passes Hosmer Lake, then dives back into the dry, lodgepole pine forest toward Sparks Lake. Trails from Hosmer Lake to Lava Lake, and from Lava Lake east, traverse unbroken forests of lodgepole pine, beargrass, and cinders. Carry water. Even the briefest cross-country travel in this 54-square-mile roadless area provides complete solitude. Explorers may search here for undiscovered lava tube caves.

The PCT offers a long-distance route the length of the Three Sisters Wilderness—52 miles from McKenzie Pass to Taylor Burn Road 600. Another rewarding long-distance challenge is the 44.1-mile hike around the Three Sisters, which follows 19.1 miles of the PCT's most scenic section.

Hiking (West Map)

An often overlooked hike in this area is the 1-mile Rainbow Falls Viewpoint Trail. It begins at gravel Road 2643, 7 miles from the McKenzie Bridge Ranger Station.

Substitute Point's abandoned lookout site is the goal of another good viewpoint hike, through 4.6 miles of forest. Linton Meadows and the PCT are 4.5 miles past Substitute Point (Buck Meadows and the Honey Lakes are even closer), offering good backpacking goals. To reach the trailhead, drive 3.5 miles past Rainbow Falls on Road 2643, then take spur Road 485 to its end.

Several day hikes on parts of the Olallie Trail begin at Horsepasture Saddle, an unsigned camp 9.3 miles up paved Road 1993 from McKenzie Bridge. A path from the saddle climbs 1100 feet in 1.5 miles to a first-rate viewpoint atop Horsepasture Mountain. A 5-mile trail northwest from the saddle follows a ridge down 1800 feet before rejoining Road 1993. A 4.5-mile hike west from the saddle traverses ridgetop meadows to McLennen Mountain. Finally, a delightful 6.5-mile segment of the Olallie Trail leads southeast from Horsepasture Saddle, past viewpoints at Taylor Castle and Lamb Butte, to Road 1993 near Wolverine Meadow.

Olallie Meadows and Olallie Mountain are both 3.5-mile day hikes (one way) away from Road 1993. The Olallie Trail continues east of Olallie Meadows 10.7 miles through forest to Horse Lake.

Castle Rock, an abandoned fire lookout site, has a panoramic view of the McKenzie Valley. A well-maintained trail to the top crosses roads in three places, making trip lengths of 1, 1.5, and 4 miles (one way) possible.

The East Fork Trail follows a splashing creek through an old-growth Douglas fir forest for 6.5 miles, from Cougar Reservoir's Echo Picnic Area to Road 1993.

The meadow on Lowder Mountain's table-like summit offers eye-level views of the High Cascades. Several trails lead there. The 4-mile route from Road 1993 (the Olallie Trail crossing) requires the least climbing. The Walker Creek Trail is a steady 6.5-mile climb.

Two exhilarating day hikes nearby are the 3.2-mile, 3000-foot climb from French Pete to Yankee Mountain's meadow, and the equally demanding climb from Walker Creek to Tipsoo Butte's viewpoint.

The popular French Pete Creek Trail winds through a forest of massive old-growth Douglas fir. A midweek visit will avoid crowds. Day hikers starting at French Pete Campground usually turn around at one of the trail's scenic bridges. A car-shuttle alternative is to start at Road 1993 and descend Pat and French Pete creeks 9.4 miles to French Pete Campground.

The Rebel Rock Trail climbs 3200 feet in 5 miles from Road 19 to a viewpoint at a former lookout site (which is actually a mile west of Rebel Rock's trailless summit). An easier trip is the 1-mile hike up nearby Rebel Creek Trail to its first stream crossing, amid 400-year-old Douglas firs.

Two 7.8-mile routes lead backpackers to the popular Mink Lake area. The heavily used Elk Creek Trail switchbacks uphill 1700 feet in its first 2 miles from Road 1964. The lesser-known Roaring River Ridge Trail, from Road 1958, avoids the initial, grueling climb. The two trails join at Corral Flat.

The Chucksney Mountain area features broad ridgetop meadows with sweeping views. Begin at Box Canyon on Road 19 and climb 3 steep miles to Chucksney Meadows. Then fork to the north 2 miles for a day hike to Chucksney Mountain's summit. Hikers with a car shuttle arrangement can continue 5 easy miles from Chucksney Meadows to Grasshopper Mountain's impressive meadow.

Grasshopper Mountain can also be the goal of two shorter hikes, either along Hiyu Ridge 4 miles from Road 1927, or up the 1.4-mile trail from Road 1929. To reach the Road 1929 trailhead, drive 13 miles from Westfir (near Oakridge) on Road 19, turn left on Road 1926 for 3 miles, then turn right on Road 1927 for 2.1 miles, and finally turn right on Road 1929 for 5.5 miles.

Climbing

The Three Sisters and Broken Top are popular with climbers chiefly because of the very scenic setting. The technical challenge is not great, and the rock itself is crumbly. Solo climbers have scaled all four peaks consecutively in a single day. Novice climbers and the area's changeable weather account for an above-average mountain rescue rate.

North Sister is trickiest. For the easiest route (level I-4), hike from Sunshine to the col between Middle and North Sister. Follow the ridge toward North Sister, passing several gendarmes on the west at the 9500-foot-level. Skirt steep scree and snow slopes to the western base of the crown-shaped summit pinnacle, then scramble up a steep chute to the top.

Of North Sister's eight additional routes, the two most difficult (levels II-5.2 and III-5.2) ascend the east face's couloir and arête. They have only been done in winter.

Middle Sister is frequently climbed from Sunshine, via the col toward North Sister. An equally easy (I-2) route ascends the south flank's scree slopes. Level II-5.2 and II-5.0 routes scale the east face glaciers' headwalls.

Broken Top is a level I-3 climb, either from Green Lakes (via the peak's northwest ridge to a crumbly pinnacle), or from Crater Creek Ditch (ascending the Crook Glacier to the crater rim's lowest notch). The north face requires level II-5.2 skills.

The Husband, via the south ridge, is a level I-3 climb.

Winter Sports

Powder snow and panoramic scenery make the Dutchman Flat-Swampy Lakes area near Mt. Bachelor ideal for Nordic skiing. Highway 46 is plowed in winter to the Mt. Bachelor ski resort, where cross-country ski rentals are available. The nearby Dutchman Flat sno-park has an extensive network of easy, marked trails through meadow and forest. Loop trips range from 1.4 to 8 miles. Snowmobiles are allowed in certain areas, notably Road 370 and the unplowed portion of Highway 46.

The open, high country between Broken Top and Tam McArthur Rim invites longer cross-country tours from Dutchman Flat. Spectacular Broken Top Crater is 6 miles (one way), via the snowed-over Crater Creek Ditch. McArthur Rim is 8 miles. Carry a compass and emergency gear.

Another trip for strong skiers is Tumalo Mountain, a 1400-foot climb to an outstanding view. Ski directly up the cone-shaped mountain—any side will do—and telemark down through the sparse forest.

Swampy Lakes is also a major Nordic center, with a network of marked trails. Popular trips from the Swampy Lakes sno-park include the easy 4.4-mile loop to the Swampy Lakes shelter, the 6.2-mile Emil Nordeen Shelter loop,

French Pete Creek (photo by Diane Kelsay and Bob Harvey)

and a 9-mile loop to the Swede Ridge shelter. An 8-mile trail connects the Dutchman Flat and Swampy Lakes sno-parks, climbing through forest behind Tumalo Mountain.

Roads 15 and 16 from Sisters are rarely plowed in winter, but, snow levels permitting, lead to rarely tried ski tours. From Road 16's snow gate, Three Creek Lake is 4.9 miles. In May or June, cars ascend Roads 15 and 1524 to Pole Creek Springs, where dramatic ski tours to Soap Creek's meadows below North Sister begin. Bring a compass and emergency gear.

Ski tours in the McKenzie Pass area are described in area 10, but the Three Sisters maps cover two additional, easy trips on Highway 242. Park at the White Branch snow gate, where plowing ends, and ski 2.5 miles to see the ice cascades of the half-mile Proxy Falls Trail, or ski 3.5 miles to the 1.5-mile Linton Lake Trail.

23. Waldo Lake

LOCATION: 59 mi SE of Eugene, 43 mi SW of Bend
SIZE: 148 sq mi, including Maiden Peak
STATUS: 58 sq mi designated wilderness (1984)
TERRAIN: lake-dotted upland forests
ELEVATION: 2480'–7818'
MANAGEMENT: Deschutes NF, Willamette NF
TOPOGRAPHIC MAPS: Waldo Lake Area, PCT Central Oregon Portion (USFS); Three Sisters (Geo-Graphics); Waldo Lake, Waldo Mountain, Irish Mountain, The Twins, Mt. David Douglas, Blair Lake, Willamette Pass, Odell Lake (USGS, 7.5')

Sailboats ply Oregon's second largest natural body of water, a brilliant blue lake so pure and clear that fish are visible 100 feet below the surface. The forests rimming Waldo Lake shelter hundreds of smaller lakes and a thorough trail network.

Patches of snow along the Waldo Lake Trail in late May

Climate

Snowfall from November to April accounts for most of the area's 60-75 inches of annual precipitation. Trails are clear of snow in late June. Headnets or repellent are necessary from early July to early August, when mosquitoes are plentiful.

Plants and Wildlife

Only two species of moss survive in Waldo Lake's renowned clear water, in part because the lake has no inlet to bring nutrients for plant life, and partly because of natural arsenic at levels hazardous to plants, but not to fish or humans.

The Charlton Butte-Cultus Lake area is frequented by bald eagles and the osprey which often roost at Crane Prairie Reservoir (a viewing blind is near Quinn River Campground). The Maiden Peak area, with the Pacific Northwest's largest stands of mountain hemlock, provides known habitat for the shy wolverine, threatened in Oregon. The meadows and high ridges west of Waldo Lake support a large Roosevelt elk herd. Black bear, cougar, bobcat, fisher, and marten are found throughout the area.

The forests of the Taylor Burn area were burned by a sheepman at the turn of the century to encourage grass growth, but the result was a vast, even-aged stand of fire-resistant lodgepole pine.

Geology

The lake basins resulted from sheet glaciation in the Ice Age. Maiden Peak, Charlton Butte, The Twins, and Cultus Mountain are the largest of the many geologically recent volcanoes in the eastern part of the area. Irish Mountain is an older, heavily eroded volcanic plug.

History

Eugene Judge John B. Waldo (1844-1907) and four companions were the first white men to travel the length of Oregon's Cascade Range, from Mt. Hood to Mt. Shasta, in 1888. Klovdahl Bay is named for an engineer whose small, abandoned dam and tunnel would have tapped Waldo Lake for irrigation and power.

THINGS TO DO

Hiking

Two of the most popular half-mile hikes are to Betty Lake (from Waldo Lake Road 5897) and to Upper and Lower Marilyn lakes (via any of four paths off Road 500). Both trips lead to views of Diamond Peak across the lakes.

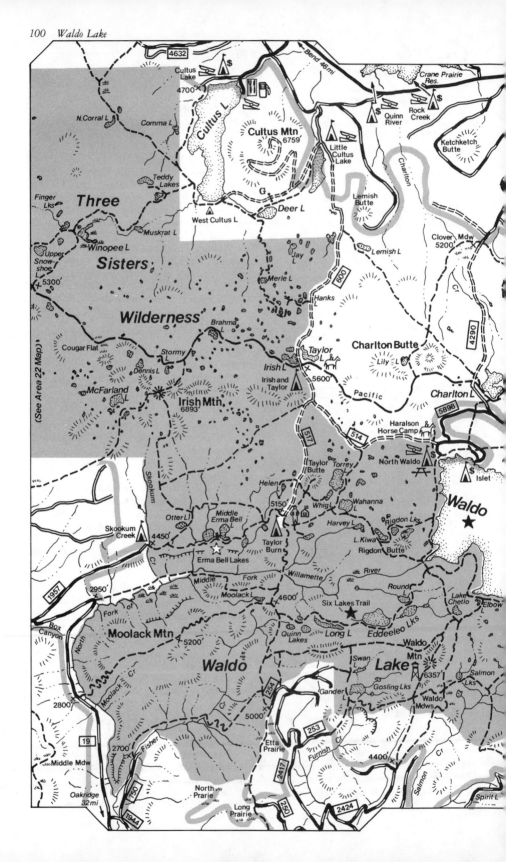

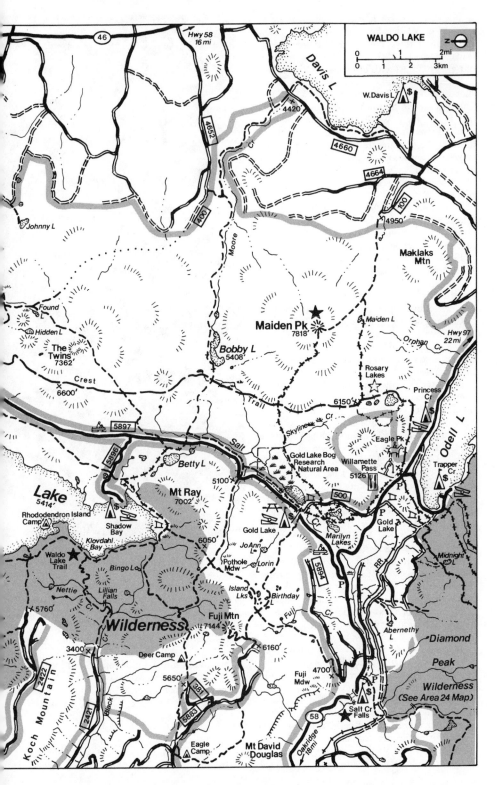

WALDO LAKE

N

0   1   2mi
0   1   2   3km

Hwy 58
16 mi

46

Davis L

4420'

W.Davis L

4652

4660

4664

400

100'

4950'

Moore Cr

Maklaks
Mtn

Johnny L

Maiden L

Found

Maiden Pk
7818'

Orphan
Cr

Hwy 97
22 mi

Hidden L

The
Twins
7362'

Bobby L
5408'

Rosary
Lakes

Princess
Cr

Crest
6600'

Trail

6150'

Skyline Cr

Eagle Pk

Odell L

5897

Salt

Willamette
Pass
5126'

Trapper
Cr

Betty L

Gold Lake Bog
Research
Natural Area

5100'

5896

Lake
5414'

Mt Ray
7002'

500

Gold
Lake

Rhododendron Island
Camp

Shadow
Bay

Gold Lake

Midnight

Klovdahl
Bay

6050'

JoAnn
L

Marilyn
Lakes

Waldo
Lake
Trail

Bingo L

Pothole
Mdw

Lorin
L

5894

Nettie

Lillian
Falls

Island
Lks

Birthday

5760'

Fuji
Cr

RR

3400'

Wilderness

Fuji Mtn
7144'

Abernethy
L

Diamond

6160'

Deer Camp

4700'

Peak

5650'

Fuji
Mdw

Wilderness
(See Area 24 Map)

381

Koch Mountain

2422

Black Cr

5883

Eagle
Camp

Mt David
Douglas

58

Salt Cr
Falls

Oakridge
18mi

2421

The Rosary Lakes nestle in a forest basin at the foot of Maiden Peak. A 3-mile section of the Pacific Crest Trail from Willamette Pass leads to large Lower Rosary Lake, traversing an old-growth forest with glimpses of Odell Lake.

Several short hikes sample Waldo Lake's shoreline. It's 2.3 miles from Shadow Bay Campground to South Waldo Shelter's meadow. From North Waldo Campground, a 3.4-mile hike reaches the lake outlet—one of the heads of the Willamette River. The shore trail traverses deep woods, occasionally coming out at narrow sandy beaches. On hot days, the chilly water and whitecapped waves invite swimming.

Also from North Waldo Campground, try hiking to the Rigdon Lakes. They're 3.2 miles away and are flanked by a little bald-topped butte with a good view.

Lily Lake is an easy 2.4 miles, mostly on the PCT, from Road 4290. The route passes lily pad ponds in the lodgepole pine forest below Charlton Butte. Minimally maintained trails east of the butte provide a loop trip option.

Cultus Lake is big, but one can hike halfway around as a day trip. It's 3.7 miles from Cultus Lake Campground to West Cultus Lake trail camp; those who plan a boat shuttle need only hike one way.

A waterfall connects popular, meadow-rimmed Middle Erma Bell Lake with its rock-lined partner, Lower Erma Bell Lake. They're 1.7 and 2.3 miles along a nearly level trail from Skookum Creek Campground. Road access is via Oakridge; drive 32 miles beyond Westfir on Road 19 to the Skookum Creek turnoff.

Gander Lake, near Swan Lake and the Goslings, usually offers a rickety raft or two for impromptu boaters. The easy 1-mile trail to Gander Lake begins at the end of Road 253. Follow paved Road 24 east of Oakridge 10.5 miles and turn left onto gravel Road 2417 for 8 miles; Road 253 is to the right.

Waldo Mountain's fire lookout and viewpoint climax a 4-mile trail. Drive to the trailhead for Gander Lake, but turn off Road 2417 (onto Road 2424) after 6 miles. From the same trailhead, a much less strenuous 2.5-mile path leads to Waldo Meadows and the nearby Salmon Lakes.

Black Creek's impressive 2000-foot-deep canyon is the start of a day hike with variety. After climbing past Lillian Falls, the 3.8-mile Black Creek Trail takes hikers to a good picnic spot on Waldo Lake's Klovdahl Bay. To reach the trailhead follow Road 24 from Oakridge to its end, then continue on Road 2421 to its end.

Interesting cinder formations and a view from Mt. Hood to Mt. Thielsen are the rewards at the former lookout site atop perfectly conical

Maiden Peak. The 5.8-mile trail gains 2800 feet at a good grade from Road 500, a half mile south of Gold Lake Campground. A next best viewpoint hike, a double summit called The Twins, requires only a 3.3-mile hike (one way), gaining 1600 feet from Road 5897.

Fuji Mountain is a cliff-topped old lookout site with an impressive view. A 1.5-mile trail reaches the peak from gravel Road 5883 (which joins Highway 58 east of Oakridge 16 miles), but many hikers prefer the 5.5-mile Fuji Mountain Trail from Gold Lake.

Two loop hikes prowl the forest east of Fuji Mountain, starting at paved Road 5897: the 9.7-mile trip from Gold Lake to Island Lakes,

The north shore of Waldo Lake

and the 9.5-mile circuit of Mt. Ray past the South Waldo Shelter.

Irish Mountain has no trail to its summit, but the PCT skirts the popular lakes about its base, and a side trail crosses its craggy shoulder. The foot of the mountain is a 4-mile day hike on the PCT from the Taylor Burn Road.

Extending deep into the wilderness, the Taylor Burn Road (numbered 600, 514, and 517) is a series of deep mudholes when wet and a rugged, high-centering track when dry. Vehicles able to survive 7 miles on this road can reach Taylor Burn Campground. From there, short hikes through the lodgepole pine forest

lead to Wahanna, Upper Erma Bell, and a half dozen other lakes.

Many people enjoy hiking—or jogging—the level, scenic 20.2 miles around Waldo Lake in a single day. If 7.2 miles a day sounds better, plan a car shuttle and backpack from Shadow Bay past the South Waldo Shelter to North Waldo Campground. Shorten the trip further by arranging to meet a boat at Klovdahl Bay or at the lake's outlet.

The Six Lakes Trail is another first-rate long-distance trail. Backpack from North Waldo Campground to the six forest-rimmed lakes. Camp, then either hike back via Taylor Burn and the Rigdon Lakes, or press on to a

Osprey roost at Crane Prairie Reservoir

prearranged car shuttle; Road 254 is closest, but quiet trails through old-growth forest also lead over Moolack Mountain, along Fisher Creek, and past the marshy meadows of the North Fork of the Middle Fork Willamette River.

Winter Sports

Though snow at Willamette Pass is often wet, an abundance of trails and scenery make the area very popular. The Gold Lake sno-park is a Nordic ski patrol base. The Willamette Pass ski resort has ski rentals.

A good beginner trip follows level 2.2-mile-long Road 500 from the Gold Lake sno-park to Gold Lake. Return via any of the Marilyn Lakes trails. Caution: the insulation of heavy snows prevents thick ice from forming on lakes. However, because skis distribute weight, skiers often can cross snow-covered lakes when hikers cannot.

Other easy trips explore the marked network of short loop trails through the forest just south of the Gold Lake sno-park. Additional loop trails are a mile beyond, at the snowed-under Trapper Creek Campground on the shore of Odell Lake.

From the Salt Creek Falls sno-park an easy half-mile glide leads through a snowed-in campground to a 286-foot waterfall, Oregon's second tallest. From the same sno-park, a marked route crosses Highway 58 and climbs 1500 feet in 4 miles on Road 5894.

The scenic basin of the Rosary Lakes is 3 miles from Willamette Pass, climbing gently on the PCT. Strong skiers can continue from Rosary Lakes to Maiden Lake, or make an 11-mile loop trip around the base of Eagle Peak. A chairlift to the top of Eagle Peak makes a number of mostly downhill tours possible.

Ready for an overnight trip? Try the 8.9-mile trek into South Waldo Shelter from the Gold Lake sno-park (via Gold Lake and Betty Lake). For an even greater challenge, ski to the view atop Maiden Peak. The 7.3-mile trail there via Road 500 gains 2800 feet, and traverses some steep, possibly icy slopes.

For tours into the Diamond Peak Wilderness, see that area's description.

Boating

In the still of the morning, canoeists can watch fish as much as 100 feet below the surface of 417-foot-deep, 10-square-mile Waldo Lake. From about 11AM to sunset, a steady southwest wind fills the sails of sailboats and creates sizable waves that keep canoeists close to shore. Choppy water can obscure rock reefs near North Waldo and Shadow Bay.

Waldo, Davis, Odell, and Little Cultus lakes have 10 mile-per-hour limits for power boats; motorized trolling is banned on Davis Lake. Cultus Lake, with no speed limit, is abuzz with waterskiers. Motors are prohibited on all other lakes.

24. Diamond Peak

LOCATION: 62 mi SE of Eugene, 64 mi SW of
Bend
SIZE: 126 sq mi, including Cowhorn Mtn.
STATUS: 82 sq mi designated wilderness (1964,
1984)
TERRAIN: snowpeak, forested uplands, lakes
ELEVATION: 4240'–8744'
MANAGEMENT: Deschutes NF, Willamette
NF
TOPOGRAPHIC MAPS: Diamond Peak
Wilderness, PCT Central Oregon Portion
(USFS); Willamette Pass, Diamond Peak,
Cowhorn Mountain, Odell Lake, Emigrant
Butte, (USGS, 7.5')

Diamond Peak is but one of the summits
rising above this area's broad forests. Four
other crags top 7000 feet, each surrounded by
their own scenic lakes and trails.

Climate

Snowfall from November through April accounts for much of the area's annual precipitation, which totals 60 inches in the west and 40
inches in the east. Most trails are snowfree by
mid-June, but hikers must cross snowfields on
the Pacific Crest Trail over Cowhorn Mountain

and Diamond Peak until about August 1. Mosquitoes are quite a problem from early July to
early August.

Plants and Wildlife

Alpine scree slopes are habitat for pikas and
marmots. They also provide footholds for lupine, penstemon, and heather. Dense mountain hemlock forests surround the peaks, leaving few openings for meadows. Lower forests
are dominated by lodgepole pine and beargrass
in the east, and by Douglas fir, rhododendrons, and huckleberries in the west. Roosevelt elk are frequent until the first snows.

Geology

The tallest peaks are the eroded remnants of
extinct, pre-Ice Age volcanoes. Odell Lake and
Crescent Lake fill the U-shaped gouges left by
glaciers, showing the ancient ice rivers' widths
and directions of flow eastward from the Cascade passes.

History

John Diamond first climbed and named
Diamond Peak in 1852 while trying to open an
Oregon Trail shortcut through the Cascades.
The "Lost Wagon Train" of 1853 set out from
Pennsylvania toward Diamond's cutoff the fol-
lowing year, and after much trouble deciding
which of the Cascade peaks was Diamond's

Diamond Peak and Mt. Yoran (at right)

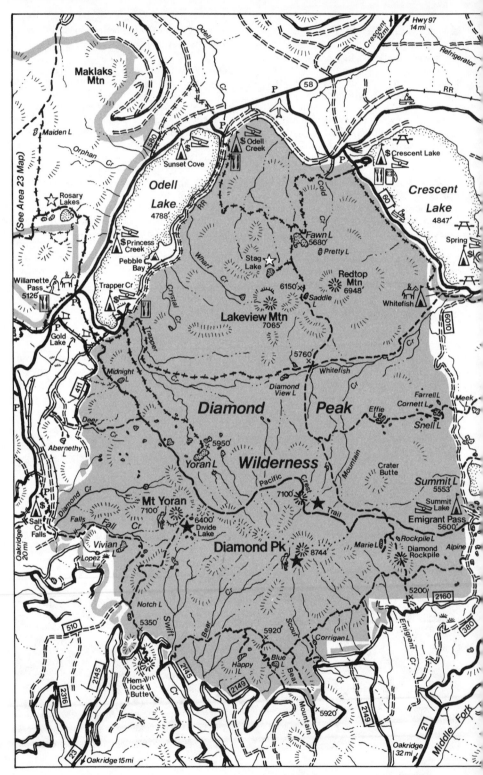

landmark, followed his sporadic blazes to Emigrant Pass, arduously hewing a trail from the dense forest. There, in mid-October, the 1,500 starving pioneers despaired at the sight of the immense, trailless forests ahead. A rescue party convinced many of them to abandon their wagons, then led them to the Willamette Valley, where they doubled Lane County's population.

THINGS TO DO

Hiking

Waterfalls, a lake, and a mountain view make the trail to Vivian Lake popular. From Salt Creek Falls Campground on Highway 58 the route follows Fall Creek 2.9 miles to a cascade among the pines. Continue another 1.1 miles for a view of cliff-faced Mt. Yoran across Vivian Lake. Before or after the hike, be sure to take the 0.3-mile side trail from the campground to 286-foot Salt Creek Falls, Oregon's second tallest.

From Willamette Pass, an easy 3.3-mile segment of the PCT leads through old-growth forest above Odell Lake to tree-rimmed Midnight Lake. Nearby, the Trapper Creek Campground serves as a starting point for two popular, ambitious day hikes to lakes with fine views of Diamond Peak. Yoran Lake is 4.3 miles on a steady uphill grade through forest, and Diamond View Lake is 5.5 miles up the Trapper Creek Trail. For solitude, avoid summer weekends.

Fawn Lake is also a popular destination, 3.8 trail miles from Odell Lake Lodge or 2.8 trail miles from Crescent Lake Lodge. Worthwhile side trips lead 1.4 miles to shallow Stag Lake, at the foot of Lakeview Mountain's impressive cliffs, and 1.8 miles up to little Saddle Lake.

Trails fan out from Crescent Lake and Summit Lake to dozens of quiet lakes among the pines. The Windy Lakes group is 3.9 miles from Road 60 at Crescent Lake; the Bingham Lakes cluster is 3 miles from Road 60.

The PCT climbs unusually high over Diamond Peak and Cowhorn Mountain to sweeping vistas on above-timberline slopes. On Cowhorn Mountain, the PCT nearly crests the craggy summit, 3.5 miles from Windigo Pass. The PCT views on Diamond Peak are 6 miles from Emigrant Pass—a long but rewarding day hike. Really energetic hikers can follow the PCT to timberline, then climb Diamond Peak's smooth southern ridge cross-country to the exhilarating summit view. The 12-mile round-trip climb requires no technical skills, only stamina.

Sawtooth Mountain overtowers a scenic, less-visited network of trails. From Timpanogas Campground, hike 1.9 miles to developed trail campsites at Indigo Lake, directly below the mountain's cliffs. Or hike halfway around Sawtooth Mountain from Timpanogas Campground to a viewpoint less than 500 vertical feet from the summit. That 4-mile route can also serve as the start of a 10-mile backpacking loop, past Cowhorn Mountain to Road 372.

To reach the Sawtooth Mountain area from Oakridge, follow Highway 58 a mile east of town, turn right on Kitson Springs Road for a half mile, turn right on paved Road 21 for 31.7 miles, head left on Road 2154 for 10 miles, then follow signs 0.2 mile to Timpanogas Campground.

Hidden on the less-visited west side of Diamond Peak are a collection of good day hikes—and prime huckleberry picking in late August. Some of the area's best wildflower meadows border Blue Lake (1 mile) and Happy Lake (3 miles) along an up-and-down trail from Road 2149.

The former lookout site atop Hemlock Butte offers a panoramic view of Mt. Yoran and Diamond Peak, and requires only a half-mile hike from Road 2145. But for mountain views, few trails can match the 4-mile path from Road 2145 to Divide Lake. The route passes narrow Notch Lake in a forest, then switchbacks up a ridge to a timberline valley of tiny lakes below Mt. Yoran's sheer face.

Trailheads on the west side of Diamond Peak are reached via Oakridge. Follow Highway 58 a mile east of town, then turn right on Kitson Springs Road (which becomes Road 23) for 16.5 miles to Road 2145.

Long-distance hikers often choose the scenic 28.7-mile section of the PCT from Willamette Pass to Windigo Pass, but there are other good routes as well. Most spectacular is the 23.7-mile circuit of Diamond Peak, starting at Road 2145. The route requires an easy

half-mile trailless climb over the ridge south of Divide Lake.

Cross-country hiking is not difficult in the high, open forests, and is especially rewarding in the lake-dotted forests between Yoran Lake and Willamette Pass, where trailside lakes are overused.

Climbing

Diamond Peak's smooth scree ridges make it a hike rather than a technical climb; neighboring Mt. Yoran requires level I-3 skills.

Winter Sports

A network of cross-country trails centers on the Nordic ski patrol shelter at the Gold Lake sno-park. Tours north of this area are described under area 23. To the south, the well-traveled PCT leads 2.7 miles at a gentle grade through forest to Midnight Lake; several return loops are possible. The unmarked 6.3-mile trail to Yoran Lake and the 7.1-mile trail to Diamond View Lake are for skiers with route-finding skills and emergency gear.

Fawn Lake is a very popular intermediate-level goal. One trail there climbs 3.8 miles from Odell Lake Lodge (ski rentals available); a route from the Crescent Lake sno-park makes the climb in 2.8 miles. A longer trip to Stag Lake is worth the extra 1.4 miles.

Skiers should avoid the tempting railroad grade along Odell Lake because of frequent high-speed trains; safer tours along Odell Lake follow forest roads above Sunset Cove.

Boating

High-elevation, 500-acre Summit Lake not only has a postcard view of Diamond Peak, it offers reliable afternoon breezes for sailboaters and an interesting shoreline for canoeists. Motors are permitted, but a 10 mile-per-hour limit prevails, and a rough dirt access road prevents crowds.

Oregon grape

25. Hardesty Mountain

LOCATION: 25 mi SE of Eugene
SIZE: 22 sq mi
STATUS: undesignated wilderness
TERRAIN: densely forested valleys, ridges
ELEVATION: 940′–4616′
MANAGEMENT: Willamette NF, Umpqua NF
TOPOGRAPHIC MAPS: *Hiking the Hardesty Wilderness* (Hardesty Mountain Study Group); Hardesty Mountain (USGS, 15′)

Soothing shades of green—moss, sword ferns, vanilla leaf—line the trails of Hardesty Mountain, where hiking is available year round, 30 minutes from Eugene.

Climate

Typically, the ridges here are snowfree by March and lower trails are open year round. Rain accounts for the area's 55 inches of annual precipitation. Nearby Mt. June was named to commemorate one year when snow lingered there until that month.

Plants and Wildlife

In the area's lush old-growth forests of Douglas fir, western red cedar, and bigleaf maple, watch for the rare Pacific giant salamander. Shiny, 7 to 12 inches long, they are easily distinguished from the orange-bellied, rough-skinned newts common in western Oregon. Also look for delicate calypso orchids on the forest floor in May and showy Washington lilies and beargrass on ridges in June. Spotted owls and osprey nest here; bald eagle nesting sites at times necessitate rerouting of trails. Lower slopes provide winter range for deer and elk.

Geology

Though dense forest conceals most rocks, the outcropping atop Mt. June reveals volcanic andesite typical of the 16- to 25-million year old Cascades.

The Eula Ridge Trail

History

The Civilian Conservation Corps built most of the area's trails 1933–38 to access lookout towers on Hardesty Mountain and Mt. June. Foundations of the towers remain.

THINGS TO DO

Hiking

The area's most popular hike is the 5-mile Hardesty Trail, which gains 3100 feet as it climbs a densely forested ridge from Highway 58 to Hardesty Mountain's former fire lookout site. Since this is a demanding trip, day hikers often break it into two halves, either starting or turning back at Crale Creek Road 5835. Another option is to start at the Road 550 trailhead, 0.9 mile from Hardesty Mountain's summit; Road 550 is an unimproved spur of Patterson Mountain Road 5840. In addition, the steep 4.2-mile Eula Ridge Trail provides the least-traveled route down from the summit.

Mt. June, an even loftier former lookout site than Hardesty Mountain, commands a much better view that stretches from Mt. Jefferson to Mt. Thielsen. A 1.1-mile trail switchbacks up to Mt. June's cliff-edged summit meadow. For a longer hike, continue eastward along meadow-topped Sawtooth Ridge on a trail lined with wildflowers, viewpoints, and rock spires. Hardesty Mountain is 3.1 miles past Mt. June on this scenic route.

To reach the Mt. June trailhead, drive east from Interstate 5 on Highway 58 to milepost 9, turn south on Rattlesnake Road for 4.6 miles, bear right on Lost Creek Road for 2 miles to an intersection with a school-bus shelter, and turn left across a bridge onto the unsigned, paved Eagles Rest Road 20-1-14 for 9.5 miles to a sign marking the Eagles Rest Trail turnoff. Continue 5 miles farther on Road 20-1-14 (which soon turns to gravel), bear left at an unmarked "Y" intersection, and then turn sharply left 0.1 mile farther onto Road 1721; the trailhead is 0.3 mile, on the right.

To avoid the final gravel section of this access route, drive on the paved Eagles Rest Road only as far as the sign indicating the Eagles Rest Trail, drive or walk the 0.6 mile dirt spur to the trailhead, and then hike this pleasant 1.3-mile path to Sawtooth Ridge.

The area's longest hike is a 9.7-mile day trip, visiting the summits of Mt. June and Hardesty Mountain before descending to Highway 58. The area does not offer good campsites for backpackers, nor trails suitable for horse use. Carry water as trails pass virtually no water sources.

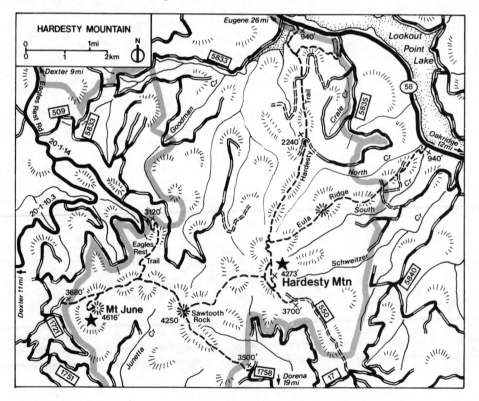

Columnar basalt flanking the North Umpqua River

26. Boulder Creek

LOCATION: 47 mi E of Roseburg
SIZE: 34 sq mi
STATUS: 30 sq mi designated wilderness (1984)
TERRAIN: steep, forested valley
ELEVATION: 1600'–5600'
MANAGEMENT: Umpqua NF
TOPOGRAPHIC MAPS: Toketee Falls, Staley
 Ridge (USGS, 7.5'); Toketee Falls, Illahee
 Rock (USGS, 15')

Boulder Creek's swimmable pools and small waterfalls are surrounded by a broad, steep valley of old-growth forests. Prominent rock spires provide technical climbing practice.

Climate
Lower trails remain snowfree and hikable all year. Winter and spring rains swell Boulder Creek, requiring knee-deep wading on trail fords. The area's annual precipitation is 60 inches.

Plants and Wildlife
Pine Bench features an old-growth ponderosa pine forest with grassy openings, unusual so far west of the Cascade summit. Elsewhere, the forest is an interesting mix of gigantic sugarpine, Douglas fir, western hemlock, droopy incense cedar, and gnarled yew. The rugged valleys are home to an estimated 30 black bear and 100 Roosevelt elk; both species are shy.

Geology
Eagle Rock and other spires of the Umpqua Rocks are eroded remnants of 25-million-year-old Old Cascades volcanoes. However, the scenic columnar basalt rimrock lining the North Umpqua River and Pine Bench is only a few thousand years old, part of a High Cascades lava flow that originated 20 miles up the North Umpqua River valley.

History
Several caves in the area preserve evidence of Indian camps. Arrowheads and other artifacts are federally protected.

THINGS TO DO

Hiking
The popular 2-mile trail to Pine Bench's shelter provides a good introduction to this area's variety. Near the trail's start, wildflower

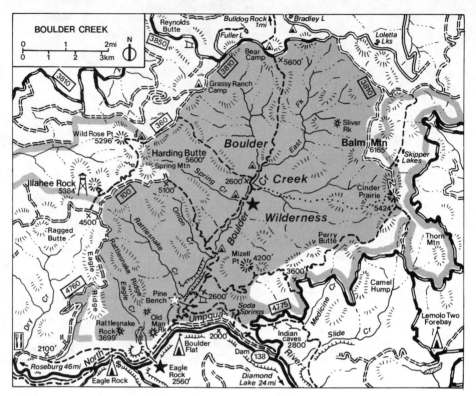

meadows at sulphurous Soda Springs offer views of the North Umpqua's basalt cliffs. Farther on, rhododendrons bloom in May in an old-growth Douglas fir forest. At Pine Bench, the ponderosa grasslands sprout with Indian pipe and other saprophytes each fall. Head west from the shelter a short distance and climb out on rocks for a breathtaking view of Boulder Creek's canyon.

To reach the Soda Springs trailhead, turn off Highway 138 onto paved Medicine Creek Road 4775 (8 miles east of the Dry Creek Store). Immediately turn left onto the Soda Springs Dam access road and follow this track for 1.2 miles, crossing a narrow bridge over the river to the trailhead.

For a longer day hike, continue north from Pine Bench 1.5 miles on the Boulder Creek Trail to a fine swimming hole at the trail's first crossing of Boulder Creek. For a good backpacking trip, cross the creek here (a knee-deep wade), then continue upstream another 2.5 miles, past several excellent campsites and three easy creek crossings, to the forks of Boulder Creek. From there the trail climbs a ridge 4 miles to Road 3810 near Bear Camp.

Two of the area's best viewpoints are Mizell Point and Illahee Rock. The 2-mile route to Mizell Point follows the faint Perry Butte Stub Trail from Road 4775 up and down to the viewpoint's 200-yard spur trail along a rocky ridge.

A lookout tower atop Illahee Rock is a short side trip from the scenic 3-mile Grassy Ranch Trail. Hike past views of craggy Bartrums Rock to the lookout, and then continue to Wild Rose Point, through meadows filled with rare Washington lilies each June. The trailhead at Road 4760 is 7 miles up from the Dry Creek Store on Highway 138.

A nearly level hike beneath the crags of the Umpqua Rocks follows a 6-mile portion of the North Umpqua River Trail from Road 4775 past Pine Bench to the Highway 138 bridge near Eagle Rock Campground.

Climbing

Eagle Rock is the largest of a cluster of rarely visited andesite crags with challenging technical climbs. Eagle Rock was first climbed in 1958 via the northern Madrone Tree Route (level I-5.2-A2). The 400-foot South Face cliffs present a level II-5.6 challenge.

Old Man Rock, rated I-5.4-A1, remained unclimbed until 1963. The spire directly north of it, Old Woman, has I-5.2 and I-5.6 routes. Other crags in the area are easier, including prominent Rattlesnake Rock (I-3).

27. Mount Thielsen

LOCATION: 72 mi E of Roseburg, 80 mi NE of
   Medford
SIZE: 126 sq mi
STATUS: 86 sq mi designated wilderness (1984)
TERRAIN: snowpeak, high forest
ELEVATION: 4260'–9182'
MANAGEMENT: Umpqua NF, Deschutes NF,
   Winema NF
TOPOGRAPHIC MAPS: PCT Central Oregon
   Portion (USFS); Mt. Thielsen, Miller Lake,
   Tolo Mountain, Burn Butte, Diamond Lake
   (USGS, 7.5')

The "Lightning Rod of the Cascades," Mt.
Thielsen's spire towers above the lakes, meadows, and high forests north of Crater Lake.

Climate

Snowfall from mid-October to April accounts for most of the area's 60 inches of annual
precipitation. Most trails are snowfree by mid-
June, but the Pacific Crest Trail may remain
blocked until mid-July. Mosquitoes are
numerous for about four weeks following
snowmelt.

Plants and Wildlife

Nearly pure stands of lodgepole pine blanket the lower areas, where the pumice and ash
soils are extremely dry in summer. Nearly pure
stands of mountain hemlock cover the higher
elevations, where lingering snow provides
summer moisture. Clark's nutcrackers, gray
jays, and golden-mantled ground squirrels are
everywhere abundant. Look for elk and red-
headed pileated woodpeckers. Diamond Lake
had no fish originally, but is now stocked to
provide 3 million trout annually.

Geology

A 5-foot-thick ground cover of lighter-than-
water pumice rock remains as evidence that
this area lay directly downwind of the cataclysmic explosion which created Crater Lake's caldera 6,600 years ago.

Mt. Thielsen, extinct for at least 100,000
years, was stripped to its central plug by the
same Ice Age glaciers which carved the basins
for Diamond Lake and Miller Lake. In 1965,
after centuries with no glaciers at all, the peak
was found to shelter two small moving ice
masses on its northern flank.

Lightning strikes the Mt. Thielsen's spire so
often that carrot-shaped "lightning tubes" and
glassy, brownish-green fulgurites of recrystal-
ized rock form at the summit.

THINGS TO DO

Hiking

The most popular of the area's many viewpoint hikes is the Howlock Mountain Trail to
Timothy Meadows. Starting from the horse
corrals at North Diamond Lake, the route
climbs through viewless forests for 3 miles be-

The east face of Mount Thielsen

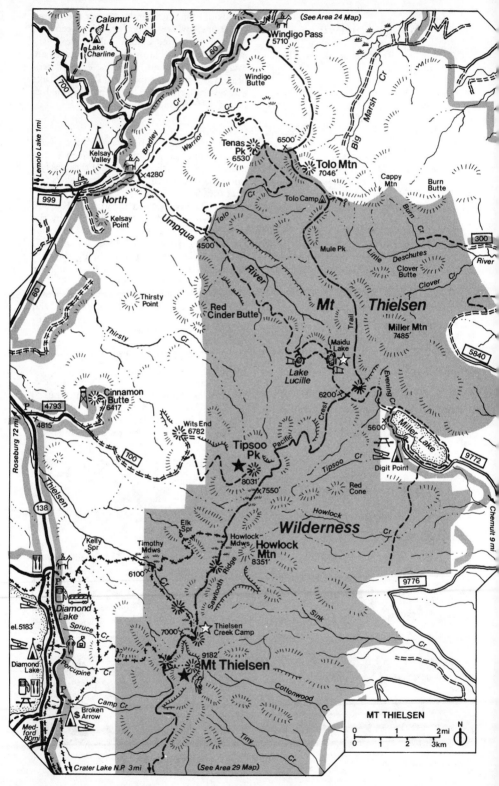

fore reaching the meadows along splashing Thielsen Creek. Here are good picnicking swales with wildflowers and glimpses of Thielsen's summit. However, it's worth climbing 2 miles farther along the creek for the astonishing view at Thielsen Creek Camp, where the peak looms like The Matterhorn.

Once at Thielsen Creek Camp, there are two tempting alternatives to simply returning via the same 5-mile route. It's only 2.6 miles farther to make a loop to the south, following the PCT to far-ranging views on the flank of Mt. Thielsen before descending to Diamond Lake via the Mt. Thielsen and Spruce Ridge trails. On the other hand, spectacular alpine scenery also lies north of Thielsen Creek Camp, on an 8.1-mile return route which follows the PCT past serrated Sawtooth Ridge and broad Howlock Meadows before descending to Diamond Lake via Timothy Meadows.

Backpacking breaks these distances into shorter hikes. The only year-round water source on Mt. Thielsen's flanks is Thielsen Creek; be sure to camp in the forest well away from the fragile clearings at Timothy Meadows or Thielsen Creek Camp, and build no fire.

Tipsoo Peak has a memorable view of Thielsen and Sawtooth Ridge. The quiet 3-mile trail there from Wits End Road 100 gains 1600 feet. From the top, it's an easy scramble down loose cinders to the alpine meadows along the PCT.

Those who have already climbed to Cowhorn Mountain on the PCT from Windigo Pass (see area 24 description) might try three rarely visited viewpoint goals south of the pass. Tolo Mountain and Tenas Peak are both 5 miles; Windigo Butte's little cone is a 1.5 mile cross-country climb.

By far the most heavily used lakeside trails are several short routes beside Diamond Lake. Quieter, and just as scenic, is the 5-mile path around Miller Lake from the Digit Point Campground. From the same trailhead, try climbing 3.5 miles to a viewpoint on the PCT, where cliffs overlook Miller Lake. Another popular hike crosses the Cascade Divide 4 miles to forest-rimmed Maidu Lake. Reach the trailhead via Road 9772, which leaves Highway 97 at Chemult.

Backpackers and equestrians have several long-distance trip options. The PCT covers 29.4 miles from Windigo Pass to the North Crater trailhead beside Highway 138, on the National Park boundary. Also, a popular 8-mile segment of the North Umpqua River Trail climbs to Maidu and Lucille lakes from the Kelsay Valley trailhead.

Throughout the area, water sources are scarce. For solitude, carry water for a dry camp

Miller Lake from the Pacific Crest Trail (photo by William L. Sullivan)

and strike off cross-country through the open, easily traversed forests.

Thousands of hikers climb—or nearly climb—Mt. Thielsen each summer. Those without technical climbing experience must settle for the excellent view at the base of the near-vertical, 80-foot summit spire (even this goal is 5 miles away from Highway 138 and 3700 feet up). Follow the Mt. Thielsen Trail from Diamond Lake, then hike south 0.3 mile on the PCT to where a track leads straight up the above-timberline scree slopes; pass the flank outcroppings of Red Rock and Black Castle on the left before heading for the southeast base of the summit pinnacle.

Climbing

Mt. Thielsen's summit pinnacle is a level I-3 climb from the southeast. For a tougher route, try the III-5.7 McLaughlin Memorial. From Thielsen Creek Camp, circle up to the peak's east face, where six rope lengths of technical work lead to the summit.

Winter Sports

Resorts at North Diamond Lake and Lemolo Lake offer cross-country ski rentals and marked winter trails. All of the hiking trails between Diamond Lake and Mt. Thielsen make good, if steep, cross-country routes. In addition, two nearly level trails head south from Diamond Lake to the North Crater sno-park on Highway 138.

The fine view at Cinnamon Butte's lookout tower is 3 miles up from another Highway 138 sno-park. The reward for climbing 1600 feet on the lookout road's steady grade is a 2-mile downhill glide.

Boating

Diamond Lake and Miller Lake offer canoeing and sailing. Motors are permitted, but with a 10 mile-per-hour limit.

28. Rogue-Umpqua Divide

LOCATION: 75 mi E of Roseburg, 56 mi NE of Medford
SIZE: 102 sq mi
STATUS: 52 sq mi designated wilderness (1984)
TERRAIN: high meadows, forested valleys, ridgetop rock outcroppings
ELEVATION: 2300'–6783'
MANAGEMENT: Rogue River NF, Umpqua NF
TOPOGRAPHIC MAPS: Garwood Butte, Quartz Mountain, Prospect, Abbott Butte (USGS, 15')

Atop a high divide west of Crater Lake, this relatively undiscovered area boasts subalpine meadows, interesting rock formations, and small lakes.

Climate
Snow covers most trails from late-November to mid-May. Annual precipitation tops 50 inches; summers are dry.

Plants and Wildlife
The ridges feature showy Washington lilies and Indian paintbrush in June and ripe huckleberries in August. The bright red snow plant, a rare saprophyte, brightens the Fish Lake area as snow melts. Forests include sugar pine and ponderosa pine on the drier eastern slopes, true firs and mountain hemlock on the ridges, and Douglas fir on the western slopes. A parklike grove of old-growth incense cedars makes a nice stop along Road 800 north of the area.

Geology
The area belongs to the heavily eroded 16- to 25-million-year-old Old Cascades. Glaciers broadened the valleys and left Buck Canyon a mile-wide cirque. A massive landslide from Grasshopper Mountain dammed Fish Lake and created Fish Lake Creek Falls. Buckeye and Cliff lakes nest atop the ancient slide.

THINGS TO DO
Hiking
The popular 3-mile trail to Fish Lake climbs through an old-growth forest, passes within earshot of 80-foot Fish Lake Creek Falls, and skirts a swamp where beaver are active. The 90-acre lake, rimmed with meadows and mountain views, was named by a group of 1889 explorers who caught 70 fish there in an hour, using venison for bait.

To reach the Fish Lake trailhead from Interstate 5, turn off at Canyonville, follow Highway 227 for 22 miles to Tiller, turn left onto Highway 46 (which becomes Road 28) for 23.5 miles, turn right on paved Road 2823 for 2.3 miles, head right on gravel Road 2830 for 1.7 miles, and turn left on Road 2840 for 0.5 mile to the trail sign.

Hikers who arrange a short car shuttle can make loop trips to Fish Lake, starting at either the Beaver Swamp trailhead, 4 miles farther up Road 2840, or at the Skimmerhorn trailhead on Road 600.

Cliff and Buckeye lakes, with close-up views of Grasshopper Mountain's sheer cliffs, are a moderate 2-mile hike (one way) from the Skimmerhorn trailhead. The view atop Grasshopper Mountain, 1.2 trail miles beyond Cliff Lake, is not to be missed.

Colorful trailside sandstone cliffs highlight a 3-mile climb to the viewpoint at Anderson Mountain's former lookout site. To reach the trailhead at Falcon Creek, turn off Highway 227 at Tiller, follow Highway 46 for 5 miles, turn right on Road 29 for 18 miles, turn right on Road 2947 for 2.5 miles, and then turn right on Road 300 for 3 miles.

Elephant Head, a sheer-sided rock bluff on the shoulder of Abbott Butte, overlooks a high meadow fringed with true firs and quaking aspen. It's a 2-mile hike along the Rogue-Umpqua Divide Trail from the Windy Gap spur road of Road 30. Road 30 is a continuation of Road 68, which branches off Highway 62, 7 miles north of Prospect.

A short car shuttle opens up another good hiking route down from Abbott Butte: the 6-mile, ridgetop Cougar Butte Trail. A stone's throw from this trail's end is Cowhorn Arch, an unusual volcanic formation. The trailhead on Road 30 can be reached either via Road 68 (described above), or via Tiller. To get there from Tiller take Highway 46 for 5 miles, turn right on Road 29 for 13 miles, and then turn right on Road 30 for 7 miles.

Hershberger Mountain not only has a good view of its own; it is also the trailhead for several day hikes. A nearly level 3-mile trail north to Hole-in-the-ground (a high meadow basin) provides a close look at Fish Mountain, tallest point in the Western Cascades. To the west of Hershberger Mountain, Grasshopper Mountain's viewpoint is 4.5 miles, past several meadows, the Cripple Creek shelter, and groves of 8-foot diameter Douglas fir.

A trip to the Rouge-Umpqua Divide can hardly be complete without a climb of Fish Mountain, the highest peak. Views range from Mt. Shasta to the Three Sisters. From the end of Road 870, walk the trail 0.3 mile south to a crest, then scramble 0.5 mile up an open trail-

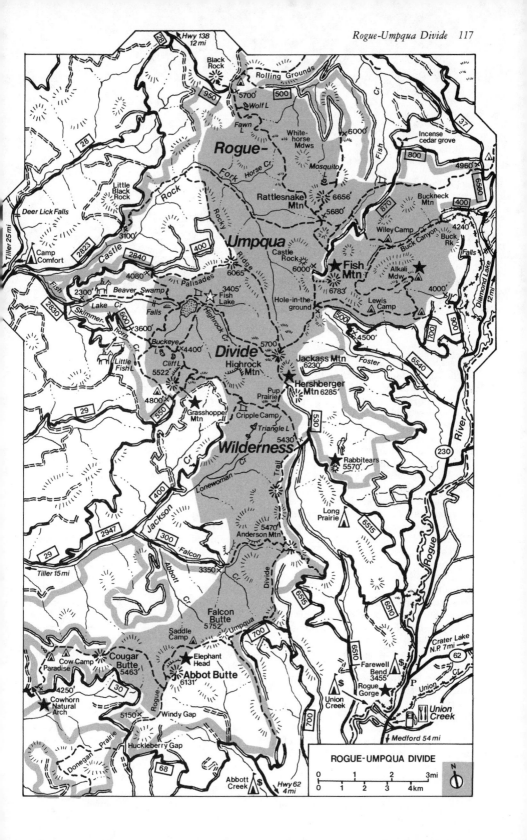

ROGUE-UMPQUA DIVIDE

Fish Lake

less ridge to the summit. Another short route to the top starts at the end of Road 500 and crosses the meadow at Hole-in-the-ground before tackling the trailless summit ridge.

To explore the high basins at the foot of Fish Mountain, try the 7-mile hike through Alkali Meadows and down Buck Canyon. June wildflowers, abundant at Alkali Meadows, include delicate pink kalmia. Plan a shuttle for this hike, driving one car from the starting point on Road 700 to the end of Road 400.

Whitehorse Meadows, in a pass overlooking the forests of Castle Rock Fork's broad valley, makes a good day hike goal. From the north, a 2.3-mile trail to the meadows from Road 950 offers a side trip to Wolf Lake. Reach Road 950 via Road 28, which joins the North Umpqua Highway 138 near Eagle Rock.

Another day hike route to Whitehorse Meadows begins at Road 870 within sight of Castle Rock's landmark crag and traverses 4 miles around Rattlesnake Mountain. Take time to hike the steep side trail to Rattlesnake Mountain's summit (a fine viewpoint — with no rattlesnakes). The car shuttle distance between Whitehorse Meadow's two trailheads is, alas, prohibitive.

Several trips require backpacking gear. One of the best is the 13-mile trail loop from Fish Lake around the base of cliff-edged Highrock Mountain, hiking through a series of high meadows and scenic passes. The trail above Fish Lake passes the area's biggest trees: Douglas fir 10 feet in diameter. Another backpacking trip, a 17-mile loop around Castle Rock Fork's upper valley, can begin at the valley's top, by Fish Mountain, or at the bottom, at Road 2823. This loop includes the recently built trail along Rocky Ridge, considered by some the area's most scenic.

The area's best known backpacking route, the Rogue-Umpqua Divide Trail, follows a ridgecrest the length of the area — 25 miles from Road 30 past Abbott Butte, Jackass Mountain, and Fish Mountain to Road 37 — and even continues 8 miles beyond, to Garwood Butte.

Climbing

Hershberger Mountain Road 6515 passes within 300 yards of the base of Rabbitears, a pair of 400-foot pinnacles first scaled in 1921. Both spires require level I-4 climbing skills.

Winter Sports

When snow levels are low, Nordic skiing is easy on segments of the 45-mile-long Upper Rogue River Trail, which roughly parallels plowed Highway 230 from Prospect to the northwest corner of Crater Lake National Park. Try the 3.5-mile trail section north from the snowed-under Union Creek Campground.

For deeper snow, try unplowed Road 6560, at the 4000-foot level. Ski past Muir Creek Falls to Buck Canyon, below towering Fish Mountain. Advanced skiers with compass and survival gear can continue west on the wilderness trail system. Beginners can prowl the level terrain between Road 900 and Highway 230.

In spring drive Road 6540 to the snow line and ski up Road 500 and the Hole-in-the-ground Trail to the high country.

29. Crater Lake

LOCATION: 64 mi NE of Medford, 49 mi NW
of Klamath Falls
SIZE: 280 sq mi
STATUS: national park (1902)
TERRAIN: cliff-edged lake, high forest, pumice
desert
ELEVATION: 3700'–8926'
MANAGEMENT: Crater Lake National Park
TOPOGRAPHIC MAPS: Crater Lake (USGS,
25'); Central Oregon Portion (USFS); *Crater
Lake National Park and Vicinity* (Wilderness
Press)

Oregon's famous national park sees a half
million visitors annually, yet away from the
paved rim road the trails are only lightly used.
On an average summer night, only a dozen
backpackers camp in the area's 259 square
miles of wilderness backcountry. In fact, the
heaviest backcountry use comes in winter,
when the snow is excellent for ski touring.

Climate

Average annual precipitation is 69 inches,
largely measured by melting the area's 45 feet
of snowfall. Snow closes most trails, and the
rim road, from mid-October to mid-June. The
eastern portion of the rim road past Mt. Scott
seldom opens before mid-July.

Plants and Wildlife

Virtually all life in the area was destroyed by
Mt. Mazama's eruption 6800 years ago. The
600 species of plants and many animals here are
evidence of ongoing repopulation. Forests,
largely of lodgepole pine, have spread nearly
everywhere but the Pumice Desert, where volcanic debris fell 200 feet deep. The Pumice
Desert's cinder soil holds so little moisture that
only occasional bunchgrass and dwarf lupine
can live there.

Crater Lake from the Rim Village (Mount Thielsen on horizon at right)

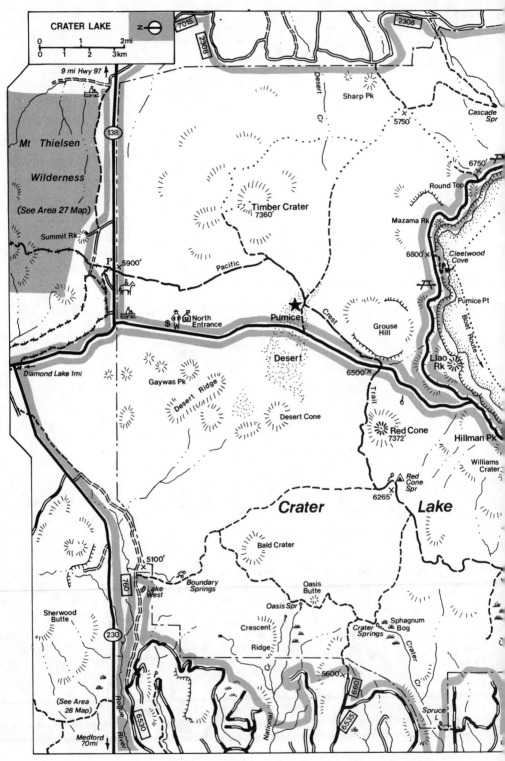

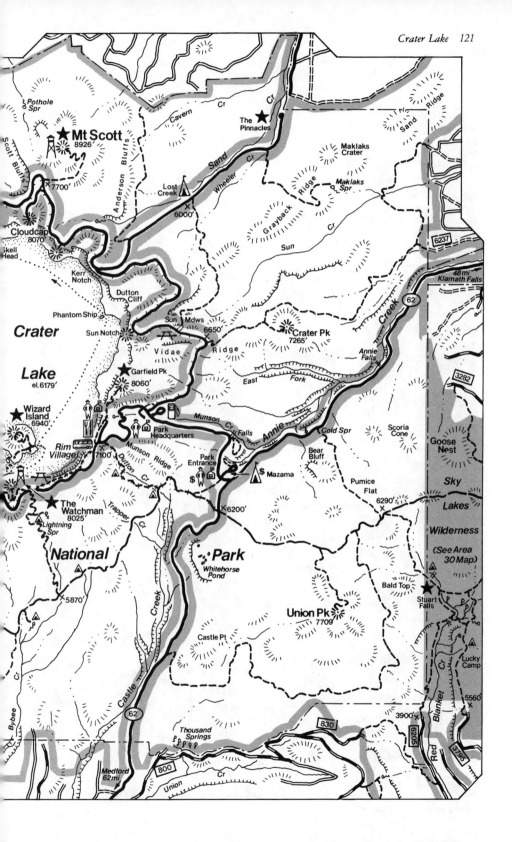

Sunrise on Sun Notch and Phantom Ship (at right)

Most, but not all, Cascade wildflowers have reestablished themselves along the lake's alpine rim. Gnarled whitebark pines clinging to the rim withstand the cliff edge's fierce storm winds because their branches are so supple they can literally be tied in knots. The dominant animal species of the rim appear to be cute golden-mantled ground squirrels and raucous, swooping Clark's nutcrackers, both of which aggressively encourage visitors to defy the park's ban on feeding wildlife.

Biologists theorize that the toads, garter snakes, and chipmunks living on Wizard Island migrated there over land when the lake was lower. The origin of the crayfish in Wizard Island's ponds remains a mystery. Rainbow trout were introduced in Crater Lake itself in 1889.

Visitors sometimes sight black bears. Though the bears generally avoid camps, hang all food 10 feet off the ground and 5 feet from a tree trunk at night.

Geology

Crater Lake fills the caldera of Mt. Mazama, which collapsed after a cataclysmic series of eruptions about 4800 BC.

Mt. Mazama first began to form about 500,000 years ago, when neighboring Union Peak and Mt. Thielsen were already extinct. At its height, Mt. Mazama was a broad, 12,000-foot mountain the size of Mt. Adams. Ice Age glaciers gouged its flanks with valleys (still visible as Sun Notch and Kerr Notch). Smaller volcanoes sprouted on its sides (Timber Crater, Red Cone, and Hillman Peak). Its slopes oozed thick lava flows (visible in cross-section as The Watchman, Llao Rock, and Cloudcap).

Then, in an eruption 100 times as massive as the 1980 Mt. St. Helens blast, Mt. Mazama suddenly exploded 14 cubic miles of pumice and ash into the sky, emptying its subterranean magma reservoir. Ash fell 10 feet deep at Klamath Marsh, and a half inch deep as far away as Saskatchewan. As the hollowed mountain collapsed, a glowing avalanche of pumice and superheated gas raced down the slopes at freight-train speeds. Gas fumaroles in the fiery avalanche deposits welded pumice together around vertical vents; later erosion exposed these as pinnacles along Annie and Sand Creeks.

Massive landslides promptly widened the caldera from 3 miles to 5 miles. Later, two cinder cones erupted on the caldera floor. Wizard Island's cone still rises 732 feet above the lake, but Merriam Cone was submerged as the caldera gradually filled with rain and snowmelt.

The deepest lake in the United States, Crater Lake has no outlet but maintains its level by evaporation and seepage. The lake's 1932-foot depth and remarkable purity account for its stunning blue color.

THINGS TO DO

Hiking

Popular day hikes lead to viewpoints on the lake rim and nearby peaks. The little-used backcountry trail system is largely dry and viewless, but it's the best bet for backpacking since camping is prohibited within a mile of the lake rim (or in summer from the rim road). Free permits for backcountry camping can be picked up all year at the Rim Village Information Center or, in winter, from the Steele Center along the south entrance road.

Other park rules: pets are prohibited on all trails. Saddle stock are limited to the Pacific Crest Trail and its spur trails leading to the lake rim; grazing is prohibited. Firearms and other hunting devices are forbidden. On the other hand, angling is permitted—no license required.

Only five hikes have views of the lake itself. Some of the best views are along the 1.7-mile trail switchbacking up 1000 feet from Rim Village to Garfield Peak, past alpine gardens of showy Davidson's penstemon, red Indian paintbrush, and spreading phlox.

Hikers with less time can take one of the 0.7-mile routes that climb 400 feet from the Rim Drive to a lookout tower amidst twisted whitebark pines atop The Watchman. The 2.8-mile Discovery Point Trail from Rim Village also leads to the Watchman.

Morning is the best time to scale Mt. Scott for the farthest-ranging views in the park— from Mt. Shasta to Mt. Jefferson on a clear day. The 2.5-mile trail climbs steadily to the lookout on this geologically recent stratovolcano.

The park's most used trail (500 hikers a day) is a steep 1-mile path from the Rim Drive down to Cleetwood Cove, where two-hour guided boat tours of the lake depart on the hour between 9AM and 3PM from early July through September. The really fun hike here, however, is to take the boat tour as far as Wizard Island, climb the .8-mile trail to its circular summit cone, then hike 2 more miles down to a quick, icy swim at one of the island's ponds. Just don't miss the last boat back to Cleetwood Cove at 3:30PM.

Craggy Union Peak lacks a lake view, but it commands a panorama of the rim peaks and of other Cascade summits. The 5.5-mile route there begins by following the PCT through a broad mountain hemlock forest south of High-

Wizard Island and the cliffs of Llao Rock

way 62. Snow covers much of the route until mid-July.

Three other peaks make interesting hikes for those seeking respite from the rim's crowds. Plan a picnic to the wildflower meadow in the summit bowl of Crater Peak, a sometimes-rugged 2.5-mile hike from the southern tip of the Rim Drive. For views of Mt. Mazama's other flank (and Cascade peaks as far north as the Three Sisters), try scaling Red Cone. It's an easy, obvious 1.5-mile cross-country hike from a turnout on the park's north rim access road, 1 mile north of the Rim Drive junction.

A third cinder cone, Timber Crater, is too well forested to offer views. Carry water on the 4.6-mile route along abandoned roads from the

Pumice Desert to the often snowy, flat summit—a crater filled to the brim by Mt. Mazama's pumice. The final half mile is cross-country.

Those staying at the popular Mazama Campground won't want to miss three short loop hikes nearby. The 1.7-mile Annie Creek loop trail from the campground passes abundant wildflowers and interesting gas-fumarole rock formations similar to those seen at The Pinnacles, in the park's distant southeast corner. Two miles farther up the south rim access road, the 1-mile Godfrey Glen loop trail follows a cliff edge past more pinnacle formations. And from the Park Headquarters, the self-guiding 0.7-mile Castle Crest wildflower

north, a good alternate route leaves the PCT near Red Cone Spring, heads for massive Boundary Springs (no camping permitted within a quarter mile), and follows a quiet road-trail to Diamond Lake. A side trip to study Sphagnum Bog's four carnivorous plant species will interest botanists with mosquito headnets and hip waders.

The area's prettiest waterfall is not within the park at all. It's 50-foot Stuart Falls, at the head of Red Blanket Creek's scenic glacier-carved valley, in the Sky Lakes Wilderness. Crater Lake visitors can hike there from Highway 62's Cold Spring turnout on a dry 5.4-mile route across forested Pumice Flat. But two shorter, more scenic trails reach Stuart Falls from the west, passing two-tiered Red Blanket Falls on the way. The nearly level 4.6-mile Lucky Camp Trail route from Road 3795 is easiest, but remains blocked by snow until mid-July. The 4.2-mile trail from Road 6205 up Red Blanket Creek is snowfree a month earlier and passes through a stately low-elevation forest, but climbs 1500 feet.

To reach Stuart Falls' western trailheads, turn off Highway 62 at Prospect, taking Road 37 east. Turn left off Road 37 in 1.1 miles to follow Road 6205 for 12 miles to its end at the Red Blanket trailhead, or turn left off Road 37 in 6 miles to follow Road 3795 for 12 miles to its end at the Lucky Camp trailhead.

Winter Sports

Within the park, Highway 62 and its short spur to Rim Village are plowed in winter, allowing Nordic skiers access to excellent tours on the snowed-under Rim Drive and surrounding terrain. Snowmobiles are out of earshot, restricted to the Diamond Lake area and the park's north access road. The lake itself is an unforgettable spectacle in winter.

The area's premier challenge, the 33-mile loop around the lake, is a two- or three-day excursion best attempted when winter's fiercest storms are over. The route is recommended for experienced skiers and snow campers only. Road cuts and slopes can calve avalanches, but the most insidious danger is being lured too close to the rim, with its unseen cornice overhangs. By late spring, volcanic grit covers the snow, slowing progress and damaging skis. Permits are required for snow campers.

When choosing day trips and tours away from the Rim Drive, remember that scenic routes on steep slopes are prone to avalanches. Map, compass, and route-finding ability are essential in the flatter areas, where viewless forests hide landmarks. The Park Service recommends that winter ski parties carry radio telemetry beepers.

garden nature-trail loop shows off the park's alpine flora.

Two trails connect the Rim Drive with the PCT and also lead to the most accessible backcountry camping. The 2.4-mile Dutton Creek Trail drops 1000 feet through viewless forest to a creekside wildflower display. The 4.1-mile Lightning Springs Trail passes a small waterfall after 1.5 miles, then becomes an abandoned forest road.

The PCT itself is uninspiring throughout the park—entirely viewless, with no water north of Red Cone Spring or south of Dutton Creek, and largely on abandoned roads. PCT hikers will want to consider hiking up Dutton Creek and along the Rim Drive instead. To the

30. Sky Lakes

LOCATION: 36 mi NE of Medford, 22 mi NW of Klamath Falls
SIZE: 220 sq mi
STATUS: 177 sq mi designated wilderness (1984)
TERRAIN: lake-dotted upland forests, peaks
ELEVATION: 3520'–9495'
MANAGEMENT: Rogue River NF, Winema NF
TOPOGRAPHIC MAPS: Sky Lakes Wilderness, PCT Central Oregon Portion, PCT Southern Oregon Portion, Jackson Klamath Winter Trails (USFS); *Crater Lake National Park and Vicinity* (Wilderness Press)

Hundreds of lakes hide among the mountain hemlock forests on the Cascade Crest between Crater Lake and Mt. McLoughlin, highest point in Southern Oregon.

Climate

The heavy winter snowpack blocks most trails until mid-June, and the Pacific Crest Trail until mid-July. Mosquitoes are so numerous after the snowmelt that headnets and zippered tents are advisable throughout July. Summers are dry, with occasional thunderstorms. Snows return in mid-October. Average annual precipitation is 40 inches.

Plants and Wildlife

The wilderness is heavily influenced by adjacent Upper Klamath Lake, which may shelter a half million birds at once during the October-November migrations. Bald eagles nesting near Klamath Lake's swamps commonly visit the high wilderness lakes. Pelican Butte is named for Upper Klamath Lake's white pelicans, unmistakable with their 9-foot wingspans.

The best time to view the teeming bird life on Upper Klamath Lake's marshy fringe is during the July and August nesting season, when a canoe put in at Rocky Point Resort (rentals available) enables birders to paddle 6 miles north up Crystal Creek, past red-necked grebes, white-headed woodpeckers, and possibly even sandhill cranes.

Sky Lakes' profusion of July mosquitoes coincides with a profusion of mosquito-pollinated wildflowers and a profusion of tiny, mosquito-eating boreal toads.

In August, the omnipresent huckleberry underbrush of the mountain hemlock forest sags with ripe fruit—especially along the Wickiup Meadow trail. By September, the huckleberry leaves turn scarlet, filling the uplands with color.

Geology

Mt. McLoughlin presents a smooth conical face toward Medford and Klamath Falls but conceals a craggy glacial cirque on its northern side. Strata exposed there show the mountain was once a tall cinder cone like nearby Pelican Butte, then erupted an armorlike covering of andesite, and finally lost its original summit when a glacier (since vanished) cut through its northern shell.

Other Ice Age glaciers scoured out most of the lake basins and gouged the deep, U-shaped valleys of the Rogue River's many forks. Nar-

White pelicans on Klamath Lake

Eagle Peak from Grass Lake, in the Seven Lakes Basin (photo by William L. Sullivan)

row Alta Lake and Long Lake did not result from glaciers, however; they lie along a possibly active fault which extends through the Mountain Lakes Wilderness to California.

THINGS TO DO

Hiking

The area's most popular hike is also the most difficult: scaling 9495-foot Mt. McLoughlin for a view of all of southern Oregon. No technical equipment is required, only the stamina to gain 3900 feet in 4.9 miles and return.

From Road 3650 hike 1.4 miles to the PCT, where there's a short spur to Freye Lake. If the lake doesn't have a nice mountain reflection, turn back and try the climb in better weather. Otherwise, follow the ridgetop trail to a frus-

trating false summit at timberline. The true top's abandoned lookout foundations lie another steep, trailless mile up a rocky ridge. Remember the route well; most search and rescue calls come for hikers who head south from the summit, missing the trail.

Other popular hikes prowl three clusters of forest-rimmed lakes: the Seven Lakes Basin, the Sky Lakes Basin, and the Blue Canyon Basin. Overused portions of some lakeshores are closed for rehabilitation—particularly in areas near trailheads.

Craggy Devils Peak towers above the Seven Lakes Basin—particularly Cliff Lake, where swimmers can high dive from cliffs into deep water. An easy 4.7-mile trail to shallow Grass Lake from Sevenmile Marsh Campground makes the entire lake basin accessible to day hikers, but it deserves a two- or three-day trip.

Backpackers to the Seven Lakes Basin won't want to miss the 6-mile loop trail over Devils Peak. Follow the PCT to a 7300-foot saddle, where a short, rugged spur trail heads for the peak's former lookout site and sweeping view.

Have another day to spend? Try an 8-mile loop to rock-rimmed Lake Ivern and slender Lake Alta. The route requires an easy half-mile cross-country traverse between the Lake Ivern Trail and the Middle Fork Trail; follow a compass bearing northwest from the Bigfoot Spring spur trail turnoff. At Lake Ivern, be

sure to take an easy quarter-mile side trip due north to a 500-foot cliff overlooking the U-shaped canyon of the Middle Fork Rogue River.

To reach the trailhead at Sevenmile Marsh, take Nicholson Road 4.3 miles west from Highway 62 at Fort Klamath, then continue on gravel Road 3334 to its end.

Less heavily used trails reach the basin from the west. The shortest, a 5-mile path from Road 3780 to Cliff Lake, climbs 1600 feet over a ridge on its way. The longest, the 9.7-mile Middle Fork Trail from Road 3790 to Alta Lake, follows a splashing fork of the Rogue

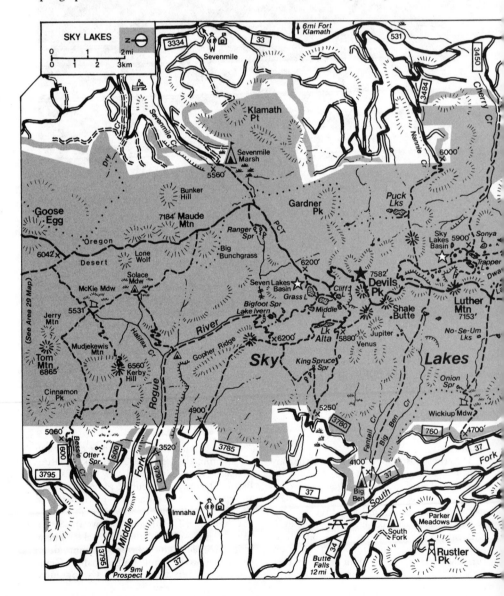

River through an old-growth forest with luxuriant, low-elevation greenery.

The Sky Lakes Basin makes up for a shortage of mountain views with an abundance of forest-rimmed lakes. The aptly-named Heavenly Twin Lakes are an easy 2-mile day hike (one way) from Cold Spring Campground. It's worth the effort to continue on a 2-mile loop trail past deep Lake Notasha, swimmable Lake Elizabeth, and large Isherwood Lake. Another good extension to this day hike heads 2 miles north to scenic Trapper Lake, in a cluster of lakes with views of Luther Mountain's rocky ridge.

Three quieter trails also make good routes into the Sky Lakes Basin. The Nannie Creek Trail from Road 3484 passes large, swimmable South Puck Lake after 2.4 miles (a good day hike goal for kids), then descends another 4.1 miles to Trapper Lake. The Cherry Creek Trail from Road 3450 arrives at that lake in 5.2 miles, but climbs 1300 feet, making the route more popular with equestrians than hikers. And from the west, the Wickiup Trail from Road 760 passes a shelter, a meadow, and lush huckleberry fields on its 5.2-mile climb to the PCT; Trapper Lake is another 3 miles.

Lakes in the Blue Canyon Basin offer reflec-

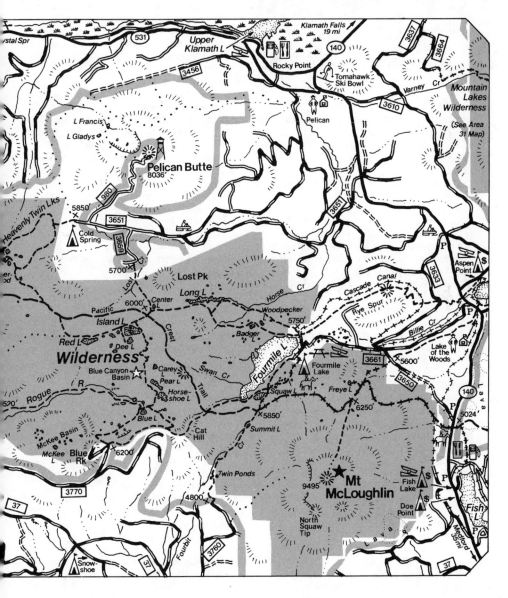

Mount McLoughlin from the Pacific Crest Trail at Shale Butte (photo by William L. Sullivan)

tions of Mt. McLoughlin's snowy northern face. Island Lake, largest of the group, is a 2.4-mile day hike along the Lost Creek Trail from Road 3659. For a good swim, try nearby Dee Lake.

Day hikers can best reach the western lakes of this basin via the Blue Canyon Trail starting at Road 3770. It's 2 miles to deep, cold Blue Lake, with its cliff backdrop, and another 0.7 mile to Horseshoe Lake's peninsula. Trailside camps are closed here to allow the fragile flora to regrow. Best bets for solitude are off-trail Pear Lake and Carey Lake.

Fourmile Lake, popular with fishermen, is the starting point of several good day hikes. The 3.6-mile route to sinuous Long Lake visits several snag-filled bays of Fourmile Lake (with views of Mt. McLoughlin) and passes wildflower meadows near pleasant Badger Lake. A 3.3-mile hike south of Fourmile Lake's outlet dam follows the sometimes-dry Cascade Canal then climbs Rye Spur to a viewpoint. From the Fourmile Lake Campground, the Twin Ponds Trail skirts shallow, grassy Squaw Lake, crosses the PCT, and descends to bouldery Summit Lake—a 2.9-mile trip.

Little-used trails in the north of this wilderness lead to McKie Meadow's shelter and Solace Meadow's cabin, both popular with equestrians. The 5.3-mile Tom and Jerry Trail to McKie Meadow from Road 600 offers a good cross-country side trip to the view atop Tom Mountain. An alternate route to McKie Meadow crosses Kerby Hill; it's steep, but features a spectacular view of the Middle Fork Rogue Canyon.

The shortest route to Solace Meadow—6.3

miles—follows the Middle Fork Trail from Road 3790, then switchbacks up the Halifax Trail through a rapid succession of botanical zones.

The nearly viewless 49.7-mile segment of the PCT between Highway 140 and Highway 62 in Crater Lake National Park manages to avoid all lakes and water sources; be sure to detour into the three major lake basins. Also be sure to take the 0.6-mile side trip to Ranger Spring, a welcome oasis. The Oregon Desert, on the northern part of the PCT route, is a lodgepole pine forest free of underbrush and notable for massive September mushrooms.

Cross-country hiking is easy and rewarding in all the upland lake basins, but particularly in the McKee Basin near Blue Rock and in the glacial cirque on Pelican Butte—areas lacking maintained trails.

Winter Sports

Marked Nordic ski trails radiate from several sno-parks along plowed Highway 140. Snowmobiles dominate snowed-under roads and are permitted on most nonwilderness trails (except the PCT and the Cascade Canal).

A good beginner tour off limits to snowmobiles follows the Lake of the Woods shoreline 1.9 miles from Highway 140 to snowed-under Aspen Point campground. Another easy route, with good views of Mt. McLoughlin, begins at the Fish Lake Resort and loops 3 miles on marked roads and trails south of that lake.

The PCT offers routes both south of Highway 140, to viewpoints in the vast lava fields around nearby Brown Mountain, and north of the highway, where it climbs steadily 3.5 miles to Freye Lake's mountain view. A 1.5-mile trail connects the PCT with Fish Lake Resort, but the closest access to the PCT is the sno-park at the junction of Highway 140 and Road 3650.

Road 3650 and the parallel Cascade Canal provide a scenic, well-graded 9.7-mile Nordic route from Highway 140 to Fourmile Lake. A shortcut to that lake, along Road 3661, is shared with snowmobiles but allows snow campers quickest access to the wilderness trail system beyond.

The area's most challenging ski tour, to the summit of Mt. McLoughlin, should only be undertaken in perfect weather by groups familiar with avalanche danger areas.

Boating

Canoes and sailboats do well on Fourmile Lake, Fish Lake, and the marshy bays and creeks of Upper Klamath Lake; motorboats are limited to 10 miles per hour in these areas.

31. Mountain Lakes

LOCATION: 38 mi E of Medford, 15 mi NW of
   Klamath Falls
SIZE: 45 sq mi
STATUS: 36 sq mi designated wilderness (1964)
TERRAIN: forested buttes, lake basins
ELEVATION: 4700'–8208'
MANAGEMENT: Winema NF
TOPOGRAPHIC MAPS: Mountain Lakes
   Wilderness (USFS); *Crater Lake* (Wilderness
   Press); Aspen Butte, Lake of the Woods S,
   Pelican Bay, Lake of the Woods N (USGS,
   7.5')

This pocket wilderness is large enough that
some of its alpine viewpoints and forest-
rimmed lakes are best seen on backpacking
trips.

Climate
Late summer brings frequent thunderstorms, but most of the area's 40 inches of annual precipitation comes as snow, which
blocks trails from early November to late June.
Mosquitoes are numerous in July.

Plants and Wildlife
Bald eagles, osprey, and a variety of ducks
from nearby Upper Klamath Lake frequent the
high lakes. The dense forests below 7000 feet
are chiefly droopy-topped mountain hemlock
and prim, Christmas-tree-shaped Shasta red
fir. At higher elevations, only gnarled whitebark pines survive. Their seeds are a primary
food source for the area's raucous Clark's nutcrackers.

Geology
This roughly circular upland was once
thought to be the eroded remnant of a collapsed 12,000-foot volcano similar to Crater
Lake's Mt. Mazama. However, the peaks here
are actually a cluster of at least four overlapping
volcanoes. Though glaciers have dissected
them severely (Mt. Carmine and Aspen Butte
were once a single cone), they were probably
never much taller than today. A feature of this
volcanic hot spot is a swarm of faults running
through the area—one of which aligned Seldom Creek's straight glacial valley.

THINGS TO DO

Hiking
Three trails climb to the 9-mile Mountain
Lakes Loop, with its lakes and scenic passes.
Because of the area's small size, permits are required for groups of more than 10—counting
persons, saddle stock, and pack animals.
   The most popular route into the wilderness
is the Varney Creek Trail from Road 3664,
which climbs among the creek's wildflowers

Varney Creek Trail

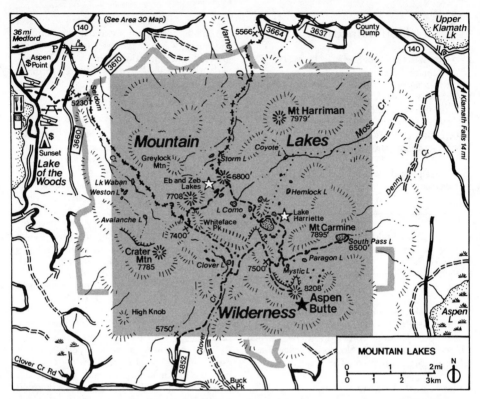

(bloom in July) 4.6 miles to Eb and Zeb lakes. These heavily visited, scenic, but shallow lakes are often warm enough for swimming.

Here most day hikers must turn about. Backpackers have more choices. Eastward, the Mountain Lakes Loop Trail heads 1.5 miles to very deep 40-acre Harriette Lake, passing Como Lake and shallow Silent and Zephyr lakes. Westward, the loop trail climbs 1 mile to a saddle, from which a 7708-foot summit with an excellent viewpoint is only a short cross-country hike away. Those ready for a grander cross-country viewpoint hike can head northeast from Eb Lake up a 2.5-mile ridge to Mt. Harriman.

Another popular trailhead, on Road 3660 near Lake of the Woods, begins a 5.4-mile path up Seldom Creek's glacial valley to the Mountain Lakes Loop. After climbing 3.3 miles on this route, look for a spur trail to grassy Waban Lake, with its seasonal profusion of tree frogs.

A third path up to the Mountain Lakes Loop, the Clover Trail, is by far the shortest and least used. It reaches small Clover Lake from Road 3852 in 2.2 miles. Most hikers veer right at the 2-mile point, following the Mountain Lakes Loop to a ridgetop overlooking Harriette Lake. Here a spur trail continues up the alpine ridge past whitebark pines, dwarfed manzanita bushes, and showy Davidson's penstemons to Aspen Butte, whose summit view makes the strenuous 4.8-mile climb from Road 3852 worthwhile. Look for Crater Lake's rim peaks, Mt. McLoughlin, and Mt. Shasta.

Backpackers hiking the 9-mile Mountain Lake Loop Trail may also want to explore the 1.7-mile spur trail eastward down a forested, but increasingly arid glacial valley to large South Pass Lake.

Winter Sports

Nordic ski trips can begin from plowed Highway 140 either at the Great Meadow sno-park near Lake of the Woods or at the County Dump near Upper Klamath Lake. Carry map, compass, and emergency gear; wilderness trails are not marked for winter use.

Great Meadow is a snowmobile center, but skiers leave noise behind when they leave Road 3660 for the Mountain Lakes Trail up Seldom Creek. Lake Waban, 4.5 miles from the sno-park, is a good goal.

From the County Dump, skiers follow unplowed roads 3.5 miles to the Varney Creek trailhead. Eb and Zeb lakes are a challenging 4.3-mile trek away.

32. Soda Mountain

LOCATION: 13 mi SE of Ashland
SIZE: 50 sq mi
STATUS: undesignated wilderness
TERRAIN: steep, mostly wooded slopes
ELEVATION: 2300′–6000′
MANAGEMENT: Medford District BLM
TOPOGRAPHIC MAPS: PCT Southern Oregon
   Portion (USFS); Siskiyou Pass (USGS, 7.5′);
   Hyatt Reservoir, Ashland, Hornbrook
   [California], Copco [California] (USGS, 15′)

The double cone of Mt. Shasta stands high on the southern horizon from the slopes of Soda Mountain, where the Siskiyou Mountains and the Cascade Range meet.

Climate

Moderate snowfall blocks the Pacific Crest Trail from about December to March or April. Annual precipitation varies from 40 inches in the upland forests to less than 20 inches in the southern oak grasslands, where summer temperatures can soar.

Plants and Wildlife

Soda Mountain stands at the apex of three biologic zones: the Cascades, the Siskiyous, and the high desert. Dark fir forests on the high, north-facing slopes resemble woods in the High Cascades. Droopy, canyon-bottom cedars and stiff-limbed manzanita brush remind one of the Siskiyous. Pungent sagebrush and juniper on the dry southern ridges belong to the Great Basin steppe.

The area is home to the showy Greene's mariposa lily (threatened in Oregon), though hikers are more likely to encounter trilliums and calypso orchids (in spring forests) or yellow-flowered rabbit brush (among fall sagebrush).

A large herd of blacktail deer from the Rogue Valley relies on the white oak grasslands of the lower southern slopes for winter browse. Other wildlife species include cougar, black bear, elk, golden eagle, and quail.

Geology

Soda Mountain is a block of 16- to 25-million-year-old volcanic rock from the heavily eroded Old Cascades, wedged between the much older Klamath Mountains to the west and the much younger High Cascades to the east.

History

Pilot Rock's landmark basalt monolith once guided gold miners and trappers toward the Siskiyou Mountains' lowest pass. Train tracks built across Siskiyou Pass in 1887 filled the final gap in a rail line around the United States'

Pilot Rock

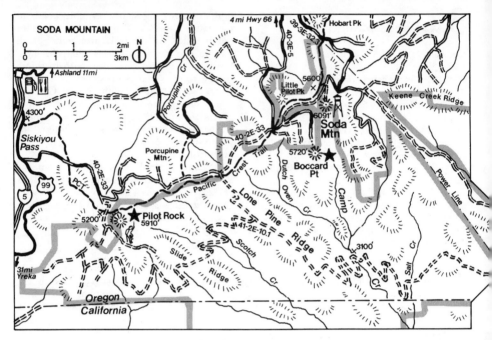

perimeter. The area remained remote enough, however, to harbor Oregon's last known grizzly bear, the legendary, 8-foot-tall Old Reelfoot, which was shot near Pilot Rock's base in 1891. Later the D'Autremont brothers attempted a train robbery at Siskiyou Pass in 1923, murdering three men. They eluded a four-continent manhunt by camping under a fallen tree beside Porcupine Creek.

THINGS TO DO

Hiking

Interstate 5 travelers can stretch their legs with a 1.5-mile forest hike on the PCT through a juniper forest to the cliffs and views at the base of Pilot Rock. From the Mt. Ashland exit, follow old Highway 99 2 miles south under the freeway, turn left on Pilot Rock Road 40-2E-33 for 1 mile, park at the PCT crossing, and hike south.

For better views of Mt. Shasta, continue hiking from Pilot Rock 6.2 miles to Soda Mountain. A short access road leads from the PCT to the lookout tower (in use each summer) on the mountain's broad, alpine summit. The PCT continues north from Soda Mountain 1.5 miles through a dense, old-growth forest before crossing Soda Mountain Road 39-3E-32.3. To reach this PCT trailhead, take Highway 66 east of Ashland 15.6 miles, turn south just before Green Springs Summit, and follow the Soda Mountain Road 5 miles.

The best view of all is at Boccard Point's rocky promontory, an easy 0.2-mile walk from the end of Baldy Creek Road 40-3E-5. From the Ashland exit of Interstate 5, take Highway 14.8 miles east, turn right on Tyler Creek Road for 1.5 miles, turn left on gravel Road 40-3E-5 for 7.5 miles to its end, and then hike south along the open, trailless ridge to the viewpoint.

Boccard Point also makes a good starting point for cross-country forays into the area's steep southern canyons. Trailless travel here is easiest through sagebrush and open grasslands along ridgetops, or along the creeks' lush growth of moss and maples. Rock outcroppings and bands of nearly impenetrable scrub oak chaparral interrupt canyon slopes. Dutch Oven Creek's many small waterfalls make good goals.

Climbing

Pilot Rock's basalt tower offers seven established mountaineering routes, including the scenic West Ridge (level I-5.3) and the South Face's broken basalt columns (level II-5.6). The West Gully, a class 3 scramble route to the summit, is commonly used by technical climbers as a descent route. A pinnacle 200 yards southeast of Pilot Rock requires level I-5.7 skills.

33. Red Buttes

LOCATION: 34 mi SW of Medford
SIZE: 130 sq mi total; 42 sq mi in Oregon
STATUS: 31 sq mi designated wilderness; 6 sq mi in Oregon (1984)
TERRAIN: rocky buttes, forested ridges, small lakes
ELEVATION: 1600'–7055'
MANAGEMENT: Rogue River NF, Siskiyou NF, Klamath NF, Oregon Caves National Monument
TOPOGRAPHIC MAPS: Red Buttes Wilderness, PCT Southern Oregon Portion (USFS); Oregon Caves, Ruch, Happy Camp [California], Seiad Valley [California] (USGS, 15')

Straddling the rocky crest of the Siskiyou Mountains, this little-visited area's trail system extends along view-filled ridges and subalpine meadows from the Pacific Crest Trail to the Oregon Caves National Monument.

Climate
Snowfall closes high trails from November to May. Summers are very dry. Annual precipitation measures 40 inches.

Plants and Wildlife
Expect frequent signs of wildlife on the trails: deer tracks, coyote scat, and palm-sized paw prints of cougar and bear. This is also a prime spot for Bigfoot fanciers; alleged sightings of ape men date to 1895. The Forest Service issued a special-use permit for a Sasquatch trap here in 1973.

The area teems with unusual flora of the Siskiyous. Knobcone pines, resembling bumpy flagpoles, dot Figurehead Mountain. Droopy weeping spruce are common. Massive incense cedars, hollowed by fire, could serve as extra camping accommodations beside Sucker Gap's shelter. A loop trail from the Oregon Caves leads to Big Tree, Oregon's largest Douglas fir. Some of the world's southernmost Alaska cedars grow on Emily Mountain, while the world's northernmost Baker's cypresses grow on Steve Peak.

June brings wildflowers familiar from the alpine Cascades as well as Siskiyou novelties, including two delicate, pink Lewisia species, best seen in Cameron Meadows.

Geology
Colorful rock cairns marking high trails here showcase the area's diversity; the rocks are up to 425 million years old (almost 20 times the age of the Old Cascades). Look for flat slate, shiny schist, green serpentinite, white marble, and speckled granite.

The ancient North American continent thrust westward here against the Pacific plate, jumbling up masses of seafloor rock—including the red peridotite forming Red Buttes' twin peaks. The collision sheared off the Siskiyou Mountains, temporarily turning them into a Pacific island 90 million years ago.

That collision's pressure also cooked limestone to marble, allowing later water seepage to create the white caverns of the Oregon Caves (now, dripstone stalactites grow there at the swift rate of an inch per decade). Finally, hot granite intrusions melted out veins of mineral-rich quartz. Gold attracted swarms of prospectors in the 1850s. Mine tailings and washed-out, "hydraulicked" river bottoms remain.

Lonesome Lake from Figurehead Mountain; Red Buttes on the horizon at left (photo by William L. Sullivan)

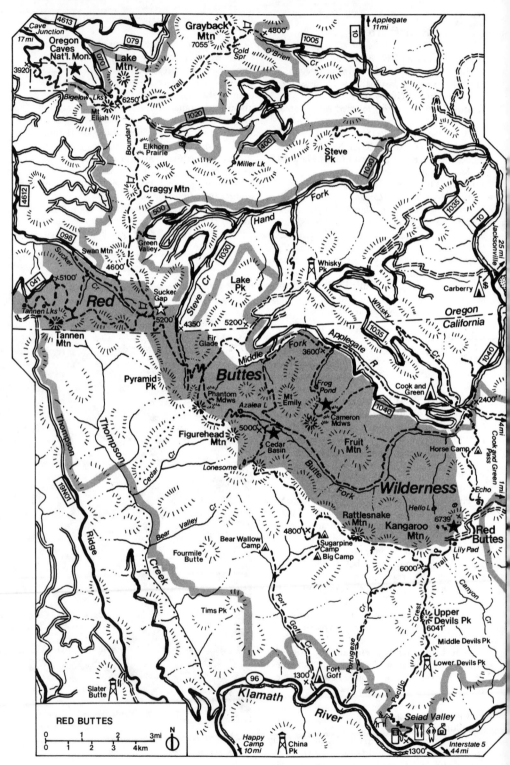

RED BUTTES

0   1   2   3mi
0   1   2   3   4km
N

THINGS TO DO

Hiking

Start with a 3.5-mile walk along the PCT from Cook and Green Pass to aptly named Lilypad Lake, at the foot of Red Buttes' double peak. Along the way take a short side trail to an overlook of Echo Lake, in a high basin. Have energy for a longer hike? From Lilypad Lake, it's a nearly level 2.6 miles to Upper Devils Peak and a look at the Klamath River 4700 feet below. For a view toward Oregon, turn off the PCT at Kangaroo Mountain and head west 2.5 trail miles to the cliff-edged pass atop craggy Rattlesnake Mountain.

In much of this wilderness, dry south-facing slopes confound cross-country hikers with impenetrable chaparral tangles of manzanita and stunted chinkapin. Open forests on northern slopes, however, invite trailless exploration. A top trip starts from the Red Buttes trailhead and circles the ruddy double peak, passing wildflower meadows, springs, and five scenic cirque lakes on a sometimes rocky 5-mile traverse, returning via the PCT.

To reach Cook and Green Pass from Medford, drive 31 miles southwest past Jacksonville, Ruch, and Star Ranger Station to the end of Applegate Reservoir. Trade pavement there for gravel Road 1050, and after 1 mile, turn right on Road 1055 (roads not shown on map). An 8-mile climb reaches Cook and Green Pass and the PCT crossing.

Cedar Basin's forested bowl features several swimmable lakes, June wildflowers, and views of rocky Figurehead Mountain. The 3.5-mile trail to Azalea Lake from Road 1040 climbs 1300 feet from the the Middle Fork Applegate River over Mt. Emily. From Cedar Basin, hike on to the rocky pass just south of Lonesome Lake for a look into the Klamath River country, swept by fire in 1987. Or climb Figurehead Mountain for views ranging from El Capitan in the western Siskiyous to Mt. Shasta and Mt. McLoughlin. A good trail on Figurehead Mountain's northwest shoulder comes within a short cross-country ramble of the summit.

To reach the Azalea Lake trailhead, drive to the end of pavement at the south end of Applegate Lake, 31 miles southwest of Medford. Take gravel Road 1040 for 4 miles to Cook and Green Campground; 1.8 miles farther on, turn left to continue on Road 1040 another 8 miles to the well-marked trailhead spur.

Visit the wildflowers at Frog Pond and Cameron Meadows with a 6-mile loop hike from Road 1040. From the meadows, scramble up a ridge to the south for a good viewpoint. Planning a car shuttle between the two trailheads will save a final 2-mile walk along Road 1040 back to the car.

Sucker Creek Gap, at the junction of the east-west Siskiyou Mountains and the north-south Grayback Range, is a cool, grassy dale surrounded by impressive old-growth cedars. Hike there from the end of Road 1030 on a 3-mile trail through Steve Creek Valley's deep forest. An even shorter 1.4-mile route to the Sucker Creek Gap shelter takes off from the end of Road 098. From Cave Junction, head toward Oregon Caves for 14.5 miles, turn south on gravel Road 4612 for 9 miles, then turn right onto Road 098.

The swimmable Tannen Lakes, nestled in forest against a backdrop of Tannen Mountain's rockslides, are a popular day hike goal. A gentle quarter-mile trail leads to the larger Tannen Lake from Road 041; East Tannen Lake is another mile along the Boundary Trail — a well-graded route that tempts hikers to continue past Sucker Gap. From Cave Junction or O'Brien, follow signs toward Happy Camp, but turn east at the Siskiyou summit on gravel Road 4812. After 4 miles branch to the right onto Road 041; the trailhead is 5 miles ahead.

Atop Lake Mountain, hikers can often spot both Mt. Shasta and the Pacific Ocean. It's easy to combine a hike there with a visit to the renowned Oregon Caves, since the trail branches off from the National Monument's Cliff Nature Trail. At the 4-mile point, weary hikers can settle for a nice view atop lesser Mt. Elijah. More energetic souls can take a side trip down to swim in the Bigelow Lakes.

Backpackers in the Red Buttes area can opt for several long-distance routes that surpass the PCT, with its grueling, 4700-foot ascent from Seiad Valley. The 18.3-mile Boundary Trail from Grayback Mountain to Tannen Lakes avoids the PCT's crowds.

Cook and Green Campground is the trailhead for three other excellent backpacking loops. A 12.5-mile trip climbs up the well-graded Cook and Green Trail to Cook and Green Pass, follows the PCT for 2 miles, then dives down past Echo Lake, back to the campground. A 20-mile forest-and-river trip follows the lovely Butte Fork Trail to Cedar Basin, then descends the Middle Fork Trail to a final 1.8-mile roadside walk back to Cook and Green Campground. But for the best sampling of this wilderness, take a 33.5-mile loop backpack from the campground to Cook and Green Pass, Red Buttes, Rattlesnake Mountain, and Cedar Basin, returning via the Butte Fork Trail.

34. Kalmiopsis

LOCATION: 33 mi SW of Grants Pass
SIZE: 672 sq mi
STATUS: 281 sq mi designated wilderness
(1964, 1978); Illinois federal wild and scenic
river
TERRAIN: steep, rugged canyons, sparsely
forested ridges; river rapids
ELEVATION: 240'–5098'
MANAGEMENT: Siskiyou NF
TOPOGRAPHIC MAPS: Kalmiopsis
Wilderness (USFS); Pearsoll Peak, Collier
Butte, Mt. Emily, Chetco Peak (USGS, 15')

Cut by the green-pooled Illinois River's rugged gorge, the Kalmiopsis is Oregon's largest but perhaps least visited forest wilderness. Seen from one of the dry ridgetop trails, jagged canyonlands spread like a vast sheet of crumpled paper. This is a land of torrential winter rains and blazing summer heat, of rare wildflowers and shy black bears.

Hikers should expect challenge as well as beauty on the steep trails. Boaters on the wild Illinois must prepare for 10 churning class 4 rapids and the monstrous, class 5 Green Wall.

Climate

Heavy rains from October to May (80 to 100 inches) swell the rivers, making crossings difficult in spring. There are no bridges. Snow usually covers trails over 4000 feet from December through March. Afternoon temperatures often exceed 90° F in virtually rainless July and August.

Plants and Wildlife

Unusual species developed during the 50 million years that the Siskiyou Mountains were an island in the Pacific Ocean. Many of these species have survived because Ice Age glaciers left most of the area untouched. Plant collecting is prohibited.

Carnivorous pitcher plants resemble green baseball bats sprouting from boggy land at springs. These plants make up for the area's poor soil by catching their own nutrients. A honey aroma lures insects into the plant's hollow stem, where tiny hairs prevent escape and enzymes reduce the catch to liquid. Also at springs, look for brilliant blue gentian and white death camas.

Rare *Kalmiopsis leachiana* fills forests with pink blooms in June. This azalealike shrub, almost entirely limited to this wilderness, is best seen at Bailey Mountain, Dry Butte, Gold Basin, and Taggarts Bar.

Forests are often Douglas fir and canyon live oak but include an odd mix of other species. Look for madrone, with peeling red bark, and chinkapin, with spiny fruit ("porcupine eggs"). Port Orford cedar and Brewer's weeping spruce, elsewhere rare, are common here.

Tail-twitching, orange Douglas squirrels scold hikers from trees. On rocky slopes, watch for western fence lizards, blue-tailed skinks, and the area's unaggressive rattlesnakes. Quiet hikers frequently surprise black bears foraging for sugarpine seeds, yellowjacket ground nests, or manzanita berries. The bears dislike dogs, but do all they can to avoid humans, typically climbing trees or fleeing on sight. Encourage this by wrapping smelly food tightly and hanging all food at night.

Geology

This portion of the Siskiyou Mountains was on the western shore of North America 200 million years ago when the continent began its present one-inch-per-year westward drift. The movement buckled up masses of sub-seafloor rock and folded Siskiyou strata like taffy.

Today, outcroppings of sub-seafloor rock (red peridotite and shiny green serpentinite) are so infertile they visibly stunt vegetation; they also provide the traces of rare, heavy metals which account for the area's many gold mining cabins and abandoned chrome mines.

The continent's westward drift also temporarily sheared off the Siskiyou Mountains, leaving them an island in the Pacific Ocean, much as Baja California has been sheared away from Mexico, or Vancouver Island from Canada. As proof of this, 45- to 90-million-year-old sea fossils are found on the eastern edge of the Siskiyous. What's more, strata in the southern Siskiyous match strata hundreds of miles away in the northern Sierras—as if the two ranges had been separated by a huge knife. The ancient strait has filled with sediment and volcanics from the Cascades.

Though new mining claims are prohibited in designated wilderness, recreational gold panning is allowed. To try, wash out heavy black sands gleaned from bedrock cracks in creekbeds in the Little Chetco River or Upper Chetco River area. Look for jasper along the Illinois River below Florence Creek.

THINGS TO DO

Hiking

The 27-mile Illinois River Trail over Bald Mountain is well graded and maintained. Nearly all other paths in the area, however, are steep, rocky miner's pack trails or bulldozed mining roads. Hikers occasionally meet four-wheel-drive vehicles even in designated wilderness, since miners with valid pre-1984 claims have keys to the road gates.

A few other cautions: beware of the shiny, autumn-red, three-leaved poison oak prolific at lower elevations. Vast brushfields of tough, red-limbed manzanita stymie most cross-country travelers. And remember that illegal marijuana is the biggest cash crop in these forests. Off-trail hikers may stumble onto possibly guarded marijuana plants near creeks and springs within a mile or two of trailheads.

The two most popular short hikes of the wilderness lead to cirque lakes high in the moun-

Sunrise from the Hawks Rest Trail at Cold Spring Camp (photo by William L. Sullivan)

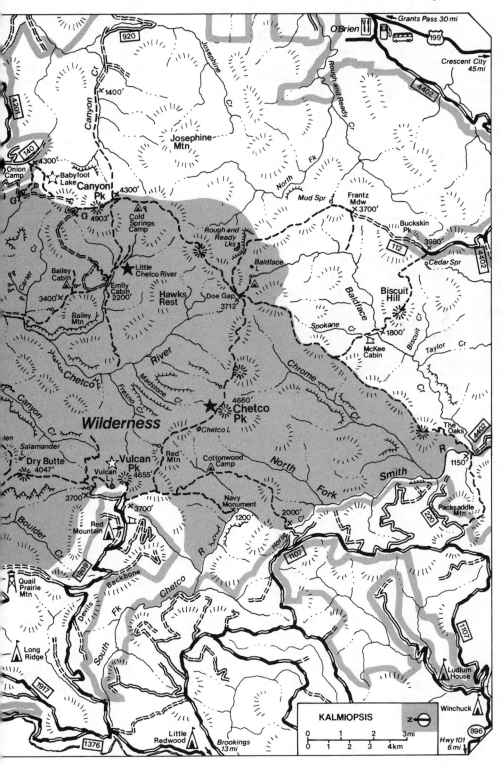

Darlingtonia, an insect-eating pitcher plant, in bloom (photo by William L. Sullivan)

tain forests: Babyfoot Lake in the east and Vulcan Lake in the west.

An easy 1-mile trail through a designated botanical area reaches Babyfoot Lake from Road 140. Continue past the surprisingly green lake through stands of droopy-limbed Brewer's weeping spruce, follow a mining road south, and return along a view-filled ridgetop trail for a 3.5-mile loop hike. For even better views of the area's rugged canyonlands—and a glimpse of the distant ocean—head for either Eagle Mountain or the abandoned lookout site atop Canyon Peak, both less than 4 trail miles from Babyfoot Lake. Reach the trailhead via Eight Dollar Mountain Road 4201, which branches off Highway 199 north of Cave Junction 5 miles.

Vulcan Lake is the same size as Babyfoot Lake (4 acres), but instead of being set in a lush forest, it fills a dramatic rock basin of rare knobcone pines below broad Vulcan Peak. The red peridotite rock shores not only exhibit glacial scratch marks of interest to geologists, but also make ideal sunbathing spots for swimmers. A well-maintained 1.4-mile trail from the end of Road 1909 crosses a scenic ridge on its way to Vulcan Lake.

Other trails near Vulcan Lake make good day trips. The old lookout site atop Vulcan Peak, with views of the Kalmiopsis and the Pacific coast, is up a 1-mile trail (gaining 1000 feet). A mostly level 4-mile ridgetop route passes Red Mountain on its way to austere Chetco Lake. Another trail with views from an open ridgetop heads north 3 miles to Dry Butte's fields of *Kalmiopsis leachiana.* Trailhead access is from Brookings; turn off Highway 101 at the north end of the Chetco River bridge, follow the road along the Chetco River 16.5 miles, and then turn right on Road 1909 to its end.

Where trails exist at all along the Chetco River's rugged inner gorge, they generally traverse canyon slopes several hundred feet above the green-pooled stream. A day hike from the western edge of the wilderness samples one such trail, a 3-mile route from a spur of Road 360 to a ford and chilly swimming hole at Boulder Creek Camp. From there, hikers can climb an extra mile to a view of the Big Craggies from Lately Prairie, or else continue 3 miles along the Chetco River for a look up Tincup Creek's gorge. To reach the trailhead, drive 23 miles up the Chetco River from Brookings, turn off Road 1376 onto dirt Road 360 for 1 mile, then switchback onto spur Road 365.

Three popular day hikes begin near the McCaleb Ranch Boy Scout camp, on the Grants Pass side of the wilderness. The main attraction of the Fall Creek Trail is its first half mile, beginning with a dramatic suspension footbridge over the Illinois River. For the two other hikes, drive up steep dirt Road 087 and park at Chetco Pass. From there, the view at Pearsoll Peak's cupola-style lookout tower—highest point in the region—is a 2.3-mile walk up a rutted road-trail. Also from Chetco Pass, it's interesting to walk the mining road west, past mostly abandoned chrome mine camps at Sourdough Flat, 3 miles to the Chetco River ford.

The popular 27-mile Illinois River Trail traverses wildflower-filled meadows along Bald Mountain's long crest, then descends through the wild Illinois River's remote inner gorge. Side trips to viewpoints at South Bend Mountain or to Collier Bar (a river ford passable from mid-June to November) can make the trip even more spectacular. Start at Briggs Creek, at the bumpy end of dirt Road 4103, and finish at a paved road 3 miles from Agness (see the Wild Rogue map, area 35). Those who can't arrange the long car shuttle can catch a Rogue River jet mail boat (available May 1 to November 1) from Agness to bus connections in Gold Beach.

Backpackers with a yen for solitude and rugged beauty will find both in the vast interior of the Kalmiopsis. The premier trip is a 42-mile trail loop from Vulcan Lake past Dry Butte, Taggarts Bar, the Little Chetco River, Emlly Cabin, Doe Gap, and Chetco Peak. Beware of dehydration, since trails follow dry ridges and canyon slopes. Carry plenty of water and study maps carefully for trailside springs and perennial streams.

Boating

Oregon's most difficult whitewater run, the Illinois River from Oak Flat to Agness packs 156 rated rapids into 35 miles. The setting is a breathtakingly stark, trailless, 4000-foot-deep canyon. The brilliant green river is so clear that mossy boulders 30 feet underwater seem within reach.

Only very experienced river runners in kayaks, narrow inflatables, or *portageable* hard boats should attempt the Illinois, and then only in April or May when water levels range between 600 and 1400 cubic feet per second (gauged at the Kerby station). The lower water of early summer turns the run to a gamut of rock dodging and boat bashing. Higher water after heavy spring rains converts Boat Eater and the Green Wall to deadly maelstroms.

Start the three-day trip at the unmarked Oak Flat launch site 13 miles west of Selma where Road 4103 dips close to the river. A box here contains free, unlimited, self-issuing permits. Drift an easy 3 miles before coming to Panther Creek and the first of many rapids that must be scouted. The next 2 miles wallop boaters with seven increasingly powerful class 3 and 4 rapids, culminating with York Creek Rapids, a 4+ churner with an underwater shelf and tall standing waves in the preferred left channel.

Boat Eater Rapids, 3 miles downriver at the mouth of Pine Creek, funnel the river past a cabin-sized boulder into a roaring suckhole with a record of trapping every third or fourth craft it meets. Boaters usually camp immediately after this class 4+ trial.

Ten miles of swift but manageable water the second day out lead to the big stuff. It starts with class 4 Fawn Falls, down a 10-foot chute into a boulder obstacle course. Hardly a half mile beyond, an ominous wall covered with green moss looms above the river, signaling all but the most athletic daredevils to *portage* the coming class 5 water.

The Green Wall Rapids drop boaters 50 feet in less than 300 yards. First comes a fast stretch of rocks and holes, then a drop through a barricade of truck-sized boulders, then another 12-

Gold miner's cabin on the Little Chetco River (photo by William L. Sullivan)

foot cascade, and finally a possible crush against the wall itself.

Three-quarters of a mile farther, Little Green Wall's class 4 rocks hang up their share of boats. Whitewater is then nonstop for 2 miles to Submarine Hole's treacherous midstream boulder, which must be run on the left side (though this positioning requires strong rowing). Exhausted river runners will find no campsite for yet another 1.7 miles.

The third day is an easy drift to the Agness pull-out on the Rogue River. The car shuttle between ends of the run totals 120 miles over several poor roads (Oak Flat–Selma–Grants Pass–Galice–Agness); if this route is closed by lingering April snow, plan on 150 miles via Crescent City and Gold Beach. Arrangements may be made through Smith Shuttle Service: call (503) 476-9010; or write 12245 Galice Rd., Merlin, OR 97532.

This chapter's map shows the 10 class 4 rapids and the Green Wall. For more detailed descriptions of these and the many lesser rapids, see *Handbook to the Illinois River Canyon* by James M. Quinn, available from Educational Adventures, Inc., PO Box 827, Waldport, OR 97394.

35. Wild Rogue

LOCATION: 27 mi NW of Grants Pass
SIZE: 224 sq mi
STATUS: 56 sq mi designated wilderness
(1978), federal wild and scenic river
TERRAIN: steep, rocky, forested river canyon
ELEVATION: 140'–5316'
MANAGEMENT: Siskiyou NF, Medford District BLM
TOPOGRAPHIC MAPS: Wild Rogue
Wilderness (USFS); Agness, Marial, Galice,
Bone Mountain (USGS, 15')

The irascible Rogue River, cutting through the mountains to the sea, is at times a string of sunny, green pools, lazily drifting past playful otter and circling osprey. But the river can also be misty mayhem—raging over Blossom Bar's boulders like a giant pinball course, swirling boats helplessly in The Coffeepot, and standing on edge in Mule Creek Canyon, a chasm so narrow boats sometimes bridge from wall-to-wall.

More than 10,000 visitors a year run the Rogue's famous whitewater. However, the beautiful 47-mile Rogue River Trail is seldom crowded, and the rest of this river's rugged 4000-foot-deep canyon remains virtually untrodden.

Climate

Toward the end of the reliably rainless, hot summers, river temperatures rise to 70° F, tempting swimmers but driving fish into cooler tributaries. Intermittent rains from September to May total 90 inches in the damp western end of the canyon but only 50 inches in the east.

Plants and Wildlife

It's easy to spot wildlife attracted to the river: deer, merganser ducks, otters, black bears (catching salmon), osprey (and their nests atop tall snags), great blue herons, kingfishers, swooping cliff swallows (with mud nests on overhangs), and water ouzels. Try identifying the many tracks on the riverbanks each morning.

The river itself teems with salamanders, newts, and over 20 species of fish, including chinook salmon, steelhead, rainbow trout,

Blossom Bar

The Rogue River Trail at the edge of the Devils Backbone

sturgeon, shad, carp, lamprey, sculpin, stickleback, and dace. Among Oregon rivers, only the Columbia provides a higher annual fish catch.

Hikers encounter scurrying lizards and blue-tailed skinks on the dry slopes. This is Oregon's only habitat for the nocturnal ringtail, a tiny, big-eared relative of the raccoon. Prospectors brought the first ringtails here from Arizona to catch mice in mines.

The Douglas fir forests include lush red cedar and rhododendron in the west, but yield to white oak and red-barked madrone in the more arid east. Brushfields of manzanita and chinkapin limit cross-country travel. May brings trailside blue iris and white beargrass blooms; expect blue lupine and California poppies in June.

Geology

Tough 150-million-year-old lava restricts the Rogue River through much of its lower gorge. A massive landslide visible just west of Whiskey Creek briefly dammed 15 miles of the Rogue in the 1880s. Unusual kettle-shaped potholes in the riverbank rock, best seen near Clay Hill Rapids, form when floodwaters swirl pebbles in depressions, drilling them deeper.

History

The river's name comes from the Tututni and Takelma Indians, whom the early French trappers called *coquins* or "rogues." Angered by a sudden influx of gold-hungry whites, the Indians massacred Rogue Valley settlers in October, 1855, and then retreated to this remote part of the river canyon for winter.

The next April, 536 U.S. cavalrymen tracked them to Battle Bar and traded fire across the river before turning back. A month later, Chief Tyee John's well-armed Indians besieged a smaller Army unit on a knoll at Illahe, where battle trenches are still visible. Relief troops from the east fled when Indians rolled rocks on them from a hillside near Brushy Bar, but soldiers from Gold Beach

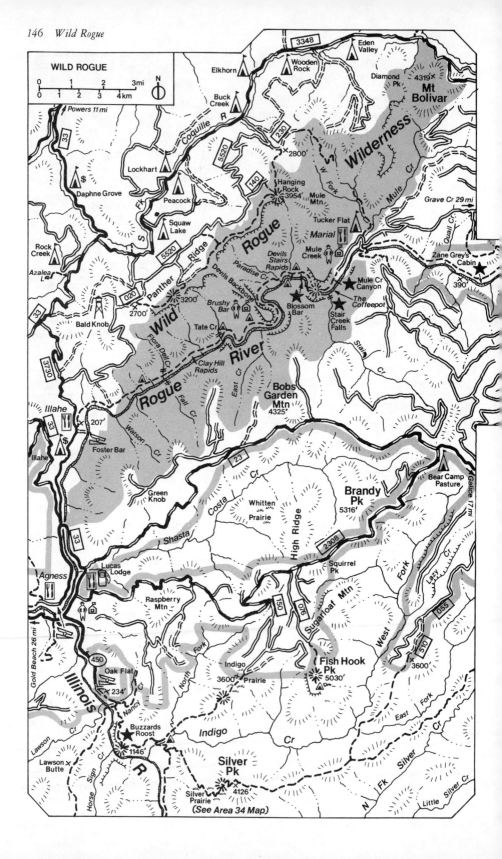

broke the siege. The Tututni and Takelma were transported north to the coastal Siletz Reservation.

In 1926, author Zane Grey bought a miner's cabin at Winkle Bar, where he fished and wrote his popular Wild West books. Few unguided parties ran the river until the late 1950s, when boatmen dynamited boulders in the most difficult rapids. Slim Pickens Rapids and Blossom Bar dropped to class 3 and class 4 whitewater, respectively.

Until 1963, mules packed mail on the Rogue River Trail from Marial to Agness,

Hikers should be alert for yellowjackets, wood ticks, rattlesnakes, and prolific growths of head-high poison oak. Campers can expect nocturnal visits by the area's numerous black bears, particularly in the Brushy Bar-Clay Hill area. Here, bears have grown bold from finding easy meals in boaters' "bearproof" cooler chests and hikers' backpacks. Hang all food at least 10 feet above ground and 5 feet from a tree trunk.

Lodges at Illahe, Clay Hill Rapids, Paradise Creek, and Marial offer meals and lodging by reservation. Scheduled daily jet boats take

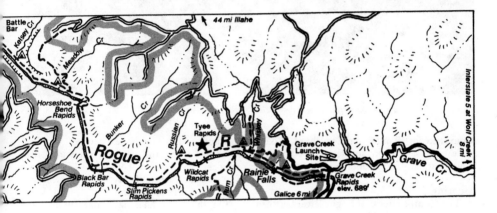

where mail boats left for Gold Beach. Although pavement now extends up the canyon to Agness, jet-powered mail boats still make the run, carrying tourists.

THINGS TO DO

Hiking

The prime trip here is the 40-mile Rogue River Trail backpack from Illahe to Grave Creek; day hikers can sample scenic parts of the route. Because the sometimes rocky trail traverses steep slopes several hundred feet above the river, it is closed to horses.

A 4.3-mile walk from Illahe to Flora Dell Creek's shady glen reaches a trailside waterfall which splashes into a swimmable pool. Those willing to drive the rutted dirt road to remote Marial, at the Rogue River Trail's midpoint, can hike 2.1 miles downriver, past inspiring viewpoints of The Coffeepot and Stair Creek Falls to Blossom Bar, a good spot to photograph frantic boaters. East of Marial, Zane Grey's tiny log cabin lies 5.7 miles up the trail. And from the Grave Creek trailhead, a 3.3-mile walk passes 15-foot Rainie Falls on the way to Whiskey Creek, where the Bureau of Land Management has preserved an historic 1880s mining cabin.

hikers from Gold Beach to the Clay Hill and Paradise Lodges between May 15 and October 15, and to Lucas Lodge in Agness between May 1 and November 1.

Surprisingly few day hikers make the trip up from the Coquille River campgrounds to the cliff-edge viewpoint at Panther Ridge's Hanging Rock. Bring binoculars to spot rafters on Blossom Bar, 3600 feet below.

The Illinois River Trail, south of Agness, offers an excellent 2.6-mile day hike (one way) to the craggy promontory of Buzzards Roost, with views both directions along this green-pooled river's canyon. Backpackers will want to hike the entire 27-mile Illinois River Trail (see area 34, Kalmiopsis, for a description). Those who can't arrange the required car shuttle can make a base camp at Indigo Creek for forays to the meadows of the rarely visited Silver Peak and Indigo Prairie areas, swept by fire in 1987.

One of the nicest day hikes in the area leads to 60-foot Silver Falls, in the narrow, fern-draped gorge of Silver Creek. Though this hike is not shown on the map, it's not difficult to locate. From Galice, drive 9 miles west on the paved Galice Timber Access Road to Soldier Camp Saddle and follow "Silver Creek" signs

Solitude Canyon, a mile downriver from Brushy Bar

from there for 10 miles to the trailhead. Hike 1 mile to Silver Creek, and then rock-hop 0.3 mile upstream to the double waterfall.

Boating

The 40-mile stretch of Rogue River between Grave Creek and Illahe is Oregon's most famous and popular three-day whitewater trip.

Rafts, kayaks, and drift boats have hardly left the launch before they hit the spray of class 3 Grave Creek Rapids. A few minutes later the increasing roar of 15-foot-tall Rainie Falls warns boaters to *portage* by lining craft down the shallow fish ladder on the right. Very large rafts often succeed in running massive Rainie Falls, passengers and all, but such vehicles later often wedge side-to-side in Mule Creek Canyon or hang up on Blossom Bar's boulders.

Beyond the falls, pull in at Whiskey Creek for a quarter-mile side trip to a well-preserved mining cabin. Downstream 1.2 miles, pull out again to scout class 4 Tyee Rapids. Keep to the far right to avoid a suckhole and then a house-sized rock. Promptly thereafter come class 3 Wildcat Rapids, concluded by a submerged, spiny-backed rock known as The Alligator.

After passing the lodge at Marial on the second day (or third, for slower drifters), boats accelerate toward class 4 Mule Creek Canyon, a chasm so narrow and turbulent that it's easy to lose an oar just when the need is greatest. After spring floods, scout from shore for logs jammed sideways. Past the canyon's final, dizzying Coffeepot comes Stair Creek's lovely side waterfall—a good swimming area.

Blossom Bar, 1.3 miles beyond, requires scouting from the right. Following this treacherous, class 4 boulder field are the Devil's Stairs, where the river drops 30 feet in a 300-yard series of chutes.

On the trip's final day, hike up to Tate Creek's shady waterfall pool, with a 25-foot natural slide of rock so smooth that swimmers can zip down its chute *sans* suits.

Campers on the heavily used riverbars and creek benches must use stoves or bring their own firewood and metal fire pans. In summer, seek out solitude by camping away from side creeks with drinkable water; for these sites, carry drinking water or purify river water.

Perhaps the greatest challenge of the Rogue River is getting a permit to launch at all. For an average year's July 1 to September 15 restricted season, the Siskiyou National Forest issues 10,000 permits by lottery from 90,000 applications.

Those without permits often sign up for a commercially guided trip (about $500) or join the mad rush of boaters during the free-for-all final weekends of September. A third alternative is to prepare for a trip in the off-season's iffy weather. By October, skies turn a misty gray and the river grows chilly, but solitude and empty campsites beckon. A few cautions: winter-high water can make the river too dangerous to run. And when snow closes the 55-mile car shuttle along twisty mountain roads (usually from November to May), the only alternative is a 180-mile paved route via Crescent City.

36. Grassy Knob

LOCATION: 51 mi S of Coos Bay, 9 mi E of Port Orford
SIZE: 39 sq mi
STATUS: 27 sq mi designated wilderness (1984)
TERRAIN: rain-forest-covered canyons and ridges
ELEVATION: 100'–2924'
MANAGEMENT: Siskiyou NF
TOPOGRAPHIC MAPS: Father Mountain, Mt. Butler, Sixes, Port Orford (USGS, 7.5')

Fog drips from the tangled forest of this virtually trailless wilderness, where ridgetops provide surprising glimpses out to Cape Blanco's fringe of ocean islands.

Climate

Heavy winter rains push the average annual precipitation over 130 inches. Summers are mostly sunny, since the area lies just inland of the coastal fog belt.

Plants and Wildlife

The rain forests here provide something precious in the heavily roaded southern Coast Range: pure, cold water. Close to 90 percent of the Sixes River's salmon spawn in Dry Creek and the South Fork Sixes River. Upriver clearcutting has pushed the Elk River's summer water temperatures to levels nearly fatal for fish, but Grassy Knob's small, shady creeks offer a cool retreat.

Here rare, old growth Port Orford cedar grow as much as 6 feet in diameter, with snaky limbs and characteristic white Xs on the underside of green leaf scales. Popular worldwide as a landscaping shrub, this fragrant cedar's small native range (five coastal counties) is shrinking rapidly. Japanese buyers pay as much as $10,000 for a single tree, since its wood is a close substitute for Japan's highly prized, and nearly extinct, hinoki cypress.

The *Phytophthora* root rot fungus, accidentally introduced here from Portland nurseries in 1944, travels easily through ground water, killing every Port Orford cedar in an infected drainage. Because the fungus can be carried in dirt on tire treads, the roadless side of Grassy Knob may be the wild Port Orford cedar's last stand.

Geology

Though largely hidden by forest, Grassy Knob's rocks consist of heavily folded and compacted seafloor sediment scraped up by the Klamath Mountains in the past 200 million years while that range slowly moved westward, overriding the Pacific plate.

History

A reconnaissance plane for a Japanese submarine dropped a 170-pound incendiary bomb into the forest between Grassy Knob and Dry Creek in 1942 in an attempt to start a forest fire. Alarmed rangers at the mountain's lookout tower radioed the Army Air Force. Because of confusion about the names of the nearby towns—Bandon and North Bend—U.S. fighters armed with antisubmarine depth charges streaked to the central Oregon town of Bend. Meanwhile, Japanese pilot Nubuo

Grassy Knob

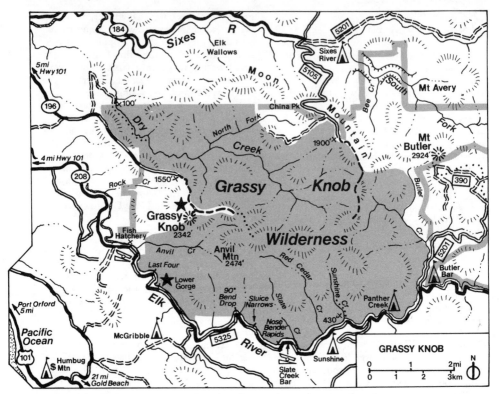

Fujita landed his plane at sea on pontoons, unbolted the wings, mounted the craft to his submarine's deck, and dived to safety.

However, the Japanese bomb failed to explode. Despite many searches, it has never been found.

THINGS TO DO

Hiking

The Grassy Knob Trail, converted to a 30-foot-wide gravel road in the waning months of the 1984 wilderness designation battle, is still the area's most interesting day hike. A barricade at the wilderness boundary keeps vehicles from this road's final 1.3 miles. The road is regrowing to forest so rapidly that it is shown as a trail on this map. Of interest are the plant succession in the trail itself, the old-growth Douglas fir forest on either side, and the view from Grassy Knob's former fire lookout site, a stone's throw from the trail's 0.3-mile mark. From the trail's end, a very roughly brushed-out trail route continues a mile to Anvil Mountain.

To drive to the Grassy Knob Trail from Port Orford, drive 4 miles north on Highway 101 and turn right on the Grassy Knob Road for 7 miles to the barricade.

Photographers looking for emerald-green glens of waterfalls, autumn-red vine maple, and droopy Port Orford cedar will want to hike the passable cross-country route up misnamed Dry Creek or ford the shallow Elk River and explore the mossy canyons of Sunshine Creek or Red Cedar Creek. For views of the area's forested ridges, try the abandoned trail to Mt. Butler from Road 390 or the abandoned road along Moon Mountain's ridgetop crest to a regenerating, 1-square-mile clearcut within the designated wilderness.

Boating

The Elk River winds between narrow rock walls, alternating emerald green pools with lots of class 4 whitewater. Launch at unmarked Slate Creek Bar, 6.35 miles by road from the take-out point at the Elk River fish hatchery. Just 0.2 mile from the launch, beware of Nose Bender Rapids, especially in low water, when this 6-foot drop's rating increases from 3 to 4. Other class 4 rapids include Sluice Narrows, 90° Bend Drop, the scenic Lower Gorge, and Last Four Rapids.

To drive to the river, turn off Highway 101 3 miles north of Port Orford. While driving to the launch site, scout the river for sweepers, the area's chief hazard.

37. Oregon Dunes

LOCATION: from Coos Bay to Florence
SIZE: 40 sq mi
STATUS: national recreation area (1972)
TERRAIN: sand dunes, ocean beach, lakes, forest
ELEVATION: 0'–500'
MANAGEMENT: Siuslaw NF
TOPOGRAPHIC MAPS: Oregon Dunes NRA (USFS); Goose Pasture, Tahkenitch Creek, Winchester Bay, Lakeside, Empire (USGS, 7.5')

Sea and sand lovers take note: here one can backpack through an oceanfront Sahara, hang glide off the top of 400-foot dunes, or gallop on 45 miles of beach. Bird watchers can count 247 species where meandering creeks cross the sand. And hikers can explore the wind-rippled sand hills that inspired author Frank Herbert to write the science fiction classic *Dune*.

Climate

A marine climate brings cool summers and wet, mild winters. Summer fogs occasionally burn off by afternoon. Spring and fall see the most sunshine. Average annual precipitation hits 85 inches.

Plants and Wildlife

On the beach itself, watch the waves for harbor seals and the spouts of gray whales (December to May).

At creek mouths, bald eagles and osprey swoop for fish. Canadian geese migrating on the Pacific Flyway stop to forage wild grains in the estuaries. In all, it's possible to tally 118 species of aquatic birds, 108 species of songbirds, and 21 species of birds of prey. In winter, hike across the south Siuslaw spit to watch hundreds of elegant tundra swans.

Rarest of the coastal birds is the small, chubby, western snowy plover, distinguished from sandpipers by its white shoulder yoke and its refusal to run piping along the beach's wet sand in search of food. Instead the plover finds sand fleas among driftwood and beachgrass near creek mouths, where it also scoops out its shallow sand nest in plain sight. Off-road vehicles (ORVs) and nest-robbing crows have cut coastal plover populations to under 100, though about 900 birds of the same species eke out a living beside desert lake playas in southeast Oregon, where ORV's are also becoming an increasing threat to their survival.

Plants and sand battle each other here on two fronts: to the east, winds shift the steep face of the high dunes 6 to 10 feet further inland each year, burying forests alive. To the west, European beachgrass (originally intro-

Patterns of sand in the dunes

Hiking is easiest on the wind-packed sand of a dune's windward side or crest

duced to stabilize sand near developments) has spread along the entire beachfront, creating a 30-foot-tall foredune that restricts sand blowing inland. Behind the foredune, winds have stripped a broad "deflation plain" of sand, allowing a succession of brush and trees to gain a foothold.

In the deflation plain behind the dunes, watch for the insect-eating sundew plant, which traps prey in its sticky drops of imitation dew. Among the alder and coast willow of the forest drainageways, look for yellow skunk cabbage and 8 of Oregon's 15 salamander species. In the spruce and hemlock forests, admire white trilliums in March, 20-foot-tall pink rhododendrons in April, and chanterelle mushrooms in October and November.

Geology

Most of Oregon's coastline is too steep and rocky to collect much sand, but here winds have repeatedly pushed waves of dunes inland across a coastal plain. Each fresh onslaught of sand buries forests, peters out, then sprouts with brush and trees of its own.

However, European beachgrass stabilized a wall-like oceanfront foredune a half century ago, blocking off the area's sand supply. The present high dunes are expected to run out of sand and stop their eastward march within 90 to 200 years. Since the stubborn European beachgrass regrows when burnt or plowed, the Forest Service has experimented with bull-

dozers breaching the foredune to set the dune-formation cycle in motion again.

The broad mudflats at the mouths of Oregon's coastal rivers are indirect products of the Ice Age. When enlarged polar ice caps converted much of the earth's water to ice, oceans dropped 300 feet and rivers cut their valleys deeper to match. When the ice melted 6000 years ago, the ocean rose into the widened river mouths. Sand and river silt have since converted these fjords to shallow estuaries.

History

The U.S. Army established Fort Umpqua on the Umpqua River spit in 1856 to watch over Indians of the Siletz Reservation to the north. In 1862, after a visiting paymaster found every officer, commissioned and non-commissioned, away on a a hunting trip, the fort was permanently closed.

Before completion of a coast highway in the 1920s, stagecoaches traveled the hard sand beaches of low tide between Florence, Reedsport, and Coos Bay. This led to public ownership of all Oregon beaches under the Oregon Department of Transportation. Beaches are now park land.

THINGS TO DO

Hiking

Short forest trails lead to the open sand, where hikers can explore dunes, tree islands, and lakes without need of marked routes. Remember that walking on the soft leeward face of a dune takes twice the time and energy of a hike on the compacted sand of a dune's crest.

Off-road vehicles are allowed in about 50 percent of the area; the noise, tracks, and danger of speeding dune buggies reduce the appeal of these zones to hikers. Beaches are subject to varying vehicle closure rules (see map) but warrant hiking regardless. The following hikes, listed from north to south, are outside ORV areas unless otherwise mentioned.

Swimmers at Cleawox Lake slide down a 100-foot sand dune into the clear water. This extremely popular lake borders both Girl Scout Camp Cleawox and Honeyman Park, a 382-unit state campground. While ORVs are banned near the south end of the lake, expect motor traffic when prowling over the dramatic dunes toward the area's interesting tree islands, Goose Pasture (a brushy bird-watching site), or the beach.

The short Siltcoos River meanders through campgrounds and dunes. A half-mile, self-guided nature trail around Lagoon Campground visits an oxbow slough of the river. From Waxmyrtle Campground, a trail and old

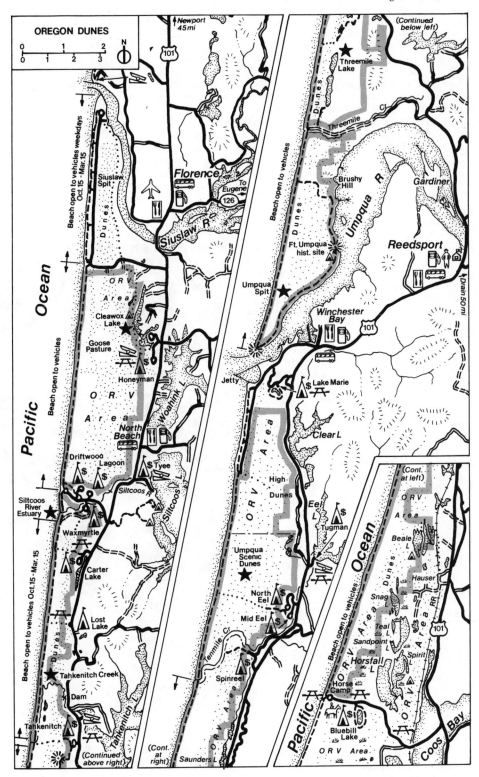

OREGON DUNES

N

0   1   2
0   1   2   3

↑ Newport
45 mi

101

(Continued below left)

Threemile Lake

Threemile

Cr

Dunes

Brushy Hill

Umpqua R

Gardiner

Siuslaw Spit

Florence

To Eugene

126

Siuslaw R

Beach open to vehicles weekdays Oct.15 - Mar.15

Dunes

Beach open to vehicles

Ocean

Pacific

O R V Area

Cleawox Lake

Goose Pasture

Honeyman

Washink L

North Beach

Driftwood Lagoon

Siltcoos

Tyee

Siltcoos R

Siltcoos

Siltcoos River Estuary

Waxmyrtle

Carter Lake

Lost Lake

Beach open to vehicles Oct.15 - Mar.15

Dunes

Tahkenitch Creek

Dam

Tahkenitch

Tahkenitch

(Continued above right)

Ft. Umpqua hist. site

Umpqua Spit

Winchester Bay

101

Jetty

Lake Marie

Clear L

O R V Area

High Dunes

Eel L

Tugman

Umpqua Scenic Dunes

North Eel

Mid Eel

Tenmile Cr

Spinreel

(Cont. at right)

Saunders L

Reedsport

↓ drain 50 mi

Ocean

Pacific

(Cont. at left)

O R V Area

Beale L

Dunes

Hauser

Snag L

Teal L

Sandpoint L

Spirit L

Horsfall L

Horse Camp

Bluebill Lake

O R V Area

101

RR

O R V Area

Coos Bay

Beach open to vehicles

O R V Area

sand road (open to vehicles from September 15 to March 15) lead 1.5 miles along the river and lower estuary past small dunes to the beach. For a pleasant short side trip prowl the sandy edge of the large beaver marsh south of this road; watch for beaver lodges.

Want a break from sun and sand? Hike 2 miles from Highway 101 through a cool, lush forest of ferns and Douglas firs to several primitive campsites on the shore of bulrush-lined Siltcoos Lake.

Some of the quietest and most spectacular sand landscapes lie between Tahkenitch Creek and remote Threemile Lake. From Tahkenitch Campground, follow a well-maintained 2.7-mile trail through stretches of deep forest to open dunes at the north end of Threemile Lake. Backpackers will find good campsites both among the dunes and in the trail's deep, sheltered forest at the sand's edge. Excellent longer hikes from here prowl north through the dunes to meandering Tahkenitch Creek or south to the Umpqua Spit.

Clams, huckleberries, dunes, and views lure hikers to the 6.5-mile-long Umpqua River Spit. For a scenic route to this vast sand peninsula, cross by boat from nearby Winchester Bay. Otherwise, park at the end of gravel on the Threemile Creek Road 100 yards short of the beach, hike south a mile on the beach, and follow a dune-buggy road inland to the dunes. Look for late August huckleberries on Brushy Hill; very low tides expose clamming mudflats along the Umpqua River below the hill. The long, rock jetty at spit's end is a good spot to watch pounding waves and ocean-going ships.

An easy warm-up hike near Winchester Bay loops a half mile around forest-lined Lake Marie at Umpqua Lighthouse State Park. Top the walk with a visit to the adjacent lighthouse.

ORVs dominate Oregon's tallest dunes, south of Lake Marie. Hikers bent on exploring these 400-foot sand mountains should watch for the red flags which ORVs display atop 9-foot antennas; dune buggies often zip over blind dune crests.

The 280-foot Umpqua Scenic Dunes nearby provide a 4-square-mile sand playground off limits to ORVs. A short forest trail from North Eel and Mid Eel Campgrounds leads to the open sand.

Beale Lake's scenic dunes, meadows, and isthmus make another good goal. Park at Hauser and hike along the railroad tracks 1 mile north to the lake.

Long-distance hikers can tramp the beach 23.7 miles from the tip of the Siuslaw Spit to the tip of the Umpqua Spit, but more interesting routes alternate beach hiking with dune exploration.

Throughout the Oregon Dunes, hikers should heed a few tips: carry plenty of water. When hiking cross-country to the beach, mark the return route through the foredune with a stick in the sand. The open dunes have few landmarks, especially in the frequent fogs; when lost, simply *listen*—the sound of surf or traffic will point the way to the ocean or Highway 101. Camp well above the beach's driftwood line (night has its high tide too), and bring a sleeping pad (sand is rock hard).

Equestrians often begin beach rides at the horse camp and loading facility near Bluebill

Lake Campground, though other beach access points are also feasible.

Boating

The coastal dunes have dammed dozens of large, many-armed freshwater lakes. Sinuous shorelines make for interesting canoe paddling. Steady west winds provide first-rate sailing conditions but can create large waves on summer afternoons. Warm water makes windsurfing practical.

Cleawox Lake, with its steep sand dune shore and long, narrow arms is the most popular nonmotorized boating site. Launch at crowded Honeyman Park.

Most other lakes have sandless forest settings and shorelines of water lilies, sedges, and cattails. Tahkenitch Lake and 5-square-mile Siltcoos Lake are heavily used by fishermen for warmwater bass and easily caught yellow perch.

Hang Gliding

Reliable west winds and unobstructed landing sites make the 400-foot-tall High Dunes an excellent practice area. Hike 1 mile east from the last parking lot south of Winchester Bay on the jetty road. Watch for ORVs.

Driftwood in the Siltcoos estuary

Folly Falls (photo by Sherry Wellborn)

38. Wassen Creek

LOCATION: 13 mi E of Reedsport
SIZE: 24 sq mi
STATUS: undesignated wilderness
TERRAIN: steep, densely forested creek valley
ELEVATION: 20'–1760'
MANAGEMENT: Siuslaw NF, Coos Bay
   District BLM
TOPOGRAPHIC MAPS: Scottsburg, Smith
   River Falls, Deer Hood Point, North Fork
   (USGS, 7.5')

In this forgotten Coast Range valley, Wassen Creek splashes over stairstep falls and eddies against dark cliffs. Side streams tumble from steep slopes of sword fern and salmonberry. Rain drips from the great, drooping branches of age-old red cedar, Douglas fir, and western hemlock.

Adventurers exploring the creek's 14 miles of trailless, twisting canyon must follow paths blazed by elk and bear—or else hike the route of the canyon's cheery water ouzels: the creekbed itself.

Climate

Torrential winter rains boost annual precipitation to 90 inches. The dry summers are free of the coastal fog which socks in Highway 101 just a few miles west.

Plants and Wildlife

In the deep forest look for white trillium and yellow Oregon grape in early spring. Rhododendrons put out pink blooms in April. By early fall both blue and red huckleberries are ripe for picking.

Expect great blue herons and Pacific giant salamanders at Wassen Lake. In old-growth woods, watch for the red top-feathers of pileated woodpeckers and the dark eyes of silent spotted owls. Kingfishers and water ouzels abound. Sea-run fish cannot leap the falls at the Devils Staircase, leaving the upper creek to small trout and bright red crawdads.

Geology

This part of the Coast Range began as mud-covered seafloor 50 million years ago. It lay directly in the path of the North American continent, which was crunching westward over the Pacific seafloor at the geologically speedy rate of an inch per year. However, a fracture in the Pacific floor lifted the Coast Range above the waves, where it became the western edge of the advancing continent.

As a result, Wassen Creek now flows over layers of weak sandstone and nutrient-poor, washed-out red clays that originated on the bottom of the sea. The area is roadless in part because roadcuts in such soils send entire hillsides sliding toward the creek. Wassen Lake itself formed when a slump dammed the creek's headwaters about 150 years ago. Snags of drowned trees still stand in the 5-acre lake.

THINGS TO DO

Hiking

Though trailless, the valley's unusual solitude and beauty inspire cross-country trips. Canyon slopes are too steep and rugged for bushwhacking, so plan to wear tennis shoes and wool socks, and wade along the creekbed itself. Wading is most pleasant in the warm weather of summer and early fall. Since the creek bottom is sandy but has some slippery mudstone, a walking stick is essential; hikers with packs will want two. Occasional parklike openings invited camping.

The easiest introduction to Wassen Creek is the 2-mile walk along the road from the Smith River. From Highway 101 at Gardiner, drive 16 miles up the Smith River (0.7 mile past the mouth of Wassen Creek) and park at a locked gate on the right. International Paper allows hikers to use this private road up Wassen Creek except when in use for logging operations. The road bridges the Smith River and then forks. Take the right fork, following the main gravel road past a private ranch, into a 1984 clearcut, across the culvert of Taylor Creek, and over some hills to a series of large concrete bridges across Wassen Creek at 1.7, 1.9, and 2.0 miles. For the adventurous, the seldom-seen Devils Staircase Falls lies 2.5 difficult trailless miles upstream. Need a head start on this challenging trek? Pick up keys to the road's locked gate at the Reedsport Office of International Paper (503) 271-3680.

To start cross-country hikes to Wassen Lake or Folly Falls drive north from State Highway 38 near Scottsburg on the Wells Creek Road (BLM 22-9-7.0) for 2.3 miles, fork left onto paved Fern Top Road (BLM 21-9-32.0) for 3.7 miles, continue *on pavement* on Wassen Lake Road (BLM 21-9-10.0) for 4.1 miles, and then watch carefully for Wassen Lake in the woods below the road. A short hike reaches this pleasant picnicking lake.

To continue to Folly Falls, climb back to the paved Wassen Lake Road, continue a mile north to gravel BLM Road 21-10-12.1, follow this 4 miles to Road 110, continue straight 1.7 miles, then turn left onto Road 119 to its end, avoiding smaller spur tracks. From here, walk down the ridge to find a trail paralleling the clearcut's edge. This rough path continues southeast into the forest down to the creek. Hang a bright marker by the creek to help locate the route back to the car for the return trip. Three rugged, trailless miles downstream are the falls, a lovely 15-foot curtain of water.

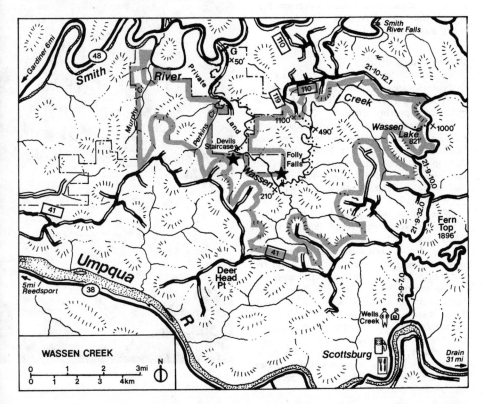

39. Oregon Islands

LOCATION: along Oregon coast
SIZE: 1477 islands/groups (1.2 sq mi)
STATUS: 56 islands/groups (0.8 sq mi)
   designated wilderness and national wildlife
   refuge (1978)
TERRAIN: small, wave-swept, rock islands
ELEVATION: 0'–327'
MANAGEMENT: Salem District BLM, Eugene
   District BLM, Coos Bay District BLM, US
   Fish and Wildlife Service
TOPOGRAPHIC MAPS: Cannon Beach,
   Nehalem, Tillamook, Cape Blanco, Port
   Orford, Gold Beach, Cape Ferrelo and other
   maps (USGS, 15')

Nesting seabirds and lolling sea lions crowd the nation's smallest and least accessible designated wilderness: surf-pounded islands scattered the length of Oregon's Pacific shore.

Climate

Wet, frostfree winters and cool, fog-shrouded summers push annual precipitation from 60 to 100 inches. Northwest winds bring fair skies; winter storms from the southwest batter the islands with 40-foot waves and high winds. Six- to twelve-foot tides submerge many rocks twice daily.

Plants and Wildlife

The islands' fascinating bird and sea mammal colonies are easily observed from mainland viewpoints, particularly with the aid of binoculars or a spotting scope.

From April to August, thousands of murres crowd the rocks to nest—the only time these black-and-white, loonlike birds visit land. Also in summer look for tufted puffins (with unmistakable, red-and-orange-striped bills) and their close relatives, the virtually neckless little auklets and murrelets.

When these birds leave for winter, other species arrive: long-necked loons, scoters (small sea ducks), and grebes (resembling clumsy, dark-backed swans). Year-round residents include five species of sea gulls and two kinds of black, crook-necked cormorants.

The brown dots one sees on these islands from a distance are often 600- to 2200-pound Steller's sea lions. Smaller harbor seals among the waves often watch humans with a curiosity rivaling our own. Also look for the spouts of gray whales, which pass here from December to February as they migrate toward Mexico, and from March to May as they return to

Alaska. Sea otters, whose fur first brought regular European trade to these shores, were driven to extinction in Oregon by 1911. An attempted reintroduction of sea otters near Cape Blanco in 1970 failed.

Most islands support few plants beyond sea palms and bobbing kelp seaweed. Others are topped with brushy salal, twinberry, and stunted spruce. Seacliff stonecrop, a thick-leaved flower threatened in Oregon, is known only from these islands.

Best wildlife viewing sites are at the Yaquina Head lighthouse 3 miles north of Newport, on the Cape Meares Loop Road west of

Tillamook, at Cape Kiwanda near Pacific City, at the state park on Cape Blanco, at Boardman State Park north of Brookings, and from the shore at Brookings itself.

In the few places where hiking on the islands is physically possible, access is prohibited to protect nesting species. Boats are allowed no closer than 200 yards to islands included in the federal wildlife refuge.

Geology

Wave erosion separated the resistant rock of these islands from the softer rock of the mainland, much as tides reduce a sand castle to the pebbles that once topped its towers. All islands north of Bandon consist of tough, black basalt. The pillow-shaped fracturing of this basalt proves it formed underwater, when lava squeezed between layers of seafloor mudstone 20 million years ago. Subsequent faulting raised the seafloor, creating the Coast Range.

The islands south of Bandon are 10 times older, belonging to the ancient Siskiyou Mountains. This fact doomed Bandon's landmark island, Tupper Rock. Composed of heavy, resistant Siskiyou blueschist prized for use in seawalls, it was quarried to the ground and now forms Bandon's south jetty.

Islands north of Boardman State Park near Brookings

California sea lion

History

Two of Oregon's offshore islands have been inhabited. Sea lion bones and clamshells remain from an Indian camp on (misspelled) Zwagg Island beside Brookings. Dutch hermit Folker Von Der Zwaag, who moved to the island in 1889 with his dog Sniff, is remembered for the trolley he devised to retrieve fresh water from the mainland automatically.

A lighthouse built with great difficulty on Tillamook Rock in 1879 was abandoned in 1957. A Portland real estate consortium purchased the island in 1980, converted the building to a mausoleum, and have since been bringing in cremated remains by helicopter.

Though an estimated 2 million birds used Oregon's offshore rocks in 1940, their numbers have declined to fewer than 500,000 because of development and fishing along the coast.

NORTHEAST OREGON

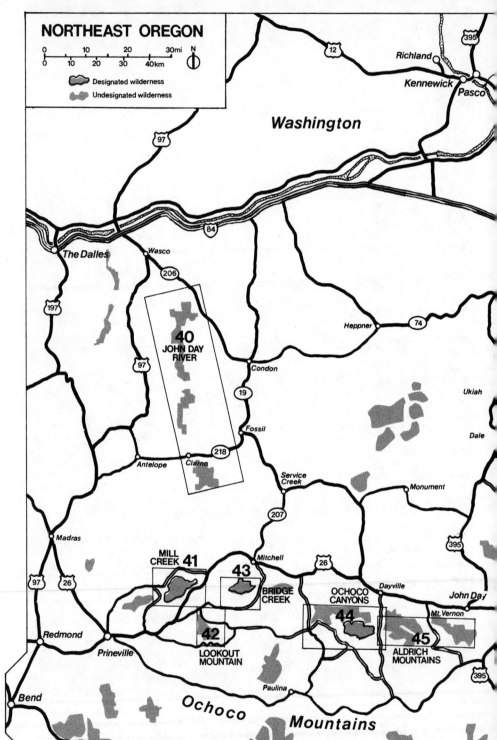

NORTHEAST OREGON

0   10   20   30mi   N
0   10   20   30   40km

Designated wilderness
Undesignated wilderness

Washington

Richland
Kennewick
Pasco

The Dalles
Wasco

Heppner

Ukiah
Dale

40
JOHN DAY
RIVER

Condon

Fossil

Service
Creek

Monument

Antelope
Clarno

Madras

MILL
CREEK **41**
Mitchell

43

BRIDGE
CREEK

OCHOCO
CANYONS
Dayville

John Day
Mt. Vernon

44

42

LOOKOUT
MOUNTAIN

45

ALDRICH
MOUNTAINS

Redmond
Prineville

Paulina

Bend

Ochoco   Mountains

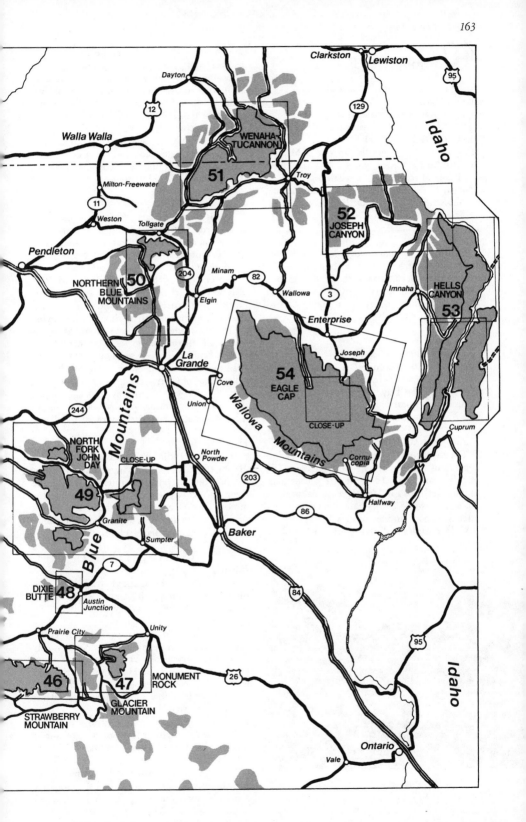

40. John Day River

LOCATION: 41 mi SE of The Dalles
SIZE: 93 sq mi
STATUS: state scenic waterway
TERRAIN: sagebrush canyonlands, river rapids
ELEVATION: 540'–3600'
MANAGEMENT: Prineville District BLM
TOPOGRAPHIC MAPS: Lower John Day River (BLM); Mitchell 2 SE, Mitchell 2 SW, Mitchell 2 NW, Chimney Springs, Bath Canyon, Shoestring Ridge, Horseshoe Bend, Indian Cove, Harmony, Esau Canyon (USGS, 7.5')

Boaters on the uncrowded John Day River sometimes float for a week through the winding, cliff-lined canyons without seeing more than a dozen people. Petroglyphs, fossils, and abandoned ranch houses make good goals for day hikes near the river.

Climate

The hot summers are virtually rainless; the freezing winters accumulate no snowpack. With just 10 inches of annual rainfall, this portion of the John Day only flows as a river because of precipitation in the distant Ochocos and Blue Mountains.

Plants and Wildlife

The sagebrush steppe here features hedgehog cactus (blooms red in April) and matlike prickly pear cactus. Look for rare yellow hairy Indian paintbrush in May. Occasional junipers dot slopes, while creeks harbor wild rose, red osier dogwood, and snowberry.

Golden eagles and prairie falcons patrol the

The John Day River at Rattlesnake Canyon (photo by William L. Sullivan)

canyon skies. Canada geese, mergansers, goldeneyes, and green-winged teals paddle ahead of boaters. The river's salmon runs died in 1889 with construction of a since-demolished grist mill dam. Steelhead, trout, bullhead, and suckers remain. Smallmouth bass, introduced in 1971, thrive.

Hikers should be alert for scorpions and rattlesnakes, though chances are greater of meeting wild horses, mule deer, coyotes, and startled, partridgelike chukars.

Geology

Fossils from the Clarno Unit of the John Day Fossil Beds National Monument indicate this area was a coastal rain forest 34 million years ago. Primitive rhinoceroses and tapirs flourished alongside ferns and avocado trees.

The creation of the Cascade Range 16 to 25 million years ago not only dried up this area by blocking moisture from the sea, it also buried the landscape repeatedly with volcanic ashfalls, preserving skeletons of saber-toothed tigers and small, three-toed horses. The many layers of red, buff, and green volcanic ash form the "painted hills" visible on the west riverbank 4 miles north of Clarno. Vast floods of Columbia River basalt 13 to 16 million years ago capped the area with a rimrock of black lava; cliffs exhibit basalt's characteristic hexagonal pillars.

History

Numerous Indian housepit sites and petroglyphs (painted rock carvings) testify to over 4,500 years of human habitation along the river. White settlers in 1866-1930 built the remote riverside ranches whose abandoned buildings remain. Be sure to leave all homesteading memorabilia in place.

THINGS TO DO

Hiking

The area's only marked trails are two quarter-mile interpretive nature paths at the picnic area of the John Day Fossil Beds National Monument near Clarno.

Spring Basin is a good spot to try cross-country hiking in the high desert. Wear sturdy shoes and carry water. From the basin's sagebrush plateau, climb to Horse Mountain's pinnacled viewpoint or explore the winding side canyons leading toward the John Day River (though the river's bank is private here). To reach Spring Basin from Clarno, drive 1.5 miles east on Highway 218, turn right onto a dirt road for 3 miles, park, and hike 2 miles up a BLM track to the east.

Walk up sandy-bottomed Rattlesnake Canyon between narrow rock walls, and then scramble cross-country up Amine Peak for one of the area's highest viewpoints. To reach the mouth of Rattlesnake Canyon, park in the same spot as for the Spring Basin hike, but then walk south along the riverside dirt road 5 miles.

Some of the area's finest cross-country hikes prowl the river's side canyons and bluffs in the BLM-owned land between Clarno and Cottonwood Bridge. Since the only public access to these remote lands is by boat, hikes must be planned in conjunction with float trips.

Climbing

The John Day Fossil Beds National Monument offers several small blocks and towers, ranging from the level I-4 Steigomonster to the II-5.2-A3 Hancock Tower.

Boating

Plan for four lazy days by raft or three thrilling days by open canoe to drift the 70 scenic miles between Clarno and Cottonwood Bridge. Timing is critical, because this undammed river varies from an unnavigable maelstrom in winter to an unfloatable dribble in September. Safe water levels (1800 to 4200 cubic feet per second, measured at the Service Creek gauging station) are most likely from April to July and again in November.

The river's wildest water, Clarno Rapids, begins 4.4 miles downstream from the Clarno Bridge launch site. This class 3, canoe-swamping section becomes a class 4 canoe-wrecker at water levels above 4000 cubic feet per second. Scout or portage on the left, remembering that Lower Clarno Rapids (class 2) lies just downstream. Beyond, however, the only serious whitewater is class 2+ Basalt Rapids, 15.9 miles from Clarno Bridge.

Expect good camping spots in the Basalt Canyon, a 4-mile-long gorge below Basalt Rapids. Then look back upriver to spot Arch Rocks' twin hoops atop a cliff. Just before Horseshoe Bend, watch the right bank for two wagons used in a 1928 movie here. Then, a mile past Horseshoe Bend, stop at Potlatch Canyon on the right to observe (but not touch) the cliff's Indian petroglyphs. Cave Bluff's river-level cavern makes a fun stop 3.5 miles further downstream. Another 10 miles along are Hoot Owl Rock, an owl-shaped clifftop pillar, and Citadel Rock, a fortress-shaped palisade. Cottonwood Bridge is the last public take-out site before a falls and the tamed Columbia's backwaters.

Many who float the John Day launch 44 miles upriver from Clarno at Service Creek. The two- to three-day run to Clarno includes class 2 rapids 6, 15, and 23 miles downriver from Service Creek.

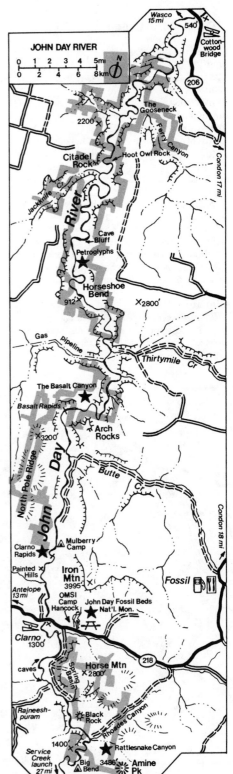

41. Mill Creek

LOCATION: 20 mi NE of Prineville
SIZE: 24 sq mi
STATUS: designated wilderness (1984)
TERRAIN: forested upland valley
ELEVATION: 3725′–6181′
MANAGEMENT: Ochoco NF
TOPOGRAPHIC MAPS: Central Oregon
   (BLM); Ochoco Reservoir, Lookout Moun-
   tain, Opal Mountain, Stephenson Mountain
   (USGS, 7.5′)

Mill Creek is a wholly-preserved Ochoco
mountain valley with excellent forest trails,
good rock climbing sites, and sweeping viewpoints. Considering that this valley lies just
one hour's drive east of Bend, it's surprising
Mill Creek is a little-known wilderness in a
generally overlooked mountain range.

Climate

The area receives only 25 inches of precipitation annually, primarily as winter snow. Summers are dry and fairly hot. Late spring and fall
are pleasant.

Plants and Wildlife

Mill Creek preserves one of the Ochocos' few
remaining climax forests of ponderosa pine and
bunchgrass. Wildfires traditionally cleared
such forests of underbrush. However, biologists worry that decades of overzealous fire sup-
pression have allowed an understory of Douglas
fir to grow, enabling future fires to reach above
the large ponderosa pines' fire-resistant trunks
to their flammable crowns.

Livestock grazing limits most other native
flora. Rocky Mountain elk, hunted virtually to
extinction here in the 1970s by teams using
aerial spotters, are repopulating.

Geology

The Ochoco Mountains formed as a string of
coastal volcanoes 40 to 50 million years ago,
before the Cascade Range existed. Twin Pillars
remain as the plug of an eroded volcano. When
the Ochoco volcanoes subsided and the Old
Cascades roared to life 25 million years ago,
massive ash deposits covered eastern Oregon,
collecting in lakes and rivers. One such rhyolite ash deposit subsequently welded together
to form the resistant tuff outcropping at Whistler Point. Look there, in the Ochoco Agate

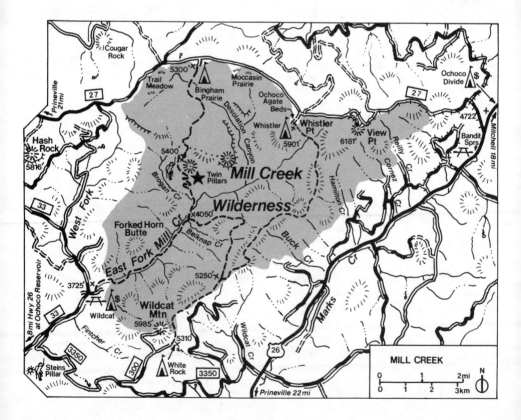

Old growth ponderosa pine on the trail to Twin Pillars (photo by Don Tryon)

Beds off Road 27, for baseball-sized thunder-eggs. The thunderegg, Oregon's state rock, forms when small cavities in the tuff fill with quartz and agate.

THINGS TO DO

Hiking

A well-maintained trail follows the East Fork of Mill Creek through an old-growth ponderosa pine forest. Start at Wildcat Campground to hike the nearly level first 3.5 miles of this trail as a pleasant, undemanding day hike. To reach Wildcat Campground from Prineville, follow Highway 26 east 9 miles to Ochoco Reservoir, then turn left for 9 miles on Road 33.

For longer hikes, Wildcat Campground is nearly always the endpoint, because its elevation is 2000 feet lower than the other three trailheads in the wilderness. A particularly scenic 8-mile trip down to Wildcat Campground begins at Bingham Prairie, off Forest Road 27, and passes the lichen-covered lava towers of Twin Pillars. Another popular 10-mile route starts at the White Rock Campground, on the shoulder of Wildcat Mountain, where a lookout tower offers views of the Ochocos and distant Cascades. A third route to Wildcat Campground, from Whistler Point on Forest Road 27, is 13 miles.

Potential backpacking campsites are plentiful throughout. Only creeks named on the map are year-round water sources.

Climbing

Twin Pillars are a pair of vertical-sided, 200 foot andesite plugs at 5500 feet, 1.5 miles from the Bingham Prairie trailhead. Though quite scenic and challenging (rated II-5.7), they are rarely climbed because of the proximity of the more challenging Steins Pillar, 3 miles southwest of Wildcat Campground on Forest Road 33. This 400-foot overhanging spire of welded tuff, unscaled until 1950, offers routes from level III-5.6-A3 to IV-5.7-A4.

Winter Sports

Ochoco Divide on U.S. Highway 22 generally has enough snow for cross-country skiing and snowshoeing from January through March. The highway is plowed in winter, allowing access to unplowed roads along the eastern edge of the wilderness. View Point makes a scenic goal, 5 miles up Road 27.

42. Lookout Mountain

LOCATION: 25 mi E of Prineville
SIZE: 26 sq mi
STATUS: undesignated wilderness
TERRAIN: forested ridges, grassy plateau
ELEVATION: 3979′–6926′
MANAGEMENT: Ochoco NF
TOPOGRAPHIC MAPS: Lookout Mountain
(USGS, 15′); Central Oregon (BLM)

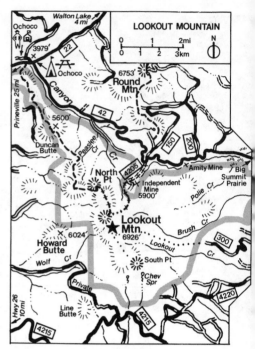

From the parklike meadows of Lookout Mountain's broad top, views stretch beyond the forested Ochoco Mountains to a string of High Cascades snowpeaks.

Climate

Winter snow accounts for most of the area's 30 inches of annual precipitation. Summers are dry and warm.

Plants and Wildlife

This is prime elk, wild horse, and mule deer range. Watch for herds in the high meadows during summer, and in the cover of low-elevation forests during winter. Open, parklike forests of ponderosa pine invite cross-country travel, while wetter northern slopes host Douglas fir and larch (with scenic orange needles in October). At the summit are subalpine fir and lodgepole pine.

Geology

A lava flow forms the flat top of Lookout Mountain. This basalt oozed from vents north of the John Day River about 25 million years ago, smothering most of the Ochoco Moun-

Mule deer buck in velvet

tains. Outcroppings of older Ochoco rock in the valleys prompted an 1873 gold rush and some cinnabar mining.

THINGS TO DO

Hiking

Two routes reach the vistas atop Lookout Mountain. A 7.5-mile trail from the Ochoco Ranger Station picnic area climbs nearly 3000 feet along a rocky ridgeline, passing frequent viewpoints. A shorter, less scenic route follows a closed jeep track 2 miles from the Independent Mine on Road 4205; hikers can easily continue through meadows from the end of the jeep track to the summit. To drive to the start of either route from Prineville, follow Highway 26 east 16 miles, then bear right on Road 22 for 8 paved miles to the Ochoco Ranger Station.

For a longer backpacking route, connect the Lookout Mountain Trail with the 7.5-mile Round Mountain Trail by hiking across Road 42. The well-marked route to Round Mountain crests that peak's summit and descends to popular Walton Lake Campground.

Winter Sports

Cross-country skiers can drive up Road 42 to snow level and ski up the snowed-in road past the Independent Mine. The reward is great, for Lookout Mountain's high, 2.5-mile-long summit meadows have the Ochocos' best snow and superlative views.

43. Bridge Creek

LOCATION: 39 mi E of Prineville
SIZE: 8 sq mi
STATUS: designated wilderness (1984)
TERRAIN: forested plateau, cliffs, slopes
ELEVATION: 4320'–6816'
MANAGEMENT: Ochoco NF
TOPOGRAPHIC MAPS: Central Oregon
   (BLM); Mt. Pisgah (USGS, 7.5'); Lookout
   Mountain (USGS, 15')

At the edge of the Ochoco Mountains' summit plateau, North Point's 600-foot cliff overlooks central Oregon and Cascade peaks from Mt. Adams to the Three Sisters.

Climate

The area receives 30 inches of precipitation annually, primarily as winter snow. Summers are dry and hot.

Plants and Wildlife

Mixed conifer thickets of Douglas fir, true fir, and larch dominate the area, with bands of lodgepole pine and ponderosa pine. Clearings of sagebrush, bunchgrass, and sparse, gnarled mountain mahogany break up the plateau forests.

Mule deer and elk find good cover and browse here year round, but especially when hunting season drives them from roaded areas. Watch for prairie falcons, goshawks, and the large, red-headed pileated woodpeckers

North Point, overlooking Ochoco Butte and Mitchell (photo by William L. Sullivan)

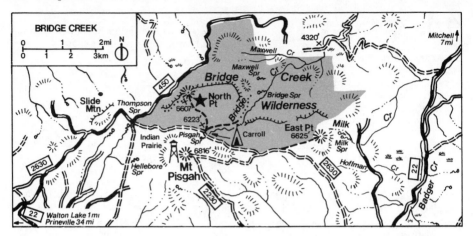

which, because of their reliance on forest snags, are an indicator species for old growth Ochoco forests.

Geology

North Point's cliff of pillar-shaped basalt columns is the edge of a lava flow capping most of the Ochoco crest. Vents north of the John Day River produced this lava about 25 million years ago.

THINGS TO DO

Hiking

The breathtaking view at North Point is an easy 1.2-mile walk up an old, closed jeep track from the Bridge Creek crossing of Road 2630, near undeveloped Carroll Campground. To reach the starting point from Prineville, follow Highway 26 east 16 miles, bear right onto paved Road 22 for 16 miles, then turn left on unpaved Road 2630 for 7 miles.

Conifer thickets stymie most off-trail hikers in this wilderness; however, frequent winds at North Point have stunted vegetation there, allowing easy and interesting cross-country hiking along the cliff edge for a mile on either side of the point. Bushwhacking becomes increasingly difficult—but possible with map and compass—for hikers intent on making a loop trip by continuing west to Thompson Spring, or along the cliff rim southeast to Bridge Creek.

East Point's rounded knoll offers lesser views; it's 1.5 miles along an arrow-straight jeep track from Road 2630.

The trail to Bridge Spring has been trampled into oblivion by the cattle which graze this sparse wilderness range each summer. Although the watershed is the domestic water supply for the town of Mitchell, Bridge Spring and Bridge Creek usually are churned to mud by hooves.

Bridge Creek's valley, from the rim near East Point (photo by William L. Sullivan)

44. Ochoco Canyons

LOCATION: 77 mi E of Prineville, 40 mi W of
   John Day
SIZE: 54 sq mi
STATUS: 21 sq mi designated wilderness (1984)
TERRAIN: steep, forested canyons, sagebrush
   slopes, rocky creeks
ELEVATION: 2840'–6871'
MANAGEMENT: Ochoco NF
TOPOGRAPHIC MAPS: Central Oregon
   (BLM); Aldrich Gulch, Wolf Mountain, Six
   Corners, Antone, Day Basin, Dayville
   (USGS, 7.5')

Three major canyons—each with its own
trail system and splashing creek—provide scenic examples of the Ochoco Mountains' remarkable transition from dense forests to
sagebrush lowlands.

Climate

Summers are hot and dry. Snowfall from
November to April brings the annual precipitation to a sparse 20 inches.

Plants and Wildlife

Water determines where there will be forest
and where sagebrush dominates in these steep
mountains. Exposed ridgetops and sunny
south slopes are brown and bald. Green swaths
of forest cling to shady north slopes and fill the
steep canyons—like biological glaciers winding downhill to the arid lowlands, where all
melts to brown again.

A hike through the forest reveals bands of
lodgepole pine, ponderosa pine parklands, and
dense Douglas fir and white fir thickets.
Spruce budworms have killed some of the
Douglas fir. At creek's edge, expect an oasis of
false Solomon's seal, coneflower, snowberry,
wild gooseberry, and delicate twinflower.

Bear, coyote, mountain lions, deer, and elk

Upper Black Canyon Creek (photo by William L. Sullivan)

Black Canyon (photo by William L. Sullivan)

are common year round. Watch for migratory cranes and geese passing overhead on their way to the Malheur Refuge to the southeast.

Geology

Black Canyon's winding, cliff-lined lower gorge, and the similar canyon of the adjacent South Fork John Day, resulted when these streams cut through the basalt lava which once flooded much of central Oregon. In Picture Gorge, 12 miles to the north, the John Day River has cut through no fewer than 17 layers of this basalt. The lava, now characterized by rusty specks of weathered olivine, spread from vents north of Dayville as far as Idaho 16 million years ago. Nonetheless, this outpouring was dwarfed a few million years later by Oregon's next round of basalt floods, which filled much of the Columbia River Basin.

THINGS TO DO

Hiking

The 11.6-mile Black Canyon Trail descends along a rushing mountain stream to a narrow, cliff-walled gorge. Before starting out from the trailhead at Wolf Mountain, take a short side trip to the East Wolf fire lookout—a tall tree topped with a crow's nest platform built in the early 1920s. No longer climbable, the lookout offers good views of Black Canyon from ground level. To find the lookout tree, walk 0.2 mile cross-country east along the canyon rim from the Wolf Mountain trailhead.

Drive to Wolf Mountain from Prineville by turning right from Highway 26 a mile east of town. Follow the paved Post-Paulina Highway 59 miles to a "Y" 4 miles past Paulina, keep

left on paved Road 42 for 8 miles. Turn right on Road 58 for a mile, then turn left onto gravel Road 5810 for 10 miles. Take Road 5840 to the right 3 miles to the trailhead.

Where Black Canyon's gorge narrows on the

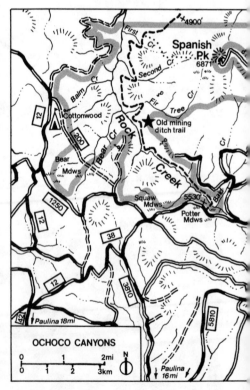

final 2 miles of the Black Canyon Trail, the path crosses the chilly, 15-foot-wide creek 12 times; bring tennis shoes for wading. Likewise, there is no bridge at trail's end across the South Fork John Day to Road 47. This river is unfordable in high water from January to April, but idles along only calf-deep in summer.

Three side trails also connect with the Black Canyon Trail: a half-mile shortcut from Road 5820 to Owl Creek, a 4.5-mile route down from Mud Springs Campground to Big Ford, and a steep, poorly marked 1.4-mile path from Big Ford to Seven Sixty Spring on Road 38.

Rock Creek's forested valley is steep, but the trail through it is not. Most of its 9 miles follow an almost perfectly level, abandoned ditch chiseled out of the canyon wall in the 1890s for gold mines once active north of here. Start at the Potter Meadows trailhead on Road 38, follow the mountain creek 2 miles, then begin the in-gully, out-ridge wanderings of the dry canal. At the 4-mile mark, the ruins of a log cabin at Fir Tree Creek make a good turnaround spot for day hikers. Five miles beyond, the increasingly rough ditch trail ends at private land. However, a trail planned for construction in 1989 will climb 2.5 miles from

the ditch trail to Spanish Peak, the area's highest point and best view. Until this handy connecting trail is complete, cross-country hikers can follow the open route to Spanish Peak with map and compass.

Cottonwood Creek meanders through the most isolated canyon of all. An often steep, 4-mile-long forest trail descends to the creek from spur Road 700 off Road 38. The path then follows Cottonwood Creek 0.8 mile downstream and joins a private dirt road leading to the Mascall Ranch at Picture Gorge.

Cross-country travel is easy enough in this wilderness along the many unforested ridgecrests, but creek-bottom conifer thickets make for slow going. One rugged but worthwhile bushwhacking route descends Balm Creek's canyon 1.5 miles from Cottonwood Campground to join the ditch trail along Rock Creek.

Winter Sports

Snowed-under ridgetop roads provide quiet routes for ski tours. Spanish Peak makes the most challenging and spectacular goal. Expect sufficient snow for skiing between December and March. Skiers must drive to snow level and park, for roads are rarely plowed.

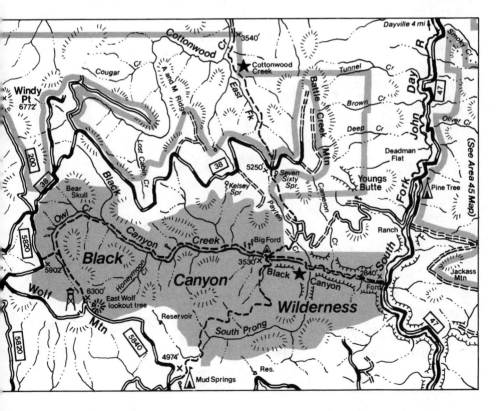

45. Aldrich Mountains

LOCATION: 11 mi W of John Day
SIZE: 91 sq mi
STATUS: undesignated wilderness
TERRAIN: broad mountains, sagebrush slopes, forest
ELEVATION: 2649'–7363'
MANAGEMENT: Malheur NF, Burns District BLM, Oregon Department of Fish and Wildlife
TOPOGRAPHIC MAPS: McClellan Mountain, Big Weasel Springs, Aldrich Mountain S, Aldrich Gulch, Aldrich Mountain N, Dayville (USGS, 7.5')

Dead Horse Mountain and Riley Creek Gorge, from a ridge near Packsaddle Gap (photo by William L. Sullivan)

This little-known range between the Ochoco and the Strawberry mountains preserves two wild areas. In the west, the Aldrich Mountain lookout rises above the forests and sagebrush gulches of the Murderers Creek Wildlife Area. In the east, a dozen peaks with bare, 2000-foot-tall shoulders cluster about McClellan Mountain.

Climate

Most of the area's scant 20 inches of annual precipitation fall as snow from November to April. Hot summer afternoons may bring thunderstorms.

Plants and Wildlife

Bighorn sheep highlight the Murderers Creek Wildlife Area, between the South Fork John Day River and the Aldrich Mountain summit. Once driven to extinction here by domestic-sheep diseases and hunting, the wild sheep increased to about 60 head since their reintroduction in 1978. They prefer Smoky Gulch and Oliver Creek's upper canyon. Sleek pronghorn antelope summer along Murderers Creek and winter in the north of the area. Elk rely on the timbered areas for winter cover, and mule deer come from as far as Strawberry Mountain for winter forage. Mountain lions,

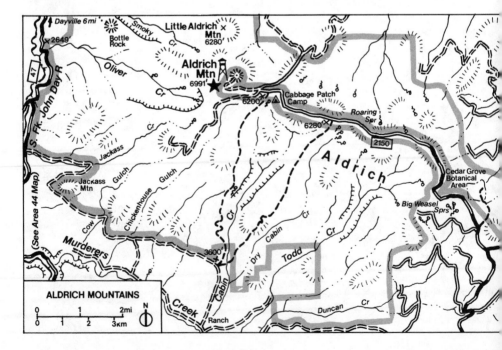

ALDRICH MOUNTAINS

coyotes, rattlesnakes, meadowlarks, and mountain cottontails are also in the area. Bald eagles winter near Dayville.

Sagebrush, bunchgrass, juniper, and yellow-bloomed rabbit brush dominate the lower elevations and south-facing slopes. Douglas fir and white fir forests cling to north slopes and cap Aldrich Mountain. Near McClellan Mountain only the canyon bottoms are forested, with stately ponderosa pine and larch.

The Cedar Grove Botanical Area preserves a biological oddity—60 acres of Alaska cedar, isolated 130 miles from other Alaska cedar stands. An easy 1-mile trail from Road 2150 leads to the grove.

Geology

The Aldrich Mountains began as seafloor mud and sand 150 to 250 million years ago. Though far from the ocean, their jumbled strata are typical of a coastal mountain range like the western Klamaths. One may conclude that before the Cascades and present Coast Range arose, Oregon's coastline ran diagonally from the Klamaths to the Blue Mountains, with the Aldrich Mountains as a seacoast ridge.

THINGS TO DO

Hiking

A steady 2.2-mile climb reaches the area's highest point, Fields Peak, with views of the John Day Valley and Blue Mountains beyond.

Find the signed trailhead by turning south from Highway 26 on Road 21 (the junction is 13 miles east of Dayville and 18 miles west of John Day); follow Road 21 for 8 miles, then turn left on Road 2160 for 2.5 miles. The trail's first mile is a steep, rutted dirt road.

Riley Creek's trail, in a wooded canyon between impressive, bare mountains, makes another good day hike. After a half mile hikers can either follow the creek cross-country to peer ahead into the creek's gorge, or follow steep trails up Riley Mountain or Dead Horse Creek to broader views. Drive Road 21 south from Highway 26 for 20 miles, then turn left on Road 2190 for 5 miles to the road's end and trailhead.

A topographic map, compass, and water are essential throughout the area, for trails are sometimes faint and many interesting routes are cross-country. This is particularly true on the steep, western flanks of Aldrich Mountain where wildlife observation is best. To spot bighorn sheep in winter, park on the South Fork John Day Road 47 between Smoky and Oliver creeks and hike cross-country up the ridge to an excellent viewpoint at Bottle Rock. In summer, start at Aldrich Mountain and hike down. Another scenic cross-country route follows the steep, open ridgetops from Fields Peak to Moon Mountain or McClellan Mountain. But don't tackle these rough, multi-thousand-foot elevation gains in poor shoes or in hot weather.

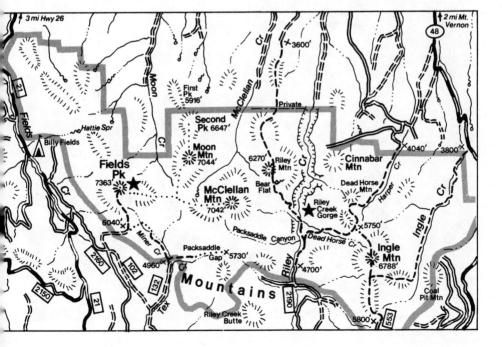

46. Strawberry Mountain

LOCATION: 4 mi SE of John Day
SIZE: 123 sq mi
STATUS: 107 sq mi designated wilderness
(1964, 1984)
TERRAIN: snowpeak, forest valleys, high
meadows, lakes
ELEVATION: 3570'–9038'
MANAGEMENT: Malheur NF, Burns District
BLM
TOPOGRAPHIC MAPS: Strawberry Mountain
Wilderness (USFS); Pine Creek Mountain,
Canyon Mountain (USGS, 7.5'); Prairie City
(USGS, 15')

For a lesson in eastern Oregon's diversity,
visit the Strawberry Range. Above the John
Day River's alfalfa fields, above an arid band of
sagebrush and juniper, dense conifer forests
rise past blue lakes, waterfalls, and alpine
wildflowers to palisades of snow-draped crags.

Climate

Since most of the area lies over 6000 feet in
elevation, snow closes trails from November to
June and lingers across high passes until mid-
July. Summers are fair and warm, with some
thunderstorms and freezing nights. Snow flurries may interrupt October's typically cool,
clear Indian summer. Annual precipitation
measures 40 inches.

Plants and Wildlife

Five of the United States' seven major biologic zones are packed into this relatively small
mountain range. Larch, the only conifer to lose
its needles in winter, spangles the high forests
with autumn gold. Other trees include Engelmann spruce, white pine, Douglas fir, white
fir, lodgepole pine, and ponderosa pine. The
area's name derives from the wild strawberries
rampant in mid-elevation forests; watch for
their fruit in July and bright red leaves in
October.

Bighorn sheep, reintroduced here after local
extinction, now thrive on Canyon Mountain.
Look for them up Sheep Gulch from Highway
395. Rocky Mountain elk and mule deer summer here in profusion, and seek shelter during
autumn hunting season. The Canyon Creek
Archery Area, south and west of Indian Creek
Butte, has been off limits to firearms each fall
since the 1930s. Other wildlife include black
bear, coyote, mountain lion, bobcat, pine
marten, ground squirrels, and golden eagles.

Strawberry Lake (photo by William L. Sullivan)

Strawberry Falls (photo by William L. Sullivan)

Geology

The western half of the Strawberry Range is a chunk of sub-seafloor buckled up from the Pacific by the westward drift of North America 200 to 250 million years ago, before the creation of the Cascades and Coast Range made this an inland area. Canyon Mountain consists of reddish peridotite, greenish serpentinite, and crumbly brown basalt—all indicative of oceanic crust.

The eastern half of the Strawberry Range, beginning at Indian Creek Butte, consists of much younger volcanic rock. About 15 million years ago, volcanoes here spewed out immense amounts of ash and lava, burying the southern Blue Mountains. Rabbit Ears is the eroded plug of one vent. Above Wildcat Basin, colored ash deposits have weathered into a scenic badlands.

Ice Age glaciers carved the many broad, U-shaped mountain valleys. They also left sandy moraines (visible in Indian Creek Canyon) and cirque lakes. Strawberry Lake formed when glacial ice retreated and the steep valley wall collapsed, blocking Strawberry Creek with a landslide.

History

Traces of gold in Canyon Mountain's peridotite launched a decade of intense placer mining in 1862, when Canyon City began as a tent town of 10,000 men. Pioneer Oregon poet Joaquin Miller lived and wrote in the boomtown during 1863-69.

THINGS TO DO

Hiking

This compact mountain range features rugged alpine scenery and a thorough trail system with room for week-long backpacking treks. Mountain lakes are rare in eastern Oregon, so the seven in this area are popular. To limit overuse, do not camp beside these small lakes, but do try the many scenic trails to less trodden meadows, ridges, and creek valleys.

From Strawberry Camp, a 1.2-mile uphill walk reaches Strawberry Lake with its photogenic backdrop of snowy crags. But save some film; another 1.1 miles up the valley, Strawberry Falls cascades 40 feet onto boulders glowing with moss. Once at the falls, day hikers have at least three options: head back, ramble on another level 0.6 mile to a good lunch stop at Little Strawberry Lake, or tackle the climb to Strawberry Mountain's panoramic viewpoint. The climb makes for a demanding 6-mile hike from trailhead to summit and gains 3300 feet in elevation, but the trail grade is good and after all, this is one of Oregon's tallest peaks.

Slide Lake is another popular destination from the Strawberry Camp trailhead. It's 4.3 miles, with Little Slide Lake just a short distance beyond. Get to the trailhead via Prairie City on Highway 26; turn south on Main Street and follow signs 11 miles to Strawberry Camp.

For a shortcut to the top of Strawberry Mountain, start at a trailhead on the southern side of the wilderness, past Indian Springs Campground at the end of Road 1640. From there, a 4.1-mile trail climbs just 1100 feet to the top. Also from the Road 1640 trailhead, a good beginner's day hike ambles 1.3 miles to High Lake's scenic basin. Those who continue 1.8 miles past High Lake up a steep pass are rewarded with a view of Rabbit Ears and Slide

Lake's glacier-carved valley. For an even broader view, hike cross-country from this pass up a cliff-edged ridge to Indian Spring Butte. To reach this trailhead, take Highway 395 south of John Day 10 miles, turn left on Road 15 for 16 miles, turn left on Road 16 for 3 miles, and take gravel Road 1640 to the left; the trailhead is 11 miles uphill.

Wildcat Basin's July wildflowers make a good goal. Take the 2.4-mile trail up from Buckhorn Meadows, at the end of Road 1520. Follow Road 15 from Highway 395 for 10 miles, turn left on Road 1520, and follow it past the Canyon Meadows Reservoir.

Two uncrowded day hike trails on the south side of the wilderness follow creeks to mountain lakes. One trail heads up Lake Creek to High Lake, and the other follows Meadow Fork past a waterfall to Mud Lake. Both routes are 3.5 miles one way. With a car shuttle, hikers can either combine the two hikes or start out at the high-elevation Road 1640 trailhead and make the trip into an easy downhill romp. From Highway 395, take Road 15 for 16 miles, head left on Road 16 for 6.5 miles to Logan Valley, then turn left on Road 934 to

Murray Campground. From there the Lake Creek trail begins 2.3 miles ahead at the end of Road 934; turn right from Murray Campground for 3 miles to reach the Meadow Fork trailhead at the end of Road 021.

Berry Creek and the East Fork of Canyon Creek splash through stately forests in deep canyons. Backpackers often take the trails along these streams when trekking to the higher country, especially to the small meadow and spring at Hotel de Bum Camp, 9 miles from the Road 812 trailhead. Day hikers will find the creekside paths soothing, but may have trouble deciding when to turn back.

The Canyon Mountain Trail offers a different challenge. Blasted into the rugged upper slopes of the Strawberry Range, this route offers lots of scenery, but very few campsites. For 15 miles between Dog Creek and Hotel de Bum there is only one reliable creek, and the flattest tent sites are in possibly windy passes. Still, the route's start makes a first-rate day hike, and it's the closest trail to Canyon City. Just take Main Street 2 miles uphill from Highway 395 and take a dirt road to the right 2.5 miles toward the abandoned

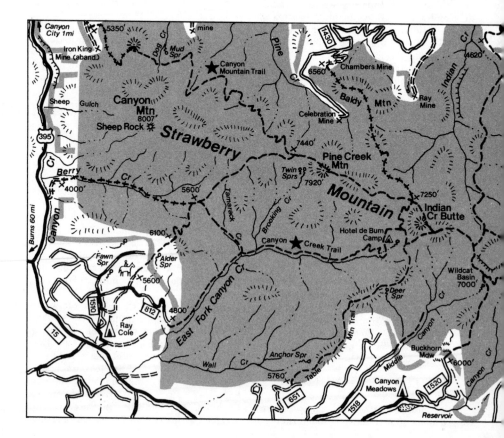

Iron King Mine.

A complete circuit of the area's high lakes makes a fun two- or three-day backpacking trip. The 15-mile loop from the Road 1640 trailhead passes Strawberry Mountain, Strawberry Lake, Slide Lake, and High Lake. Add 2 miles if starting from Strawberry Camp. Allow time for side trips.

To really experience the Strawberries, try backpacking the entire length of the mountain range's crest. It's 42 miles, starting with the Skyline Trail's forested ridge in the east and ending with the Canyon Mountain Trail's rugged slopes in the west.

Winter Sports

There's plenty of snow in these mountains but it's a challenge to get to it when most access roads are unplowed. When snow covers low elevations from January to March, one solution is to park along plowed Highway 395 at the (state-owned) Berry Creek Ranch. Ski or snowshoe over the little bridge across Canyon Creek and head up Berry Creek.

Another midwinter option is to park 2 miles up Canyon City's Main Street and ski the Iron King Mine road 2.5 miles to the Canyon Mountain Trail. The first 2.4 miles of this trail are not too rugged, yet offer excellent viewpoints.

Paved roads 14, 15, and 16 are also plowed, giving skiers access to excellent snow on the south and east sides of the Strawberry Mountain Wilderness. From the summit of Road 14 (5899 feet) ski up side Road 101 and the woodsy Skyline Trail. From Road 16 in Logan Valley (not shown on the map), ski up side Road 1640. Snowed-under Indian Springs Campground is 8 miles along this road; adventurers can snow camp at Indian Springs and continue 7 miles to the summit of Strawberry Mountain itself.

Strawberry Lake in winter is a goal worth a journey. Expect snow to block the unplowed access road 2 to 8 miles short of the trailhead.

Some of the best snow, and best views, are atop Baldy Mountain on the Pine Creek Trail. The access Road 1430, though unplowed, is seldom blocked by snow more than 2 or 3 miles before the trailhead at the Chambers Mine. This road joins Highway 26 east of John Day 6 miles.

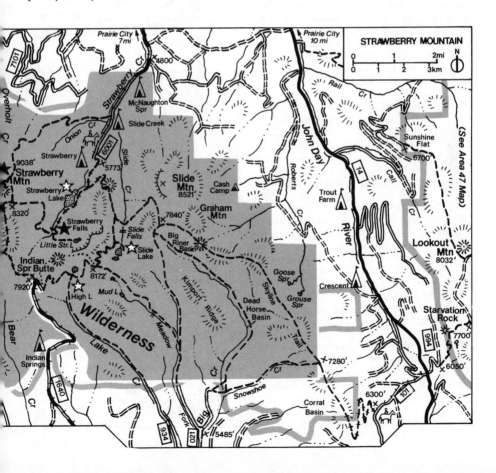

47. Glacier Mountain and Monument Rock

LOCATION: 26 mi E of John Day, 52 mi SW of Baker
SIZE: 91 sq mi, including Wildcat Creek area
STATUS: 31 sq mi designated wilderness (1984)
TERRAIN: steep, forested canyons, open ridges
ELEVATION: 4300'–8033'
MANAGEMENT: Malheur NF, Wallowa-Whitman NF
TOPOGRAPHIC MAPS: Bullrun Rock, Little Baldy Mountain, Deardorff Mountain, Rastus Mountain (USGS, 7.5'); Prairie City (USGS, 15')

At the southernmost edge of the Blue Mountains, this area's alpine, once-glaciated ridges offer views across much of eastern Oregon. The canyon forests are dense enough to shelter the reclusive, bearlike wolverine.

Climate
The John Day Valley funnels winter storms and summer thundershowers eastward to the mountain ridges here. As a result the area receives 40 inches of annual precipitation, twice as much as the surrounding, arid lowlands. Expect snow to block trails over 6000 feet from November to May. Summer brings hot days and chilly nights.

Plants and Wildlife
A wolverine sighted west of Table Rock in 1980 provides rare evidence that this unusual animal still exists in Oregon. Named "skunk bear" for its habit of scenting uneaten food, and *Gulo gulo* (Latin for "glutton glutton") for its diverse appetite, the wolverine resembles a small, bushy-tailed, gray-headed bear. Though only 18 to 42 pounds, its ferocity successfully drives coyotes, bears, and even mountain lions away from contested carrion.

Wolverines and mountain lions are among the few predators that dare to eat porcupines, a locally abundant species. Watch for porcupines during the day on low tree limbs (where they gnaw on bark and sleep), and at night in human campsites (where they eat sweaty backpack straps and fishing rod handles for the salt).

The unstocked Little Malheur River preserves a population of rare, red-banded trout. The area's 70 bird species include the creek-loving water ouzel and the red-headed pileated woodpecker.

Ponderosa pine and juniper sparsely forest the lowlands and dry south-facing slopes. Al-

pine meadows, June wildflowers, and spire-shaped subalpine fir top the high ridges. Thickets of mixed conifers crowd other areas.

Geology
Glacier Mountain, Lookout Mountain, and Little Baldy Mountain are glacial horns, their sides steeply scalloped by the U-shaped valleys of vanished Ice Age glaciers. That the equally high Monument Rock area shows so little of this scenic glacial topography remains a puzzle.

The rocks are mostly 15-million-year-old

lava and ash from vents near Strawberry Mountain, but an outcropping of much older, more mineralized rock on Bullrun Mountain and Mine Ridge has spawned several small mines.

History

The lichen-covered 8-foot cylindrical stone monument atop Monument Rock may have been erected by pioneer sheepherders. The Snake Indians who once roamed here are not known to have built such megaliths, but did leave pictographs on a natural rock arch at Reynolds Creek.

THINGS TO DO

Hiking

The area's high ridges feature easy trails to dramatic viewpoints. Even the road to the Lookout Mountain trailhead, dirt Road 548, provides thrilling views as it traces a narrow ridgeline from Sheep Mountain. From Road 548's gate, the tops of Lookout Mountain and Glacier Mountain are a half hour hike away, but require some cross-country scrambling. A popular day hike continues past the gate on the abandoned road (now maintained as a trail) along the nearly level ridgeline 4 miles to Little

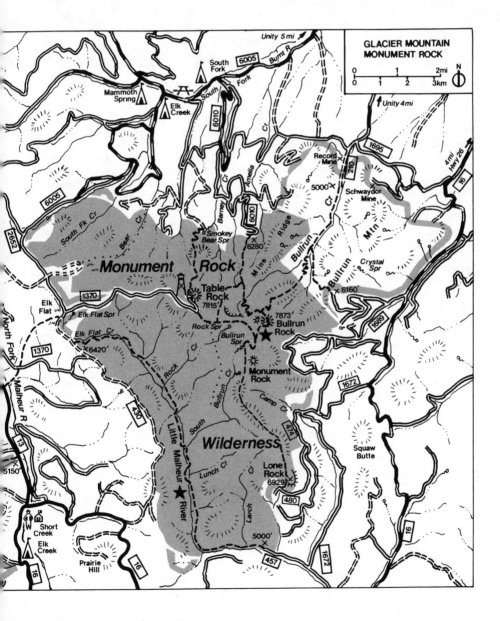

The John Day Valley, from Little Baldy (photo by William L. Sullivan)

Baldy Mountain's summit meadow, and the best view of the John Day Valley.

Reach Road 548 from Prairie City by turning south on Main Street; drive 24 paved miles southeast on what becomes Road 14, turn left 1 mile past the road's summit onto dirt Road 1665 for 4 miles, then turn left on Road 548 to the trailhead.

The fire lookout tower on Table Mountain is a good place to begin a visit to the Monument Rock area. After taking in the view, backtrack a half mile down the lookout road and take a level 2-mile stroll along an ancient dirt road to Bullrun Rock's 150-foot cliffs. A fork of this trail winds close to Monument Rock and continues 5 miles along a scenic ridgecrest to Lone Rock.

To reach the Table Rock lookout from Highway 26, drive west from downtown Unity up the South Fork Burnt River 16 miles following Road 6005, turn left on Road 2652 for 2 miles, then take Road 1370 to the left. To reach the trailhead from Prairie City instead, turn south from Highway 26 on Main Street, follow a paved county road southeast 9 miles, turn left onto Road 13 for 12 miles, then take Road 1370 to the left.

Several streamside trails in deep forest offer cool retreats during summer's heat. The 2-mile path up Reynolds Creek traces this moss-banked, splashing stream well into its shady canyon. To visit this area's interesting natural rock arch, leave the Reynolds Creek Trail just after a major gulch appears on the left, 1.6 miles from the trailhead. Scramble 0.3 mile up a ridge to the left to a large basalt outcrop with the arch, some Indian pictographs, and a nice view of the valley. To get to the trailhead from

Highway 26, take Prairie City's Main Street southeast 8 miles, then turn left on Road 6210 for 4 miles to the Reynolds Creek bridge.

A 10-mile trail follows the Little Malheur River from Road 457 to the river's source at Elk Flat. The best day hike starts at the bottom and aims for a lunch stop near aptly named Lunch Creek. Beyond, the trail crosses the river four times, requiring cold wades or log crossings. Reach the trailhead via main Road 16; at the Little Malheur River bridge turn onto Road 457 and follow it to its end.

Sheep Creek's trail has the advantage that day hikers who arrange a car shuttle can easily make the trip one way downhill. It's 6.5 miles from the Road 548 gate at Lookout Mountain to Road 13 at the bottom. In October the creek's broad glacial valley glows with bright orange quaking aspen and larch.

The Bullrun Creek Trail starts out with 2 easy miles of hiking in a steep-sided canyon, but then climbs 2000 feet in 3.5 miles up a ridge to Bullrun Rock. Drive to the trailhead from Highway 26 by heading west from downtown Unity on a paved road for 1 mile, then turning left onto gravel for 4 miles. Jog to the right on Road 1695, then follow Road 210 to the trail.

One of the more accessible and popular hikes climbs past Starvation Rock, a large basalt monolith, to Road 548 on the narrow ridge between Sheep Rock and Lookout Mountain. Backpackers and equestrians can use this path as a connector between the Glacier-Monument and Strawberry Mountain trail systems, which are here less than 2 miles apart (see area 46 map).

48. Dixie Butte

LOCATION: 26 mi NE of John Day, 50 mi W of
  Baker
SIZE: 19 sq mi
STATUS: undesignated wilderness
TERRAIN: forested butte and bench cut by creek
  valleys
ELEVATION: 4000'−7592'
MANAGEMENT: Malheur NF
TOPOGRAPHIC MAP: Bates (USGS, 15')

Dixie Butte from the Davis Creek Trail (photo by William L. Sullivan)

This prominent, cone-shaped butte over-looks a broad slope of pristine forestland—a wilderness island in an otherwise heavily roaded and logged portion of the Blue Mountains.

Climate

Snow blocks the Davis Creek Trail from about Thanksgiving to late April, the same period during which the Dixie Mountain Ski Area operates. The 30 inches of annual precipitation are chiefly snow. Summers are dry.

Plants and Wildlife

Mule deer and elk rely on the area for browse, and for cover during fall hunting season. Larch trees and creekside golden currant bushes provide orange foliage in October. The virtually unbroken forests are mostly Douglas fir and white fir, with some ponderosa and lodgepole pine.

Geology

Though shaped like a volcano, Dixie Butte was born of water. The peak's rocks are seafloor sediments buckled up by the Blue Mountains when they were a coastal range 200 to 250 million years ago. Lava flows from the Strawberry Mountains 15 million years ago covered the plateau below the Davis Creek Trail.

History

Southern gold prospectors here during the Civil War christened Dixie Butte and (Jefferson) Davis Creek to spite the Union men who named the area's new county for Ulysses S. Grant.

THINGS TO DO

Hiking

The Davis Creek Trail contours 5.5 miles through Dixie Butte's forests. The creeks feature small log bridges, and elk often show themselves along the way. After the hike, plan to drive to the Dixie Butte lookout tower for an overview of the trail's route, as well as a bird's eye view of the snowy Strawberry Mountains across the John Day Valley.

Winter Sports

The snowed-under roads looping through the foothills of Dixie Butte make ideal cross-country ski trails. Start at the Dixie Mountain Ski Area (warming hut, rope tow), and remember the route taken, since as many as six roads converge at intersections. In midwinter, park at Austin Junction for a nearly level 3.2-mile jaunt along Road 2614 to icy Davis Creek.

The area's premier challenge is the 5.5-mile climb up Road 2610 to the summit's un-matched winter view. Beware of avalanche danger on steep roadsides.

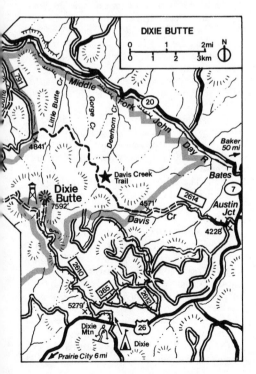

49. North Fork John Day

LOCATION: 61 mi S of Pendleton, 13 mi W of
Baker

SIZE: 617 sq mi

STATUS: 190 sq mi designated wilderness
(1984)

TERRAIN: snowy mountain ranges, rugged
river canyons, forested benchlands, cirque
lakes

ELEVATION: 3356'–9106'

MANAGEMENT: Umatilla NF, Wallowa-
Whitman NF, Malheur NF, Vale District
BLM

TOPOGRAPHIC MAPS: North Fork John Day
Wilderness (Sylvan Services); North Fork
John Day Wilderness (USFS); Anthony Lakes,
Bourne, Elkhorn Peak, Crawfish Lake, Mt.
Ireland, Trout Meadows, Greenhorn, Pearson
Ridge, Tower Mountain (USGS, 7.5');
Desolation Butte, Bates, Dale (USGS, 15')

The largest wild area in the Blue Mountains,
this sprawling complex of wilderness lands encompasses two entire mountain ranges—the
craggy Elkhorns and the Greenhorns—as well
as a major river, the North Fork John Day.
Here roam the largest share of the Blue Mountains' 52,000 elk and 150,000 mule deer.

Though separated by paved or well-graveled
roads, each of the units of this wilderness has
plenty of room for day hikes or long backpacking trips. Not to be missed are the Elkhorn
Crest Trail's 24 miles of alpine scenery and the
North Fork John Day River Trail's 25 miles of
winding gorge. In addition, Anthony Lake offers a Nordic skiing center with access to the
wilderness in winter.

Climate

Snowfall is heaviest in the Elkhorn Mountains, where the Anthony Lake Ski Area usually operates from Thanksgiving to April 15.
Snow blocks hiking trails over 7000 feet until
early July; the lower part of the North Fork
John Day River Trail is clear of snow as early as
April.

Annual precipitation hits 45 inches in the
Elkhorns, but drops to 20 inches in the western
canyons. Summers are dry. October, though
generally pleasant, may bring sudden snowstorms. Night temperatures can dip below
freezing year round.

Plants and Wildlife

This is elk country, where 800-pound bulls
with 5-foot-wide antlers bugle challenges to
rival males each fall. More than twice as large

as the mule deer, which are also common here,
elk bulls assemble harems of up to 60 cows during the August to October rut. In this season,
listen at dawn or dusk for the bulls' bugles:
snorts that rise to a clarinetlike whistle and end
with several low grunts. Also look for saplings
stripped of bark to mark territory, and elk wallows—small bogs dug by hooves and laced
with urine as a bull's private orgy site.

Many of the area's deer and elk winter in the
Bridge Creek Wildlife Area south of Ukiah,
but others remain, able to survive in this high
country's heavy snows by shifting daily between north- and south-facing slopes. The
north-facing canyon slopes with dense conifer
forests provide shelter from snow and wind.
South-facing slopes are sparsely forested, allowing winds to expose the dried grass which
elk rely on for food.

Summer hikers find bright green moss,
shiny-leaved twinflower, and pink-bloomed
prince's pine on the shady north slopes of canyons, while sunny south slopes feature wild
strawberry and huckleberry on a dry floor of
pungent ponderosa pine needles.

High in the Elkhorn Mountains, rock-lined
lakes appear to have just been released from a
glacier's grip; others have filled in to become
marshy wildflower-filled meadows. Lower
basins have grown over with subalpine fir and
Engelmann spruce.

Dead and dying conifers throughout much
of the area are evidence of the mountain pine
beetle, which bores into pine bark, and the
spruce budworm, which feeds on new needles
of Douglas fir, grand fir, and spruce. Not all
barren conifers are dead, however; larch
normally sheds its needles for winter, span-
gling the forest with orange foliage each
October.

Recovering from widespread dredging of
stream gravels for gold in 1920-54, the North
Fork John Day River now provides spawning
grounds for 70 percent of the John Day River's
steelhead and 90 percent of its Chinook
salmon. The fish runs, which peak in late August, help feed a population of bald eagles.

Geology

The granite and scrambled sedimentary rock
here reflect the Blue Mountains' history as a
volcanic range paralleling the coast 30 to 200
million years ago. Erosion has stripped away
the old volcanoes, revealing the granite of their
magma chambers. When magma cools slowly
to form large-crystaled granitic rock, gold and
silver collect along the rock's quartz veins—
hence this area's colorful mining history.

Columbia River basalt flows buried the area
about 15 million years ago. Erosion stripped

Aerial view of Baldy Lake and Ireland Mountain

this lava from the Elkhorn and Greenhorn Mountains when they later rose. Finally, Ice Age glaciers scalloped the ranges with scores of U-shaped glacial valleys.

History

Sumpter, Bourne, Granite, and Greenhorn are picturesque gold mining boomtowns dating from an 1862 gold strike. Ancient prospects, tailings, and a few small active mines dot hills near the towns, though the easy placer diggings are gone. An abandoned gold dredge near Sumpter once churned many valleys in these mountains to gravel wastelands.

Part of the North Fork John Day River Trail follows an abandoned mining ditch once used to bring water to gold sluices. The Forest Service is gradually acquiring many of the old claims and gold mining log cabins within the wilderness.

THINGS TO DO

Hiking

The most popular day hikes explore the Elkhorn Mountains' alpine scenery. Anthony Lake, ringed with rugged peaks, is easy to get to from Interstate 84, making it the only destination in the entire area likely to be crowded.

A nearly level 1-mile warm-up hike from the Anthony Lake Campground passes Lilypad Lake and skirts rugged Gunsight Mountain to Black Lake. Another easy 1-mile hike starts at the south end of Anthony Lake and ascends Parker Creek to the Hoffer Lakes along a self-guiding nature trail. From Hoffer Lakes, however, the area's best view is just another 1.5 miles away and 1000 feet up; continue on a long switchback to The Lakes Observation Point, atop a craggy ridge.

For an excellent sample of the high Elkhorns' scenery, take the 7-mile loop trail from Anthony Lake entirely around Angell Peak and Gunsight Mountain. The well-built path gains only 1300 feet along the way, passing wildflowers in Crawfish Meadows and a view of Dutch Flat Lake's bowl-shaped hanging valley.

Crawfish, Van Patten, Red Mountain, and Summit lakes are noteworthy day hike goals in the northern portion of the Elkhorns. Each lake lies in its own high glacial basin, between 1.2 and 1.5 miles from a trailhead.

Rock Creek Lake fills a breathtakingly stark, treeless cirque, backed by the cliffs of the Blue Mountains' highest peak, 9,106-foot Rock Creek Butte. Mountain goats frequent the cliffs behind the lake. Both routes to this lake require 2200-foot climbs: the 4-mile trail

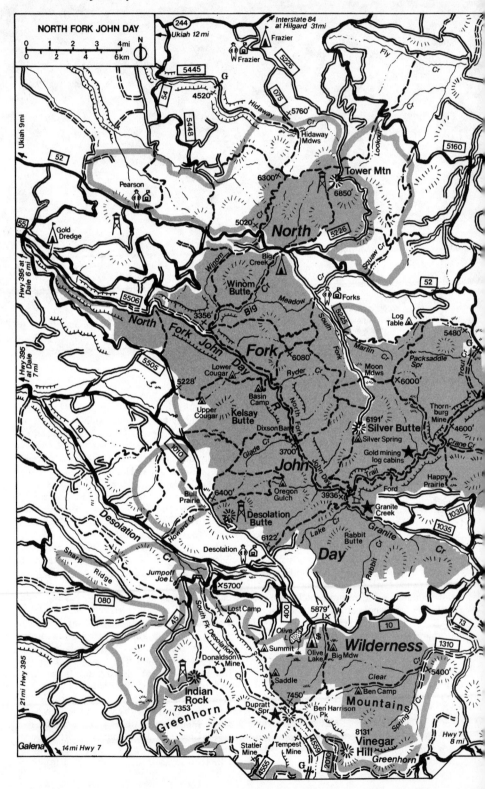

NORTH FORK JOHN DAY

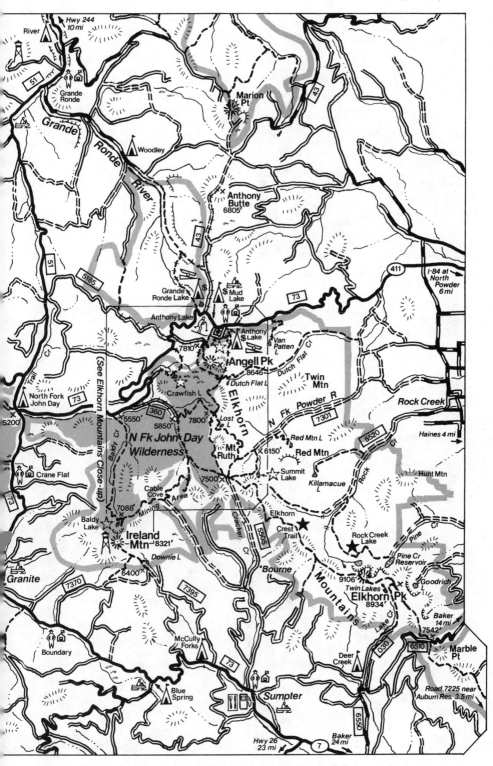

Gunsight Butte and Anthony Lake (photo by William L. Sullivan)

from Road 5520 and the 3-mile path from Pine Creek Reservoir. The last 2 miles of dirt road to Pine Creek Reservoir are rugged even for four-wheel-drive vehicles; plan to park and walk.

For a taste of the Elkhorn Crest Trail, start at Road 6051 near Marble Point and hike 4 miles along the ridge to the Lake Creek Trail junction. From there, switchbacks lead 0.7 mile down to Twin Lakes; more energetic souls can scramble up trailless Elkhorn Peak for a view of Baker and the distant Wallowa Mountains. Hikers who've planned a car shuttle can head home via the steep 3-mile Lake Creek Trail to Road 030.

On the west side of the Elkhorns, the wildflowers of Cunningham Cove and the view at Nip and Tuck Pass lure hikers up a steep, switchbacking, 3.5-mile trail from Peavy Cabin at the end of Road 360. Nearby, a 6-mile trail up the quiet Baldy Creek Valley from Road 73 leads to Baldy Lake, overtowered by Ireland Mountain. For a path to Ireland Mountain's lookout tower, however, start from Road 7395 out of Sumpter. The 2.5-mile trail climbs 2000 feet. Don't miss the short side trip to Downie Lake.

The Greenhorn Mountains, dotted with small, active mines, offer trails and old mining tracks among broad, subalpine summits. Dupratt Spring is one of the most scenic goals, at a rocky pass between the deep, glacier-carved valleys of South Fork Desolation Creek and Granite Boulder Creek. Three day hikes lead

Gold mining cabin on the North Fork John Day River Trail (photo by William L. Sullivan)

there. Shortest is the 3-mile mining track from the Vinegar Hill lookout road. A 5-mile trail climbs to Dupratt Spring along Summit Camp's forested ridge from a spur of Road 400. And the 6-mile Princess Trail follows the view-filled Greenhorn Mountain crest to Dupratt Spring from the Indian Rock lookout tower.

The winding 25-mile canyon traced by the North Fork John Day River Trail offers new vistas at every bend: forests plunging down 1000-foot slopes into the brawling stream, rustic log cabins among lodgepole pines, and towering rock outcroppings. Should the weather turn, even the private log cabins are left unlocked as emergency shelter (though many have rats and leaky roofs).

Day hikers can easily sample this impressive canyon trail at three points. The most popular route follows Granite Creek 3.5 miles from Road 1035 to a footbridge across the North Fork John Day and a meadow with an old log cabin. At the canyon's eastern end, hikers starting from the North Fork John Day Campground can follow the river 3 miles to a bridge across rushing Trout Creek. At the canyon's western end, Road 5506 provides a third river-level access to the North Fork John Day River Trail.

Those unable to arrange a car shuttle for end-to-end backpacking trips along the Elkhorn Crest or North Fork John Day River Trails should consider several loop hike alternatives. A 31-mile loop from the Granite Creek trailhead climbs from Dixson Bar to Moon Meadows before returning via Wagner Gulch and the upper portion of the North Fork John Day River Trail. A 29-mile loop from the North Fork John Day trailhead at Road 5506 climbs the Winom Creek Trail to the Tower Mountain lookout, then returns along the Big Creek Trail. And a 16-mile loop near the Desolation Guard Station climbs from Road 45 up the scenic South Fork Desolation Creek Trail to Dupratt Spring, then returns past Saddle and Lost Camps; save time to scramble up 400 feet to Ben Harrison Peak's view.

Climbing

The Elkhorn Mountains feature granite cliffs (rare in Oregon) up to 300 feet tall. Though scenic, the area lacks named routes and crowds of climbers because of its remoteness and the fact that all peaks have walk-up sides.

Winter Sports

The Anthony Lake Ski Area provides use of 6 miles of groomed Nordic trails for a fee. However, Nordic skiers and snowshoers have many other options.

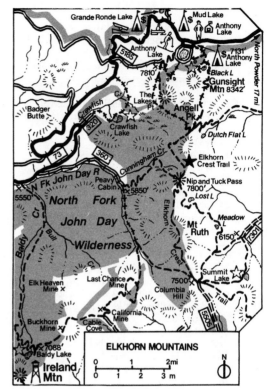

Start with an easy 1-mile jaunt around Anthony Lake or to nearby Black Lake. Then try snowed-under Road 43 north of the Grande Ronde Campground; it follows a nearly level ridgeline with outstanding views for 7 miles to the slopes of Anthony Butte.

Iced-over Crawfish Lake is another fun trip. Ski there cross-country from the top of the Anthony Lake Ski lift, or ski along Road 73 (unplowed west of the Anthony Lake ski area) to either of two 1.5-mile trails to Crawfish Lake.

Van Patten Lake, set in a narrow basin below Van Patten Ridge's cliffs, is a nice 1.5-mile ski tour up from Road 73.

Take the Anthony Lake chairlift to start the dramatic 7-mile loop around Angell Peak. Pass up this challenging trip if weather or avalanche danger threatens.

Boating

The North Fork John Day is not generally considered navigable through its wilderness portion due to boulders and low water levels. Raft and kayak trips on the North Fork commence at Dale and follow 40 miles of class 2+ whitewater to Monument.

Motorless boats are allowed on small, scenic Anthony Lake.

50. Northern Blue Mountains

LOCATION: 26 mi E of Pendleton, 9 mi NW of La Grande
SIZE: 233 sq mi
STATUS: 32 sq mi designated wilderness (1984)
TERRAIN: plateaus cut by steep, partly forested canyons
ELEVATION: 2000'–6064'
MANAGEMENT: Umatilla NF, Wallowa-Whitman NF
TOPOGRAPHIC MAPS: Bingham Springs, Andies Prairie, Tollgate, Blalock Mountain, Jubilee Lake, Gibbon, Thimbleberry Mountain, Duncan, Drumhill Ridge, Summerville (USGS, 7.5')

One of the roughest barriers confronting Oregon Trail pioneers in the 1840s, the northern Blue Mountains still harbor enough wilderness to challenge hikers and hide elk.

Climate

Autumns are renowned both for delightful Indian summer weather and surprise blizzards. Shade is at a premium during summer's heat, since less than half the area is forested. Annual precipitation—mostly winter snow—ranges from 20 inches in the arid southwest to 45 inches in the eastern uplands. Ski season at Spout Springs is from mid-November to mid-April.

The North Fork Umatilla Wilderness (photo by William L. Sullivan)

Plants and Wildlife

Road building and logging have largely been confined to the area's plateaus, leaving wilderness in the steeply dissected canyonlands. There, only the relatively wet and shady north-facing slopes support forests (chiefly white fir). As a result, nearly every ridge offers a view to the south of forest and a view to the north of seemingly uninterrupted, dry grasslands, giving the illusion that one is always on the edge of a steppe.

The low-elevation creekbanks sprout lush foliage: sword fern, wild ginger, Oregon grape, yew, alder, wild cherry, stinging nettle, and snowberry. Look for beaver ponds and gnawed trees along the North Fork Umatilla. Expect to find boggy wallows made by bull elk along the North Fork Meacham and Five Points Creek.

Geology

The northern Blue Mountains do not resemble their southern cousins. Forty miles to the south the Blue Mountains are craggy, granite peaks. Here the range consists of dissected basalt tablelands.

The difference is that when the Columbia River lava flows spread out from the Grande Ronde area 15 million years ago, they topped the southern Blue Mountains with a thin, easily eroded layer. Here, flow upon flow of lava buried the landscape 4000 feet deep. Even when subsequent uplifting allowed creeks to cut the leveled terrain into a jagged canyonland, the older rocks presumably below have still not been exposed.

History

This mountain range once divided the Cayuse and Nez Perce Indians. Lookingglass Creek commemorates Nez Perce leader Apash-wahay-ikt, dubbed Chief Lookingglass because he often carried with him a hand mirror.

The first white men here were crossing the continent to establish a fur-trading post at Astoria in 1812. In 1827 botanist David Douglas hiked to the Blue Mountain crest and found 4-foot-tall yellow lupine blooming—possibly the rare Sabine lupine, found only in these uplands.

In 1836, missionaries Marcus and Narcissa Whitman crossed the range on a primitive route now maintained by the Forest Service as the Whitman Trail: south of Mt. Emily, across Five Points Creek and Meacham Creek, then down Horseshoe Ridge toward Walla Walla. Marcus Whitman returned in 1843 leading a wagon train. Within five years, 9000 settlers

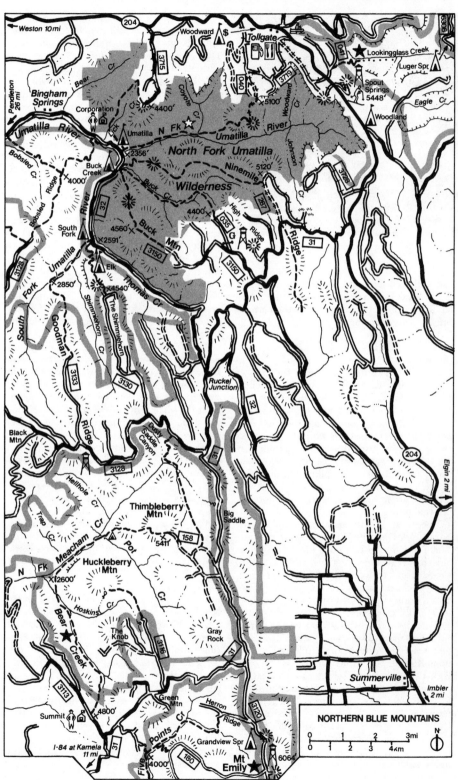

Rocky Mountain elk

had followed on what became the Oregon Trail, winching their wagons onto the tablelands west of La Grande to avoid the narrow, brushy canyon bottoms.

THINGS TO DO

Hiking

A cluster of campgrounds near the forks of the Umatilla River form the hub of eight radiating hiking trails. All of these paths gain some 2000 feet on their way to progressively higher and more compelling canyon viewpoints; however, the trails which follow creeks climb gently at first, while the ridge trails start out briskly. Since none of the eight routes connects, up-and-back day hikes are in order. Those who wish to hike the trails only downhill must arrange car shuttles to the remote upper trailheads.

The most heavily used trail follows the North Fork Umatilla River 3 miles from Umatilla Campground to a good picnic spot in an old-growth fir forest at the mouth of Coyote Creek. Here crowds thin out, for the trail, which had been nearly level, suddenly switchbacks 3 miles up grassy Coyote Ridge to Road 040 on Tollgate's plateau.

Three less-crowded trails nearby also feature rushing streams. One accompanies Buck Creek for an easy 3.8 miles before climbing 1.3 miles up to Road 035. Another path traces the South Fork Umatilla River 2.3 miles before taking off up Goodman Ridge 1.5 miles to Road 3133. Finally, the Lick Creek Trail forks off from the North Fork Umatilla River Trail near its beginning, then contours past some canyon slope viewpoints before ascending Lick Creek's ravine. The upper trailhead at Road 3715 is 4 miles distant.

Of the four ridge trails near the Umatilla River campgrounds, the switchbacks up Ninemile Ridge climb with the gentlest grade. That route extends 7 miles to Road 287. As with all of the local ridgeline hikes, the first mile has most of the elevation gain while the remaining miles follow an open, view-filled crest.

The 5.5-mile trail up Bobsled Ridge starts out with a few switchbacks that lessen its steepness. However, there are two ridge trails nearby that more closely resemble bobsled runs: the steep 4-mile route up to Buck Mountain's ridge and the (unmarked) very steep 1.5-mile Shimmiehorn Trail to Road 3130.

The area's largest roadless tract has been named Hellhole by the Forest Service—a name which misrepresents the area's lovely canyon scenery. For proof of this, try the trail down Bear Creek from the Summit Guard Station. The route gradually descends 6 miles through a cool, old-growth forest, then follows the clear North Fork Meacham Creek 2.5 miles to a grassy campsite at Pot Creek before climbing 3.5 miles to flat-topped Thimbleberry Mountain.

Mt. Emily is not only the area's highest point, with a sweeping view across the Grande Ronde Valley to the Wallowa Mountains, it's also near the start of a quiet forest trail that's surprisingly close to downtown La Grande. Near the Mt. Emily turnoff on Road 3120, follow Road 180 for 4 miles to the trailhead. The path switchbacks down 1 mile to Five Points Creek. Here, either head upstream 3.3 miles to a trailhead on Herron Ridge, or turn downstream, following the creek 5.5 miles to a ford and dirt road at Camp One, just 7 miles northwest of La Grande via backroads marked as the route of the old Whitman Trail.

For canyon solitude, try Lookingglass Creek. A good trail switchbacks 1.5 miles down from the Spout Springs area to the creek, but from there on, hikers are on their own.

Winter Sports

Highway 204, plowed in winter, provides Nordic skiers with access to snowed-under roads on the tablelands fringing the North Fork Umatilla Wilderness. Expect competition from snowmobiles on routes near Tollgate. A good strategy is to head for canyon rim viewpoints, particularly the ones at the upper wilderness trailheads. The trails themselves, especially the one on Ninemile Ridge, are also skiable for short distances. Turn back when they begin descending sharply to lands of less snow. Warm up at Spout Springs, a major winter center with three lifts, two day lodges, and a restaurant.

51. Wenaha-Tucannon

LOCATION: 50 mi N of La Grande, 28 mi E of
Walla Walla
SIZE: 363 sq mi total; 122 sq mi in Oregon
STATUS: 277 sq mi designated wilderness; 104
sq mi in Oregon (1978)
TERRAIN: steep, partly forested river canyons,
dissected plateaus
ELEVATION: 1700'−6387'
MANAGEMENT: Umatilla NF
TOPOGRAPHIC MAP: Wenaha-Tucannon
Wilderness (USFS)

This huge canyonland on the Oregon-Washington border supports the nation's highest elk population density. The excellent trail network, popular with equestrians, has room for week-long backpacking trips.

Climate

Snowfall from late November to April averages 8 to 12 feet at Oregon Butte and 1 to 2 feet along the Wenaha River. Trails to 4000 feet elevation are clear of snow by early May, but higher routes may be blocked until June. August afternoon temperatures often exceed 100° F, while fierce winters bring weather as cold as -40° F and occasionally freeze the Grande Ronde River. Sudden snowstorms may interrupt autumn's cool, clear weather.

Plants and Wildlife

Elk dominate the area, but whitetail deer and big-eared mule deer are also plentiful. The herds move down from the mountains in winter to the Wenaha Wildlife Area, where the state supplies them with supplemental feed. These feeding stations are probably the best spot in Oregon to observe elk and deer. For a look at the herds, drive the road from Troy along Eden Bench from mid-January to late May.

Other mammals include the whistling marmot, Columbia ground squirrel, snowshoe hare, black bear, mountain lion, coyote, bobcat, and marten. Bald eagles winter along the Grande Ronde River. Chukar and grouse startle hikers by bursting out of trailside brush.

The trailside brush with elegant white berries is snowberry. When Lewis and Clark passed north of here they collected snowberry seeds and brought them to Thomas Jefferson, who delighted in the "very handsome little shrub" and presented a bush to Lafayette's aunt in Paris as a gift from America.

Old growth cottonwoods, fir, and ponder-

Mouth of the Wenaha River Canyon, from the road to Flora (photo by William L. Sullivan)

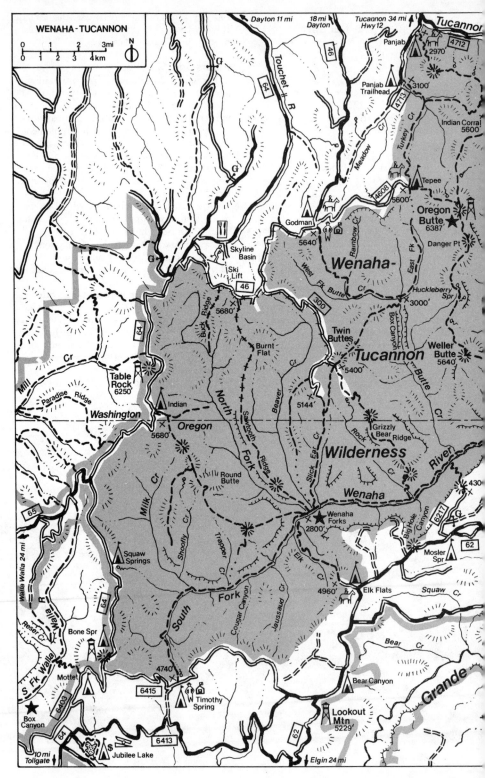

WENAHA - TUCANNON

0   1   2   3mi
0 1 2 3 4km
N

Dayton 11 mi
18 mi Dayton
Tucannon 34 mi Hwy 12
Tucannor
Panjab
4712
2970
4713 3100'
Panjab Trailhead
Indian Corral 5600
Touchet R
64
46
Meadow Cr
4608
Turkey Cr
5600
Tepee
Rainbow Cr
Godman
5640
Oregon Butte 6387
Danger Pt
Skyline Basin
West Fk Butte
East Fk Cr
Huckleberry Spr
3000'
Ski Lift
46
300
Box Canyon
Wenaha-
Buck Ridge
5680
Burnt Flat
Twin Buttes
Weller Butte 5640
Tucannon
Table Rock 6250
Paradise Ridge
Mill Cr
64
Indian
5144'
5400'
Beaver Cr
Butte Cr
Washington
Oregon
5680
North Fork
Sawtooth Ridge
Slick Ear Cr
Grizzly Bear Ridge
Rock Cr
Wilderness
River
430
65
Round Butte
Milk Cr
Shoofly Cr
Trapper Cr
Wenaha Forks
2800'
Wenaha
Big Hole Canyon
6217
Walla Walla 24 mi
Squaw Springs
Mosler Spr
62
Elk Cr
Elk Flats
Squaw Cr
64
Walla Walla R
Reser Cr
South Fork
Cougar Canyon
Jaussaud Cr
4960'
Bear Cr
Bone Spr
Grande
Mottet
4740
6415
Timothy Spring
Bear Canyon
S Fk Walla Walla
6403
Box Canyon
64
6413
62
Lookout Mtn 5229'
10 mi Tollgate
Jubilee Lake
Elgin 24 mi

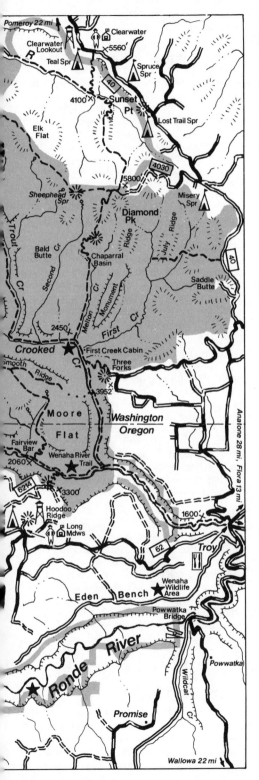

osa pine line the Wenaha River. Sparse bunch-grass covers the steep canyons' dry, south-facing slopes. Dense mixed conifer forests cover north slopes and tablelands. Expect wild-flowers in June and the beautiful red foliage of nonpoisonous sumac bushes in October.

Geology

This area was the main source of the Colum-bia River lava flows which buried the landscape from Utah to Astoria 15 million years ago with up to 5000 feet of basalt. For proof of this look in the canyons, where stream erosion has cut deep into the old lava plain. Running verti-cally through the basalt layers are occasional, wall-like outcroppings of jointed rock, looking almost like stacked cordwood. These are dikes, formed when the lava oozed up from the earth and squeezed into cracks on the way.

The distinctive red layers between rimrock levels are old soil horizons, indicating that thousands of years of forests had time to grow between lava eruptions.

History

The name Wenaha is Nez Perce, for this was once the *ha* ("domain") of Wenak, a Nez Perce chief. Similarly, the Imnaha River to the east was the ha of Chief Imna.

THINGS TO DO

Hiking

Part of the wonder of this area is its enormity. Even day trips open vistas of seem-ingly endless canyonlands, wild rivers, and rugged ridges.

Troy (population 58) offers the only river-level trailhead on the Oregon side. Start here for a 6-mile walk up the Wenaha's arid, wind-ing canyon to the footbridge and broad gravel bar at the mouth of Crooked Creek. Troy can be reached year round by gravel road from Bog-gan's Oasis, Washington, which is 32 miles south of Lewiston on Highway 129. To get to Troy from Enterprise, take Highway 3 north to the ghost town of Flora (the road is icy in winter), then take a steep gravel road 13 miles west to Troy.

A good way to sample the area's rugged scenery is to hike from a canyon rim down to one of the rivers. Of the many possible routes, here are three which are neither too steep nor too long: the Hoodoo Trail switchbacks 2.2 miles from Road 6214 to a narrow part of the Wenaha River's chasm near Fairview Bar, losing just 1300 feet. A 3.5-mile route from the Three Forks trailhead loses 1600 feet on its way to Crooked Creek and the Forest Service cabin at First Creek. And finally, those who

The Wenaha River (photo by William L. Sullivan)

prefer a longer, gentler trail through forest might try the 5-mile path from the Elk Flats Campground down 2100 feet to Wenaha Forks. The canyon-bottom flat at Wenaha Forks features big cottonwoods, snowberry, and gravel bars.

Other day trips follow ridgelines to high viewpoints. Start at Indian Campground on Road 64 for a 3.4-mile walk to Round Butte and a view down the length of the Wenaha River; the final quarter mile to the summit is cross-country. A different day trip climbs to the fire lookout on Oregon Butte, the highest point in the wilderness. The view is well worth the 2.2-mile hike from Tepee Campground.

Trailheads on the southwest side of the wilderness are best reached via Walla Walla or Tollgate. From Walla Walla, take Highway 12 east 3 miles and turn right onto paved Mill Creek Road, which becomes Road 65. From Tollgate—located on Oregon Highway 204 halfway between Weston and Elgin—take gravel Road 64 for 11 miles to the popular Jubilee Lake Campground, shown on the map.

Much of the vast backcountry can only be reached by overnight trips. Don't miss the 31.3-mile Wenaha River Trail from Timothy Spring Campground to Troy. This well-maintained route requires no major fords. The Forest Service's elaborate footbridge across the North Fork Wenaha, left high and dry when that fork changed course, has been replaced by a log conveniently felled by beaver.

Of the many possible loop trips, here are three suggestions for exploring the interior wilderness: an 18.2-mile route begins at the Twin Buttes trailhead on Road 300, follows Grizzly Bear Ridge's mesa to the Wenaha River, then returns to Twin Buttes via Wenaha Forks and Slick Ear Creek. For a 29.2-mile

loop, start at Diamond Peak, follow the ridge to Indian Corral, descend Trout Creek and Crooked Creek, then return via the trail up Melton Creek. A spectacular 41-mile loop visits Oregon Butte, Moore Flat, Crooked Creek, and Indian Corral; one can get to this loop from any of the eastern trailheads.

Just west of the Wenaha-Tucannon area, the South Fork Walla Walla River rushes through Box Canyon, a rocky gorge where stream-loving water ouzels dip and sing. At one point the popular trail here is a mossy ledge lapped by the river and overtowered by basalt cliffs. Day hikers can reach Box Canyon by switch-backing down 1800 feet in 2.3 miles from Mottet Campground on a good trail; cross the footbridge at Reser Creek and amble downstream 1 or 2 miles into the canyon. Backpackers can start at the head of the South Fork Walla Walla Trail at Road 65 and continue 18 miles to either of two trailheads. One is at the end of the South Fork Walla Walla Road (13 miles west of Milton-Freewater); the other climbs to a spur road a half mile northwest of Target Meadows Campground, near Tollgate.

Winter Sports

The best access to winter snow is via Dayton, Washington. Take Fourth Street to plowed Road 64 and the Skyline Basin ski area. From there, ride the lift to the canyon rim and set out on snowshoes or cross-country skis. Snowed-under Roads 46 and 300 provide well-defined, nearly level ridgetop routes with views into the North Fork Wenaha River canyon. The trail along narrow Buck Ridge stays level for 2 miles (then descends dangerously). Another tour from Road 46 climbs slightly for 2.5 miles to Burnt Flat's plateau.

Boating

The Grande Ronde River winds through a 2400-foot-deep canyon of steep forests and interesting basalt formations. Canoeists can navigate the river except in April to June's high water, which kayakers often prefer. Low water grounds most craft in September.

The run begins at Minam on Highway 84, follows the Wallowa River 8.5 miles to Rondowa, then continues down the Grande Ronde River 28.5 miles to Powwatka Bridge, 8 miles south of Troy. All rapids in this section can be scouted by boat. The most serious of these is the (class 3) Minam Roller, 1.5 miles below the Minam launch.

From Powwatka Bridge, boaters can continue 26 miles to Boggan's Oasis (on the Enterprise-Lewiston highway), and then another 26 miles to Heller's Bar on the Snake River. In low water The Narrows, below Boggan's Oasis, poses a class 4 hazard.

52. Joseph Canyon

LOCATION: 20 mi N of Enterprise
SIZE: 39 sq mi
STATUS: undesignated wilderness
TERRAIN: steep, sparsely forested canyon
ELEVATION: 2400'–4920'
MANAGEMENT: Wallowa-Whitman NF
TOPOGRAPHIC MAPS: Table Mountain,
    Shamrock Creek, Paradise (USGS, 7.5'); Sled
    Springs, Elk Mountain (USGS, 15')

Birthplace of the Nez Perce Indian leader, Chief Joseph, this stark canyon features the same kind of awe-inspiring scenery as the larger, but less easily accessible Hells Canyon nearby.

Climate

The canyon's wildflowers bloom and the bunchgrass greens from April to June. In summer, the canyon bottom temperatures top 100° F. Fall is dry, infrequently interrupted by brief snowstorms. Winter temperatures remain below freezing for weeks at a stretch. Highway 3, though plowed of snow, is often icy and treacherous from December to March. Annual precipitation measures an arid 15 inches.

Plants and Wildlife

The canyon's sides are corrugated with steep gulches; forest grows on north-facing gulch slopes and bunchgrass grows on dry south-facing slopes. This results in the distinctive strips of vegetative cover popular with elk, who need to shift between shelter and grazing areas, especially in winter.

An extensive forest fire in 1986 performed the maintenance work traditionally reserved for wildfire here: clearing out deadfall, brush, and mixed conifer thickets, while leaving much of the old-growth ponderosa pine intact.

Bring binoculars to distinguish raptors in flight: golden and bald eagles, goshawks, Cooper's hawks, and sharp-shinned hawks. All of these nest here, as do blue grouse, ruffed grouse, and chukars. Joseph Creek and its tributaries provide spawning grounds for salmon and steelhead.

Joseph Canyon and Table Mountain

Geology

This canyon exposes some of the state's most interesting basalt formations. The area was a major source of the colossal Columbia River basalt flows 15 million years ago. Not only are dozens of horizontal basalt flows visible in cross-section, but basalt dikes show as vertical stripes, formed when the upwelling lava squeezed into cracks. The basalt has eroded into cliffs, caves, and crags, including domed Haystack Rock.

When the land here began to rise about 13 million years ago, creeks swiftly cut canyons into the lava plain, following the area's north-south fault lines.

History

Chief Joseph, leader of the Wallowa band of the Nez Perce, was born in a cave along this portion of Joseph Creek. The original 6.5-million-acre Nez Perce Reservation of 1855 included Joseph Canyon. A divisive 1863 treaty left the tribe with only a small tract of land in Idaho. The Wallowa band refused to sign the treaty or to recognize it. President Grant upheld their right to the Wallowa Valley and Joseph Canyon in 1873, but under mounting pressure from settlers, the Army in 1877 ordered the Indians to leave, setting in motion the Nez Perce's famous, ill-fated march toward freedom in Canada.

THINGS TO DO

Hiking

Begin with a visit to the Joseph Canyon Viewpoint on Highway 3. West of the highway stretches an unassuming plain of forest and wheat fields, while to the east the land

suddenly falls away into a gaping, 2100-foot-deep chasm.

The Davis Creek Trail offers the gentlest route into this canyonland. The trail begins 9 miles south of the Joseph Canyon Viewpoint at the end of spur Road 170 and descends 1.3 miles to Davis Creek, whose long, V-shaped valley forms a major branch of Joseph Canyon. Day hikers can lunch along Davis Creek and return. Backpackers will want to continue north to Joseph Creek (9.5 miles from this trailhead) and allow a day to prowl the deeper canyon there before returning, perhaps via Swamp Creek and the connector trail over Starvation Ridge.

Adventurers with good shoes and sound knees can hike to the bottom of the Joseph Canyon in just 2 miles by following the steep, abandoned Wilder Trail down from the Joseph Canyon Viewpoint on Highway 3. To avoid

the cliffs below the viewpoint, first hike north along the canyon rim 0.2 mile, then descend a rounded ridge past the remains of a log cabin. The faint trail heads southwest halfway down, but is easy to lose.

At the bottom, another unmaintained route follows the winding creek through its cliff-edged gorge—a narrow oasis of green shaded by noble ponderosa pines. Bring creek-wading sneakers, for the cold, calf-deep creek crosses the narrow canyon often. Private land blocks creek bushwhackers 2.3 miles downstream from the Wilder Trail terminus and 6.8 miles upstream at the Joseph Creek Ranch.

The grassy edge of Table Mountain's forested plateau affords a sweeping view of the entire canyon and the distant Wallowa Mountains. Haystack Rock provides an easy cross-country goal across the grassy slopes from Road 4650.

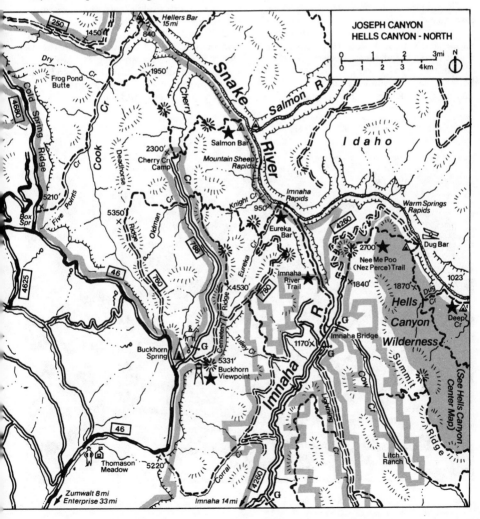

53. Hells Canyon

LOCATION: 80 mi E of Baker, 36 mi E of
  Enterprise
SIZE: 977 sq mi total; 666 sq mi in Oregon
STATUS: 334 sq mi designated wilderness; 198
  sq mi in Oregon (1975, 1984), federal wild
  and scenic river, national recreation area
TERRAIN: immense unforested chasm,
  whitewater river, forested tablelands,
  snowpeaks, lakes
ELEVATION: 840'–9393'
MANAGEMENT: Hells Canyon NRA, Vale
  District BLM
TOPOGRAPHIC MAPS: Hells Canyon
  Wilderness, Wild and Scenic Snake River
  (USFS)

The deepest gorge on earth, Hells Canyon inspires awe for its sheer size. From the gentle wildflower meadows on its rim, this chasm gapes like the ragged edge of a broken planet. Basalt rimrock and stark, treeless terraces alternate downward toward a tiny curve at the bottom — the brawling whitewater of the mighty Snake River, over a vertical mile be-low. And stacked 9000 feet high on the Idaho rim loom the crags of the snowy Seven Devils Mountains.

Climate

Two different climates prevail here at once: heavy snows drape the alpine rim from November to May or June, while the relatively balmy, but much more arid canyon bottom receives less than 10 inches of precipitation in an entire year. Summer temperatures often hit a sweltering 100° F along the river but remain in the 70s on the rim, where nights can freeze in any season. Spring and fall are pleasant in the canyon.

Plants and Wildlife

Bring binoculars to spot big-eared mule deer and herds of up to 100 elk from miles away in this open canyonland. Also watch for mountain goats, with shaggy coats and spike horns, and bighorn sheep, with curling horns. The black bears in Hells Canyon are a distinctive cinnamon brown. This is the only site in Oregon with a recent sighting of a wolf.

Birds include great blue herons and non-migrating geese, enticed to year-round residency by the river's mild climate.

Hells Canyon from the trail below Buckhorn Viewpoint (photo by William L. Sullivan)

The Snake River itself provides rare habitat for giant white sturgeon up to 12 feet long. Sea runs of salmon and steelhead died forever from the upper Snake River system when the Idaho Power Company built the Hells Canyon, Oxbow, and Brownlee dams in 1958-64 with inadequate fish-passing facilities. The company has since built a hatchery on the Rapid River in an attempt to perpetuate Snake River strains of fish in the free-flowing Salmon River system.

In April and May the canyon slopes glow green with bunchgrass. Flowers include tiny pink phlox and prickly pear cactus. In June, red Indian paintbrush and yellow desert parsley carpet the alpine meadows interspersed with forest along the rim. The canyon turns brown in summer, but balsamroot brightens river benches with miles of little sunflowers. Summer is the only likely time to spot rattlesnakes. By October most gulches flame with the beautiful scarlet leaves of nonpoisonous sumac bushes. Sumac's relative, poison oak, grows on a few riverbanks.

Geology

This enormous chasm did not exist as recently as 15 million years ago, for Columbia River basalt flows of that age are continuous across the Oregon and Idaho rims.

Surprisingly, Hells Canyon was not carved by the Snake River. The ancestral Snake flowed across southern Oregon to the sea. When Great Basin faulting lifted large chunks of eastern Oregon about 13 million years ago, the Snake backed up, creating a lake over most of southern Idaho. Meanwhile, north-south fractures from the Great Basin faults allowed Columbia tributaries to cut deeply into the new northern Oregon uplands, carving the parallel canyons of the Imnaha, Salmon, and an unnamed creek that dead-ended in Hells Canyon. When this unnamed creek cut its canyon to the edge of the huge lake in Idaho, the waters suddenly poured northward to the Columbia, and the Snake River raged into Hells Canyon.

The canyon cuts through 4000 feet of Columbia River basalt to expose the older surface below. This light gray rock, forming the Snake's rugged Inner Gorge, consists of jumbled sedimentary and volcanic strata laid down on the seafloor 200 million years ago, then scraped up into an ancient coastal range by the westward-moving continent.

At first it seems puzzling that the tablelands bordering Hells Canyon slope upward to the canyon's edge. However, the Earth's crust floats on a molten mantle. When creation of Hells Canyon removed some 500 cubic miles of rock here, the crust floated upward like an emptied gravel barge. This in turn caused the

Suicide Point, from the Oregon side (photo by William L. Sullivan)

river to cut the canyon still deeper. The Seven Devils Mountains, between the vast, empty canyons of the Salmon and Snake, have bobbed highest of all.

Ice Age glaciers ground out the many lake basins in the Seven Devils Mountains and rounded the valleys of the Imnaha River, Rapid River, and upper Granite Creek.

History

Pit house depressions along Tryon Creek testify to ancient habitation, as do petroglyphs at Willow Bar and elsewhere. Vandalism by pottery- and basket-seekers threatens study of the estimated 160 to 200 archeological sites in the canyon. Even arrowheads and old bottles are federally protected.

Nez Perce Indians under Chief Toohoolhoolzote established domination of the canyon by obliterating a Shoshone village at Battle Creek. In 1877, U.S. Army negotiators trying to convince Oregon Nez Perce to move to a small Idaho reservation took Toohoolhoolzote hostage. Sullenly, the Wallowa band's Chief Joseph led 400 Indians and several thousand head of Appaloosa horses and cattle toward the reservation. The tribe marched down the Imnaha River and managed to cross the Snake in flood stage. A 3.7-mile portion of the amazingly rugged route they followed is preserved as the Nee-Me-Poo (Nez Perce for "the real people") Trail. A shoot-out near the reservation, however, sent the tribe on a four-month tactical retreat, ending with defeat just 30 miles short of permanent sanctuary in Canada.

Hells Canyon frustrated explorers seeking a navigable river route west, notably an 1811-12 overland expedition to Astoria. In 1870 a

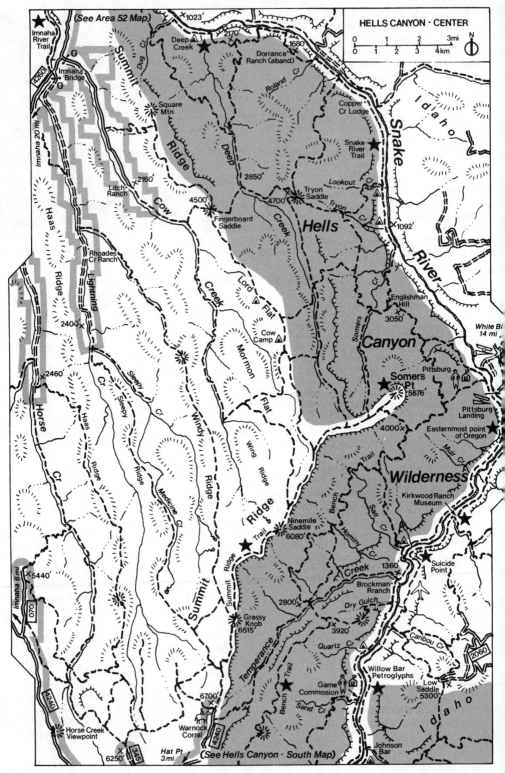

HELLS CANYON - CENTER

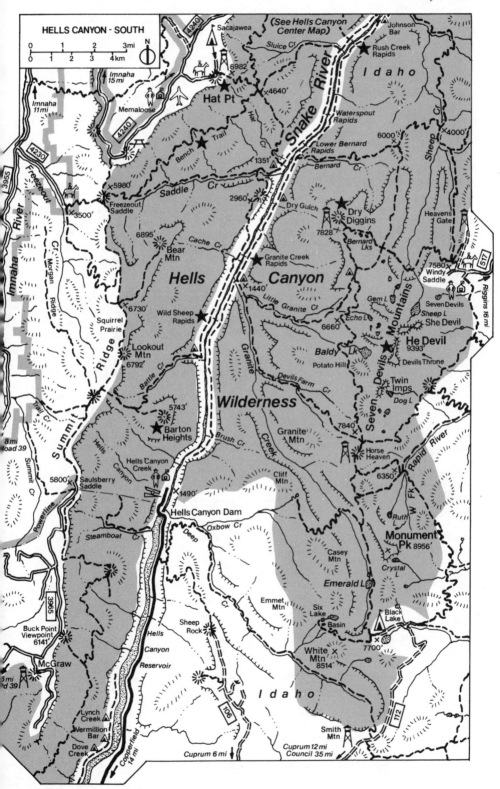

HELLS CANYON - SOUTH

Scale: 0 1 2 3mi / 0 1 2 3 4km N

(See Hells Canyon Center Map)

Sacajawea

Johnson Bar

Rush Creek Rapids

Idaho

Sluice Cr

×6982

×4640'

Waterspout Rapids

6000'

×4000'

Sheep Cr

Imnaha 15 mi

Imnaha 11 mi

Memaloose

Hat Pt

Hat Cr

Lower Bernard Rapids

Bench Trail

1351'

Bernard Cr

Heavens Gate

517

×5980

Saddle Cr

2960'

Dry Gulch

Dry Diggins

7828'

Bernard Lks

×3500'

Freezeout Saddle

6895

Cache Cr

Granite Creek Rapids

7580×

Windy Saddle

Bear Mtn

Hells

Canyon

×1440'

Little Granite Cr

Gem L

Seven Devils

Sheep L

She Devil

Riggins 16 mi

6730'

Wild Sheep Rapids

Echo L

6660'

Mountains

He Devil

9393'

Squirrel Prairie

Lookout Mtn

6792'

Battle Cr

Granite

Baldy Lk

Devils Throne

Potato Hill

Seven

Twin Imps

Dog L

8 mi Road 39

5743'

Barton Heights

Brush Cr

Wilderness

Devils Farm Cr

7840×

Devils

Horse Heaven

Summit Ridge

Creek

Granite Mtn

6350×

Rapid River

Hells Cr

Hells Canyon Creek

Cliff Mtn

W Fk

5800×

Saulsberry Saddle

×1490'

Ruth

Powerline

Summit Cr

Trail Cr

Hells Canyon Dam

Steamboat Cr

Deep

Oxbow Cr

Casey Mtn

Monument Pk 8956'

Crystal L

3965

Cr

Emerald L

Black Lake

Buck Point Viewpoint 6141

Sheep Rock

Emmet Mtn

Six Lake

Basin

7700'

McGraw

Hells Canyon Reservoir

White Mtn 8514

112

3 mi d 39

Lynch Creek

Vermillion Bar

Copperfield

106

Smith Mtn

Idaho

Dove Creek

Cuprum 14 mi

Cuprum 6 mi

Cuprum 12 mi

Council 35 mi

Imnaha River

Morgan Ridge

Freezeout Cr

3955

4230

4240

steamboat built on the upper Snake River ran the canyon downriver, but lost 8 feet of its bow in the process.

A copper and gold strike at Eureka Bar in 1900 brought regular steamboat service from Lewiston to the mouth of the Imnaha River. A 125-foot ship winched herself up the river with the aid of giant iron rings still visible in the cliffs above Wild Goose and Mountain Sheep rapids. The ship lost power on a 1903 run, drifted backward into Mountain Sheep Rapids, bridged the 62-foot-wide canyon there, and broke in half. Visible at Eureka Bar are remains of the steamboat landing and a huge, never-completed ore mill.

In 1887, a group of seven Idaho cowhands robbed and murdered 32 Chinese gold miners panning river gravel at Deep Creek. Chinese numerals still mark the wall of the miners' crude rock shelter. The robbers buried their loot at the scene; one vial of gold dust turned up there in 1902.

Homesteaders built hardscrabble ranches in the canyon bottom during 1910-30. The Forest Service has acquired most of the abandoned ranches and has restored the Kirkwood Ranch's clapboard ranch house and log bunkhouse as a museum of that era.

THINGS TO DO

Hiking

Nearly all of the trails crisscrossing this huge, open canyonland provide shake-your-head-in-wonder viewpoints. The area is so remote, however, that trailheads require long drives on poor dirt roads. Many of the rugged trails involve wearying elevation gains of up to 6000 feet. And expect that rarely used paths (not described here) will be faint and hard to follow.

Several lookout towers reachable by car provide good starting points. Most popular is Hat Point, near the middle of the Oregon rim. Day hikers can savor views of the Seven Devils from wildflower meadows along the start of the trail switchbacking down from Hat Point. Drive Highway 82 to Joseph, then continue 30 miles to pavement's end at Imnaha (gas, general store). Hat Point is one and a half hours beyond Imnaha on a 24-mile, steep, rutted dirt road.

A slightly better road leads to Buckhorn Viewpoint, on the northern part of the Oregon rim (see the map for area 52). The scenery here extends to the jumbled canyonlands at the mouths of the Imnaha and Salmon rivers. For the best view, however, drive past the lookout tower a mile or two until Road 780 becomes too rough for cars, then hike out Cemetery Ridge. To drive to Buckhorn Point, turn off

Highway 82 between Enterprise and Joseph, then follow signs 42 miles to Zumwalt, Thomason Meadow, and Buckhorn.

The most popular viewpoint on the Idaho side is the Heavens Gate lookout tower, close to the Seven Devils' crags. From Highway 95 at Riggins, Idaho, take gravel Road 517 for 17 miles to the trailheads at Seven Devils Lake and Windy Saddle, then drive north 1.5 miles to the lookout.

Only a few hikes in the area are short enough and level enough to qualify as day trips. Three of these begin with a 20-mile drive north of Imnaha on gravel Road 4260 (see the map for area 52, p. 198). There, from the Imnaha Bridge at Cow Creek Ranch, a delightful 4.5-mile trail follows the raging Imnaha River through a cliff-edged defile to the Snake River and Eureka Bar's mile-long gravel beach. Here, prowl the ruins of Eureka's gold mill and watch boats run Eureka Rapids.

The Nee-Me-Poo Trail, tracing Chief Joseph's route, begins 2 miles past the Imnaha Bridge on Road 4260. This 3.7-mile path climbs 900 feet to the excellent view at Lone Pine Saddle before descending to Dug Bar.

Dug Bar is one of only two trailheads actually on the Snake River in Hells Canyon. The last 8 miles of road there, past Imnaha Bridge, are too rough for trailers. A good 4-mile trail from Dug Bar crosses some bluffs to Deep Creek's bar, where an old Chinese miners' camp overlooks the Snake River and cliffs.

Pittsburg Landing, the other river-level trailhead in Hells Canyon, is the start of the Idaho shore's popular Snake River Trail. An up-and-back day hike along the trail's first 5 miles penetrates the narrows opposite Oregon's easternmost point and reaches the museum at Kirkwood Ranch. To drive to the trailhead from Highway 95 at White Bird, Idaho, take dirt Road 493 for 16 miles to Upper Pittsburg Landing. After a rain, this grueling road is passable only by cars with chains or four-wheel drive.

Backpacking or horseback trips are needed to reach most of the trails in this enormous wilderness. Hells Canyon is exceptionally well suited to horse use. Keep in mind that open fires are banned within a quarter mile of the Snake River from July 1 to September 15. Fragile streambank and lakeshore areas see such heavy use that visitors are advised to keep campsites and stock 200 feet away from water.

The commercial jet boats roaring up and down the river detract from the wilderness atmosphere but provide backpackers with an alternative to dusty trailheads. For about $85 per person, any of three jet boat outfitters will take backpackers from Lewiston to the Idaho shore at Pittsburg Landing or Johnson Bar and back. Prices from Pittsburg Landing to Johnson Bar are about $25. The short run from Hells Canyon Dam to Wild Sheep Rapids (where hikers can join either the Idaho or Oregon Snake River trails) costs about $20. Most outfitters do not operate in winter. For names and schedules, contact the Lewiston office of the Hells Canyon National Recreation Area, 3620-B Snake River Ave., Lewiston, ID 83501; (208) 743-3648.

The Idaho Snake River Trail is not only spectacularly scenic, it's nearly level for 35 miles from its start at Pittsburg Landing to its end at Brush Creek, 3 miles short of the Hells Canyon Dam. At Suicide Point, the trail has been blasted from sheer cliffs nearly 500 feet above the river. Four major side trails climb

6000 feet into the Seven Devils Mountains, increasing the options for longer treks.

The Oregon shore's Snake River Trail is equally scenic, but longer (56 miles from Dug Bar to Battle Creek), and climbs sharply away from the river on five occasions. Side trail options abound. Most notable are the route up Dry Gulch to the Bench Trail, trails from Sluice Creek and Saddle Creek to Hat Point, the Saddle Creek Trail to Freezeout Saddle, and the Battle Creek Trail to Saulsberry Saddle.

The Summit Ridge Trail hugs the Oregon rim. Somers Point's remote view is 14 miles from the Warnock Corral trailhead north of Hat Point. South of Hat Point, the Summit Ridge Trail continues another 13.5 miles from Road 4240 to Saulsberry Saddle. Side trails lead to photogenic Snake River vistas atop Bear

Abandoned homestead east of Deep Creek on the Snake River Trail (photo by William L. Sullivan)

Prickly pear cactus by the Snake River (photo by William L. Sullivan)

Mountain and Barton Heights. To reach the Saulsberry Saddle trailhead from Joseph, drive toward Imnaha 8 miles, turn right onto Road 39 for 30 miles, then turn left onto Road 3965 for 16 miles to its end.

The Bench Trail zigzags through the canyon halfway up, passing grassy slopes, stands of big ponderosa pines, and tumbling creeks. Try a portion of this route for variety on a longer trek, or hike the rugged bench the length of the canyon—63 miles from the Freezeout Creek trailhead to Dug Bar, via Freezeout Saddle, Englishman Hill, Tryon Saddle, and Deep Creek.

Private land blocks access to trailheads along Cow Creek and Lightning Creek. For permission to pass the gates here, contact Jack McClaren of the Cow Creek Ranch near Imnaha Bridge.

There are those who swear the best canyon view is at Dry Diggins in Idaho, and that the most scenic loop hike circles the Seven Devils Mountains. A 25-mile trip combines the two. From Road 517 at Windy Saddle, a 7-mile trail to the lookout tower at Dry Diggins dips 1000 feet crossing Sheep Creek's glacial valley. Continue south to the less spectacular Horse

Heaven lookout. Return to Windy Saddle along the range's east face. The trail passes only the Bernard Lakes; the area's many other lakes are up in high cirques and require cross-country climbs.

Boating

Huge canyon scenery and several huge rapids make the Snake River a popular float trip. Plan on two to eight days from the boat ramp below Hells Canyon Dam, depending on whether the goal is Pittsburg Landing (32 miles), Hellers Bar at the mouth of the Grande Ronde River (79 miles), or Lewiston (104 miles). Be forewarned that all the big whitewater thrills jam into the first 17 miles below the dam. For this stretch, ranger-issued permits are required from the Friday before Memorial Day through September 15. Self-issuing permits suffice for the slower water below. For permit reservation information call (208) 743-2297.

Wild Sheep Rapids, 6 miles below Hells Canyon Dam, can easily flip 18-foot rafts. This class 5 whitewater, the longest on the river, concludes with big diagonal waves that must be run head-on. Two miles beyond lie Granite Creek Rapids, where a large submerged rock in the river's center creates a variety of unpredictable class 4 turbulence—class 5 at high flow levels.

Lower Bernard Creek Rapids, at river mile 12 below the dam, make a 6-foot, class 4 drop that washes out in high flows. Beyond it 1.3 miles, Waterspout Rapids develop a class 4 suckhole at certain levels; better scout it. The final rapid requiring scouting is Rush Creek, at river mile 16, with a boat-hungry, class 4 hole on the Idaho side.

This is no river for open canoes or rafts under 12 feet, though jet boats and rafts with up to 30 passengers are allowed. The National Recreation Area provides toilets and tables at 39 heavily used riverbench campsites (camping is not allowed at the Hells Canyon Dam). Each year landing beaches grow smaller as upriver dams silt in, blocking the supply of fresh sand. Open campfires, never encouraged, are specifically banned in the nonwilderness corridor (a quarter mile on either side of the river) from July 1 to September 15. Bring camp stoves, portable charcoal grills, or fully enclosed wood stoves with screened chimneys. There is no firewood along the river.

The Snake is runnable year round, with 70° F water and low flows in summer, chilly water and some squalls in fall, cold weather in winter, and very challenging high water in spring.

54. Eagle Cap

LOCATION: 7 mi S of Enterprise, 21 mi E of La
  Grande
SIZE: 715 sq mi
STATUS: 560 sq mi designated wilderness
  (1964, 1972, 1984)
TERRAIN: snowpeaks, high lakes, alpine
  meadows, valley forests
ELEVATION: 2700'–9845'
MANAGEMENT: Wallowa-Whitman NF
TOPOGRAPHIC MAP: Eagle Cap Wilderness
  (USFS)

This wilderness in the Wallowa Mountains encompasses Oregon's largest single alpine area. Here are wildflower meadows and ice-bound lakes. Of the 29 mountains in Oregon over 9000 feet tall, 17 are here. Presiding at the hub of eight radiating valleys rises 9595-foot Eagle Cap.

Climate

Wettest area east of the Cascades, the Wallowas collect 60 inches of precipitation each year. Heavy winter snows close most trails from about the end of October to the start of July. Snowdrifts cling to high passes into August, but the lower Minam River Trail clears of snow as early as April. High water from snowmelt can make river fords difficult in May and June.

Mosquitoes can be thick in lake basins throughout July, when wildflowers are at their peak. Come prepared for brief afternoon thundershowers in July and August. September often brings clear Indian summer weather with freezing nights.

Plants and Wildlife

Rocky Mountain bighorn sheep, reintroduced here in 1971 after local extinction, now number about 30. In winter, bring binoculars to spot them on the slopes above the Lostine River near Pole Bridge Picnic Area. In spring they lamb on high ledges, where the young's only predators are golden eagles. In summer these curly-horned sheep range into the high country, where males butt heads during the November rut. Also watch for the area's 20 spike-horned mountain goats which winter on Sacajawea Peak. Easier to find, however, are mule deer; many winter on the moraines of Wallowa Lake.

The little, round-eared "rock rabbits" whistling warnings to each other from the Wallowas' alpine rockslides are pikas. These cute, industrious animals clip and sun-dry large

Panorama of the Wallowa Mountains' high peaks from Mount Howard

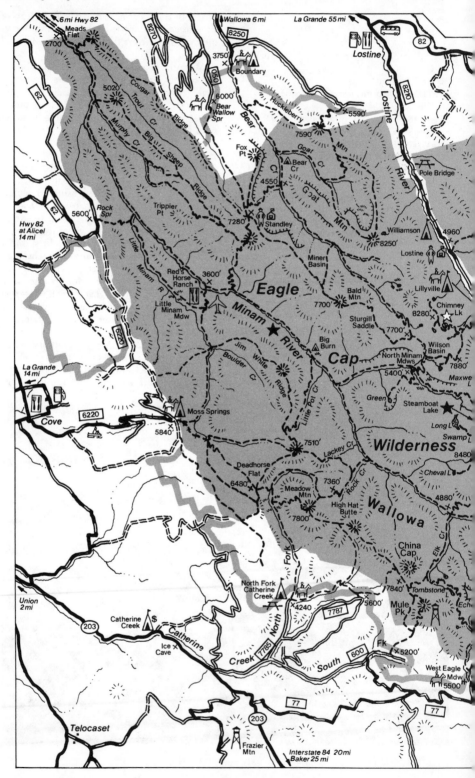

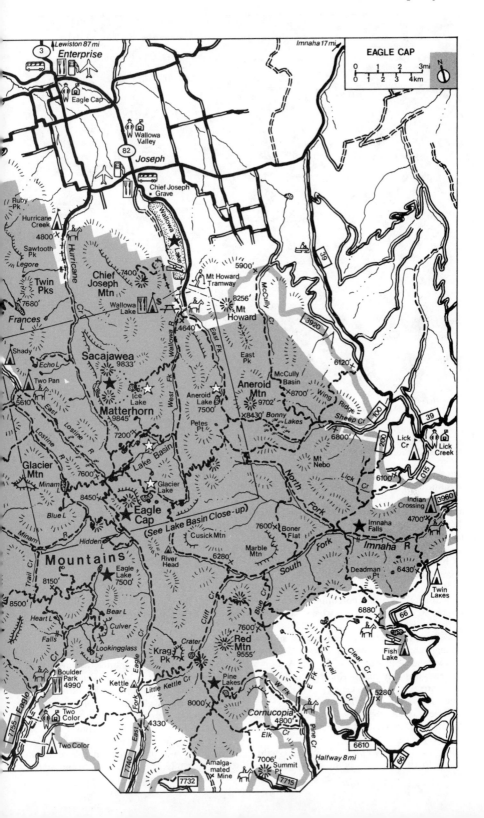

EAGLE CAP

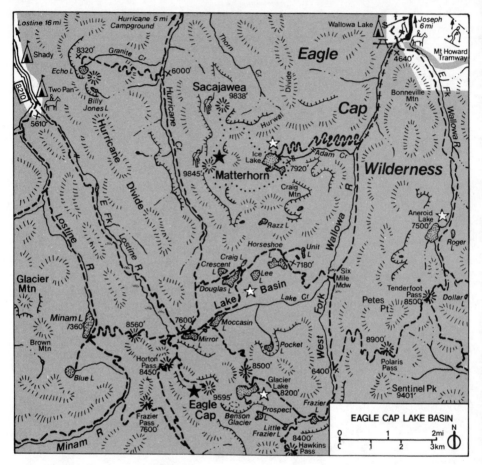

EAGLE CAP LAKE BASIN

0   1   2mi
0   1   2   3km
N

piles of grass and wildflowers, then store them in tunnels under rockslides, where the pikas winter without hibernating. One of their few predators here is the weasel-like marten, which likewise does not hibernate. The marten may travel 15 miles a night through treetops in pursuit of squirrels.

Chipmunks and black bears are numerous enough that backpackers must hang food at night for safe keeping. Campers also report nighttime visits from porcupines that chew fishing rod handles and sweaty backpack straps for their salt.

Wallowa Lake attracts geese, ducks, and occasional whistling swans in winter. Summer bird-watchers can watch for the rare Wallowa gray-crowned rosy finch. Known chiefly from just three locations—Glacier Lake, Petes Point, and a tarn near Tenderfoot Pass—this finch feeds on numbed insects that have fallen onto high snowfields. Its winter home remains a mystery.

July brings an impressive show of wildflowers to the area's many alpine meadows—most notably at the Bonny Lakes south of Aneroid Mountain. Buttercups, yellow monkeyflower, and purple pedicularis brighten wet areas, while drier fields host blue lupine, aster, scarlet gilia, bluebells, and heather.

Douglas fir and lodgepole pine dominate the forests. The twisted trees at timberline are whitebark pine and limber pine—both sporting five-needle clusters and limbs so flexible they can literally be tied in knots. Limber pine, identified by its longer cones, grows nowhere else in Oregon but the Wallowas.

Geology

The predominantly granite Wallowas have been called America's Little Switzerland, and in fact resemble the Alps geologically.

Many of the Wallowas' jumbled strata began as seafloor sediment. Greenstones forming the peaks directly south of Wallowa Lake are 250-million-year-old metamorphosed seafloor basalt. The stunning white marble and contorted limestone of the Matterhorn and Marble

Ice Lake and, at right, The Matterhorn (photo by William L. Sullivan)

Mountain began 200 million years ago as compacted seashells. Dark outcroppings are usually slate and shale — 150-million-year-old seafloor mud.

All this rock was buckled up from the Pacific by the advancing North American continent and then cooked by magma bubbling up from below 100 million years ago. The magma cooled slowly to form granite. Next, erosion must have nearly leveled the mountain range, for Columbia River basalt flows 15 million years ago successfully blanketed the entire area with lava. Shortly afterwards, Great Basin faulting lifted the Wallowas as much as 5000 feet above the surrounding plain, allowing stream erosion and glaciers to strip the basalt from most of the range. Basalt rimrock still tops ridges along the lower Minam River.

Ice Age glaciers ground out U-shaped valleys and basins for the area's 58 named lakes. The last major glacial advance left the smooth moraines which dam Wallowa Lake on three sides. Today eastern Oregon's only glacier, tiny Benson Glacier, survives near Glacier Lake.

History

The Wallowa band of Nez Perce occupied a winter village on the site of the present Wallowa Lake State Park until their flight in 1877 under Chief Joseph. The names of Joseph and his U.S. Army adversary, General Howard, now grace opposing mountains across Wallowa

Lake. A lakeside cemetery contains the grave of Joseph's father, the elder Chief Joseph.

The 1885 boomtown of Cornucopia produced $15 million in gold before its mines closed in 1941.

THINGS TO DO

Hiking

Ninety percent of all visits by horseback riders and hikers begin at just three adjacent trailheads: Wallowa Lake State Park, Hurricane Creek Campground, and Two Pan Campground. As a result, trails in this central area are crowded, camping space is tight, and some lakeshores are roped off altogether as restoration sites. For solitude, skip the Lake Basin. The Wallowas have four other lake clusters and 400 miles of quieter trails.

Scenic Wallowa Lake offers only a few paths short enough for day hikers. For an easy panoramic view, ride the gondola to the top of Mt. Howard. From there, hike the open ridge (no trail needed) 2.5 miles up to 9447-foot East Peak. To avoid the gondola fare, climb the nearby trail to Chief Joseph Mountain instead. It's 7 miles to the base of the peak's summit cliffs, with vistas of Wallowa Lake all the way. The classic day hike from Wallowa Lake, however, is the dusty, 6-mile climb to the rustic log cabins at beautiful Aneroid Lake.

Chimney Lake is one of several good day hike goals from dirt Road 8210 south of Lostine. The popular, 4.4-mile route from Lillyville Campground to Chimney Lake climbs 2500 feet; it's worth continuing another mile to Hobo Lake in order to scramble to the view atop 8831-foot Lookout Mountain. Another option is to take a fork of the trail to Chimney Lake and cross a pass to less-visited John Henry Lake in Wilson Basin—6.5 miles from Road 8210. Nearby, the switchbacking 4-mile trail from Shady Campground up to Maxwell Lake is also quiet. And two popular trails begin at Two Pan Campground, at the end of Road 8210. One leads to large Minam Lake in 5.7 miles, while the other reaches the East Lostine River's beautiful meadows and a view of Eagle Cap in just 2.8 miles.

For a look at the vast canyonlands in the northwest of the wilderness, climb the steep 2-mile trail from Road 8250 to Huckleberry Mountain's former fire lookout site. Or, farther west, take the much gentler 5-mile trail from Bear Wallow Spring to Standley Guard Station's 1932 cabin; best canyon views are a mile beyond, to the south. Drive to Bear Wallow Spring via Road 8270, which leaves Highway 82 a mile east of Minam.

Day hikers can sample the lower Minam River's rugged, V-shaped canyon by hiking down the canyon's side 3.5 miles from Rock Spring on Road 62. A second, once popular trailhead to the lower Minam River was at Meads Flat. A locked gate now blocks the private road there, but equestrians can still reach the old trailhead by riding up the river itself 7 miles from the Highway 82 bridge at Minam.

On the south side of the Wallowas, the Mule Peak lookout offers a view extending to the Blue Mountains. A steep 7.4-mile loop trail from Road 600 includes the 3200-foot climb to the lookout.

The headwaters of Eagle Creek fan out in U-shaped valleys to nearly a dozen lakes in different high mountain bowls. From West Eagle Meadow on Road 77, hike 4.9 miles to Echo Lake. The trail gains 1700 feet (a gentle climb by Wallowa standards); Traverse Lake is 1.6 miles beyond and another 500 feet up.

Eagle Lake, in a spectacular cirque rimmed by 9000-foot peaks, is 6.7 trail miles from Boulder Park on Road 7755—almost too far for a day trip. Closer goals from the same trailhead include Lookingglass Lake (6.2 miles), Bear Lake (5.8 miles), Culver Lake (5.2 miles), and Heart Lake (4.3 miles). Elevation gain to these timberline pools averages 2300 feet.

The eastern edge of the Wallowa Mountains is also uncrowded. A nearly level path follows the rushing Imnaha River from Indian Crossing Campground on Road 3960; Imnaha Falls provides an ambitious 6.3-mile destination.

To reach the trailhead from Joseph, drive 8 miles toward Imnaha, turn south on Road 39 for 28 miles, then turn right on Road 3960 for 9 miles to its end.

Most hikers headed for the wildflower fields at Bonny Lakes trudge up the long, crowded Aneroid Lake Trail. However, the 4.5-mile trail up Sheep Creek from Road 100 is shorter, and only climbs 900 feet on its way to the lakes (Road 100 is too rough for passenger cars). Looking for an even less visited wildflower patch? Try McCully Basin, 5.5 miles up from a spur of Road 3920.

Backpackers and equestrians in the wilderness should note camping is banned within 200 feet of any lake. Stock cannot be grazed or confined within 200 feet of lakes. Group size is limited to 6 in the Lake Basin and 12 elsewhere in the wilderness. And campers are not allowed to cut firewood from standing trees, alive or

dead. Downed firewood is scarce; bring a camp stove.

The most popular goals for overnight trips are the fragile lakes overtowered by the Matterhorn and Eagle Cap. Before taking the trail south from Wallowa Lake to this spectacular high country, however, consider that there are no trailside camping sites for 8 or 9 miles uphill. Camping and stock grazing are banned at Six Mile Meadows on the West Fork Wallowa River. At Ice Lake (7.9 miles) and Horseshoe Lake (9 miles) most level, wooded ground is closed for restoration. And campfires are prohibited within a quarter mile of Mirror, Moccasin, Upper, Sunshine, Glacier, Prospect, Little Frazier, Pocket, Blue, Razz, and Ice lakes. Expect to search away from trails or lakes for a low-impact campsite.

Ice Lake is a scenic timberline base for hikers scaling Oregon's sixth and seventh tallest mountains, the Matterhorn and Sacajawea Peak. Though high enough to warrant caution, the route from the lake gains only 1900 feet and requires no special gear or use of hands. A ridge between peaks allows ambitious hikers to reach both summit viewpoints on the same trip.

Stark, island-dotted Glacier Lake climaxes an 11.8-mile trail ascending the West Fork Wallowa River past Six Mile Meadow, through a rocky gorge, and past Frazier Lake. For a scenic 27-mile loop trip, continue north from Glacier Lake across a pass (with a sweeping view) and return through the Lake Basin.

Eagle Cap is not the area's tallest peak, but its summit view is unsurpassed, and a register box at the top immortalizes those who make the trip. A 2.5-mile trail leads there from Mirror Lake, which in turn is 6.5 miles from the Two Pan Campground trailhead.

Aerial view of Twin Lakes, looking up the Imnaha River valley

The Matterhorn (photo by William L. Sullivan)

To appreciate the enormity of the Matterhorn's 1800-foot, west-facing marble cliff, hike up Hurricane Creek 7.5 miles to the mountain's base—or, better yet, climb to Echo Lake across the valley for a bird's eye view. The lake is 8.3 miles from the trailhead near Hurricane Campground; the final 3 miles are steep.

Frances Lake fills an alpine valley in the midst of bighorn sheep country, where open slopes tempt hikers to scramble up nearby 9000-foot peaks. The 9.1-mile trail from Road 8210 gains 3200 feet before dropping 800 feet to the lake.

Steamboat Lake and North Minam Meadows highlight an uncrowded region of peaks, lakes, and winding glacial valleys. An 11-mile route from Two Pan Campground climbs 2900 feet, then drops to Steamboat Lake, with its ship-shaped rock formation. North Minam Meadow's mile-long pasture lies 5.5 miles beyond. The quickest route back to civilization from the meadows climbs through Wilson Basin and descends to Lillyville Campground (11.8 miles).

Goat Mountain and Huckleberry Mountain connect to form a hairpin-shaped alpine wall through the northwestern canyonlands. For a 29.5-mile trip through the area, hike from Boundary Campground up Bear Creek and Goat Creek to Huckleberry Mountain, and then follow the ridgetop trail south to a viewpoint at Little Storm Lake. Return by hiking the length of Huckleberry Mountain.

Want to track a river to its source? Take the Minam River Trail 46 miles to Blue Lake's alpine cirque. The rugged lower canyon is V-shaped; higher up, the valley is heavily forested and cut to a U shape by vanished glaciers. Privately owned Red's Horse Ranch offers meals, accommodations, and a bridge 9.9 miles into the wilderness from the Rock Spring trailhead on Road 62.

The closest trailhead to Interstate 84, Moss Springs Campground is the starting point for a relatively gentle, 20.4-mile loop trail along the forested Little Minam River Valley and alpine Jim White Ridge.

From North Fork Catherine Creek Campground nearby, a more strenuous 18-mile loop trail heads up the creek past a large, privately owned meadow, climbs to Meadow Mountain's view, then returns via a timberline pass on High Hat Butte's shoulder.

Part of the appeal of scenic Tombstone Lake is the difficulty of getting there. It's roughly 9 miles from any of the three closest trailheads, and all routes cross high passes.

Start at Cornucopia, a rustic, semi-abandoned mining boomtown, for the 7.1-mile hike to Pine Lakes. Walk the closed road up the West Fork of Pine Creek to the Queen Mine's ore tramway. A footbridge there leads to the trail proper. Some antique mining machinery remains at the alpine lakes. For a loop trip, continue south around Cornucopia Peak to Elk Creek (16.4 miles in all), or head north past Crater Lake around 9555-foot Red Mountain (25.8 miles).

Climbing

Although all peaks have walk-up sides, granite cliffs provide technical challenges in Yosemitelike rock. The Matterhorn's 1800-foot marble west face is toughest of all. Winter ascents of the Matterhorn and Sacajawea can be undertaken with snowshoes or even skis from Ice Lake.

Winter Sports

A good warm-up jaunt for Nordic skiers traverses the snowed-under park and shore of Wallowa Lake at the end of plowed Highway 82. Nearby, the trail up the West Fork Wallowa River is gradual enough for skiers, but the Chief Joseph Mountain Trail has more viewpoints.

Those hoping to spot mountain goats or bighorn sheep can park at snow level on the roads up Hurricane Creek or the Lostine River and continue on skis. Check with the Forest Service for avalanche danger; Hurricane Creek won its name from the swaths of broken trees left not by windstorms but by snowslides.

A ski trip from the snowmobile loading point on Road 6220 near Cove climbs the road 4 miles to Moss Springs Campground, then continues on trail 2 miles to the Little Minam River. The road portion gains 1600 feet; the trail drops 400 feet.

Steens Mountain from the Alvord Desert

SOUTHEAST OREGON

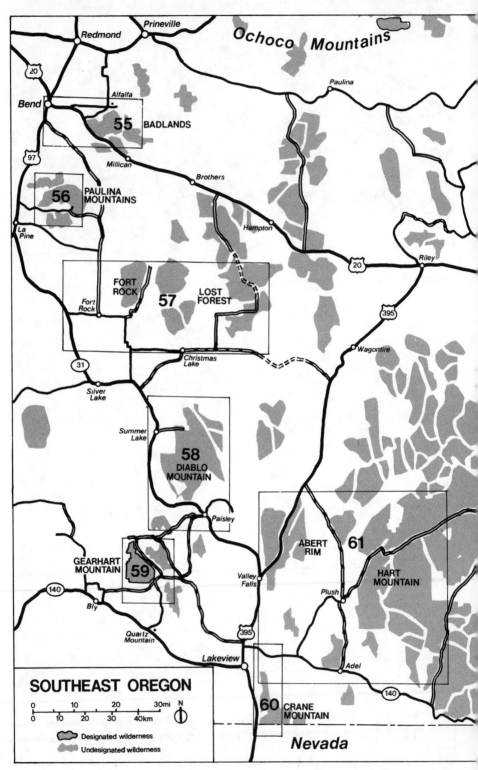

SOUTHEAST OREGON

Designated wilderness
Undesignated wilderness

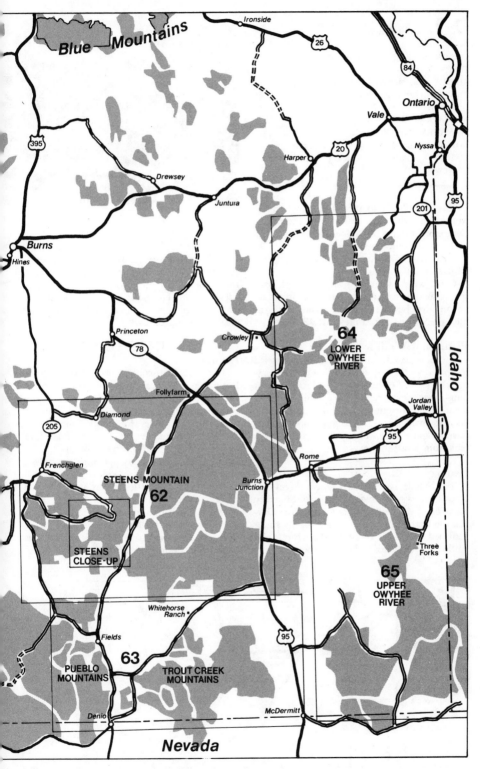

Blue Mountains

Ironside

26

84

Ontario

Vale

395

Nyssa

Harper

Drewsey

20

201

Juntura

95

Burns

Hines

Idaho

Princeton

Crowley

64
LOWER
OWYHEE
RIVER

78

Follyfarm

Jordan
Valley

Diamond

205

95

Frenchglen

Rome

STEENS MOUNTAIN

62

Burns
Junction

STEENS
CLOSE-UP

Three
Forks

65
UPPER
OWYHEE
RIVER

Whitehorse
Ranch

95

Fields

63

PUEBLO
MOUNTAINS

TROUT CREEK
MOUNTAINS

Denio

McDermitt

Nevada

55. Badlands

LOCATION: 10 mi E of Bend
SIZE: 50 sq mi
STATUS: undesignated wilderness
TERRAIN: juniper-forested lava plain, sandy
   basins
ELEVATION: 3400′–3865′
MANAGEMENT: Prineville District BLM
TOPOGRAPHIC MAPS: Central Oregon
   (BLM), Alfalfa, Horse Ridge, Millican,
   Powell Buttes SW (USGS, 7.5′)

Just 10 miles from sprawling Bend, but a world apart, this maze of lava formations, ancient juniper trees, and hidden sandy basins is a little-known wilderness retreat.

The Badlands

Climate

Cold, windy winters give way to pleasant spring weather as early as March. Summers are hot and dry, but fall arrives cool and clear. Annual precipitation measures just 12 inches.

Plants and Wildlife

An old-growth forest of scenic, gnarled juniper dots these rugged lava lands, increasing the feeling of isolation by blocking most long-range views. Sagebrush adds its pungent desert smell. Bright yellow and orange lichens encrust many rocks. Watch for mule deer, lizards, and signs of bobcats. Evening brings bats from lava tube caves.

Geology

This basalt lava flow's rugged ridges and caves formed when molten rock continued to move beneath the flow's hardened crust. During the wetter climate of the Ice Age, a since-vanished lake in the Fort Rock-Lost Forest area spilled north across the lava here to the Crooked River, leaving narrow cuts and smoothed water channels along Dry River's bed. Pumice and ash dusted the lava repeatedly from eruptions at distant Mt. Mazama (Crater Lake) and Mt. Newberry (Paulina Mountains). This ash, plus windblown sand, created the area's sandy openings.

THINGS TO DO

Hiking

The best cross-country exploration routes begin along Highway 20 or the dirt road on the area's southern edge. Hikers can follow the course of long-extinct Dry River, climb up craggy basalt ridges for views, photograph 200-year-old junipers, hunt for small lava caves, or head for the interior of the area in search of secluded, sandy openings — excellent campsites for high desert study.

Bring good boots for the rough rock and plenty of water (there is none here at any time of year). Also pack a compass; the lack of landmarks in this level, forested lava land can be disorienting. The occasional, overgrown ruts of old, meandering roads offer little guidance.

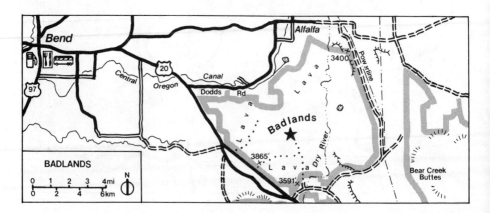

56. Paulina Mountains

LOCATION: 23 mi S of Bend
SIZE: 51 sq mi
STATUS: undesignated wilderness
TERRAIN: forested peaks, high lakes, lava
  flows, cinder cones
ELEVATION: 4750'–7984'
MANAGEMENT: Deschutes NF
TOPOGRAPHIC MAPS: Paulina Peak, East
  Lake, Lava Cast Forest, Fuzztail Butte (USGS,
  7.5')

The Paulina Mountains are remnants of the ancient Newberry volcano. As at Crater Lake, the original summit collapsed. Unlike Crater Lake, however, this 5-mile-across caldera features two large lakes, two obsidian flows, eight popular campgrounds, and a scenic trail around the entire, roadless rim.

Climate

Patches of snow remain in the campgrounds and ice still fringes the lakes when crowds arrive for the opening of fishing season here in late May. Snow blocks the higher Rim Trail until July. By August all streams are dry except Paulina Creek. Winter snows, commencing in November, account for most of the area's 15 to 30 inches of annual precipitation.

Plants and Wildlife

A lodgepole pine forest covers almost the entire area. Big ponderosa pines grow at lower elevations. The woods harbor wildlife typical of both the Cascades and the high desert, though raucous gray jays and inquisitive golden-mantled ground squirrels seem prevalent. The state stocks East Lake and Paulina Lake with 300,000 trout annually.

Geology

This volcanic hot spot marks the western end of the Brothers Fault Zone, a line of recent eruptive centers running from here to Idaho. This major fault, and the jumble of Great Basin faults south of it, resulted from the North American continent's shearing collision with the Pacific seafloor's plate. Oregon is being stretched diagonally, and lava is leaking through the ensuing cracks.

The remains of the Newberry volcano form one of Oregon's most massive and least-noticed mountains. Countless thin basalt lava flows stack here into an enormous shield shape 25 miles in diameter and 4000 feet above the sur-

Nature trail at the Big Obsidian Flow

rounding plain. From the highways at the mountain's perimeter, however, the overall silhouette seems low. More impressive are the hundred parasitic cinder cones dotting the mountain's flanks like molehills in a giant's garden.

After the Newberry volcano had been built of basalt, the magma became richer in silica, causing more violent eruptions of pumice. Hollowed by explosions and massive lava outpourings, the volcano collapsed inward, leaving the Paulina Mountains as the rim of a gaping caldera. Eruptions continued inside the caldera; two obsidian flows and the 1900-year-old Central Pumice Cone have separated Paulina and East lakes.

At the Lava Cast Forest, a fluid basalt flow surged through a stand of large trees, then ebbed, leaving the trees encased with lava up to the flow's highest level. The trees burned, but their lava shells retain even the checked pattern of the wood.

THINGS TO DO

Hiking

A paved, 1-mile interpretive trail extends through the Lava Cast Forest. The gravel road there joins Highway 97 just opposite the turnoff to Sunriver.

Another short nature trail, this one inside the Paulina Mountains' caldera, begins on Road 21 a mile east of Chief Paulina Campground. The half-mile path visits a huge, glassy obsidian flow and Lost Lake at the flow's end. For a better overview of this spectacular flow, drive a half mile further on Road 21, then take a dirt road to the right another half mile. The trail beginning there climbs 900 feet in

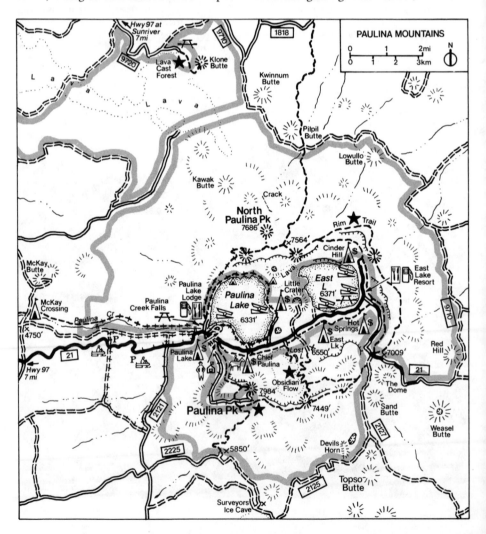

3.6 miles to a viewpoint atop the caldera rim. From there, the obsidian flow looks like dark chocolate cake dough poured into a gigantic pan.

For a level walk, try a section of the 7.3-mile trail around Paulina Lake. The route passes two campgrounds on the north shore accessible only by boat or trail, an obsidian flow on the northeast shore, and some summer homes on the south.

A dirt road climbs to the area's most popular view and highest point, Paulina Peak. Here the vista extends from the peaks of the Cascades to Fort Rock in the high desert.

The 21-mile Rim Trail passes scores of other viewpoints—all less crowded than Paulina Peak, and all within range of day hikers. Head north from Paulina Lake Lodge on this trail for increasingly fine views of Paulina Lake. At the 4-mile mark, make an easy cross-country side trip to the summit of North Paulina Peak for a view of Bend and possibly even Mt. Adams.

Those who prefer to climb less for their views can join the Rim Trail at 7009 feet, where it meets Road 21 above East Lake. From this pass, head north along the broad, nearly level rim top, or drive a quarter mile south on Road 2127 and hike the narrow, up-and-down rim west toward Paulina Peak, 5.9 miles away.

Hikers here must carry water, and backpackers must plan on dry camps. Cross-country travelers will find solitude and unobstructed hiking outside the caldera area. The most interesting goals on the mountains' flanks are the dozens of small cinder cones, many with summit craters.

Horse-loading ramps are located both at Chief Paulina Campground and at Swamp

Paulina Peak

Wells Campground, north of the area on Road 1816. The 17-mile route between the two campgrounds passes North Paulina Peak and crosses Roads 9710 and 1818. Near Chief Paulina Campground, use the trail paralleling Road 21 to avoid meeting motor traffic. To reach Swamp Wells Campground from Bend, drive 3 miles south on Highway 97, turn left on Road 18 for 6 miles, branch right onto Road 1810 for another 6 miles, then turn left on Road 1816 to its end.

Winter Sports

Clear weather, dry snow, and plowed access make these mountains attractive to snowshoers and Nordic skiers despite the presence of snowmobiles. Two methods work to avoid the noisy snow machines: visit on a weekday, or steer clear of their favored haunts—the snow-covered humps of the Big Obsidian Flow, the road up Paulina Peak, and the lakeshores.

From the uppermost sno-park on Road 21, follow the snowed-under road 2.5 miles to the Paulina Lake Lodge, open year round. Explore the lakeshore or head north up the Rim Trail for viewpoints. Don't miss icy Paulina Creek Falls, below a picnic area 0.3 mile from the lake.

If Road 21 has too much traffic, two much quieter, parallel routes also lead to the lake. Just north of Road 21, a snowed-under dirt road follows powerlines to the lodge. Still farther north, confident trackers can cross Paulina Creek and search for the Paulina Creek Trail.

Boating

Paulina Lake and East Lake are both large enough for sailing and scenic enough for rowing or canoeing. Sail over the hot springs near the southeast shore of East Lake. Squalls and choppy water can appear quickly. Motors are allowed.

Banded obsidian in the Big Obsidian Flow

57. Fort Rock and Lost Forest

LOCATION: 64 mi S of Bend
SIZE: 286 sq mi
STATUS: undesignated wilderness
TERRAIN: high desert plain, lava beds, sand dunes
ELEVATION: 4290'–5585'
MANAGEMENT: Lakeview District BLM
TOPOGRAPHIC MAPS: Cougar Mountain, Sixteen Butte, Fox Butte, Hogback Butte, Jacks Place, Crack In The Ground, Fossil Lake, Sand Rock, Moonlight Butte, Mean Rock Well (USGS, 7.5')

The high desert here is full of curiosities: Oregon's largest inland sand dunes, Fort Rock's imposing citadel, Hole In The Ground's enormous crater, Crack In The Ground's fissure, a "lost" forest of ponderosa pine, and three large lava beds.

Climate

Studies of tree rings in the Lost Forest show the current, bleak 9 inches of annual precipitation has been the average here for over 600 years. A foot of snow may fall in very cold December and January. In July and August, afternoon heat can be withering. Clear skies are the rule.

Plants and Wildlife

The Lost Forest's puzzle is how a 5-square-mile stand of ponderosa pine thrives in a sagebrush steppe with barely half the rainfall usually required for such stately trees. There are no other ponderosas for 40 miles. The answer is that during the wetter climate of the Ice Age, pines grew throughout southeast Oregon. This relict grove survives where rainfall collects in windblown sands underlain by the impermeable hardpan of an ancient lakebed. Oregon's largest juniper, with a trunk 18 feet around, is also in the Lost Forest.

More than a century of intense cattle grazing cleared the high desert savannah of its original grassy cover, allowing sagebrush and juniper to spread. Ungrazed "islands" within lava flows here provide a rare glimpse of ungrazed bluebunch wheatgrass and other hard-pressed native species.

Bald eagles winter here, relying for carrion on mule deer that die during harsh weather. Many local and migratory birds gather at Cabin Lake Campground's spring; a public blind there provides first-rate bird-watching. Throughout the area, bobcats and coyotes hunt jackrabbits, cottontails, and kangaroo rats.

Geology

The fresh-looking volcanism here is a by-product of an east-west fault zone extending from Newberry Crater to Jordan Craters near Idaho. When the Ice Age brought heavier rains, a 170-foot-deep lake collected in the Fort Rock and Christmas Lake valleys. Eruptions during that time met surface water and exploded in blasts of steam and rock, leaving rimmed craters, or *maars*. Mile-wide Hole In The Ground looks like a meteorite crater, but is actually a maar. Fort Rock, another explosion crater, lay in water deep enough that waves eroded its once-sloping rim to sheer, 320-foot-tall walls. Maars at Flat Top and Table Mountain later filled to the brim with basalt.

Bones preserved at Fossil Lake reveal this enormous Ice Age lake attracted camels, elephants, horses, and a profuse bird population of flamingos, gulls, and cormorants. Winds have collected the vanished lake's sands into miles of dunes as tall as 60 feet near Fossil Lake.

Most of the Devils Garden Lava erupted from a low, U-shaped vent in the extreme northeast of the flow. When the basalt's crust hardened, lava flowed on underneath, leaving lava tubes like Derrick Cave. South of Derrick

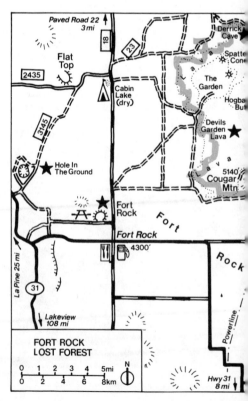

Old growth juniper partly buried by sand dunes at Lost Forest

Cave, a line of small vents formed many circular spatter cones 5 to 30 feet across and two larger cones, the 400-foot-wide Blowouts. The soupy, pahoehoe lava of this flow left a relatively smooth surface with ropy wrinkles. In the south of the flow, collapsed lava tubes left sinuous depressions and circular dips which filled with pumice from the eruption of the Newberry volcano (Paulina Mountains) 1900 years ago.

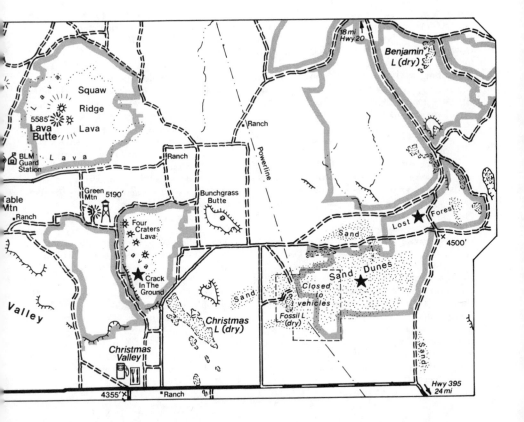

Fort Rock

Both the Squaw Ridge Lava Bed and the Four Craters Lava Bed consist of much more rugged, blocky, aa lava. Crack In The Ground, at the edge of the latter flow, is a 2-mile-long tension fissure.

History

Archeologists here rocked the scientific world in 1938 with the discovery of 75 sandals over 9000 years old, pushing back estimates of man's arrival in North America. The sandals, woven from sagebrush bark, were found in Cow Cave in a bluff just west of Fort Rock. Flourishing wildlife at the area's once-huge Ice Age lake apparently attracted early hunters. Artifacts found in caves on nearby Cougar Mountain date back 11,900 years.

THINGS TO DO

Hiking

From the Fort Rock State Monument picnic area, walk below the rock's imposing outer walls to observe the wave-cut terraces and cliff swallow nests there, or explore the "fort's" open center for penstemon wildflowers and views across the valley. In the evening, watch for owls leaving perches on the eastern rim.

The Lost Forest and nearby sand dunes offer easy and rewarding cross-country hiking. In the Lost Forest, climb a small basalt outcropping near the forest's center for a view, hike to the forest's eastern edge for a look at sand dunes encroaching there, or photograph artistically gnarled juniper trees. Then trek southwest into the dunes' vast Saharan landscape to let the kids romp in the sand. To reach the area, drive east 8 miles on paved road from Christmas Valley's general store, turn left on a dirt road 8 miles to a "T" intersection, and take a dirt road

right another 8 miles. Dune buggies make the eastern dunes hazardous on Memorial Day or Labor Day weekends.

Crack In The Ground is a 2-mile-long basalt slot 10 to 70 feet deep and often so narrow that it is bridged by boulders. Winter ice remains in its depths year round. Drive 8 miles north of Christmas Valley to the crack's northern end, then hike south; the first mile is well traveled. North of the crack, energetic hikers can cross a rugged lava flow to four prominent cinder cones.

The Devils Garden Lava Bed attracts both hikers and volcanologists. From the dirt road at the flow's northeast corner, hike to the flow's main vent, a row of spatter cones, and Derrick Cave. Bring lanterns, warm clothes, and hard hats to explore this lava tube. Above ground again, hike a mile southwest of Derrick Cave over rough lava to reach Little Garden, an old lava dome island in the fresher basalt flow.

For an overview of the smoother, southern part of the Devils Garden flow, make the short climb up Cougar Mountain. Then head north from that summit across the lava to find small sandy openings and desert solitude.

The highest point and best view in the area is atop Lava Butte, 3 miles from a road over the extremely rugged Squaw Ridge Lava.

Hikers should carry plenty of water. Fort Rock and Cabin Lake Campground have the only public sources of drinking water. All lakes and streambeds are dry. Wear sturdy boots when hiking on the area's sharp, rugged lava flows. Expect dirt roads to be badly rutted, slow, and unsigned. Side roads can be confusing, and after a rain, mud can stop even four-wheel-drive vehicles.

58. Diablo Mountain

LOCATION: 73 mi S of Bend, 49 mi N of
  Lakeview
SIZE: 244 sq mi
STATUS: undesignated wilderness
TERRAIN: high desert rimrock, brush-covered
  sand, alkali flats
ELEVATION: 4130′–6145′
MANAGEMENT: Lakeview District BLM,
  Oregon Department of Fish and Wildlife
TOPOGRAPHIC MAPS: Diablo Peak, Ana
  River, South of Ana River, Loco Lake, Sharp
  Top, Bull Lake, St. Patrick Mountain (USGS,
  7.5′)

Tundra swan on frozen Summer Lake in February

From this fault-block mountain's 1800-foot
eastern cliff, views extend across high desert
hills and salt lakebeds to distant Cascade
peaks. Birdlife thrives at Summer Lake's
refuge.

Climate

July and August afternoons top 100° F. Intensely cold December and January bring light
snows. Spring and fall are pleasant. Annual
precipitation is a scant 9 inches.

Plants and Wildlife

Marshes north of Summer Lake attract bald
eagles and whistling swans in winter, migratory species in spring and fall, and white
pelicans, Canada geese, and sandhill cranes in
summer. The best bird-watching is during
March and April.

Unusually salt-tolerant plants survive in
Summer Lake's vast alkali flats, including
three spiny shrubs: greasewood, shadscale, and
hopsage (blooms brilliant orange in July).
Sagebrush dominates Diablo Mountain, but
May brings wildflower shows of yellow,
orange, and red Indian paintbrush.

Bobcats are common in uplands, but they're
shy. Watch for sage grouse and flocks of western bluebirds. Raptors nest in rimrock.

Geology

Great Basin faults left the impressive, east-
facing scarps of Winter Ridge and Diablo
Mountain. Summer Lake, with no outlet, is
the salty remnant of a 40-mile-long Ice Age
lake.

THINGS TO DO

Hiking

From the Wildlife Refuge Campground on
the Ana River, walk Summer Lake's marshland
dikes to spot birds and muskrat.

Diablo Mountain's breathtaking, 1800-foot
cliff deserves an overnight trip, but a 4.5-mile
(one way) day hike also reaches the summit.
Drive east from the Summer Lake store 7 miles
to a fenceline. Hike east and north around the
fenceline to the peak.

Wildcat Mountain is the best viewpoint in
the south, a 1-mile cross-country hike from either of two dirt roads. North of the area, drive
past the area's only brushless dunes to the base
of Rocky Butte, then explore cliff-rimmed
Sand Canyon.

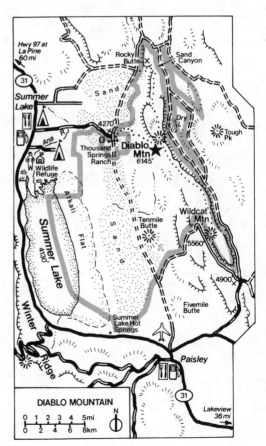

59. Gearhart Mountain

LOCATION: 36 mi NW of Lakeview, 66 mi E of
  Klamath Falls
SIZE: 72 sq mi
STATUS: 35 sq mi designated wilderness (1964,
  1984)
TERRAIN: forested ridges, cliffs, valleys
ELEVATION: 5700'–8364'
MANAGEMENT: Fremont NF
TOPOGRAPHIC MAPS: Gearhart Mountain
  Wilderness (USFS); Coleman Point,
  Coffeepot Creek, Lee Thomas Crossing,
  Cougar Peak (USGS, 7.5'); Fishhole Moun-
  tain (USGS, 15')

Picturesque cliffs and rock domes top this
long, low-profile mountain. Nearby, Dead
Horse Rim and Coleman Rim feature clifftop
viewpoints and stately stands of old-growth
ponderosa pine. Throughout, lush meadows
dot high, once-glaciated valleys.

Climate

Summer days shine clear and seldom hot in
this forested upland. Be prepared for possible
afternoon thunderstorms and frosty nights.
Snow blocks the Gearhart Mountain Trail's
crest from November to mid-June. Snow covers Dead Horse Rim, Coleman Rim, and most
roads from early December to the end of April.
Winters can be extremely cold. Annual precipitation ranges from 20 inches at Gearhart
Mountain to 14 inches in the east.

Plants and Wildlife

The parklike stands of ponderosa pine here
survive wildfire well. Because old-growth
ponderosas lack low branches, fires burn brush
and grass without reaching the trees' crowns.

Ponderosa pine

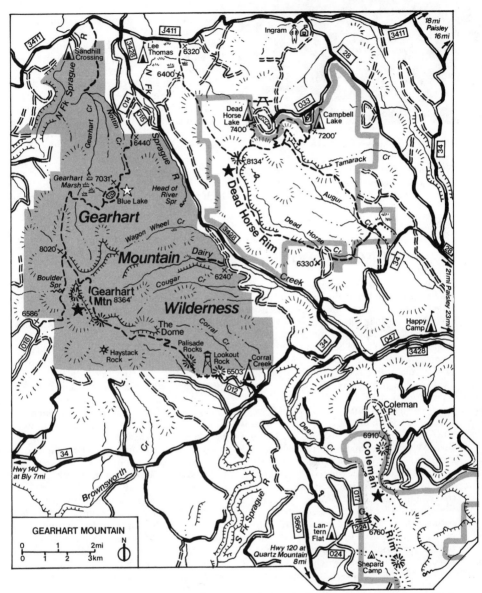

GEARHART MOUNTAIN

0   1   2mi
0   1   2   3km

Ponderosa bark, which turns orange after a century or more in the sun and develops a pleasant vanilla smell, features a jigsaw-puzzle surface that flakes off during fires to remove heat from the trunk.

The smaller, denser lodgepole pines burn easily in forest fires, but reseed profusely because their cones open after a fire's heat. Many lodgepole pines have been killed by mountain pine beetles, making room for white pine, and at high elevations, supple-limbed whitebark pine. Lodgepoles have two needles to a cluster, while ponderosas have three. Other local pines have five.

Mammals here include mule deer, black bear, coyotes, and porcupine. Listen for litttle, round-eared pikas whistling from their rock-slide homes.

Geology

Both Gearhart Mountain and Dead Horse Rim began as shield-shaped volcanoes built of many thin basalt layers. The older of the two, Gearhart Mountain may once have stood 10,000 feet high. Erosion uncovered the resistant lava which forms its summit cliffs, The Dome, and Haystack Rock. Ice Age glaciers scooped out the impressive U-shaped valleys of

Dead Horse Rim (photo by Wendell Wood)

Gearhart Creek, and Dairy Creek. Dead Horse Creek drains the broad caldera of the Dead Horse volcano.

Coleman Rim's cliff is the scarp of a fault block, like most cliff-edged mountains in the Great Basin.

THINGS TO DO

Hiking

From the north end of the popular, well-graded Gearhart Mountain Trail an easy 1.6-mile hike reaches often-crowded Blue Lake and a view of the long, low mountain 4.4 trail miles beyond. To drive to the trailhead from Paisley (on Highway 31 between Lakeview and Summer Lake), take Mill Street west from town 1 mile, turn right onto gravel Road 3411 for 27 miles, turn left on Road 3428 for 1.6 miles, turn right on Road 015 for a half mile, and turn right on Road 014 to its end.

From the south end of the Gearhart Mountain Trail, day hikers starting at Lookout Rock's tower sometimes stop at The Dome, 3 miles in. However, the cliffs, views, and meadows become increasingly spectacular for the next 2.8 miles, from The Dome to the trail's high point below Gearhart Mountain's summit cliffs. To reach the trailhead from Paisley, drive west of town on Mill Street (which becomes gravel Road 33) for 19 miles, turn left on Road 28 for 2 miles, turn right on Road 3428 for 8 miles, switchback to the left on Road 34 for 5 miles, then turn right on Road 012 to its end.

On a clear day, hikers atop Gearhart Mountain's summit can spot Steens Mountain, the Three Sisters, and even Mt. Lassen. Take the trail from Lookout Rock 4.8 miles to a pass, then hike the trailless, but easily followed open ridge another mile to the top. No special gear or use of hands is required.

The Boulder Spring Trail offers a quiet shortcut to Gearhart Mountain's high country. This 2.7-mile route climbs from a ponderosa pine forest at Road 018 to a trail junction on the peak's shoulder, passing the meadows at Boulder Spring on the way. To reach the trailhead from Bly (between Klamath Falls and Lakeview), take Highway 140 a mile east of town, turn north for a half mile on a county road, turn right on Road 34 for 4 miles, turn left on Road 335 for 1.5 miles, and turn right on Road 018 for 7 miles.

Dead Horse Rim, though nearly as tall as Gearhart Mountain, sees much lighter use. For a 1.5-mile warm-up hike here, take the trail between Campbell Lake and Dead Horse Lake campgrounds. Connecting trails switchback up to the rim's 8134-foot summit. The shortest route to the top, however, is the 1.7-mile path beginning at the west end of Dead Horse Lake. After soaking in the view at the rim's high point, hikers can explore trails along the forested ridgecrest 4.3 miles south to a Weyerhaeuser road or 4.5 miles north to Road 3411. Beaver ponds obscure the path near the Road 3411 trailhead; the Forest Service has scheduled trail reconstruction here for 1988.

Cross-country hiking is easy in the area's open forests; bring a compass and topographic map. At Gearhart Mountain and Dead Horse Rim, strike off from established trails to follow ridges or find meadows in high creek basins. Old trails at Dairy Creek and to Gearhart Creek from Road 3411 provide good starts. Likewise, cross-country hikes are the way to explore Coleman Rim's interesting ridgecrests, old-growth ponderosa pine forests, and meadows. Two routes lead to Coleman Rim from the undeveloped Lantern Flat Campground on Road 024. Either drive 0.7 mile past Lantern Flat on Road 024 and hike east through aspen-filled meadows (known as Shepard Camp), or drive north from Lantern Flat 0.7 mile on Road 017 and hike abandoned Road 224 east to meadows along the rim.

Backpackers can hike the entire 12.1-mile Gearhart Mountain Trail or simply spend a few days in the high country exploring from a base camp. Firewood is scarce and fire danger often high; bring a camp stove. Saddle stock are allowed within 200 feet of open water in the designated wilderness only for watering, loading, or travel on trails.

Winter Sports

Though none of the roads in the area are plowed in winter, cars can usually drive from Lakeview or Bly to the Corral Creek Campground (elevation 5960 feet) by early April. From there, ski or snowshoe 2 miles up to the Lookout Rock tower and another nearly level mile to Palisade Rocks.

Boating

Small craft do well on half-mile-long Dead Horse Lake and smaller Campbell Lake; no motors allowed.

60. Crane Mountain

LOCATION: 5 mi E of Lakeview
SIZE: 61 sq mi
STATUS: undesignated wilderness
TERRAIN: forested fault block mountain, high meadows
ELEVATION: 5200'–8454'
MANAGEMENT: Fremont NF
TOPOGRAPHIC MAPS: Crane Mountain, Crane Creek, Lakeview NE, Horse Prairie (USGS, 7.5')

Highest point in south-central Oregon, Crane Mountain lifts its sudden scarp above the sagebrush flatlands and shore marshes of vast Goose Lake.

Climate
Very cold winters whiten the mountain's crest by late November; the snow lingers to late May. Summer temperatures are pleasantly mild. With only 20 inches of average annual precipitation, blue skies predominate.

Quaking aspen

Plants and Wildlife
May and June bring wildflower displays to the high meadows covering much of this long mountain. Expect Indian paintbrush, aster, arrowhead balsamroot, clarkia, penstemon, phacelia, yarrow, and spreading phlox. In fall, white-barked quaking aspen brighten the gulches with brilliant orange leaves. Evergreen trees range from spire-shaped subalpine fir at the highest elevations to mountain mahogany on dry slopes and tall ponderosa pine in lower forests.

Bighorn sheep have been reintroduced here, though hikers are more likely to spot mule deer, jackrabbits, porcupines, and coyotes. Goose Lake's tremendously varied bird population, which peaks during spring and fall migrations, includes pelicans, herons, tundra swans, geese, and many ducks. Bald and golden eagles soar above the mountain and lake during winter.

Geology
Great Basin faulting has chopped much of southeast Oregon into broad valleys and blocky mountains. The huge fault scarp forming

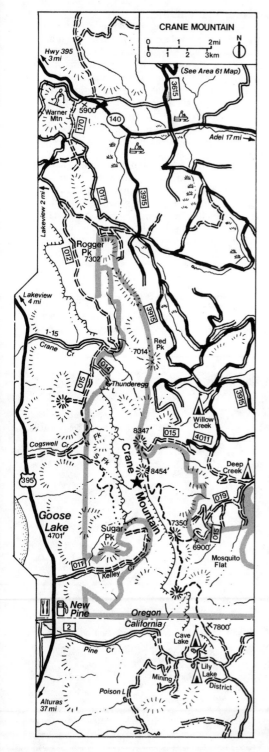

Crane Mountain's abrupt western cliffs continues north 40 miles to Abert Rim. Once-level basalt layers have been hoisted 3700 feet to the top of Crane Mountain, exposing underlying John Day rhyolite tuff on the mountain's western flank. Rockhounds find agate nodules and thundereggs in this rhyolite layer east of Highway 395.

The optimistically named Highgrade Mining District uncovered small amounts of gold-bearing quartz in the basalt flows capping the southern end of Crane Mountain. The find still puzzles geologists; basalt is usually a hopeless place to look for gold.

Older residents in the area recall when Goose Lake drained via the Pit River to the Sacramento. Irrigation has since lowered the lake, leaving it land-locked and increasingly saline.

THINGS TO DO

Hiking

Start with an overview of the area from a former lookout site on Crane Mountain's crest. Dirt Road 015 leads there but is a little rough for passenger cars; consider parking at the junction with gravel Road 4011 and walking the final 2.2 miles. Just before Road 015 ends, the Crane Mountain National Recreation Trail branches south. This scenic 8.7-mile route parallels the rim's edge into California. The highest point on Crane Mountain is a mile south along this trail and a short scramble west.

At one point, Crane Mountain narrows to a knife-edged ridge between the valleys of Kelley Creek and Deep Creek. Hike to this 7350-foot saddle for an easy day trip. To get there, drive south from Highway 140 on Road 3915 for 15 miles, turn right on Road 4015 for 1.3 miles to Deep Creek Campground, turn left on Road 019 for 2 miles, and continue uphill on rutted dirt Road 015 for 1.5 miles. From here, walk up an old 1-mile jeep track to the Crane Mountain Trail and nearby saddle.

The high meadows and open forests lend themselves to cross-country exploration. One route follows the series of knolls on the crest between Rogger Peak and Red Peak. A more rugged route follows a bench halfway up the face of Crane Mountain from Kelley Creek to Cogswell Creek.

Winter Sports

The Warner Mountain Ski Area operates a T-bar lift and day lodge from mid-December to mid-March, depending on snow conditions. The area serves as a base for cross-country ski trips south on snowed-under roads toward Crane Mountain.

61. Abert Rim and Hart Mountain

LOCATION: 25 mi NE of Lakeview, 93 mi SW of Burns
SIZE: 840 sq mi
STATUS: undesignated wilderness; 430 sq mi national wildlife refuge
TERRAIN: high desert block mountains, ephemeral lakes
ELEVATION: 4237′–8405′
MANAGEMENT: US Fish and Wildlife Service, Lakeview District BLM, Fremont NF
TOPOGRAPHIC MAPS: Lake Abert N and S; Little Honey Creek; Crook Peak; Drake Peak; Priday Reservoir; Adel; Guano Lake; Rock Canyon; Lone Grave Butte; Alger Lake; Jacobs Reservoir; Hart Lake; Warner Peak; Swede Knoll; Beatys Butte NW; Murphy Waterholes; Flook Lake; Campbell Lake; Flagstaff Lake; Rabbit Hills SW, NW, and NE; Bluejoint Lake W and E; Sixmile Draw (USGS, 7.5′)

Pronghorn antelope and bighorn sheep roam the edges of the nation's tallest fault-scarp cliffs. Marshes at the Warner Lakes attract pelicans, cranes, and swans. In the uplands, sagebrush plains stretch to the horizon.

Climate

As upland snow melts from March to May, wildflowers bloom, dry lakes fill, and mud may close some dirt roads. July and August afternoons can top 100° F though nights are cool. Fall brings mild days and frosty nights. Sub-zero snowstorms close the Plush-Frenchglen road and Highway 140 east of Adel periodically between December and March. Blue sky presides 300 days a year in this region of only 9-to 20-inch annual precipitation.

Plants and Wildlife

Graceful pronghorn antelope browse sagebrush throughout the area. North America's swiftest animals at up to 70 miles per hour, they flash their white rumps and release a musk when alarmed to flight. The Hart Mountain National Antelope Refuge reports an average of 100 to 300 head; most winter in Nevada.

Overhunting and domestic sheep diseases drove bighorn sheep to extinction in Oregon by 1915. Twenty of the curly-horned sheep reintroduced at Hart Mountain from British Columbia in 1954 multiplied with such success that animals have since been trapped here and released at many southeast Oregon locations. About 400 now live on rimrock ledges from Hart Mountain to Poker Jim Ridge, with smaller herds on the cliffs of Fish Creek Rim and Abert Rim.

Warner Lakes' marshes sustain elegant egrets, awkward white pelicans, eared grebes, ruddy ducks, geese, and many other birds. Visit in March or April for the spectacular spring migrations.

Bald eagles, golden eagles, and prairie falcons nest in rimrock ledges; Fish Creek Rim

Abert Lake and Abert Rim

averages four aeries built of sticks per mile.
Ask refuge rangers for the best spots to watch
sage grouses perform their peculiar strutting,
puffing, gurgling courtship displays at the
crack of dawn from mid-March to mid-May.

Twelve species of sagebrush grow here. Silver sage graces alkali playas. In rich soils, big
sagebrush reaches 15 feet tall with 8-inch-
diameter trunks. Near big sage, expect profuse
displays of Indian paintbrush, larkspur, buckwheat, and sage buttercups in spring. The low
sagebrush of rocky, high elevations protects
different spring flowers: bitterroot, crag aster,
and goldenweed. The rarest plants in the area
are salty Lake Abert's endangered Columbia
watercress, South Abert Rim's delicate blue-
leaved penstemon, and Guano Creek's
threatened Crosby's buckwheat.

In fall, quaking aspens in rim gulches turn
stunning yellow and orange. Small groves of
ponderosa pine—remnants of a vast Ice Age
forest here—survive near Hart Mountain's
Blue Sky Hotel camp and on Abert Rim east of
Valley Falls. The snowier Warner Mountains
about Drake Peak support fir forests.

Geology

Though history records no major earth-
quakes here, the rocks do. Very fresh-looking
fault scarps at Abert Rim, Poker Jim Ridge,
Hart Mountain, and Fish Creek Rim show that
blocks of earth have shifted 2400 feet verti-
cally, leaving plateaus and gaping lake valleys.
The landscape here must have been mostly flat
10 million years ago, for Steens Mountain
basalt flows of that age cover all these dis-
jointed rims. Hot springs and the Crump
Geyser suggest ongoing crustal activity.

The Ice Age brought rain instead of ice to
this warm region. Lake levels rose about 200
feet, unifying the Warner Lakes and connecting Lake Abert with Summer Lake (see area
58). Beaches of these once-huge lakes remain as
gravel terraces on valley edges near Plush and
along Poker Jim Ridge. Now even Lake Abert
and Hart Lake run dry in lean years.

Jasper, agate, and opal have been found on
Hart Mountain's western face. The wildlife
refuge allows collection of 7 pounds of rocks
per person.

History

Northern Paiute Indians sailed these lakes
on rafts of bundled bulrushes to hunt ducks
and gather eggs in disposable cattail baskets.
Petroglyphs remain at Hart Lake, Colvin Lake,
and the southern tip of Fish Creek Rim. Caves
in the rimrock overlooking Guano Lake may
have been occupied in the Ice Age. All artifacts
are federally protected.

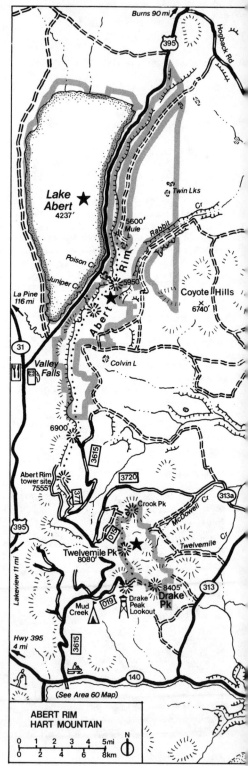

ABERT RIM
HART MOUNTAIN

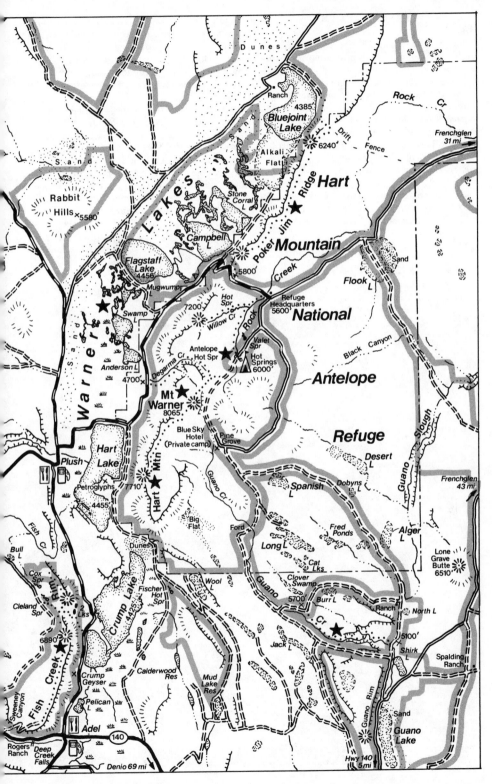

THINGS TO DO

Hiking

There are no marked trails, but rim edges, creeks, and ridges offer abundant natural pathways in this open landscape.

Drive slowly along the gravel road from Plush toward the Hart Mountain refuge, watching with binoculars for birdlife in the Warner Lakes and for bighorn sheep on the eastern cliffs. Where the road crests Poker Jim Ridge, hikers can follow the rim northwest for views across the often dry lakes below. Backpackers can hike the rim 12 miles to Bluejoint Lake.

At the refuge's Hot Springs Campground, relax in Antelope Hot Springs' 104° F natural pool. Drinking water is 1 mile down the road at Valet Spring.

Hiking routes radiate from this camp-ground. Follow Rock Creek 5 miles downstream to the refuge headquarters, passing beaver ponds along the way. Or hike 4 miles northwest onto the plateau at the head of Willow Creek to visit a bighorn sheep corral and get an impressive rim-edged view of Flagstaff Lake.

Mt. Warner, the refuge's highest viewpoint, makes a good goal for day hikers (or backpackers headed on to Hart Mountain's plateau). Since the jeep track nearest to Mt. Warner's eastern cliffs is impassable to most cars, it's best to start either on the road a mile south of Hot Springs Campground or at Guano Creek's scenic ponderosa pine grove near private Blue Sky Hotel. From either point the summit is 4 miles away and 2000 feet up.

Permits are required to camp anywhere in the refuge except Hot Springs Campground.

The Warner Lakes and Poker Jim Ridge

It's best to obtain these from the Lakeview office: Box 111, Lakeview, OR 97630; (503) 947-3315. The headquarters at the refuge is often unstaffed. The refuge also bans off-road vehicle travel, excessive noise, and destruction of live plants; firearms are restricted.

Abert Rim's stark face may look unhikable, but a little-known 2-mile trail from Highway 395 takes hikers right to the top. The unmaintained, well-graded route follows Poison Creek to a breathtaking overlook of alkalifringed Lake Abert, 1700 feet below. From the top, it's easy to follow the rim 4 miles north to a dirt road at Mule Lake. Hardy hikers interested in a loop back to Highway 395 can take Juniper Creek's rugged, trailless canyon down; it's 3 miles south of Poison Creek. For a 21-mile backpack, trek Abert Rim all the way from Mule Lake to the site of the former Abert Rim lookout tower on Road 377.

Pronghorn antelope

Little-known Fish Creek Rim raises its cliffs 2400 feet above the Warner Lakes, providing a view across 5 miles of thin air to Hart Mountain. The best routes for cross-country exploration follow the rim's edge or descend through a break in the rimrock 3.5 miles from Cleland Spring to the Plush-Adel Highway at Crump Lake. Drive to the upper rim by taking paved Road 313 north from Highway 140 for 12 miles; turn right on a rough dirt road for 8 miles, then park and hike east.

For a break from sagebrush, try the fir forests and quaking aspen groves of the Drake Peak area. Here a half dozen rounded, grassy peaks cluster about the once-glaciated basins of Twelvemile and McDowell creeks. From the Drake Peak Lookout (which is not on Drake Peak) walk or drive a rough dirt road 1 mile east, park, and then hike onward along an open ridge another mile to Drake Peak's real summit. To scale scenic Twelvemile Peak, park at the crest of the rough dirt road and walk a ridge 2.5 miles north.

Guano Creek is a misnamed oasis. Park at the creek crossing north of Shirk Lake and hike up this green-banked stream as it meanders between low rimrock walls. From Adel, drive 21 miles east on Highway 140, and then take a dirt road 13 miles north.

On all hikes, carry plenty of water. After spring all lakes and streams are dry or undrinkable due to salinity or cattle pollution. Also, dirt roads shown by dashed lines on the map are probably impassable for passenger cars; inquire locally.

Hang Gliding
Abert Rim's 2000-foot west scarp faces the west wind, and thermals off Lake Abert allow long soaring. To launch, pack gliders up the 2-mile Poison Creek trail.

62. Steens Mountain

LOCATION: 63 mi S of Burns
SIZE: 1548 sq mi, including Alvord Desert and Sheepshead Mountains
STATUS: undesignated wilderness
TERRAIN: snow-capped fault-block mountain, glaciated canyons, desert playas, sagebrush hills
ELEVATION: 4025'–9733'
MANAGEMENT: Burns District BLM, Vale District BLM
TOPOGRAPHIC MAPS: Alvord Desert, Steens Mountain to Alvord, Steens Mountain to Page Springs, Page Springs to Diamond (Desert Trail Association); Fish Lake, Wildhorse Lake, Alvord Hot Springs, Home Creek Butte, Juniper Lake, Johnny Creek NW, Mickey Springs, and 29 other maps (USGS, 7.5'); Adel (USGS, 1:250,000)

A snowy landmark for all of southeast Oregon, 50-mile-long Steens Mountain looms a vertical mile above the Alvord Desert's stark alkali flats.

Huge, U-shaped gorges dissect the western flank of Steens Mountain's 9733-foot-tall plateau. Rushing western streams lead to the Donner und Blitzen River, which winds through a rimrock-lined canyon on its way to the bird-rich marshes of the Malheur National Wildlife Refuge. The vast, treeless Sheepshead Mountains stretch to the northeast, a jumble of sagebrush ridges and dry lakebeds.

Cross-country hiking routes and a 77-mile segment of the Desert Trail lead to the popular uplands of Steens Mountain and dozens of lesser-known attractions.

Climate

A sign at the foot of the Steens Mountain Loop Road notes, "Storm area ahead. Weather may change from clear to blizzard in a few minutes. No shelters available." Winter snow and gates block access to the Steens' uplands from October 31 to July 1. However, summer on the mountain is generally cool and clear with freezing nights. Prepare for thundershowers and possible July mosquitoes or gnats. Avoid trees and high places during lightning storms.

April, May, and June are pleasant below 6000 feet, with abundant wildflowers and water. In these months, the Alvord Desert and other playas may become lakes. July and August bring blazing heat to lower elevations, with little or no shade. Fall is cool but bone dry; the Sheepshead Mountains and many other areas will have no water. December to

Pike Creek Canyon on Steens Mountain's eastern face

Sunrise at Mickey Hot Springs

February, fiercely cold winds rake the region.

Annual precipitation drops from 20 inches on Steens Mountain to just 7 inches in the Alvord Desert—Oregon's driest spot.

Plants and Wildlife

Five life zones band the mountain. Above 8000 feet, expect bunchgrass, colorful rock-encrusting lichens, and a blaze of August wildflowers. Steens paintbrush, moss gentian, a dwarf blue lupine, and showy Cusick's buck-

wheat grow atop Steens Mountain and nowhere else in the world. In high cirques, look for bleeding heart, shooting star, bitterroot, buttercup, and wild onion. A herd of over 200 bighorn sheep also likes these cirques; watch for them from the East Rim overlook.

Quaking aspen groves dot the 6500- to 8000-foot zone, with flashing leaves in summer and orange foliage in fall. Look for (but do not deface) the bawdy graffiti Basque shepherds carved in the aspen's white bark near

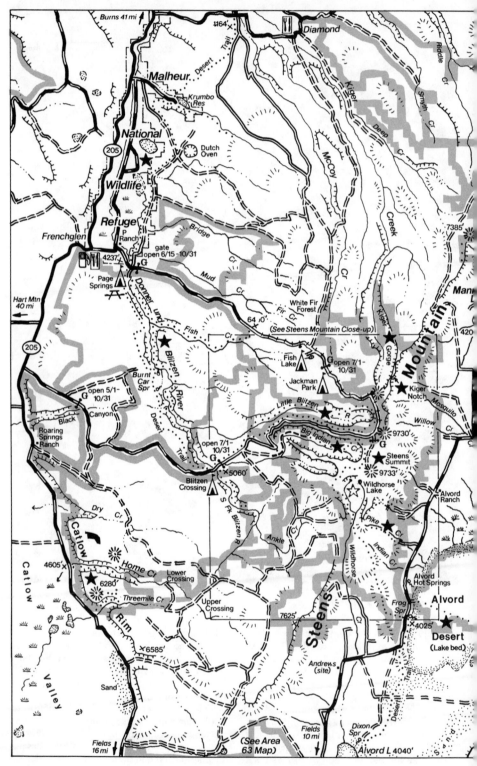

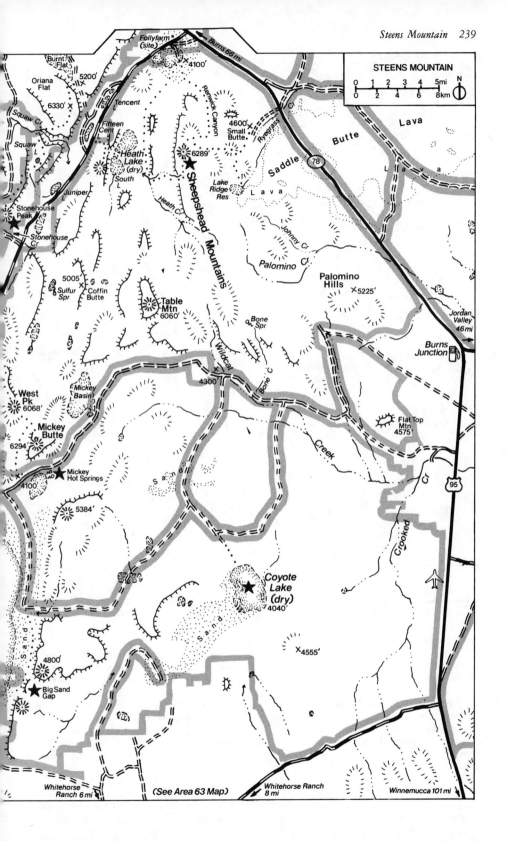

STEENS MOUNTAIN

0 1 2 3 4 5mi
0 2 4 6 8km
N

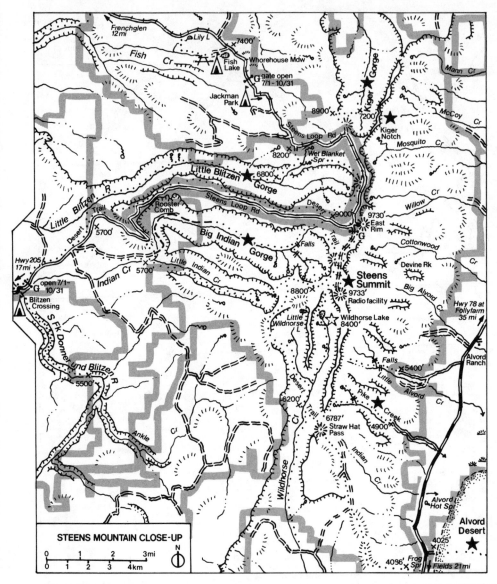

STEENS MOUNTAIN CLOSE-UP

old camps in Little Blitzen Gorge and Whorehouse Meadows. Beldings ground squirrels and marmots thrive here, as do July flowers: Clarkia, monkeyflower, and prairie star.

Juniper and low sagebrush dominate between 5500 and 6500 feet elevation. Listen at dawn for sage grouse strutting and puffing in courtship displays March to mid-May. Wild horses and antelope run here, especially on the benchlands west of Blitzen Crossing. Jackrabbits, coyotes, and rattlesnakes are common. May brings blooms of penstemon, buckwheat, and (in the Stonehouse Creek area) rare Biddle's lupine.

Below 5500 feet, tall sagebrush rules. Watch for young burrowing owls standing about their ground holes in June. At small, multi-entranced burrows, listen for the thumping of long-tailed kangaroo rats scolding within. The kit fox, once thought extinct in Oregon, still hunts the southern Sheepshead Mountains by night. Lizards abound.

Alkaline playas such as the Alvord Desert are virtually devoid of life, but salt-tolerant species cling to their sandy fringes: bright green greasewood bushes, leafless orange iodine bush, saltgrass, and spiny shadscale. Silver sage covers other dry lakebeds, such as Follyfarm Flat. Spadefoot toads emerge en

Table Mountain from Mickey Basin

masse from the ground after rains. Antelope ground squirrels scamper even in summer heat, shaded by curled white tails.

Huge flocks of migrating birds begin arriving at the Malheur National Wildlife Refuge in late February: snow geese, lesser sandhill cranes, whistling swans, and pintails. The spectacle peaks from mid-March to mid-April. Greater sandhill cranes nest in April, when migrant curlews, avocets, and stilts arrive. Songbirds pass through in April and May. By June grass is so tall at the refuge that birds are more often heard than seen. Watch for muskrats in the refuge's canals, and porcupines and great horned owls in streamside willow thickets.

Since creeks here have had no outlet to the sea for millennia, unusual fish species have evolved, including redband trout and the Catlow tui chub. Wildhorse Lake, Mann Lake, and Juniper Lake have been stocked with Lahontan trout.

Geology

All rocks here are volcanic: layers of dark basalt lava and light rhyolite ash. When this rock erupted about 15 to 20 million years ago, it covered all of southeast Oregon 4000 feet deep, leveling the landscape. The massive eruptions here matched the Columbia River basalt floods in northeast Oregon. But the Steens basalt is different—full of big feldspar crystals.

Then North America's shearing collision with the Pacific crustal plate stretched Oregon diagonally, shattering southeast Oregon into north-south-aligned basins and ranges. Steens Mountain rose entirely in the past 5 to 7 million years, while the Catlow Valley and Alvord Desert fell. The Sheepshead Mountains consist of smaller rims and basins. Hot springs indicate continuing fault movement.

The Ice Age brought increased precipitation. A lake filled the Alvord Basin 200 feet deep all the way to Coyote Lake, but found no outlet. Glaciers formed on Steens Mountain, gouging five U-shaped canyons 2000 feet deep. The canyons only left fingers of the original Steens plateau intact, and even these were breached by glaciers at Rooster Comb and Kiger Notch.

After the Ice Age ended about 10,000 years ago, eruptions along the Brothers Fault Zone produced rugged, fresh-looking basalt flows at Diamond Craters (north of Diamond) and the Saddle Butte Lava Bed.

Today, look for smooth bedrock polished by glaciers at the head of Big Indian Gorge. Along Pike Creek and Little Alvord Creek, exposed ash formations contain thundereggs, agates, and petrified wood. And in desert basins, note where wind has stripped the ground to "desert pavement," fields of pebbles stained brown by "desert varnish," a crust of oxides.

History

Seminomadic Northern Paiute Indians lived in brush lean-tos and caves in this area, relying chiefly on jackrabbits for meat and fur. Peter Skene Ogden led beaver trappers to the area's creeks in 1825-29. Army Major Enoch Steen battled the Paiutes and named the mountain in 1860. The Army established seven forts ringing the Steens Mountain area in the late 1860s, exiling Indians to reservations at Yakima and later Burns.

Pete French built a cattle empire here during 1872-97; his P Ranch near Frenchglen is now owned and maintained by the Malheur Wildlife Refuge. By 1901, Basque and Irish shepherds were grazing over 140,000 head of sheep on Steens Mountain, obliterating once-lush grasslands. Domestic sheep were banned from the mountain in 1972 but cattle still range on virtually all public lands—even the delicate wildlife refuge.

THINGS TO DO

Hiking

The area's most spectacular views are just a short walk from the Steens Mountain Loop Road. Drive this rugged route up from Frenchglen 23 miles and hike a half-mile spur road to an overlook of colossal Kiger Gorge and Kiger Notch. Walk another half mile north along the rim; at that point, a very steep scramble trail descends 1400 feet to the valley floor.

Next, drive 3 miles further along the Loop Road and walk a spur road 0.4 mile to the East Rim's breathtaking vista of the Alvord Desert. Then, from the same parking spot on the Loop Road, hike south on a gated road 2.5 miles to the Steens' highest point, with Wildhorse Lake in a gaping canyon below. A very rough trail drops 1300 feet down to the lake.

The Desert Trail traversing Steens Mountain is not a specific footpath but rather a general corridor marked by cairns. Hikers must pick their own route through the open, generally treeless terrain. A topographic map and compass are essential. To see the most, plan to backpack. Since dead sagebrush is the only firewood, bring a camp stove.

In the Steens uplands, follow the Desert Trail and its alternate routes through any of four colossal gorges. Expect wildflowers, plenty of springs, scenic quaking aspen, and waterfalls. Start the 9-mile route along the Little Blitzen River either at the steep trail down from Wet Blanket Springs, or at the canyon mouth (park on the Steens Loop Road at a curve 3.5 miles from Blitzen Crossing and traverse a slope north).

Begin hikes up Big and Little Indian canyons from the Steens Loop Road, too. Drive 5 miles east of Blitzen Crossing to a hairpin curve and hike down the steep hillside to where the creeks meet. It's 11 miles via either canyon to the Steens Loop Road near East Rim Viewpoint, but only confident hikers should attempt to scramble up the rugged headwalls of these canyons.

A 15-mile section of the Desert Trail traverses impressive Wildhorse Canyon on the way from the Steens Loop Road to Frog Spring, on the Fields-Follyfarm Road. Side trips explore the alpine basins of Wildhorse and Little Wildhorse lakes.

The Donner und Blitzen River cuts a 400-foot-deep, rimrock-lined canyon through the

Coyote on the west side of Steens Mountain

sagebrush tablelands south of Page Springs Campground. The Desert Trail route parallels this canyon across the tableland. It's rougher but more interesting to hike up the canyon bottom from Page Springs. Expect to wade occasionally. Fish Creek's side canyon is also worth exploring.

North of Page Springs, the Desert Trail follows Malheur Wildlife Refuge backroads. Camping is banned on refuge lands, as are horses, open fires, swimming, and rock collecting.

The east side of Steens Mountain also offers interesting day hikes and overnight trips. Check the gas gauge before driving the Fields-Follyfarm Road to the Alvord Desert. If the desert lakebed is dry, hike out onto the cracked, alkali surface a few miles to experience this remarkably empty playa and to admire the view of snowy Steens Mountain. Better yet, camp in the desert, continue to the greasewood-covered sand hummocks of the far shore (7 miles distant), prowl Big Sand Gap's canyon, and climb to the rimrock viewpoints nearby.

For this and other desert hikes, do not travel in midsummer heat, carry a gallon of water for each day, and bring a hat or cloth for shade. Expect roads shown by dashed lines to be passable only by four-wheel-drive vehicles.

Conclude a visit to the Alvord Desert with a relaxing soak in the Alvord Hot Springs, easily visible 100 yards from the Fields-Follyfarm Road. The Alvord Ranch owns the springs but allows the public to use the site. Reward this courtesy by keeping the area free of litter.

Driving north from the Alvord Desert, choose one of Steens Mountain's steep eastern canyons to explore on a day hike. Pike Creek and Little Alvord Creek are favorites, with waterfalls, rugged rock narrows, wildflowers, and views of the desert playa below. Start hiking at the end of the dirt roads leading up these creeks. Rocks and streamside brush make these cross-country hikes rough. Expect to detour uphill to the right several times to circumvent cliffs along Little Alvord Creek.

Mickey Hot Springs feature shifting steam vents, mud pots, and turquoise "glory pools" as hot as 210° F. Walk about this harsh area and nearby playa, or climb treeless Mickey Butte for a bird's-eye view of Steens Mountain.

The Sheepshead Mountains are the most barren and forbidding-looking hills in Oregon. And therein lies their secret charm. For even when spring fills the creeks and fires the sagebrush slopes with wildflowers, there are no crowds in this huge world of hidden canyons, cliffs, and valleys. To sample this range, hike 2 miles east from Fifteen Cent Lake (on

The Alvord Desert

the Fields-Follyfarm Road) through a canyon to hidden Heath Lake's playa, and scale an unnamed rim nearby for a view. To see more, backpack south from Follyfarm Flat at Highway 78, hike up Renwick Canyon, follow the high rim of the Sheepshead scarp, descend North Heath Creek's canyon, and return to Follyfarm—23 miles in all.

Try these other utterly uncrowded scenic areas for hiking:

The far northern end of Steens Mountain. Hike north from Stonehouse Peak's castle-shaped rock along a 7000-foot rim or explore the lakes and aspen groves near perennial Squaw Creek.

Catlow Rim. Walk up the canyons of Threemile Creek or Home Creek between sheer, 1300-foot walls and hike to a rim-edged overlook of Catlow Valley and distant Hart Mountain.

Coyote Lake. Devotees of pure desert delight that this desolate playa is even more remote than its Alvord Desert twin.

Runners compete each August on Oregon's highest 10-kilometer course, the Steens Rim Run from Fish Lake to the 9730-foot East Rim. Record time is 47 minutes.

Winter Sports

Powder snow and far-ranging winter vistas are plentiful on Steens Mountain's crest, but difficult access and treacherous weather stop all but the most accomplished snow campers from skiing or snowshoeing there. Sudden whiteouts and freezing winds can occur in any month. Arrange with the Burns District BLM office (503) 573-2071, to pick up snow gate keys at Campers Corral, near Page Springs Campground. In April, expect snow to block the road at least 3 miles before Fish Lake.

63. Pueblo Mountains and Trout Creek Mountains

LOCATION: 105 mi S of Burns, 100 mi N of Winnemucca

SIZE: 682 sq mi, including Rincon Creek and Alvord Peak

STATUS: undesignated wilderness

TERRAIN: fault-block mountains, creek canyons, desert flats

ELEVATION: 4040'–8634'

MANAGEMENT: Burns District BLM, Vale District BLM

TOPOGRAPHIC MAPS: Pueblo Mountains, Alvord Desert (Desert Trail Association); Chicken Springs, Little Whitehorse Creek, Doolittle Creek, Oregon Canyon Ranch, Van Horn Basin, Ladycomb Peak, and 16 other maps (USGS, 7.5'); Adel, Jordan Valley (USGS, 1:250,000)

South of the desolate Alvord Desert, the Pueblo Mountains surprise hikers with high meadow basins nestled against snowy cliffs. In the Trout Creek Mountains, a dozen creeks have cut scenic, rimrock-lined canyons into a high tableland.

Van Horn Creek Canyon in the Pueblo Mountains

Climate

In the Pueblos, snow blocks the Desert Trail from November to late May. Wildflowers peak in June. July and August are only hot in the lowlands. Sudden storms bring lightning and occasionally even snow in summer.

In the Trout Creek Mountains, the snowpack melts and wildflowers appear in early May. Heavy cattle grazing from July 1 to September 15 diminishes midsummer appeal. Fall is cool and dry.

Annual precipitation, just 7 inches in the lowlands, creeps to 15 inches in the Trout Creek Mountains and 20 in the Pueblos.

Plants and Wildlife

Unusual fish have evolved here, cut off from the sea for millennia. The 90° F alkaline hot springs at Borax Lake support their own species, the 2-inch-long Borax chub. The only fish in the branches of Willow Creek or Whitehorse Creek are native Whitehorse trout, typically 6 to 10 inches long. Trout Creek's fish are redband trout, while the branches of Oregon Canyon Creek and McDermitt Creek host a hybrid of native Lahontan trout and introduced rainbow trout.

Sagebrush and bunchgrass dominate, but

willow and quaking aspen turn streams into linear oases. On open slopes, mountain mahogany develop elongated tree crowns—a result of browsing below and shearing winds above.

Wildflowers in meadows include blue lupine, sunflowerlike balsamroot, phlox and the showy Bruneau mariposa lily. In dry areas, look for delicate penstemon and pink bitterroot. Along creeks expect tall larkspur, mint, and 3-foot-tall bluebells.

Oregon Canyon is a veritable museum of rare and endangered wildflowers: red buttercup, Lemmon's onion, two-stemmed onion, and bristle-flowered collomia. The Pueblos' Cottonwood Creek harbors one of the northernmost populations of Mormon tea, a green, leafless bush used to brew a mild stimulant. Oregon's only long-flowered snowberry bushes grow along Fifteenmile Creek.

Beavers work virtually every stream. Bighorn sheep live in the Pueblos, but mule deer are more often sighted. Partridgelike chukars by the hundreds cluck in lower canyons of the Pueblos. Listen for the California quail's three-syllable call, the western meadowlark's territorial songs, and the omnipresent Brewers sparrow. Watch for sage grouse and prairie falcons.

Mountain mahogany, trimmed by cattle below and wind above (photo by William L. Sullivan)

Geology

Steens Basalt lava and ash buried all of southeast Oregon 15 to 20 million years ago. Great Basin faulting then hacked the flattened landscape into block-shaped, tilted plateaus such as these two ranges. Fault scarps here have exposed the older rock beneath the basalt. Granite, greenstone, and schists along the eastern base of the Pueblos and in canyons of the western Trout Creek Mountains contain gold, copper, and mercury.

Two enormous, violent volcanoes on faults in the Trout Creek Mountains collapsed about 14 million years ago, leaving 15-mile-wide, Crater-Lake-style calderas. The lakes filled with sediment and breached their rims. Willow Creek and McDermitt Creek now drain the two basins. A long arc of cliffs between Disaster Peak and the head of Oregon Canyon marks the McDermitt Caldera rim.

History

The 1860's Pueblo Mining District gave the range its name. Look for stone cabin ruins in Denio Canyon and along the Pueblos' Willow Creek. Mining continues in Denio Basin.

The Rose Valley Borax Company once shipped 400 tons of borax per year from Borax Lake to Winnemucca via 16-mule-team wagons. The Nature Conservancy now leases the lake to protect its ecosystem.

Whitehorse Ranch, headquarters for John Devine's cattle empire during 1869-89, remains a showplace of the old West.

THINGS TO DO

Hiking

The popular Desert Trail route parallels the Pueblo Mountains' crest for 22 miles from Denio to Fields. Day hikers can sample the route at Denio Canyon and from the Domingo Pass Road near Roux Ranch. Backpackers can take side trips to the 8634-foot summit of Pueblo Mountain (southeast Oregon's second highest point) or along the cliff-edged ridge to the west. Other side routes ascend Cottonwood Creek, Colony Creek's canyon meadows, and Van Horn Creek's narrow, rugged gorge.

In the Pueblos, 48 cairns mark the cross-country route of the Desert Trail. Although each rockpile is within sight of the last, it's still easy to miss the cairns; a topographic map and compass are essential. All other hiking routes are unmarked, but the open terrain invites cross-country travel and animal trails simplify most canyon routes. Water sources are plentiful in the high Pueblos and along major streams in the Trout Creek Mountains; elsewhere, carry a gallon per day. Sagebrush is the only firewood; use a camp stove.

Borax Lake makes a fascinating day hike goal. Park at Soap Lake amid brush-covered sand dunes and fields of Apache teardrops (wind-polished obsidian). Hike a mile to Borax Lake, passing a sod house and rusting borax vat, and then continue 2 miles north along a string of algae-colored hot springs, turquoise "glory pools," and steam vents to alkaline Alvord Lake's sandy shore.

For a desert challenge, hike the Desert Trail 25 miles across sagebrush flats from Fields to the Alvord Desert (see area 62 map). The Steens, Pueblos, and Trout Creek Mountains

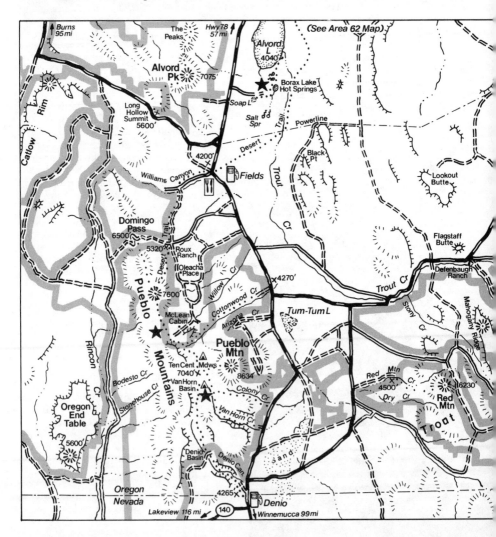

look deceptively near all the way. Avoid mid-summer's blazing heat. The only water source is Dixon Spring, 14 miles from Fields.

In the Trout Creek Mountains, hikers often begin excursions from base camps at Mud Spring or Chicken Spring. From Mud Spring, hike east 2 miles to an overlook of 1600-foot-deep Oregon Canyon. Many possible routes lead to the bottom. Backpackers can prowl Oregon Canyon Creek's forks and botanize. Less difficult access to this canyon requires permission to cross the Echave Ranch downstream.

Whitehorse Creek's many-branched canyon lies 1 mile west of Mud Spring. Pick one of many routes down through breaks in the rimrock and explore side canyons for beaver dams, waterfalls, and colonnades of spire-shaped rock formations.

From Chicken Spring, drive south 5 miles to McDermitt Creek and hike up the North or South Fork to high meadows amid extensive stands of quaking aspen. From there, back-packers can continue 15 miles down Little Whitehorse Creek's winding, rimrock-lined canyon.

Orevada View, this range's highest area, is a 8506-foot plateau overlooking cone-shaped Disaster Peak and four states. The 4-mile cross-country route across the plateau skirts private land at Sherman Field.

Winter Sports

Fierce winter weather limits skiing or snow-shoeing in the Pueblo Mountains to experts. By late March the snow level is typically at 5600 feet, but winds have sorted things into icy slopes and awkward drifts.

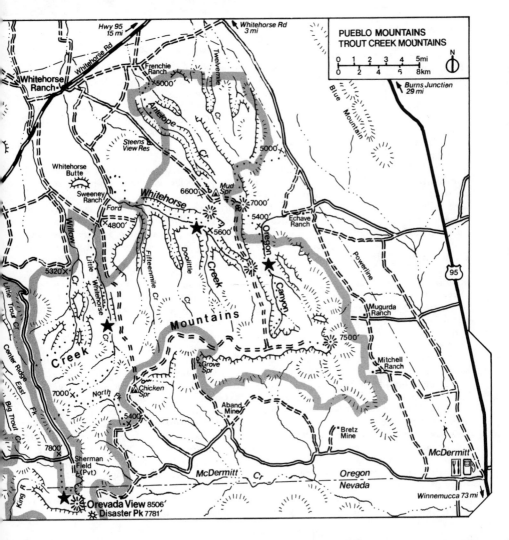

64. Lower Owyhee River

LOCATION: 40 mi S of Ontario, 104 mi E of
Burns
SIZE: 792 sq mi
STATUS: federal wild and scenic river,
undesignated wilderness
TERRAIN: cliff-lined desert river, colored rock
formations, lava
ELEVATION: 2670'–6000'
MANAGEMENT: Vale District BLM
TOPOGRAPHIC MAPS: The Elbow, Pelican
Point, Rooster Comb, Diamond Butte,
Jordan Craters N and S, The Hole In The
Ground, Rinehart Canyon, Lambert Rocks,
Owyhee Butte, and 25 other maps (USGS,
7.5'); Jordan Valley, Boise (USGS,
1:250,000)

The Honeycombs (photo by Don Geary)

Whitewater boaters on this desert river drift
into a remote world of towering stone canyons,
wild rapids, cliffside caves, and rock pinnacles.
Hikers can follow the canyon too, or investi-
gate the colored crags of The Honeycombs.
Nearby, Jordan Craters Lava Bed features spatter cones and Coffeepot Crater.

Climate

Blue sky and frosty nights predominate
from April to June, but even in this popular
season the desert climate can bring surprise
snow flurries or 100° F heat. July and August
are too hot for travel, but autumn's coolness
again allows hiking. The very cold winter
brings only light snows to this region of just 11
inches of annual precipitation.

Plants and Wildlife

One hundred fifty wild horses and 200
bighorn sheep roam the rock gulches east of
Owyhee Reservoir; in the winter they're joined
by an average of 850 mule deer. Commonly
sighted smaller wildlife include white-tailed
antelope ground squirrels, rattlesnakes, and
lizards.

The river and reservoir attract 150 species of
songbirds and numerous waterfowl. Bald eagles come to hunt these birds and usually stay
until the reservoir is drained for winter. Another good birding spot is Batch Lake, a cluster
of marshy potholes amid the Jordan Craters
lava. Look for white pelicans, sandhill cranes,
and egrets.

Sagebrush dominates here, though juniper
survive atop the tallest peaks and gnarled hack-
berry trees hug some river benches. The only
pine trees, at last count, were 49 ponderosas on
a ridge south of Leslie Gulch. The ashy soils of

this area have produced a wealth of rare wildflowers. Ertter's grounsel, MacKenzie's phacelia, Owyhee clover, two species of milk
vetch, and grimy ivesia are known chiefly from
Leslie Gulch. A new penstemon was identified
in the early 1980s north of Dry Creek Buttes.

Geology

Erosion carved the colored badlands and
rock pinnacles here from compacted volcanic
ash deposits as much as 2000 feet thick. Sand-
wiched throughout this immense ash layer are
resistant basalt lava flows also 15 to 20 million
years old. This volcanic activity may have
dammed the ancestral Snake River, for the
ash's stripy strata indicate lakebed deposition.

The old basalt now forms a rimrock cap at
Table Mountain, Red Butte, and many other
places. The partially welded ash of The
Honeycombs contains weak spots that have
eroded into caves, ledges, and honeycomb-like
indentations. Paleontologists unearthed horse,
bear, camel and antelope fossils from ash near
Red Butte. Succor Creek State Park allows
amateur collecting of thundereggs, agates, and
petrified wood from ash deposits there.

Coffeepot Crater and Lava Butte vented the
Jordan Craters Lava Beds within the past 9000
years. Look for lava tubes and spatter cones
near these two source vents. The relatively
smooth, ropy surface of these pahoehoe-style
lava flows has been jumbled by pressure ridges,
cracks, domes, and collapsed caves. Jordan
Craters sits atop the Brothers Fault Zone,
source of a string of recent eruptions across
southeast Oregon.

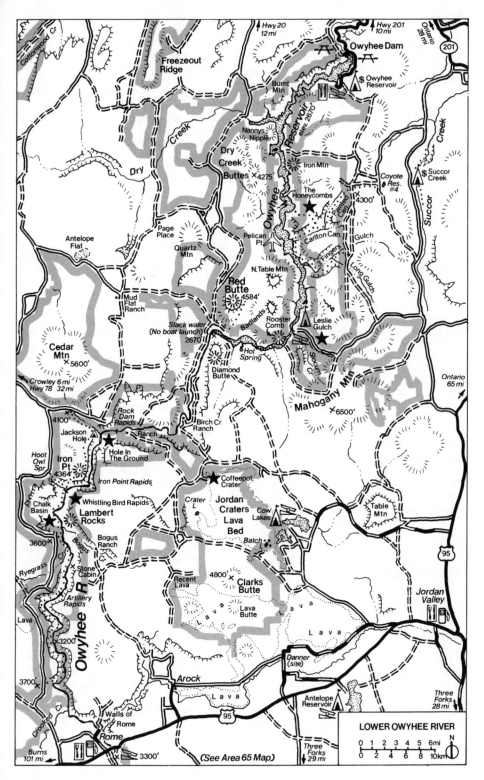

LOWER OWYHEE RIVER

0 1 2 3 4 5 6mi

0 2 4 6 8 10km

N

History

Cave campsites, petroglyphs, and arrow-heads indicate humans have lived along the Owyhee River for 12,000 years. The name Owyhee—a 19th-century spelling for Hawaii—commemorates two Hawaiians hired by early beaver trappers and killed here by Indians in 1819. Fish runs on the Owyhee died when the Owyhee Dam was built in the 1930s. The reservoir now teems with black crappies; the river supports small populations of catfish, suckers, and carp.

THINGS TO DO

Hiking

Boats provide a good way to reach many hiking areas. While drifting the Owyhee north of Rome, stop at Chalk Basin to spend a day exploring the colored rock formations and delicately fluted cliffs there. Not far downstream, stop at a huge, river-level cave near Whistling Bird Rapids and hike up a sandy-bottomed gulch past rock narrows and dry waterfalls to Hoot Owl Spring. From the same base camp, another good cross-country hike climbs up 1300 feet in elevation to the canyon rim and Iron Point, practically overhanging the river.

From the Owyhee Reservoir, hikable sandy washes lead to The Honeycombs, gulches lined with pinnacles. The formations are most concentrated north of Carlton Canyon, but extend to Three Fingers Gulch and Leslie Gulch. Rugged passes provide routes between canyons.

From the south end of Owyhee Reservoir, climb to viewpoints at Rooster Comb and Red Butte. Between these lies a colorful badlands of rounded hills.

No boat? Then drive to these hikes. A dirt road north from Rome comes within a 2-mile walk of scenic Chalk Basin, and within 4 miles of Iron Point. Those driving via Burns can take a shortcut to this area by turning left off Highway 78 at Follyfarm Junction, 66 miles from Burns. Take the gravel Crowley Road 25 miles, turn right on dirt Riverside Road 5 miles, and then turn right for another 6 miles to a junction. The right fork leads toward Chalk Basin and Rome. Or take the left fork 2 miles, park, and hike 4 miles down a gulch to reach Jackson Hole—where the Lower Owyhee Canyon is at its deepest and narrowest.

The road to Leslie Gulch is well marked; The Honeycombs are trickier to find overland. To get there, drive south from Ontario 32 miles on Highway 201, turn right onto the dirt Succor Creek Road for 6 miles, turn left onto an unmarked dirt road for 6 miles, take a fork to the right for 2 miles, and then take a left fork for another 2 miles to the watering tank

labeled number 4. From here hike west on a jeep track 2 miles to the head of Painted Canyon. The further one hikes down this canyon, the more dramatic it becomes.

Wear sturdy boots to explore Jordan Craters' lavaland. Coffeepot Crater is the most popular day hike goal, though Batch Lake's wildlife and Lava Butte's lava tubes are also of interest.

Backpackers can spend a few days exploring The Honeycombs, or else prowl the Owyhee's rim from Jackson Hole to Chalk Basin. From Chalk Basin it's possible to hike 24 miles south along the trailless riverbank toward Rome; hike up to the road before hitting private land at Crooked Creek.

On all hikes, bring plenty of water. Pure water sources are limited to infrequent springs along the Owyhee River. A U-shaped tent peg helps tap these dribbles, but by late summer many are dry. Water from the Owyhee River, Owyhee Reservoir, and (misnamed) Dry Creek must be treated.

Boating

First floated in 1953, the 63-mile stretch of Owyhee River between Rome and the reservoir has become a popular four- to five-day trip. Intermediate-level rafters and kayakers generally portage or line through the class 4 rapids (Whistling Bird and Rock Dam). Caution is most important, for losing a boat on this very remote desert river means trouble. No permits are required.

Upstream snowmelt makes the river runable only in April and May (kayaks sometimes run until mid-June); bring gear for cold weather. There are few springs, so carry a day's supply of drinking water. Motors are banned on the river.

The first serious whitewater, class 3 Artillery Rapids, comes 17.5 miles down from the Rome launch site. Twelve miles beyond, stop on the left to scout or portage Whistling Bird Rapids. A slab of canyon wall has tumbled into the river here on the right, forcing boaters hard left. Three miles downstream, Iron Point Rapids provide a class 3 drop at a sharp right riverbend. The last major hurdle comes 7 miles farther along, where an abandoned rock dam partially blocks the river. In low water, line boats on the right. In high water, experts run the dam's middle or left side.

Owyhee Reservoir's slack water at mile 55 leaves boaters 8 miles to paddle (4 hours for rafts) to the Leslie Gulch ramp. Rest after 3 miles at the south shore hot springs.

Canoes and sailboats do well on the reservoir despite competing powerboats. Shoreside campsites abound.

65. Upper Owyhee River

LOCATION: 105 mi SE of Burns
SIZE: 820 sq mi
STATUS: federal wild and scenic river,
    undesignated wilderness
TERRAIN: sheer-walled river canyons,
    whitewater, sagebrush tablelands
ELEVATION: 3300'–6500'
MANAGEMENT: Vale District BLM, Oregon
    Land Board
TOPOGRAPHIC MAPS: Three Forks,
    Whitehorse Butte, Skull Creek, Indian Fort,
    Dry Creek, Scott Reservoir, Drummond
    Basin, No Crossing, Rawhide Pocket,
    Rawhide Springs, Guadaloupe Meadow,
    Brewster Reservoir, and 19 other maps
    (USGS, 7.5'); Jordan Valley (USGS,
    1:250:000)

Oregon's wildest whitewater river cuts a
dramatic, 1000-foot-deep slot through the
sagebrush tablelands where Oregon, Idaho,
and Nevada meet. Drift boaters here pass
cliffside caves and hot springs on their way to
raging Widowmaker Rapids. Hikers either
follow the branching canyon's arid rims or
trace the canyon bottoms, wading when
streams careen between sheer cliffs.

Climate
In April and May, when the river is high
enough to be run, prepare for unpredictable
weather: balmy blue sky, freezing nights, sear-
ing heat, or even snow. After a rain, dirt roads
may be impassably muddy—especially the
final mile to Three Forks. The only bridge in
the area is at Rome; all other crossings are
fords, made difficult by early spring runoff.
May and June are best for hiking in the
uplands. Plan canyon-bottom hikes for September or October when streams are low and
fordable. Avoid the freezing winds of winter or
the scorching heat of July and August. Annual
precipitation measures just 11 inches.

Plants and Wildlife
Watch for kingfishers and water ouzels
along the water's edge, fat chukars in the side
gulches, and raptors nesting in the rimrock:

The Owyhee Canyon just below the Three Forks launch site

Widowmaker Rapids, moments before the whitewater stripped this raft of both boaters and gear

golden eagles, buteos, and prairie falcons. Sage grouse, jackrabbits, and rattlesnakes are more numerous here than anywhere else in Oregon.

Sagebrush and bunchgrass dominate this treeless terrain. Plant life in the canyons remains pristine, for cliffs restrict cattle grazing to the uplands. Phlox and evening primrose provide delicate flowers in spring. Rabbit brush and sunflowerlike balsamroot bloom yellow in fall.

Geology

During immense volcanic eruptions 15 to 20 million years ago, rhyolite ash exploded from vents and basalt lava spread across this entire area. Later, as the land gradually rose, the Owyhee River cut downward, exposing the orange welded ash layers and black basalt flows in canyon walls.

THINGS TO DO

Hiking

Three Forks, a remote ford near the confluence of three major Owyhee River branches, serves as a base for cross-country exploration of this trailless canyonland. Before setting out, put on boots that can get wet.

Start with a 2-mile hike up the main Owyhee River (wading two tributaries along the way) to one of the finest swimable hot springs in the state. Next, put the wet boots back on and try walking up the North Fork's streambed a few miles into that river's inner gorge, where calm, wall-to-wall water reflects the towering canyon above. For a more rugged day hike, explore the Middle Fork's slotlike canyon 3 or 4 miles up from its mouth. The Middle Fork may stop flowing altogether by fall, but leaves deep, wall-to-wall pools that require chest-deep wades.

Streamside cliffs and swift water prevent hikers from following the main Owyhee riverbank downriver from Three Forks. However, it's possible to hike atop the canyon rim all the way to Rome. The 40-mile route requires few detours (Soldier Creek is the only major side canyon to circumvent), but has no water.

Antelope Creek and the West Little Owyhee River both have long, deep, scenic, and very remote canyons. Cross-country hikers following these canyon bottoms must wade some pools and boulder-hop across a few rockslides, but they can discover towers, caves, columns, chutes, and colored rock walls. To get there, take a four-wheel-drive vehicle from Three Forks across the North and Middle Fork fords,

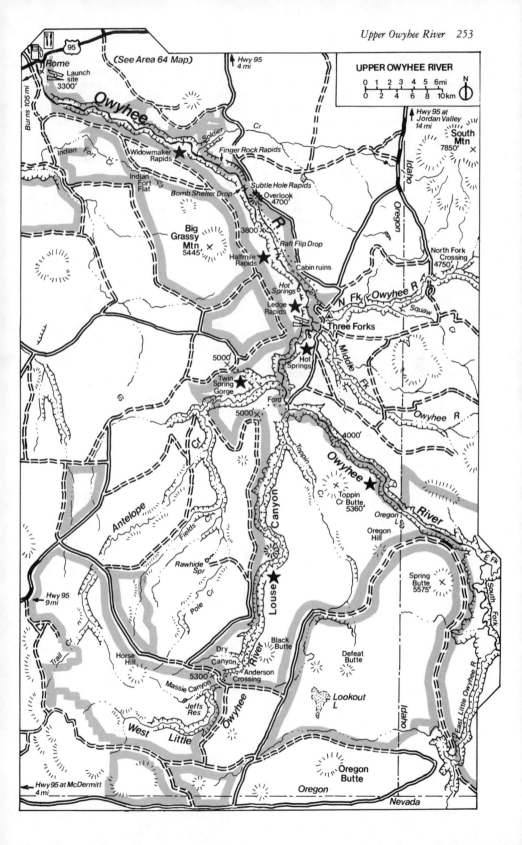

drive 3 miles up to the tablelands, turn right, descend 5 miles to the Owyhee River, and park. From there, wade the Owyhee (generally feasible by June) to the nearby canyon mouth of the West Little Owyhee River; Antelope Creek's 700-foot-deep chasm begins 2 miles downstream.

A better road reaches the upper portion of the West Little Owyhee River's canyon. Turn east off Highway 78 at a gravel road 40 miles south of Burns Junction. Follow the road 15 miles, and then turn right for 20 additional miles to Anderson Crossing. From here the canyon extends 30 miles downstream.

Boating

The 35 miles of Owyhee River between Three Forks and Rome provide one of the most challenging and scenic runs in the state. No permits are required. The run can only be made in April or May. Possible cold weather and cold water these months make hypothermia a danger; wet suits are advisable.

Just 1.5 miles below the deceptively calm waters of the Three Forks launch site, the rushing, narrow chutes of Ledge Rapids leave many a boater swimming through a rugged, quarter-mile-long rock garden. Scout this class 4+ whitewater carefully from the left side; there is no easy way out of this remote desert canyon for those who have lost their boat.

Seven miles beyond Ledge Rapids stop at a sharp right bend to scout Halfmile Rapids ahead. This class 4+ rapids begins with rocks jutting into the current on the right and continues with a full half mile of rough water. After only a 100-yard lull, boaters face Raft Flip Drop's big wave (class 3-4).

Subtle Hole (class 3+), at river mile 14 below Three Forks, is longer than Raft Flip Drop. Bomb Shelter Drop (class 3) follows immediately; pull left in order to stop at the interesting cave below it. Three miles beyond, two rocks in midstream mark the start of Finger Rock Rapids (class 3).

Class 5+ Widowmaker Rapids, at river mile 20.5, must be portaged by all but daring experts in medium-length rafts. Part of this fall's treachery is that it's preceded by a half mile of class 3 rapids. Begin a difficult portage on the right before the river ahead disappears between huge boulders. This chute, sometimes briefly mistaken for the Widowmaker itself, is actually a class 3 drop that fills boats with water, making them unmanageable at the brink of Widowmaker's 10-foot waterfall immediately ahead.

Another, less frequented Owyhee River whitewater run begins near the town of Owyhee, Nevada, and follows the South Fork Owyhee to Three Forks.

Telemarking on South Sister; Broken Top, Green Lake in background (photo by Talbot Bielefeldt)

Appendix A: State Trail Plan

A network of existing and proposed long-distance trails links many of Oregon's wild areas. Four trail routes cross the entire state. Other routes follow rivers or serve as connectors between Oregon's population centers and the longer trail routes.

The Pacific Crest Trail and routes east of the Cascades are open to both hikers and equestrians. However, all long-distance trails west of the Cascade summit (except the North Umpqua River Trail) are for hikers only.

The Pacific Crest Trail (PCT) follows the Sierra Nevada and Cascade Range on a 2500-mile route from Mexico to Canada. Though some California portions of the trail remain uncompleted, the Forest Service dedicated the final link of Oregon's 424-mile section in 1987. Begun in the 1920s as the Oregon Skyline Trail, the route was one of two trails authorized by Congress in the 1968 National Trail Systems Act. Today the well-marked route, built with a wide tread and gentle grade, has become so popular that sections near highway trailheads may be quite dusty by late summer. Snow closes much of this high-elevation trail from mid-October to early July. Several guidebooks detail the route (see Appendix D).

The Oregon Coast Trail (OCT), now 75 percent complete, uses the open sands of Oregon's public beaches for much of its 360-mile route between Washington and California. Forested trail

segments lead hikers over headlands. Gray cedar posts mark completed sections, notably the northernmost 64 miles from Fort Stevens (on the Columbia River) to Garibaldi (near Tillamook). Several guidebooks cover this all-season route (see Appendix D).

The Desert Trail (DT), crossing Oregon's southeast corner, explores high desert mountain ranges, rimrock canyons, and wide-open landscapes where sagebrush dominates. Rock cairns mark the trail's general route, allowing travelers to pick their own way through the open terrain. Trail markers and published trail guides define the completed 118-mile section between Denio (on the Nevada border) and Diamond Craters (south of Burns).

The Desert Trail Association, cooperating with the Bureau of Land Management, proposes continuing the trail as far as Mexico and Canada. The planned route south traverses Nevada to connect with an existing southern Californian portion of the Desert Trail. The route north briefly joins the New Oregon Trail in the Blue Mountains, and then crosses Hells Canyon and Idaho to follow the Continental Divide National Scenic Trail to Canada.

The New Oregon Trail (NORT), 57 percent complete, follows the crests of four mountain ranges on its 1300-mile route from Oregon's westernmost point at Cape Blanco to the state's easternmost point in Hells Canyon. The NORT connects the trans-state Oregon Coast Trail and Desert Trail, and follows a portion of the Pacific Crest Trail. The route, first hiked end-to-end by William L. Sullivan in 1985, also incorporates two earlier long-distance trail proposals: the Ochoco Trail and the Blue Mountain Trail.

Nearly all of the existing trail segments of the NORT traverse wild areas, and are thus included in this book. Hikers can fill trailless gaps by following logging roads and highway shoulders, although the route is still unmarked. Snow blocks high portions of the mountain ranges in winter.

The Columbia Gorge Trail leads from the Portland area through the Columbia Gorge, where it crosses the Pacific Crest Trail. Hikers can currently follow the route 25 miles from Sheppards Dell State Park (near Bridal Veil Falls) to Starvation Creek (near Viento State Park). Plans would extend the route east to Hood River and west to Troutdale, in order to join the 40-Mile Loop around Portland. Weather rarely closes this low-elevation route, even in winter.

The 40-Mile Loop, latest addition to the State Trail Plan, began as a 1910 proposal to link

Forest Park trails with a 40-mile route encircling Portland. Growth of the city has lengthened the mapped loop to 140 miles, but the trail's original name remains. Currently hikable throughout, the loop connects popular existing trails in Forest Park, Washington Park, Tryon State Park, and Delta Park with a variety of sidewalk and roadside walking routes.

The Indian Ridge Trail, largely undeveloped and unhikable, follows ridgelines from Silverton through Silver Falls State Park and Bull of the Woods Wilderness to the Mt. Jefferson Wilder-

ness and Pacific Crest Trail. Calapooya and Mollala Indians heading for the Cascades' hunting and huckleberry fields established this ridgetop route to avoid the dense brush of the river valleys. The State Trail Plan proposes reopening the route to hikers.

The Corvallis To The Sea Trail currently offers only 15 miles of completed trail, including the Corvallis-Philomath bike path, a trail at Marys Peak, and trails in the Drift Creek Wilderness. The proposed 90-mile route would cross the Coast Range and connect with the Oregon Coast Trail.

The Eugene To PCT Trail has been completed as far as Oakridge from the Pacific Crest Trail (at Bobby Lakes, north of Maiden Peak). This 34-mile section follows forested ridges usually snow-free from June to November. Volunteer trail-building efforts proceed on the proposed 40-mile, valley-bottom route that would continue from Oakridge to join the Eugene-Springfield bike path network.

The North Umpqua Trail provides 59 miles of completed trail along this forested and often cliff-lined river from its headwaters—Maidu Lake in the Mt. Thielsen Wilderness. The completed section extends from the Pacific Crest Trail to the village of Steamboat. Volunteers propose continuing construction downriver 40 miles to Roseburg.

The Rogue River Trail consists of two widely separated, completed sections. The popular Lower Rogue River Trail extends 40 miles from Grave Creek to Illahe, traversing the rugged Wild Rogue Wilderness. The little-known Upper Rogue River Trail climbs 45 miles from Prospect to the northwest corner of Crater Lake National Park. A proposal to connect the two trail segments suggests a nonriver route through Wolf Creek.

The Metolius-Windigo Trail features a completed, 45-mile path through central Oregon's pine forests. The route primarily attracts equestrian use and serves as a low-elevation alternative when the nearby, high-elevation Pacific Crest Trail is blocked by snow.

The trail crosses Highway 20 at Indian Ford, 5 miles northwest of Sisters. To the north of Highway 20, the path skirts Black Butte and follows Green Ridge, overlooking the Metolius River. To the south, the trail continues as far as Three Creek Lake, near Broken Top. A Forest Service proposal would eventually extend the route south to join the Pacific Crest Trail in the Mt. Thielsen Wilderness.

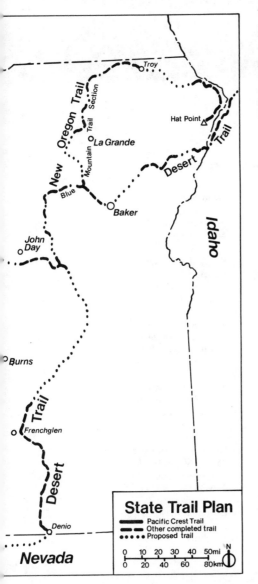

State Trail Plan

▬▬▬ Pacific Crest Trail
▬ ▬ ▬ Other completed trail
• • • • Proposed trail

0   10   20   30   40   50mi
0   20   40   60   80km

A windstorm shrouds Diablo Mountain with alkali dust

Appendix B: Managing Agencies

UNITED STATES FOREST SERVICE (USFS)*

Pacific Northwest Regional Office
319 SW Pine St.
Portland, OR 97208
221-2877

Deschutes National Forest
211 NE Revere St.
Bend, OR 97701
388-2715

Fremont National Forest
34 D St.
Lakeview, OR 97630
947-2151

Malheur National Forest
139 NE Dayton St.
John Day, OR 97845
575-1731

Mt. Hood National Forest
2955 NW Division St.
Gresham, OR 97030
667-0511

Ochoco National Forest
PO Box 490
Prineville, OR 97754
447-6247

Rogue River National Forest
PO Box 520
Medford, OR 97501
776-3600

Siskiyou National Forest
200 NE Greenfield Rd.
Grants Pass, OR 97526
479-5301

Siuslaw National Forest
4077 SW Research Way
Corvallis, OR 97333
757-4480

Umatilla National Forest
2517 SW Hailey Ave.
Pendleton, OR 97801
276-3811

Umpqua National Forest
704 SE Cass St.
Roseburg, OR 97470
672-6601

* The long-distance area code throughout Oregon is 503.

Wallowa-Whitman National Forest
PO Box 907
Baker, OR 97814
523-6391

Willamette National Forest
PO Box 10607
Eugene, OR 97440
687-6522

Winema National Forest
PO Box 1390
Klamath Falls, OR 97601
883-6714

BUREAU OF LAND MANAGEMENT (BLM)
Oregon State Office
825 NE Multnomah
Portland, OR 97208
231-6274

Burns District
74 S Alvord St.
Burns, OR 97720
573-5241

Coos Bay District
333 S 4th St.
Coos Bay, OR 97420
269-5880

Eugene District
1255 Pearl St.
Eugene, OR 97401
687-6651

Lakeview District
1000 9th St. S
Lakeview, OR 97630
947-2177

Medford District
3040 Biddle Rd.
Medford, OR 97501
776-4174

Prineville District
185 E 4th St.
Prineville, OR 97754
447-4115

Salem District
1717 Fabry Rd.
Salem, OR 97306
399-5646

Vale District
100 Oregon St.
Vale, OR 97918
473-3144

OTHER AGENCIES
Confederated Tribes of the
Warm Springs Indian Reservation
Warm Springs, OR 97761
553-1121

Crater Lake National Park
Superintendent's Office
Crater Lake, OR 97604
594-2211

Crooked River National Grassland
2321 E 3rd St.
Prineville, OR 97754
447-4120

Hells Canyon National Recreation Area
PO Box 490
Enterprise, OR 97828
426-3151

The Nature Conservancy
1234 NW 25th
Portland, OR 97210
228-9561

Oregon Caves National Monument
National Park Service
Cave Junction, OR 97523
592-3400

Oregon Department of Fish and Wildlife
506 SW Mill St.
Portland, OR 97208
229-5403

Oregon Dunes National Recreation Area
855 Highway Ave.
Reedsport, OR 97467
271-3611

Oregon State Parks and Recreation Divison
525 Trade St. SE
Salem, OR 97310
378-6305

US Fish and Wildlife Service
PO Box 111
Lakeview, OR 97630
947-3315

Fish Lake

Appendix C: Topographic Map Publishers

Bureau of Land Management (BLM)
PO Box 2965
Portland, OR 97208
231-6281

The BLM publishes several topographic maps for $1 each: the *Lower Deschutes River,* the *Lower John Day River,* and *Central Oregon.* In addition, the BLM's planimetric maps for eastern Oregon can be extremely useful both for driving the maze of dusty tracks near roadless areas and for hiking within the roadless areas themselves. The *Steens Mountain Recreation Lands* map ($1) covers Steens Mountain, the Alvord Desert, the Pueblo Mountains, and most of the Sheepshead Mountains and Trout

Creek Mountains. Other areas in eastern Oregon are covered best by the BLM's 30-minute quadrangle series; these 66 black-and-white maps, scaled 1 inch to 1 mile (1:63,360), cost $2 each and cover an area 25 miles wide by 34 miles long. All BLM maps show public and private land ownership.

Desert Trail Association
PO Box 589
Burns, OR 97720

This non-profit association organizes hikes, distributes a monthly newsletter *(Desert Trails),* and publishes topographic maps of the Desert Trail route. The maps include detailed notes for following the trail route, but are broad enough to cover alternative hiking terrain. The five maps available in Oregon so far (more are planned) cover the Pueblo Mountains, the Alvord Desert, Steens Mountain, the Donner und Blitzen River, and the Malheur Wildlife Refuge. Price is $3, postpaid.

Geo-Graphics
225 SW Broadway, Suite 418
Portland, OR 97205
241-9287

This publisher offers three high-quality topographic maps of popular Cascades wilderness areas. The *Mt. Hood Recreation Map* ($7.95 plus 50 cents postage) covers the Mt. Hood Wilderness at a scale of 1:24,000 on the front, and the Columbia, Badger Creek, and Salmon-Huckleberry Wildernesses at a scale of 1:100,000 on the back. The *Mt. Jefferson Recreation Map* ($5.95 on plain paper, $7.95 on waterproof paper, plus 50 cents postage) covers a 10-mile-by-15-mile area about the peak itself at 1:24,000. The *Three Sisters Recreation Map* ($7.95 plus 50 cents postage) covers the entire Three Sisters Wilderness and half of the Mt. Washington and Waldo Lake wildernesses at a scale of 1:70,000. The maps are also available at some bookstores and outdoor stores in northwest Oregon and Bend.

Green Trails
PO Box 1272
Bellevue, WA 98009
(206) 232-2119

Green Trails publishes 15 topographic maps for Oregon, covering the Northern Oregon Cascades at a scale of 1:69,500. These frequently updated maps each cover about 12 by 18 miles, showing trails, cross-country skiing routes, and other recreational data. The maps are available in many outdoor stores in northwest and north-central Oregon, but can also be ordered direct from the publisher. Up to four maps cost $2.25 each, postpaid; five or more cost $1.95, postpaid. Orders of less than 10 maps are folded and mailed. Orders of 10 or more are shipped flat via UPS.

Hardesty Mountain Study Group, c/o ONRC
1161 Lincoln St.
Eugene, OR 97401
344-0675

The $2.95 guidebook, *Hiking the Hardesty Wilderness,* includes a topographic map of the Hardesty Mountain area. Order it from the Oregon Natural Resources Council (ONRC), adding $1 postage.

United States Forest Service (USFS)
PO Box 3623
Portland, OR 97208
221-2877

The USFS publishes convenient topographic maps for designated wilderness areas under their management, generally at a scale of 1:62,500. However, maps are not complete for most of the areas designated since 1979, and the completed maps often exclude roadless areas. The USFS also offers special topographic maps covering the Pacific Crest Trail through Oregon, trails in the Columbia Gorge, and winter ski trails in certain areas. Finally, non-topographic recreation maps cover each of the 13 National Forests in Oregon, showing major roads, most trails, and other data at a scale of 1:126,720. All of these maps are reasonably priced at $1 apiece. District offices generally stock all the maps, while ranger stations only keep maps of local interest on hand.

To keep track of the latest Forest Service roads, try the $3 *District Transportation Maps* for each district. Most of the National Forests' 57 Oregon ranger districts offer copies of these frequently updated maps to the public on request. Often topographic, always awkwardly large, the maps attempt to show every Forest Service road and trail at a scale of 1:62,500.

United States Geological Survey (USGS)
Box 25286 - Denver Federal Center
Denver, CO 80225
(303) 236-7477

USGS topographic maps come in several sizes: their 7.5-minute series maps show great detail but can be unwieldy for large areas (in Oregon 1 minute is approximately 0.8 mile). Their 15-minute series maps, though larger, date from the 1950s and do not show many newer roads. USGS maps with a 1:250,000 scale span 100 miles but show insufficient detail for most uses.

USGS topographic maps are available at a few outdoor stores and bookstores, but maps can also be ordered direct. The 7.5-minute and 15-minute maps cost $2.50 postpaid; the 1:250,000 series maps and special 25-minute Crater Lake map cost $4 postpaid. Send the map name, state, and series type along with full prepayment. The USGS ships maps rolled. They do not accept telephone orders, but will send a free state index map on request.

Many university and college libraries in Oregon stock all Oregon USGS topographic maps and allow them to be checked out or photocopied.

Crawfish Lake (photo by William Sullivan)

Appendix D: Selected Bibliography

PLANTS AND WILDLIFE

Animal Tracks of the Pacific Northwest by Karen Pandell and Chris Stall (The Mountaineers, 1981).

The Audubon Society Field Guide to North American Mammals by John O. Whitaker, Jr. (Knopf, 1980).

A Field Guide to the Cascades & Olympics by Stephen R. Whitney (The Mountaineers, 1983).

A Field Guide to Pacific States Wildflowers by Theodore F. Niehaus (Houghton Mifflin, 1976).

A Field Guide to Western Birds by Roger Tory Peterson (Houghton Mifflin, 1961).

Flora of the Pacific Northwest by C. Leo Hitchcock and Arthur Cronquist (University of Washington Press, 1973).

Mountain Flowers by Harvey Manning and Bob and Ira Spring (The Mountaineers, 1979).

Northwest Trees by Stephen Arno and Ramona Hammerly (The Mountaineers, 1977).

Oregon's Great Basin Country by Denzel and Nancy Ferguson (Maverick Publications, 1978).

Trees to Know in Oregon by Charles R. Ross (Oregon State University Extension Service, 1975).

Wildflowers 1: The Cascades by Elizabeth Horn (Touchstone Press, 1972).

Wildflowers 2: Sagebrush Country by Ronald J. Taylor and Rolf W. Valum (Touchstone Press, 1974).

GEOLOGY

Fire & Ice: The Cascade Volcanoes by Stephen L. Harris (The Mountaineers, 1980); out of print.

Geology of Oregon by Ewart M. Baldwin (University of Oregon Bookstore, 1964).

Pages of Stone: Geology of Western National Parks and Monuments, Vol. 2 by Halka Chronic (The Mountaineers, 1986).

Roadside Geology of Oregon by David D. Alt and Donald W. Hyndman (Mountain Press Publishing, 1978).

HISTORY

Bridge of the Gods, Mountains of Fire: A Return to the Columbia Gorge by Chuck Williams (The Mountaineers, 1980).

East of the Cascades by Phil F. Brogan (Binfords & Mort, 1964).

Jam on the Ceiling by J. Wesley Sullivan (Navillus Press, 1987).

Oregon Geographic Names by Lewis A. McArthur (Western Imprints, 1982).

Hells Canyon by William Ashworth (Hawthorn Books, 1977).

HIKING

50 Hiking Trails—Portland & Northwest Oregon by Don and Roberta Lowe (Touchstone Press, 1986).

60 Hiking Trails—Central Oregon Cascades by Don and Roberta Lowe (Touchstone Press, 1978).

62 Hiking Trails—Northern Oregon Cascades by Don and Roberta Lowe (Touchstone Press, 1979).

100 Oregon Hiking Trails by Don and Roberta Lowe (Touchstone Press, 1969).

Calapooya Trails by Jerold Williams (Calapooya Books, 1982); out of print.

Crater Lake National Park and Vicinity by Jeffrey P. Schaffer (Wilderness Press, 1983).

Day Hikes in Central Oregon by Virginia Meissner (Meissner Books, 1981).

Desert Trails monthly newsletter (Desert Trails Association).

Emergency Survival Handbook by Robert E. Brown (The Mountaineers, 1984).

Gorp, Glop & Glue Stew: Favorite Foods From 165 Experts by Yvonne Prater and Ruth Mendenhall (The Mountaineers, 1982).

A Guide to the Kalmiopsis Wilderness (Siskiyou National Forest, 1985).

Guide to the Middle Santiam and Old Cascades edited by Julie Ambler and John Patt (Marys Peak Group, Sierra Club, 1981).

A Guide to the Trails of Badger Creek by Ken and Ruth Love (Signpost Books, 1979).

A Hiker's Guide to the Oregon Coast Trail by David E.M. Bucy and Mary C. McCauley (Oregon Parks and Recreation Division, 1977).

A Hiker's Guide to Oregon's Hidden Wilderness, Bull of the Woods, (Central Cascades Conservation Council, 1978); out of print.

Hiking the Bigfoot Country by John Hart (Sierra Club Books, 1975).

Hiking the Great Basin by John Hart (Sierra Club Books, 1981).

Hiking the Hardesty Wilderness (Hardesty Mountain Study Group, 1981).

Hiking Light by Marlyn Doan (The Mountaineers, 1982).

McKenzie Trails by Jerold Williams (Calapooya Books, 1979); out of print.

The Mount Jefferson Wilderness Guidebook by Tony George (Solo Press, 1983).

Northwest Trails by Ira Spring and Harvey Manning (The Mountaineers, 1982).

The Olallie Scenic Area Guidebook by Tony George (Solo Press, 1983).

Oregon Coast Hikes by Paul M. Williams (The Mountaineers, 1985).

Oregon Coast Range Wilderness edited by Sherry Wellborn (Siuslaw Task Force, 1980).

The Pacific Crest Trail, Vol. 2: Oregon and Washington by Jeffrey P. Schaffer and Bev and Fred Hartline (Wilderness Press, 1986).

Umpqua Wilderness Trails by Mike Anderson (Mike Anderson, 1978); out of print.

Unobscured Horizons, Untravelled Trails: Hiking the Oregon High Desert by Bruce Hayse (Oregon High Desert Study Group, 1979); out of print.

Willamette Trails (Willamette National Forest, 1979); out of print.

CLIMBING

A Climbing Guide to Oregon by Nicholas A. Dodge (Touchstone Press, 1975).

Mountaineering: The Freedom of the Hills, Fourth Edition, edited by Ed Peters (The Mountaineers, 1982).

Oregon Rock: A Climber's Guide by Jeff Thomas (The Mountaineers, 1983).

WINTER SPORTS

Cross-Country Ski Gear, Second Edition, by Michael Brady (The Mountaineers, 1988).

Cross-Country Skiing by Ned Gillette and John Dostal (The Mountaineers, 1988).

Cross-Country Ski Routes of Oregon's Cascades by Klindt Vielbig (The Mountaineers, 1984).

Oregon Ski Tours by Doug Newman and Sally Sharrard (Touchstone Press, 1973).

Snowshoeing, Third Edition, by Gene Prater (The Mountaineers, 1988).

BOATING

Boater's Safety Handbook edited by Robert E. Brown (The Mountaineers, 1982).

Canoe Routes: Northwest Oregon by Phil Jones (The Mountaineers, 1982).

Handbook to the Illinois River Canyon by James M. Quinn (Education Adventures Inc., 1979).

Handbook to the Rogue River Canyon by James M. Quinn (Educational Adventures Inc., 1978).

John Day River Drift and Historical Guide by Arthur Campbell (Frank Amato Publications, 1980).

Soggy Sneakers: Guide to Oregon Rivers (Willamette Kayak and Canoe Club, 1986).

Wild Rivers of North America by Michael Jenkinson (Dutton, 1981).

◆INDEX◆

Note: **Bold face** indicates major wild areas and their discussions. *Italic* page numbers refer to maps.

About the photographer:

DIANE KELSAY'S insightful nature photography has appeared in *Backpacker*, *Wild Oregon*, and *Travel Oregon*. She is perhaps best known for her synchronized, multi-image slide shows, including the "Oregon" show (featured at Expo 86 in Vancouver, B.C.), a show for the Oregon High Desert Museum near Bend, a presentation used with Mason Williams' "Of Time and Rivers Flowing" concerts, and a show on the Galapagos Islands (which placed first at a 1986 Northwest Regional Multi-image Festival). A long-time resident of Springfield, Oregon, Ms. Kelsay is now a partner of In Sync Productions in Fort Collins, Colorado.

ABOUT THE AUTHOR

WILLIAM L. SULLIVAN began backpacking in Oregon at the age of 6 and has been in love with adventure ever since. At 17 he left high school to study at remote Deep Springs College in the California desert, where his duties included milking cows by hand. He went on to earn a B.A. in English from Cornell University and an M.A. in German from the University of Oregon. He and his wife Janell Sorensen bicycled 3000 miles through Europe, studied at Heidelberg University, and built a log cabin by hand on Oregon's Siletz River.

To research this guide, Sullivan backpacked 1360 miles across the state—from Oregon's westernmost shore at Cape Blanco to the state's easternmost point in Hells Canyon. The "New Oregon Trail" he blazed on that two-month solo trek has since been included in the State Trail Plan by the Oregon State Park and Recreation Division's Recreational Trail Advisory Council.

A freelance writer since 1980, Sullivan has written for *Sierra, Oregon Magazine,* and *The Mother Earth News.* His books include *The Cart Book* and two recently completed works, *Joaquin* and *Listening For Coyote.* He and Janell live in Eugene with their children Karen and Ian.

William L. Sullivan (Photo by Tim Lillebo)

About the Oregon Natural Resources Council

The Oregon Natural Resources Council (ONRC) is Oregon's largest conservation network. A nonprofit, tax-exempt corporation, ONRC is composed of over 85 local and statewide conservation, sporting, education, business and outdoor-recreation organizations and more than 3000 individual members. The Council addresses major conservation and natural-resource-management issues facing Oregon's forests, rivers, rangelands and coast. Wilderness protection, especially through legislation, is a premier organizational priority and is viewed as vital for both environmental and economic purposes. The areas described in this book *are* that resource.

With a full-time staff of twenty, including regional field coordinators who live and work in each corner of Oregon, ONRC's strength is its strong and active grass-roots citizen network of volunteers. The Council coordinates public involvement in Oregon conservation issues at the agency-planning level, represents its members in court, and lobbies with them directly at the State Legislature and in Congress. Its educational programs provide information and assistance to all members of the public interested in management of Oregon's lands, waters, and natural resources.

ONRC is a publicly supported educational, scientific and charitable organization dependent upon private donations and citizen support. It receives no government funding. Memberships and contributions are tax-deductible.

Main Office
3921 SE Salmon St.
Portland, OR 97214
(503) 236-9772

Western Regional Office
1161 Lincoln Street
Eugene, OR 97401
(503) 344-0675

Northwest Field Office
Box 9
Prairie City, OR 97869
(503) 820-3714

Southeast Field Office
Box 848
Bend, OR 97709
(503) 388-0089

Southwest Field Office
Box 638
Ashland, OR 97520